D0216050

COGNITIVE FOUNDATIONS
OF MUSICAL PITCH

OXFORD PSYCHOLOGY SERIES

EDITORS

DONALD E. BROADBENT   JAMES L. McGAUGH
STEPHEN KOSSLYN   ENDEL TULVING
NICHOLAS J. MACKINTOSH   LAWRENCE WEISKRANTZ

Cognitive Foundations
of Musical Pitch

CAROL L. KRUMHANSL

Department of Psychology
Cornell University

OXFORD PSYCHOLOGY SERIES NO. 17

New York   Oxford
OXFORD UNIVERSITY PRESS
1990

4p

Oxford University Press

Oxford   New York   Toronto
Delhi   Bombay   Calcutta   Madras   Karachi
Petaling Jaya   Singapore   Hong Kong   Tokyo
Nairobi   Dar es Salaam   Cape Town
Melbourne   Auckland

and associated companies in
Berlin   Ibadan

Published by Oxford University Press, Inc.,
200 Madison Avenue, New York, New York 10016

Oxford is a registered trademark of Oxford University Press

Library of Congress Cataloging-in-Publication Data
Krumhansl, Carol L.
Cognitive foundations of musical pitch / Carol L. Krumhansl.
p.   cm.—(Oxford psychology series ; no. 17)
Bibliography: p.
Includes index.
ISBN 0-19-505475-X
1. Music—Psychological aspects.   2. Musical pitch.
3. Cognitive psychology.
I. Title.   II. Series.
ML3830.K76   1990   89-9312
781'.11—dc20   CIP   MN

9 8 7 6 5 4 3 2 1

Printed in the United States of America

05/30/91

For Jane L. Ward

Preface

Cognitive Foundations of Musical Pitch considers the problem of how listeners encode, organize, and remember pitch patterns in music. The work seeks to explicate the nature of listeners' knowledge of how pitch structures are formed, identify musical properties that shape this knowledge, and characterize the process through which sequences of sounds become coherent, memorable, and meaningful. The approach taken is that of cognitive psychology, in which laboratory methods examine the nature of mental representations and processes. Previous publications have described a number of the studies. They are summarized here together with new results, allowing richer connections to be drawn between the empirical findings. Theoretical and methodological issues surrounding the laboratory studies are also examined. The experiments focus primarily on pitch structures in traditional Western music. This choice of focus is based on the large corpus of literature in music theory that deals with this style. This literature has been important for designing the experimental materials and interpreting the results. A number of studies extend the methods to music outside this tradition. Throughout, care has been taken to provide adequate background in experimental methods and music theory so that no special background is needed to follow the major arguments. However, the reader will naturally discover certain topics to be of greater interest than others depending on his or her special expertise.

This project has evolved over a period of more than a decade, during which there has been remarkable progress in the study of music perception and cognition. Landmarks of this era include the appearance of the journal *Music Perception,* Deutsch's *The Psychology of Music,* Lerdahl and Jackendoff's, *A Generative Theory of Tonal Music,* Sloboda's *The Musical Mind,* Dowling and Harwood's *Music Cognition,* the translation into English of Francès's *The Perception of Music,* and many important articles in professional journals. No attempt has been made here to summarize this rapidly developing field; only the literature of most direct relevance to the present investigations is reviewed.

The project owes a tremendous debt to many individuals and institutions. My greatest debt, of course, is to my numerous collaborators on the studies reported here. I would especially like to acknowledge the contributions of Roger Shepard, who encouraged the work from the beginning and was responsible for crucial methodological innovations, and Jamshed Bharucha, who formulated the theoretical framework for understanding the results on musical harmony. The research has been generously supported by grants from both the National Science Foundation and the National Institute of Mental Health. The first draft of the monograph was written while I was a fellow at the Center for Advanced Studies in the Behavioral Sciences in Stanford, California. Revisions were undertaken in part while I was on a sabbatical leave at the Institut de Recherche et Coordination Acoustique/Musique in Paris. Both leaves were supported by the National Science Foundation. Valuable suggestions on earlier drafts of the chapters were made by any number of thoughtful people, including William Austin, Caroline Palmer, Michael Kelly, Mary Babcocke, Mark Schmuckler, Roger Shepard, Desmond Sergeant, Muriel Bell, Lynn Cooper, James Cutting, and Reid Hastie. I am deeply thankful for the encouragement and wealth of constructive suggestions made by my readers for Oxford University Press: John Sloboda, W. Jay Dowling, and Fred Lerdahl. Monica Howland, Paula DiSanto Bensadoun, and Christopher Hopkins prepared many of the figures.

Ithaca, New York   C.K.
April 1989

Contents

COGNITIVE FOUNDATIONS
OF MUSICAL PITCH

1. Objectives and methods

Listening to music, we hear the sounds not as isolated, disconnected units, but integrated into patterns. Our perceptual experience goes beyond sensory registration of single musical events. Sound elements are heard in context, organized in pitch and time, and are understood in terms of their functions within that context. The absolute pitch of a particular tone is less important to the listener than the intervals it forms with surrounding pitches. Each pitch participates in extended melodic and harmonic patterns. Similarly, the absolute duration of a musical event is less important than its relationship to neighboring events with which it combines to form metrical and rhythmic units. In taking context into account, the listener apprehends increasingly larger temporal groupings. The listener appreciates the organization of a musical work by assigning significance to the sounded elements according to their roles in the musical context, and by integrating them into the broader pattern.

Certain musical relationships are explicit in the music; these are features or properties of the music that can be derived more or less directly from the sounded sequence. Examples are the ratios of pitch frequencies and durations, and the repetition of melodic and rhythmic patterns. To say that such aspects of musical structure are explicit in the music, however, does not necessarily imply they are perceived. To understand the listener's response to music, it is necessary to specify which of the potentially available features of the music are realized by the listener, how they are processed and remembered, and how they contribute to an appreciation of the overall plan of the piece of music. It cannot be assumed that this experience is a direct mapping of the external musical events, although some objective musical features may have direct psychological correlates.

The listener's experience of a particular musical sequence is driven and constrained by the sounds registered by auditory mechanisms and processed by available mental resources. Furthermore, the construction of the music itself must respect the listener's capacities for appreciating structured auditory information. That is, the way musical materials are formed must take into consideration certain inherent limitations and special capabilities of the listener. It is possible, for instance, that particular pitch combinations predominate in music because they are perceived as consonant or pleasing, and this may be a consequence of peripheral auditory mechanisms for registering pitch. Simple ratios of durations, such as 2 : 1 and 3 : 1, may be more readily perceived and more accurately remembered, and thus more commonly employed in the formation of metrical and rhythmic units. Or, to take another example, the duration of rhythmic and pitch patterns may reflect limitations in memory capacity. All this suggests that music psychology must seek to understand the interdependencies between the structured sound material of the music and the listener's capacity for apprehending and remembering relations among the sounded events.

In discussing this problem, it may be useful to distinguish the objective (external) musical stimulus from the subjective (internal) experience of music as indicated in Figure 1.1. The objective musical attributes can be divided into those that the listener does and does not perceive. This classification would, presumably, depend on the listener's training and experience. Some attributes of music are probably accessible even to naive listeners because they fit with general principles of psychological organization. For example, there may be natural tendencies to group elements on the basis of similarity of pitch or timbre, locate phrase boundaries at relatively long pauses, and notice periodic repetitions of temporal patterns. More extensive experience may be required to perceive other attributes. This experience might enable the listener to hear a melody as a variation of another, recall the lyrics that accompany it, or associate it with a sociocultural context in which it is conventionally played. More important, however, the listener may interpret the sounded events in terms of a system of knowledge that specifies the ways in which musical passages tend to be constructed within a relevant musical style system. In addition, there are undoubtedly features of music that can be objectively specified but cannot be perceived. This may be due to the listener's limited ability to discriminate along objective auditory dimensions, to limitations in memory, or to a mismatch between the underlying organizational scheme of a composition and natural tendencies to perceive auditory information in a particular way. These limitations may in some cases be overcome through perceptual learning or by special instruction or additional descriptions. However, there are inherent bounds to the ways in which music can be perceived due to the nature of the human psychological system for perceiving music.

In a similar way, the subjective experience can be divided into aspects that do and do not correspond to objective musical structures. Various considerations suggest a rather direct mapping between certain objective properties of music and the listener's organized internal representation. The construction of music reflects certain intuitions about the listener's capacities for internalizing relations existing between the sounded events. It takes into account predispositions to organize pitch and time in particular ways. For example, pitch materials may tend to be categorized in terms of a limited number of pitch classes, and periodically regular metrical units may be preferred. Simple patterns of melodic contour and rhythmic grouping may facilitate the formation of larger perceptual units.

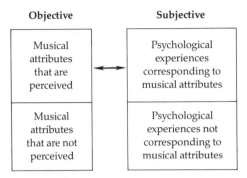

Objective   Subjective

Fig. 1.1. Objective musical attributes are distinguished from subjective musical experiences. In some cases there is a fairly direct mapping between attributes that can be objectively specified and attributes that are perceived, indicated by the arrow. Other objective musical attributes may not be perceived, and some aspects of the listener's experience may be difficult to trace to objective musical attributes.

Moreover, the listener may have abstracted and internalized structural regularities from experience with a musical idiom. This knowledge may include the pitch intervals in musical scales, probable combinations of simultaneous and successive pitches, and characteristic rhythmic patterns. Once acquired, this knowledge may serve as a framework for precisely encoding, organizing, and remembering new musical sequences written in the musical idiom. The present investigations focus on that part of the musical experience that can be traced quite directly to objective musical structures. Other aspects of the subjective experience, such as emotional responses, personal associations, or visual imagery evoked by the music, may be quite indirectly related, or unrelated, to objective musical attributes. Consequently, they are difficult to study systematically using the methods of cognitive psychology to which we now turn.

The approach of cognitive psychology

The methods and theoretical orientation of the research to be presented are those of cognitive psychology. Cognitive psychology is a subarea of experimental psychology concerned with describing human mental activity. A diverse collection of activities has been considered by investigators in the field, including encoding and interpreting perceptual information such as visual patterns and speech, learning and remembering perceptual and linguistic information, organizing and executing motoric and linguistic behaviors, as well as reasoning, problem solving, and decision making. The cognitive psychologist is generally less concerned with the occasional exception or special case than with the more general rules governing human cognition. Furthermore, the focus is less on describing the experience of specially trained or exceptional individuals than with cognitive capacities exhibited more generally. Finally, the motivation is not to provide a prescriptive account of human behavior—what individuals should do on logical or rational grounds—but to arrive at a descriptive account of what individuals actually do when engaged in cognitive activities.

Investigations in various areas have led to the view that cognitive activity requires complex mental structures and processes. That is, observable behaviors can only be understood if we presuppose a mental system that encodes, transforms, and combines information. Out of this work have emerged various characterizations or models of the cognitive system. Certainly, areas of cognitive activity are not yet fully understood, and important theoretical issues remain unresolved, particularly about the most appropriate format for describing or representing internal structures. However, the field has now evolved to the point where quite precise questions have been formulated, laboratory techniques for investigating those questions have been devised, and various conceptual systems for summarizing and communicating the empirical observations have been developed.

As a complex human activity, music perception is naturally an area of interest to cognitive psychology. However, introducing this domain of inquiry raises anew basic questions about how best to formulate the questions to be investigated, how to compile observations that bear on these questions, and finally how to devise a descriptive framework for communicating the results obtained. In general terms, the aim is to describe the human capacity for internalizing the structured sound materials of music by characterizing the nature of internal processes and representations. In making choices about the most fruitful kind of analysis, a variety of considerations must be weighed.

The musical materials employed in the experiments should not be so impoverished that only a small subset of the potentially relevant internal structures are evoked or engaged. For example, presenting tones in isolation or in random combinations would not reveal the nature of internal structures with specifically musical content. The materials should, in some sense, be representative of actual music. On the other hand, complex musical materials evoke a multiplicity of responses that may be difficult, if not impossible, to disentangle. Moreover, detailed analyses of the response to particular pieces of music may inadvertently lead to overgeneralizations of the results obtained; the conclusions reached may depend strongly on the particular musical context and be largely uninformative with respect to broader questions. Only to the extent that the materials are representative of a broad class of music can experimental results be generalized. In the end, the selection of materials depends to some extent on one's interests and intuitions about the most fruitful questions to be investigated experimentally.

Significant questions also arise about the kinds of behaviors or responses that are to be measured. Various considerations come into play here as well. The cognitive psychologist is interested in describing an internal system that cannot be examined directly. Consequently, its properties must be inferred from external, observable behaviors. For the most part, musical experience is not well suited to verbal description, which may be one reason why music has received less attention than other cognitive activities. Although one component of training in music is the acquisition of terminologies for characterizing musical structure (and these often take a verbal form, although other symbolic devices are also used), not all listeners or even performers have sophisticated skills in music analysis. If one is interested in understanding the musical experience of listeners with diverse levels of training, then the observed responses should not require special knowledge of established descriptive systems. A similar argument applies to responses requiring production, such as music transcription, playing an instrument, or even singing. Nonetheless, the observations made should be musically relevant, that is, they should be matched in some way to the experience itself. The observations made are informative only to the extent that the mode of response mirrors essential components of the internal systems engaged in listening. Here again, a considerable degree of intuition is involved.

Other important considerations in choosing behaviors to be recorded come from the experimental methodologies of cognitive psychology itself. The researcher seeks a systematic body of observations that are well suited to treatment by various analytical techniques. The available techniques restrict the kinds of observations that can be treated. Moreover, to understand the relationship between the music and the listener's experience, it is essential to vary properties of the external musical event and trace how these changes affect the pattern of responding. In this connection, we speak of the external musical event as the stimulus, and the changes made in the stimulus as experimental manipulations.

For this strategy to be informative, considerable understanding of the relevant stimulus attributes or properties is required. It is essential to control irrelevant properties of the stimulus, and to change or manipulate only those of interest. Potentially separable properties must not be experimentally covaried or confounded if the pattern of response is to be interpreted unambiguously. Finally, the variables manipulated should be musically relevant. This requires that the manipulated stimulus attributes correspond to appropriate conceptualizations about the way music is constructed. If this general strategy is carried out successfully, it leads to a scientific account of particular aspects of the musical experience. Admittedly, one could still argue about the choice of stimulus materials, the nature of the response required, the interpretation of the data, and generality of the conclusions. However, as a minimum, these arguments take place in the context of a controlled and systematic body of observations about the musical experience.

Contemporary cognitive psychology is closely aligned with other subfields of the cognitive sciences, particularly philosophy of mind, linguistics, and artificial intelligence. It should be clear, however, that cognitive psychology differs in certain fundamental ways from these other fields, despite their overlapping concerns. Cognitive psychology is, at the core, an empirical approach to understanding human thought and experience. This means that theories are developed from and constrained by observations about human behavior made largely in laboratory situations. The conclusions, or generalizations, reached are intended as summary descriptions of the external behaviors observed in response to controlled external situations.

In its reliance on laboratory methods, cognitive psychology is patterned closely after the physical sciences. With this alliance comes a concern for quantification. Advances in these other scientific disciplines have come largely through successful measurement of physical attributes and the discovery of lawful relationships among them. Special problems arise, however, in quantifying psychological properties. At the most fundamental level, these problems arise because the observations are of some external correlate of the internal system, and not of the internal system itself. The measurements are thus indirect, making it necessary to employ a variety of approaches. To the extent that different approaches converge on the same results, it can be argued that we are describing the internal system and not the effects of some particular method of measurement. Moreover, observable behaviors are notably complex and variable, and so it is necessary to constrain the mode of responding and record aspects that can be coded precisely. Mathematics provides numerical structures well suited to this, and therefore we tend to record quantifiable aspects of responses. In involving mathematics, however, we must be careful not to make unwarranted assumptions about the nature of the measured quantities. The kind of conclusions that are justified on the basis of particular kinds of data is the subject of considerable theoretical analysis and debate.

Despite the difficulties, quantification is unavoidable. The variable nature of human behavior impels us in that direction. Under what are seemingly identical external circumstances, different individuals will respond differently, and the same individual will respond differently on different occasions. Even so, we intuitively believe that there are underlying regularities and lawful principles operating. To uncover these, we routinely employ statistical and other analytical methods. Although a technical understanding of these methods will not generally be necessary for what follows, the empirical work presented should be understood with an appreciation for the difficulties involved in quantifying psychological attributes and achieving general statements in the face of considerable variability.

The final issue concerns the choice of listeners to participate in the experiments. This choice interacts with a variety of other considerations, including the objective of the experiment, the nature of the materials employed, and the kind of response that is to be measured. Because cognitive psychology is directed at describing mental capacities exhibited quite generally, the majority of studies do not employ participants with extraordinary talents or severe deficits. However, even the general population includes large variations in the extent of musical talent, training, and performing and listening experience. If we are especially interested in how musical knowledge is acquired, then a variety of strategies can be followed. One strategy is to take a developmental approach, using listeners of different ages. Another strategy is to select listeners so that they have different levels of musical training or prior experience with the kinds of materials used in the experiment. Alternatively, the experiment can provide extended experience with a particular set of materials and trace how this experience changes the pattern of responding. If, however, we are less concerned with the process of acquisition, and more concerned with describing a fully developed cognitive system for processing musical materials, we tend to employ listeners with considerable training and experience. In any case, because music background may affect the results, care must be taken to assess participants' music backgrounds and treat the data in a way that allows for the possibility of individual differences.

The plan of the research

Having described in general terms some of the considerations involved in studying music from the perspective of cognitive psychology, I turn now to more specific methodological and theoretical issues surrounding the work described in the following chapters. The experiments summarized here are directed at characterizing the listener's internal system for processing pitch structures, focusing primarily on those found in traditional Western music. I will refer to this music as tonal-harmonic to indicate, first, that it is tonal in the sense of being organized around a central reference pitch (tonic) and, second, that harmony is important for establishing the tonal framework. The aim is to describe what the listener knows about pitch relationships in this style, how this knowledge affects the processing of sounded sequences, and how this system arises from stylistic regularities identifiable in the music.

In tonal-harmonic music, three distinct types of basic elements can be identified: single tones, chords, and keys. Although pitch is continuously variable, Western tonal music selects from the potentially infinite set of pitches a relatively small set of discrete pitch categories. This property, in fact, holds true for most (if not all) musical cultures. In Western music, there are 12 pitch categories in each octave range, with a total of about eight octaves in musical usage. Both psychologically and compositionally, however, a natural identification exists between corresponding pitches in different octaves (that is, pitches one or more octaves apart), and so the set of musical tones can be described as 12 pitch categories or classes. Chords in tonal-harmonic music consist of three or more tones sounded simultaneously, although the same harmony can also be expressed as successively sounded tones. Diatonic triads, three-tone chords built on the seven tones of the diatonic scale, form the core of harmonies in eighteenth- and nineteenth-century music. A musical key is defined by its tonic and its scale (or mode, which is usually major or minor). The tonic is one of the 12 pitches in an octave range, and the scale is a specific pattern of intervals defined relative to the tonic. The major and minor scales and twelve tonics give rise to a total set of 24 keys.

The construction of these elements will be treated in considerably more detail later. For the present purposes, it is important to note only that tonal-harmonic music is constructed from small sets of basic elements. Consequently, it is possible to measure experimentally the degree to which they are perceived as related to one another. The experiments constituting the basic line of inquiry follow this approach quite directly. The studies assess the perceived relationships between elements, either of the same type (e.g., between tones) or of different types (e.g., between tones and keys). For reasons of practicality, the sets are restricted in certain ways. The tones employed in the studies all have simple harmonic spectrums, employ equal-tempered tuning, and are generally restricted to a one-octave range. The experiments do not consider various borrowed or altered chords, and do not employ modes other than major and minor. These restrictions, although they ignore characteristics of potential interest, permit interdependencies between perceptual relations for elements of different types to be evaluated in a straightforward way.

In the basic experiments, the elements of interest (tones or chords) are presented singly or in pairs following a musical unit, such as a scale or chord cadence, that would be expected to establish a particular key quite unambiguously. The listeners are required to judge, using a numerical scale, how related the presented elements are, either to each other, or to the established key. Some justification for this procedure is needed. The rationale for presenting tones in key-defining contexts is that key, or tonality, has important implications for the way in which tones and chords are used in simultaneous and successive combinations. Moreover, the key establishes hierarchies of structural significance for tones and chords. Certain of these elements are more central or important within the tonality, with other elements functioning in relation to these central elements. It will be argued that this kind of hierarchical ordering is an essential point of contact between the way in which tonal-harmonic music is constructed and the psychological system that organizes, interprets, and remembers music of this style.

The rating task required of the listener is simply to make a judgment on a numerical scale about the degree to which different elements are related. The instructions to listeners do not specify the particular features or attributes to be considered in arriving at their decision. The task is open-ended and unconstrained, except by the particular musical materials presented and the mode of responding—the numerical scale. In defense of the method, it turns out that there is considerable consistency in the results obtained. Different listeners exhibit similar patterns of responses, and the same individual tends to produce the same or nearly the same response on different occasions when the identical musical stimulus is presented. This internal consistency lends some support to the method. Moreover, it is possible to interpret the patterns obtained in terms of various music-theoretical concepts, serving as a source of external validation for the experimental task.

Tasks of this sort have found useful application in a wide variety of domains. Measures of relatedness or proximity take different forms, including the frequency with which two things co-occur, the probability that two things are confused or misidentified as each other, and numerical ratings about the similarity between objects in the domain of interest. Because data of this general sort arise in various ways, analytical techniques have been devised for their treatment. These techniques require that a measure of relatedness has been obtained for every pair, or at least most pairs, of objects within the set under consideration. The techniques then reduce this set of numbers, which is usually quite large, to a form, or representation, that expresses the underlying patterns contained in the complex set of data. Usually the form of the representation is that of a spatial configuration or map, a graph or tree structure, making the relationships among the elements relatively easy to understand. For this reason, these techniques have proved fruitful as exploratory methods for discovering patterns in complex data that may otherwise be difficult to uncover. These methods are used frequently in the experiments reported here. As a matter of subsidiary interest, however, it turns out that characteristics of the data obtained in the experiments on music perception make them not entirely suited to analysis by existing methods, suggesting desirable extensions and modifications.

These basic experiments describe the perceived relationships between the three types of elements of tonal-harmonic music in an abstract sense. The measurements are presumed to reflect part of a system of knowledge summarizing how the elements are generally employed within the style. Any particular piece exhibits its own unique features: melodic figures, rhythmic and metrical groupings, patterns of repetitions, variations and developments, harmonic progressions, and modulations between keys. These features are apprehended by the listener, in part, by reference to more abstract knowledge about pitch structures. For example, encoding and remembering a melodic figure is influenced by appreciating how its component tones function within the scale of the key. Or, to take another example, a shift between keys is traced by the listener through understanding the multiple functions of the sounded chords within the different keys. Thus, the experience of longer and more complex sequences is assumed to engage the abstract knowledge about pitch structures and be influenced by it. To establish this, various experiments were conducted in conjunction with the rating studies. Some of the experiments are concerned with how tonality affects the listener's ability to remember component elements in longer melodic and harmonic sequences. Certain variables manipulated in these memory studies are those that emerge as important in the rating studies, so the memory data provide a source of convergent evidence. Other experiments employ the rating methods in conjunction with relatively extended and complex sequences, permitting comparisons with the simpler and more abstract materials.

The choice to focus on tonal-harmonic music was based on two primary considerations. First, I was concerned with investigating the knowledge of pitch structures resulting from relatively extensive experience with a musical style. It seemed that information about the final form this knowledge takes could suggest processes through which it is acquired. The availability of listeners to participate in the experiments who were familiar with this style was important, then, in choosing this focus. The second consideration was the extensive body of music theory and analysis treating this idiom. This literature identifies general stylistic principles of organization that could aid in constructing the stimulus materials. Inasmuch as the stimulus materials incorporate features typical of the style, the results obtained have a reasonably wide range of generality. Moreover, the terminology of music theory provides a useful means of interpreting and communicating some of the empirical results. Finally, it was hoped that the perceptual studies might provide a psychological explanation for some of the principles articulated in more theoretical treatments of music. It should be emphasized, however, that the experimental methods do not depend on a particular idiom; they can be extended to other styles when appropriate modifications are made in the stimulus materials. This approach was taken in a number of studies that explore the perceptual effects of music outside the tonal-harmonic tradition. These provide information about the perception of music in less familiar styles that can be compared with the results for tonal-harmonic music.

Outline of the following chapters

The basic empirical results, outlined in Figure 1.2, describe the perceived relationships between tones, chords, and keys. Chapter 2 begins with experiments that measure the degree to which each chromatic scale tone fits with key-defining contexts such as scales, tonic triads, and chord cadences. The results show that a context defining a major or minor key imposes on the set of tones a well-defined ordering of structural significance or stability. This ordering is called a tonal hierarchy. The tonal hierarchies of different keys can be used to produce a quantitative measure of the degree to which the keys are related to one another. The argument is based on the idea that keys are related to the extent that their tonal hierarchies are similar. The analysis that produces a spatial representation of key distances from the tonal hierarchies completes Chapter 2.

The next two chapters are also concerned with tonal hierarchies. Chapter 3 asks what objective properties of music are correlated with the tonal hierarchies measured in the experiments. Two possibilities are examined in detail: tonal consonance and the statistical distribution of tones in tonal-harmonic music. Strong correlations are found between the tonal hierarchies and the durations and number of occurrences of tones in various compositions, suggesting a mechanism through which the tonal hierarchy is internalized. These findings suggested the key-finding algorithm described in Chapter 4. This simple algorithm takes as input the durations of each of the 12 chromatic scale tones in a musical segment; these values are then matched to the tonal hierarchies of all possible major and minor keys. The algorithm returns a set of values indicating the relative strength of each possible key. The algorithm is applied to initial segments of a number of compositions, and to segments throughout a single composition to trace key changes within this piece.

Chapters 5 and 6 turn to the question of how tones are heard in relation to one another. The experiment that is central to Chapter 5 presents all possible pairs of successive tones following a context that defines either a major or minor key. Listeners judge how closely related the first tone of the pair is heard as being to the second. These data are then analyzed to determine the variables influencing the listeners' judgments: distance on the chroma circle, distance on the circle of fifths, and the position of the two tones in the tonal hierarchy of the context key. The judgments are compared with statistical summaries of the frequency with which melodic intervals appear in tonal-harmonic music. The judgments depend on temporal order and key context, which limits the utility of spatial models for representing perceived pitch relations. This problem is treated more theoretically in Chapter 6, which proposes three principles of contextual dependency. These principles, which account for various general patterns found in the experiment of Chapter 5, are also supported by a number of pitch memory studies described in Chapter 6. Other principles governing perceptual organization of pitch sequences are also summarized briefly.

The next two chapters examine the perceptual relationships that obtain for chords. Chapter 7 begins with two experiments that measure the relative structural significance of all possible major, minor, and diminished chords in major and minor key contexts. A well-defined harmonic hier-

	Tones	Chords	Keys
Tones	*Chapter 5*	*Chapter 7*	*Chapter 2*
Chords	*Chapter 7*	*Chapter 8*	*Chapter 7*
Keys	*Chapter 2*	*Chapter 7*	*Chapters 2, 7*

Fig. 1.2. Schematic outline of the organization of the chapters that describe the basic experiments. These explore the perceived relationships in tonal-harmonic music between elements of three types: tones, chords, and keys. Other chapters present material related to these basic experiments.

archy emerges that is considered in light of a number of possible influences, namely, tonal consonance, the statistical distribution of chords in tonal-harmonic music, and the positions of the component tones in the tonal hierarchy of the context key. Chapter 7 closes by demonstrating that the harmonic hierarchy gives rise to a measure of key distance virtually identical to that obtained from the tonal hierarchy. Chapter 8 summarizes a number of studies measuring the degree to which different chords are perceived as related to one another. These perceptual judgments depend strongly on the tonal context according to the principles of contextual dependency proposed in Chapter 6. Supporting results are obtained from studies of memory for chord sequences, also described in Chapter 8. The chapter concludes with a summary of the commonalities found for tonal and harmonic structures.

Chapters 9 and 10 summarize four detailed case studies of the psychological effects of pitch structures in more complex musical sequences. The four experiments all use the same methodology introduced in Chapter 2. Chapter 9 begins with an investigation of how the sense of key develops and changes as a harmonic sequence unfolds in time. The next experiment tests the possibility that two keys can be perceived simultaneously when the musical context employs materials of two different keys in parallel. Chapter 10 considers two musical styles outside the Western tonal-harmonic tradition. One study examines the perception of pitch structures in materials drawn from two compositions in the style of 12-tone serialism. The other study takes a cross-cultural approach, using rāgs from North Indian music. Each of these case studies reveals special psychological capacities and limits for perceiving complex musical sequences.

The final chapter steps back from the empirical results to consider what they reveal about the psychological basis of musical pitch structures. Certain properties of pitch systems are identified that may be important for accurate encoding and memory. A number of traditional and novel pitch systems are analyzed for the presence or absence of these properties. The chapter concludes with a summary of the empirical findings, and a discussion of what they indicate about the nature of the perceptual and cognitive abilities underlying our musical experience.

2.   Quantifying tonal hierarchies and key distances

The experiments reported in this chapter assess the degree to which single musical tones are perceived as being related to tonal centers, or keys. The experiments provide a quantitative measure of the hierarchical ordering imposed on the individual tones in tonal contexts. In music-theoretical terms, the ratings might be identified with the relative stability or structural significance of tones as they function within tonal contexts. It will be argued that this hierarchy is, in some sense, basic to the structuring of music itself and also to the psychological response to music. This identification of a music-theoretical construct and a pattern of psychological data, then, represents a point of contact between the structure contained within the music and described by music theory, and the listener's response to that structure.

One very general feature of music is that one particular pitch is established as a central reference pitch. This pitch is called the tonic, or tonal center. The means of emphasizing the tonic and organizing the other elements around it vary considerably across musical styles. In most cases, the tonic is emphasized both melodically and rhythmically; it is sounded with relative frequency and with longer duration; and it tends to appear near the beginning and end of major phrase boundaries and at points of rhythmic stress. Other mechanisms for establishing the tonal center may also be used. For example, in classical Indian music the tonic appears in the form of a drone that is sounded continuously throughout the rāg, often accompanied by another tone, called the secondary drone. In Indonesian music, the gong tone (the most important pitch) is sounded at the end of major melodic sections together with the gong. In traditional Western music, tonality is associated with a system of harmony, with certain chords and chord sequences acting as important indicators of the tonal center.

In twentieth-century Western music, compositional techniques have evolved that represent significant steps away from the basic principles of tonal harmony. Examples are extreme chromaticism, the construction of chords not assignable to traditional harmonic functions, the simultaneous employment of materials from more than one key, and serial (12-tone) techniques. In some of these cases, the music is structured so as to deny or prevent reference to a single, stable tonal center. The effect of these techniques on the listener is a topic of considerable psychological interest, and certain cases will be considered later. Despite these developments in the West, much contemporary music, as well as music in other cultures, adheres to the basic principle of tonality that, defined in its most general sense, is the centering of the pitch materials around one particular tone.

A number of considerations suggested that the most appropriate place to start the exposition was with the tonal hierarchy imposed on tones by key contexts in Western music. First, the experimental method is quite simple and illustrates certain issues in experimental design. Second, there are relatively clear intuitions and theoretical predictions for this case; other cases with less clear predictions will be presented later. Third, the techniques of data analysis introduced here, correlation and multidimensional scaling, are used again in numerous other studies. Finally, the results obtained here parallel those found in other areas of human cognition and perception, suggesting that a general psychological principle is operating in the particular musical case considered.

Briefly, this general psychological principle is that particular perceptual and conceptual objects have special psychological status. This notion appears in a variety of contexts in the psychological literature, notably in the work of the Gestalt tradition and more recent work by Garner (1970), Rosch (1975), Rosch and Mervis (1975), and Goldmeier (1982). The basic idea is that within categories certain members are normative, unique, self-consistent, simple, typical, or the best exemplars of the domain (sometimes called "prototypes"). They are reference points to which other category members are compared. To illustrate with some examples that have been investigated experimentally, colors are often described with respect to "focal" colors, such as red, green, blue, and yellow. A color may be described as off-red or brownish-red, with implicit reference to a "focal" red. Similarly, numbers are rounded off to other numbers with special cognitive status, such as multiples of tens and hundreds. One says that 9 is almost 10, or that 95 is almost 100. Certain visual forms seem somehow "better" than others, because they are simpler, more regular, or more symmetric. The other, less regular forms are described as variants of these "good" forms. Thus, for example, a line may be described as almost vertical, and a quadrilateral figure as almost a square. These are all examples in which the elements are described in reference to certain other elements having special status within the category.

From a psychological point of view, the existence of singular, central, or prototypical elements within categories is thought to reflect a drive toward maximizing the efficiency of coding or minimizing the complexity of cognitive objects (Goldmeier, 1982, p. 57). This is, in Rosch's terms (1978), the principle of "cognitive economy"; one seeks a system of internal coding that is best suited for making distinctions that are relevant to the domain in question, at the same time conserving finite cognitive resources. In her work, this is codified in a structural theory, sometimes called cue validity, in which the best members of categories are those having the greatest number of features in common with other elements of the category and the fewest features in common with members of other categories. It should be noted, however, that psychologically special category members may exist even when the objects cannot be decomposed into discrete features. The example of color, mentioned earlier, is a case in which cue validity theory based on discrete features does not apply.

Empirical support for psychological reference points consists of two related kinds of findings. The first establishes that elements can be rated reliably in terms of "goodness" (Garner, 1970) or typicality (e.g., Rips, Shoben, & Smith, 1973; Rosch & Mervis, 1975). That is, observers agree with one another when asked to make ratings about how good an exemplar each member is of the category. This establishes a kind of hierarchical ordering on the elements in the category, often expressed in quantitative terms. The second kind of finding shows that the hierarchical ordering influences various measures of perceptual or cognitive processing. For example, "good" figures are remembered better, and are subject to fewer distortions than are less "good" figures (e.g., Goldmeier, 1982). The hierarchical ordering is also reflected in the speed with which observers classify category members, the time required and the number of errors made when learning novel classifications, the order of acquisition of concepts in children, the order and probability of item output, judgments of the degree of relatedness between elements, and various linguistic forms for describing category membership. (See Rosch, 1978, for a summary of these empirical findings.) In summary, considerable empirical work supports the general notion that human cognitive and perceptual systems invest certain elements with special status: these elements are given priority in processing, are most stable in memory, and are important for linguistic descriptions.

The tonal hierarchy

This description of a hierarchical ordering of category members would seem readily applicable to tones in tonal contexts. A tonal context designates one particular tone as most central. The other tones all have functions specified with respect to this tone, in terms of their relatedness to the tonic and secondary reference points established by the tonic. This suggests the operation of a system of reference points in music similar to those emerging from studies in other domains. One important difference should be noted at the outset, however. Whereas other perceptual and cognitive reference points are fixed, the tonic depends on the particular context. No tone is inherently more "tonic" than others, in contrast to, for example, certain colors that appear to be inherently more "focal" than others.

The relative stability of a tone may depend to some degree on its treatment within a particular compositional context as, for example, by the degree to which it is stressed metrically or rhythmically, its place in the contour of a melodic line, its pitch range, and the timbre and dynamics with which it is sounded. However, it is presumed that there is a more abstract, invariant hierarchy of stability that is typical of a musical style more generally, and that this more abstract hierarchy is an important characteristic contributing to the perceived stability of each tone within a complex musical sequence. In this connection, Bharucha (1984b, p. 421) makes the following useful distinction between "event hierarchies" and "tonal hierarchies":

Event hierarchies describe the encoding of specific pieces of music; tonal hierarchies embody our tacit or implicit knowledge of the abstract musical structure of a culture or genre. The tone C may occur many times in a musical piece; each occurrence is a distinct musical event. But all the occurrences are instances of a class of tones (tokens of a type) denoted by "C." In the context of a given piece of music, an event hierarchy represents the functional significance of each occurrence of a C relative to the other sounded tones, whereas a tonal hierarchy represents the functional significance of the class of all C's relative to the other pitch classes.

It is with the latter kind of hierarchy that the present experiments are concerned.

The notion of an abstract tonal hierarchy is suggested in theoretical descriptions of musical structure, in which it is expressed using a variety of terms. Stability will be taken here to be the basic term and to be loosely identified with other terms used, such as relative structural significance, priority, resolution (versus tension), and rest (versus activity). It is taken to refer to the dimension along which musical tones differ, with some tones producing an unstable effect and requiring resolution, and other tones producing a stable effect and giving a sense of completion. Central to the work of L. B. Meyer (1956), this concept of stability is intimately connected to his notions of emotion and meaning in music. Tonal stability plays a central role in numerous other treatments of musical structure, but in Meyer's presentation it takes on specifically psychological content in which he generalizes Gestalt theory to relate principles of tonal organization to the listener's response.

In addition to the psychological functions ascribed by Meyer to the concept of musical stability, his treatment is notable in two other respects. First, it is striking how similar his language is to that used in connection with perceptual and cognitive reference points in the psychological literature summarized earlier. Second, his treatment gives very specific predictions about the ordering expected for Western tonal music, which can be compared to the empirical results presented later. For these reasons, the following passage from L. B. Meyer (1956, pp. 214–15) is interesting:

The term "tonality" refers to the relationships existing between tones or tonal spheres within the context of a particular style system . . . ; some of the tones of the system are active. They tend to move toward the more stable points in the system—the structural or substantive tones.

But activity and rest are relative terms because tonal systems are generally hierarchical: tones which are active tendency tones on one level may be focal substantive tones on another level and vice versa. Thus in the major mode in Western music the tonic tone is the tone of ultimate rest toward which all other tones tend to move. On the next higher level the third and fifth of the scale, though active melodic tones relative to the tonic, join the tonic as structural tones; and all the other tones, whether diatonic or chromatic, tend toward one of these. Going still further in the system, the full complement of diatonic tones are structural focal points relative to the chromatic notes between them. And, finally, as we have seen, any of these twelve chromatic notes may be taken as substantive relative to slight expressive deviations from their normal pitches.

Meyer also points out that this hierarchy has correlates in the names of the notes in various theoretical systems for describing music. Basic names are given to the normative tones, and other tones are described in relation to these. He notes that in Western music the less stable tones in the scale have names that reflect their relationship to the most stable tones, the tonic and the dominant (a fifth above the tonic). The third scale tone is called the mediant because of its position between the tonic and the dominant. The seventh degree of the scale (one scale step below the tonic) is called the leading tone because it "leads to" the tonic. The second degree of the scale (one scale step above the tonic) is called the supertonic. The fourth scale tone, which is a fifth below the tonic, is called the subdominant, and the sixth scale tone, midway between the subdominant and the tonic, is called the submediant. Meyer described analogous naming schemes in theoretical systems for both Indian and Chinese music.

These parallels between musical structure and psychological reference points are suggestive. The parallels indicate the possibility that principles of organization applicable to music resemble those in other cognitive and perceptual domains. To substantiate this parallel, it is necessary to test empirically whether similar effects to those studied in other areas are found in music. As the first step, we investigate the psychological ordering imposed on the set of chromatic tones by contexts establishing Western major and minor keys. The measurement of this hierarchy is the focus of this chapter. The second step is to establish that the elements that dominate in the quantified hierarchy have special perceptual and cognitive status, with other elements heard in relation to them. Experiments reported in later chapters establish that patterns of perceptual and memory judgments conform to those found in other psychological domains in which reference points are presumed to operate.

The first probe tone study: individual differences with a major-key context

The method used to quantify the hierarchy of stability is called the probe tone method, which was introduced in a paper by Krumhansl and Shepard (1979). We observed that when an "incomplete" scale is sounded, such as the successive tones C, D, E, F, G, A, B, this creates strong expectations about the tone that is to follow. The tonic itself, C, is heard as the best completion, and it seemed to us that this was largely unaffected by whether the tone C was in the octave next to the penultimate B, or in some other octave. Other tones complete the sequence somewhat less well, and the degree to which this was the case appeared to be a function of the musical relationship between the final tone and the tonic implied by the incomplete scale. This, then, suggested that a way to quantify the hierarchy of stability in tonal contexts would be to sound incomplete scale contexts with all possible tones of the chromatic scale (which we call "probe tones"), and ask listeners to give a numerical rating of the degree to which each of the tones completed the scale.

In our first experiment, we used both ascending and descending incomplete C major scales. The ascending scale was sounded in the octave below middle C; it consisted of the sequence of notes C, D, E, F, G, A, B. The descending scale began two octaves above middle C; it consisted of the notes, C, B, A, G, F, E, D. The probe tone came next, and the listener's task was to rate it as a completion of the scale context (1 = "very bad" to 7 = "very good"). The probe tones were the equal-tempered semitones (the tones of the chromatic scale) in the octave range from middle C to the C an octave above. Thus, the 13 probe tones were C, C♯, D, D♯, E, F, F♯, G, G♯, A, A♯, B, and C' (the octave above middle C). The tones were produced on an electronic organ, using the flute stop as the best readily available approximation to a pure sine wave tone. Our second experiment used the same incomplete scale contexts, but the tones were produced by computer using digitized sine waves converted to analog form. In addition, this second experiment also included as probe tones the quarter tones between the chromatic scale tones. (A quarter tone is halfway between the adjacent chromatic scale tones on a logarithmic scale.)

The participants in these experiments were university students of diverse musical backgrounds. In analyzing the results from the study, we noticed three distinct patterns and were interested in seeing whether the differences depended on prior musical experience. The first pattern is shown at the top of Figure 2.1. It turned out that the subjects producing this pattern were those who, in our unselected sample, had the most training on average (years instruction = 7.4; years performing = 5.6). The pattern can be characterized in the following way. The tonic received the highest rating, followed by the other scale tones, and the nonscale tones had the lowest ratings. Listeners' responses did not depend strongly on whether the scale context ascended from below or descended from above the range of final probe tones; both contexts resulted in virtually the same pattern. In addition, approximately equal ratings were given to the low and high tonics, independently of context. (This experiment also included one listener with absolute pitch, that is, the ability to identify notes by name in the absence of a known reference pitch. That subject's results were similar to those of this first group of listeners, only with maximal ratings given to the first, third, and fifth scale degrees.)

The second pattern of results found in this study is shown in the center of Figure 2.1. For these listeners, the ratings for the tonic were consistently higher than those for the other tones, although the rating for the tonic tone farther from the scale context (in pitch difference) was somewhat lower than that for the tonic tone closer to the scale context. There was a consistent effect of membership in the diatonic scale, although the effect was reduced compared to the first group of listeners. These results were produced by listeners in our sample who had an intermediate level of training on average (years instruction = 5.5; years performing = 3.3).

The bottom of Figure 2.1 shows the results for the listeners with the least amount of training on average (years instruction = 0.7; no performing experience). As can be seen in the crossing functions, there was a strong effect of the distance of the final probe tone from the preceding context. Tones closer in pitch to the context were preferred over those more distant. In this case, there was a reduced effect of tonic function that generalized only weakly to the tonic distant from the scale context, and the effect of scale membership found for other listeners was virtually absent.

These effects were found both when the tones were produced on the electronic organ in our first experiment, and when they were computer-generated sine wave tones in our second experiment. We did not find that the quarter tones in our second experiment were given consistently lower

---

Fig. 2.1.   Each tone of the chromatic scale ("probe tone") was presented following an ascending or descending incomplete C major scale context in the first probe tone experiment (Krumhansl & Shepard, 1979). Top panel shows results for listeners with the greatest musical training; middle panel shows results for listeners with an intermediate level of musical training; lower panel shows results for listeners with the least musical training. Copyright 1979 by the American Psychological Association. Adapted by permission of the publisher.

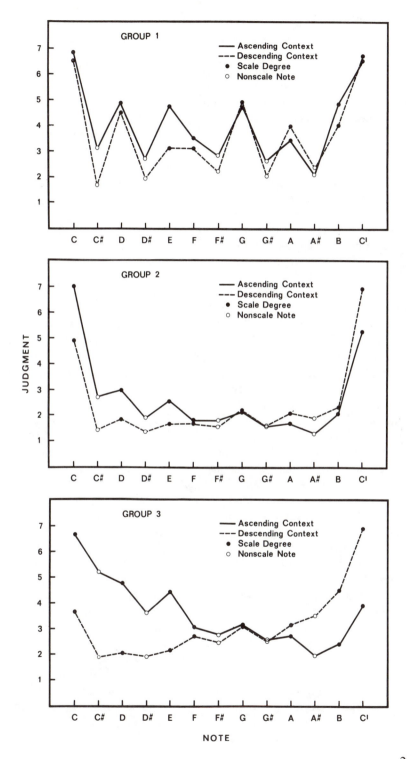

23

ratings than were the chromatic scale tones, as we had expected. Rather, the ratings for the quarter tones were approximately equal to the average of the ratings of the neighboring chromatic scale tones. We concluded that, under the circumstances being tested, listeners are unable to make these fine discriminations, and that the quarter tones are assimilated to their chromatic scale neighbors. However, in a subsequent experiment conducted by Jordan (1987) using a slightly different methodology, differences were found between quarter tones and chromatic scale tones. In that experiment, the probe tones were presented in the same octave range as the scale context, and consistently lower ratings were given to the quarter tones than the chromatic scale tones. Thus, the different results might be attributable to the difficulty listeners in the Krumhansl and Shepard study (1979) had in judging the quarter tones with respect to the scale context presented in a different octave. Jordan (1987) found no evidence of finer discriminations when the scale range was further subdivided into eighth tones.

To summarize, Krumhansl and Shepard (1979) showed different patterns of responding in the probe tone task, and these were quite consistently related to the extent of the listener's music background. Listeners with the least training emphasized the dimension of pitch height. The strength of octave equivalence and the hierarchy of tonal functions increased for listeners with more musical experience. One possible interpretation of these results is that extensive experience is required for knowledge of the tonal hierarchy to be acquired. This interpretation is equivocal, however. It may be that listeners without formal musical training do have knowledge of the relative structural significance of tones in tonal contexts, but simply approached the experimental task with a nonmusical attitude, choosing what may have seemed like a more logical strategy of basing their responses on pitch height differences to the exclusion of other, more musical characteristics. Alternatively, or in addition, the large leaps between the context tones and some of the other probe tones may have made the coding of such characteristics as scale membership difficult and induced a focus on overall pitch height differences.

A more recent developmental study by Speer and Adams (1985) provides additional information concerning the effects of training and experience. That study used almost exactly the methodology of the Krumhansl and Shepard study (1979) with only very minor modifications in the mode of responding. Their subjects were children in first, third, fifth, seventh, or ninth grade, more than half of whom had not had private music lessons. The stimulus materials were essentially identical to those used in our study, with ascending and descending scale contexts followed by each of the possible probe tones. Their listeners were instructed to say how good or bad the last note sounded "when it comes right after the other ones."

They found that musically trained listeners in all grades showed a preference for diatonic over nondiatonic tones, for tonic triad tones (the first, third, and fifth scale tones) over other diatonic tones, and for the tonic over the other triad tones. For musically untrained listeners, a developmental sequence appeared. First graders showed only a weak preference for diatonic tones over nondiatonic tones. Third graders showed a more consistent preference for diatonic tones over nondiatonic tones, and also a preference for the tonic over other tones of the triad. Fifth, seventh, and ninth graders showed all the relevant musical distinctions as listeners with musical training. (This pattern of acquisition is similar to that found by Krumhansl and Keil (1982). In that study, children were asked to judge pairs of tones presented in tonal contexts. The distinction between diatonic and nondiatonic tones appeared earlier in development than the distinction between tones in the diatonic scale.)

What is important to note in the present context is that explicit musical training in both the Speer and Adams (1985) and Krumhansl and Shepard (1979) studies led to a pattern of responding that reflects musically relevant distinctions between tones. The developmental study showed, however, that training is not necessary for this pattern to be produced; untrained listeners have, by fifth grade, acquired all the relevant distinctions. A subsequent study by Speer and Meeks (1985) found these distinctions were also made by some untrained second grade students. We did not find these distinctions for our untrained adult listeners, supporting the notion that these listeners may have adopted an alternative strategy in performing the experimental task.

Replication and extension to minor-key contexts

A subsequent probe tone experiment, reported by Krumhansl and Kessler (1982), was undertaken to replicate and extend the results of the first study. In this second experiment, we included a variety of different contexts to ensure that the basic findings of the first experiment generalized to other contexts. We assumed that the scale context of the first study established the expected key; this assumption would be supported if similar ratings were given when different contexts thought to imply the same key were used. In this second experiment, we used as contexts: complete scales (with the tonic tone sounded in both the first and last position), tonic triads (the I chords), and three different chord cadences (IV V I, VI V I, and II V I). (The Roman numerals indicate the scale degree of the root of the chords. For example, IV in C major designates a diatonic triad built on the fourth scale degree, F.)

These context types were also sounded in both major and minor keys to see whether analogous patterns would be found for the two modes. In addition, a variety of different tonal centers or keys were used to make sure that our findings in the first experiment did not depend on the choice of C as the tonic. It seemed to us unlikely that there would be differences between keys of the same type (major or minor) that depended on the particular tonic. This intuition would be supported if the rating data, when transposed to a common abstract tonic, contained similar patterns.

A major objective of this experiment was to obtain ratings of probe tones that were as stable and reliable as possible, so that they could be used in connection with subsequent experiments with more complex musical contexts. For this reason, various procedures were adopted. The experimental session began with a number of practice trials, representing the variety of contexts and probe tones used in the actual experiment. Listeners were instructed to try to use the rating scale consistently, and to use the entire range of the scale as much as possible. In addition, each block (group) of trials began with a number of practice trials to orient the listener to the particular context used in that block of trials. The same context was used in a number of blocks, so that listeners made multiple judgments about the same context–probe tone combinations. These "exact replications" can be used to assess the reliability of the ratings. The order of the probe tones was selected randomly, with different orders in different blocks of trials. The reason for this is that there may be carry-over effects from trial to trial such that the rating for one probe tone may be affected by the ratings given to probe tones on previous trials. Using different random orders in different blocks of trials would be expected to average out these carry-over effects. Finally, different blocks of trials, using different contexts, were presented in different orders for the purpose of averaging out any carry-over effects between blocks of trials for different listeners.

We also did two things to minimize the effects of influences that are not specifically musical. First, to decrease the chance that nonmusical response strategies would be adopted, listeners had to have at least 5 years of formal instruction in music. In fact, our participants had an average of approximately 11 years of instrumental and/or voice lessons, had performed for an average of 12 years in instrumental groups and 2 years in choral groups, and were listening to music an average of 23 hours per week. However, we did not want listeners to have had extensive training in music theory, because we wanted the results to be based on the listeners' perceptual response rather than on theoretical knowledge. One of our listeners had had a very basic course in music theory; the remaining listeners had no formal music theory background.

Second, we attempted to minimize the effect of pitch height differences between the context and probe tones, which strongly affected the responses of the least musically oriented listeners in the earlier study. We used complex tones consisting of sine wave components distributed at octave intervals over a five-octave range. Single tones (such as those in the scale contexts and the probe tones) consisted of 5 sine wave components in a five-octave range from 77.8 Hz to 2349 Hz (an example is shown at the top of Figure 2.2). Triads (in the tonic chord and cadence contexts) consisted of 15 sine wave components sounded over the same five-octave range, with 5 components for each of the three chord tones in each of the five octaves (as shown at the bottom of Fig. 2.2). An amplitude envelope was imposed over this frequency range, such that the components at the low and high ends of the range approached hearing threshold. Tones produced by this method have an organlike quality, with no well-defined lowest or highest pitch and approximately the same overall pitch height. They have appeared in a number of contexts. Stuckenschmidt (1969) reports that Ernst Krenek electronically generated sounds using a similar method in the oratorio *Spiritus Intelligentiae Sanctus* (1955–1956) to create a sense of acoustic infinity. Shepard (1964) also used the method to produce an illusion of a continuously rising pitch sequence; he called them "circular" tones because after a series of steps (in which the component sine waves are shifted up and new components are added at the low end of the range) the sequence returns to the original starting point. Recently Deutsch and colleagues (1986a, 1987; Deutsch, Moore, & Dolson, 1986; Deutsch, Kuyper, & Fisher, 1987) have been using tones of this sort to study what is called the "tritone paradox" in which some listeners hear a tritone as ascending while others hear it as descending. Technical details of our specific application of the method can be found in Krumhansl, Bharucha, and Kessler (1982). For present purposes, this method of stimulus production minimized overall pitch height differences, so that the tones differed primarily in terms of their position within the tonal scale (which was the variable of real interest).

One final difference in method from the previous study (Krumhansl & Shepard, 1979) should be mentioned. In that study, the contexts were "incomplete" scales, and the listener's task was to rate how well the various probe tones completed the scale. In the present experiment, because of the nature of the contexts used, the task was to rate how well the final probe tone "fit with" the context in a musical sense. The effect of this change in instructions can be assessed by comparing the results for the major contexts from this experiment with those of the previous study.

Ten listeners participated in the experiment, and produced rating responses that were quite reliable as assessed in a number of ways. An individual listener produced similar responses on different trials containing the same context and probe tone combinations ("exact replications"). In addition, different listeners agreed quite well with one another, and methods for exploring possible differences between subjects uncovered no consistent patterns related to the extent of the listener's music background. This would be expected given the selection of listeners, who were quite homogeneous in their level of training. Moreover, substantially the same patterns were found for different major and different minor contexts when the ratings were transposed to compensate for the different tonics. For example, the ratings for the C major contexts agreed well with the

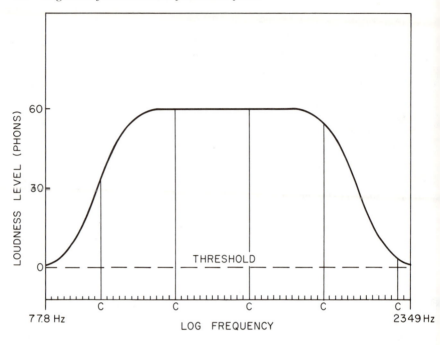

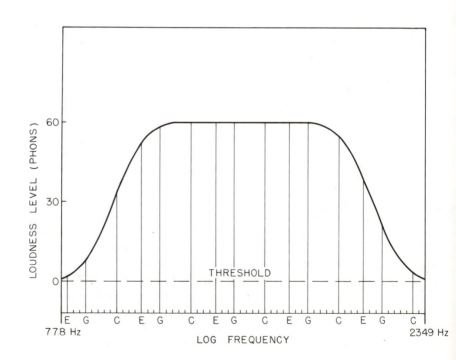

ratings for the A major contexts when the two sets of data were transposed to a common tonic.

The rating data also did not depend strongly on the particular context chosen to establish the intended key. That is, the responses did not, in general, depend on whether the context was a scale, a tonic triad chord, or one of the three chord cadences. Statistical tests showed high consistency across the different kinds of contexts. However, the results for the tonic triad chord context and the three cadence contexts were more similar to each other than these were to the results for the scale context. The differences can be characterized in the following way. When a scale context was used, somewhat higher ratings were given to the scale tones near the final tonic; slightly higher ratings were given to the second, sixth, and seventh scale tones, and slightly lower ratings were given to the third scale tone. These differences in the ratings can be traced back to differences between the contexts themselves, but it should be emphasized that they were quite minimal. Because of them, however, we elected to form a composite rating profile from the tonic triad chord and the three cadence contexts, all of which were very similar to one another. (The average ratings for these contexts are given in Table 2.1 and plotted in Figure 2.3.) These values are the average of the ratings given in the various blocks of trials, transposed to a common tonic, and averaged across the tonic triad and three chord cadence contexts. The values are shown with respect to C major and C minor keys, but it should be remembered that the results come from a number of different key contexts transposed to a common reference tonic, taken to be C.

With the major key context, the highest rating was given to the tonic itself, C (for the reference key of C major), followed by the fifth scale degree (G), the third scale degree (E), and the remaining scale tones (D, F, A, and B). The lowest ratings were given to the nonscale pitches: C♯(D♭), D♯(E♭), F♯(G♭), G♯(A♭), A♯(B♭). Thus, the results strongly confirmed the hierarchy of stability predicted by L. B. Meyer (1956), which was given earlier. In addition, the results of the major contexts generally replicated those of the earlier experiments (Krumhansl & Shepard, 1979) for listeners with the most musical training. These findings suggest that the various changes in method, including the different instructions and musical contexts, did not significantly affect the results. The rating profiles from this experiment, however, showed somewhat finer

Fig. 2.2. Loudness envelope used to determine the relative amplitudes of the 5 sine wave components of the "circular" tones and the 15 sine wave components of the "circular" chords used in the experiment of Krumhansl and Kessler (1982). The technique (Shepard, 1964; Krumhansl, Bharucha & Kessler, 1982) produces tones and chords with approximately equal overall pitch height and no well-defined lowest or highest pitch. Copyright 1982 by the American Psychological Association. Adapted by permission of the publisher.

Table 2.1. Probe tone ratings

Tone	Context	
	C Major	C Minor
C	6.35	6.33
C♯/D♭	2.23	2.68
D	3.48	3.52
D♯/E♭	2.33	5.38
E	4.38	2.60
F	4.09	3.53
F♯/G♭	2.52	2.54
G	5.19	4.75
G♯/A♭	2.39	3.98
A	3.66	2.69
A♯/B♭	2.29	3.34
B	2.88	3.17

Source: Krumhansl and Kessler (1982).

distinctions than those of the earlier study, probably because of the larger number of observations made in this experiment and the somewhat higher levels of music training among the participants.

A similar pattern holds for minor keys. Again, the highest rating was given to the tonic tone, C. Following this were the third (E♭) and fifth (G) scale pitches. Note that, unlike the major contexts, the minor contexts produced higher ratings for the third scale degree than for the fifth scale degree. This may reflect that the third scale degree is the tonic of the closely related, relative major of the minor key (the relative major and minor keys differ in mode and in the location of their tonics, but consist of the same set of scale pitches; the relative major of C minor is E♭ major). Again, the remaining scale pitches are given the next highest ratings, and the lowest ratings overall were given to the nonscale pitches.

The effects just described were found to be highly reliable when statistical tests were performed. Moreover, the quantitative ratings accorded well with qualitative music-theoretical predictions. That is, the ordering corresponds to the musical dimension variously known as relative stability, structural significance, priority, resolution, and rest. The pattern of probe tone ratings in Table 2.1 and Figure 2.3, then, can be considered to be an indicator of a psychological orientation to a musical key. A musical key establishes a hierarchical ordering on the set of 12 tones of the chromatic scale, and this hierarchy is distinctive for each key. The next chapter considers various possible determinants of the hierarchy of stability. However, before addressing this question, an additional analysis of the probe tone rating data will be presented.

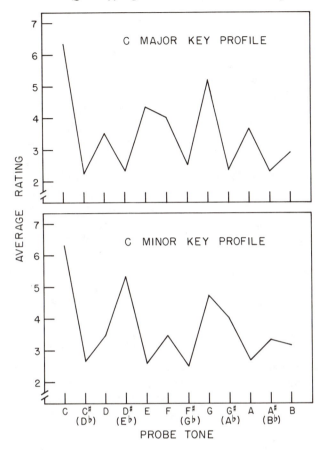

Fig. 2.3. Probe tone ratings from the study by Krumhansl and Kessler (1982) shown with reference to a C major key (top) and a C minor key (bottom). The data were produced by experienced musicians following contexts that were tonic triads and chord cadences. Copyright 1982 by the American Psychological Association. Adapted by permission of the publisher.

A derived measure of interkey distance

This section considers whether the experimentally measured tonal hierarchies can be used to produce a measure of interkey distance. The issue of interkey distance arises in music-theoretical descriptions of traditional Western tonal-harmonic music because of the compositional practice of modulating, or changing, between keys. A musical composition is typically written in one main or "home" key, but modulations between keys are frequently found. That is, a composition moves from the main key to one or more other keys, usually returning again to the original key. This practice is codified in various descriptions of interkey distance, in which keys are considered close if modulations between them are relatively frequent.

The distance between major keys is represented by the "circle of fifths," shown in Figure 2.4. The name derives from the tonics of neighboring keys that are separated by an interval of a fifth. Around the circle, neighboring keys have scales that share all but one pitch. For example, the scale of the key of C major (C, D, E, F, G, A, B) has all but one tone in common with the scale of the key of G major (G, A, B, C, D, E, F♯). The same property holds for all other pairs of major keys that are adjacent on the circle of fifths. This means that key signatures of neighboring keys on the circle differ only by one sharp or flat. (A "key signature" refers to the number and names of the pitches in a specific key that must be flatted or sharped to produce a diatonic scale. For example, the key signature of G major is one sharp [F♯]; the key signature of E♭ major is three flats [B♭, E♭, and A♭].) When enharmonically equivalent tones (tones with different names but played the same in equal-tempered tuning (e.g., F♯ and G♭) are identified, the pattern of interkey relatedness folds back on itself to form a closed circle. Table 2.2 shows the scale tones of seven neighboring major keys on the circle of fifths.

When minor keys are introduced, the problem of defining interkey distance is complicated considerably. Minor scales take a number of different forms, shown in Table 2.2. The "natural" minor scale contains the same pitches as a major scale, only beginning on the sixth scale degree of the major scale. For example, the scale tones of the natural A minor scale

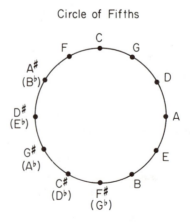

Fig. 2.4. Circle of fifths showing relationships between major keys. Neighboring keys have tonics separated by an interval of a fifth, their scales share all but one tone, and their key signatures differ only in terms of one sharp or flat.

Table 2.2. Tones of major and minor scales

Seven Neighboring Major Keys on the Circle of Fifths

Eb Major	Bb Major	F Major	C Major	G Major	D Major	A Major
C	C	C	C	C		
					C♯	C♯
D	D	D	D	D	D	D
Eb	Eb					
		E	E	E	E	E
F	F	F	F			
				F♯	F♯	F♯
G	G	G	G	G	G	
Ab						G♯
	A	A	A	A	A	A
Bb	Bb	Bb				
			B	B	B	B
C	C	C	C	C		

Three Forms of A-Minor Scale

Natural A and Descending Melodic	A Harmonic	A Ascending Melodic
A	A	A
B	B	B
C	C	C
D	D	D
E	E	E
F	F	
		F♯
G		
	G♯	G♯
A	A	A

(A, B, C, D, E, F, G) are exactly those of C major (C, D, E, F, G, A, B), only the minor scale begins on the sixth scale degree (A) of C major. However, when chords are formed in minor, the seventh scale pitch (G in A minor) is usually raised by a half step (to G♯). This produces what is called the "harmonic" minor scale. One important consequence of raising the seventh scale degree is that the chord built on the fifth scale degree, the dominant, is a major chord. Finally, both the sixth and seventh scale degrees (F and G in the key of A minor) tend to be raised in ascending melodic lines to minimize the large gaps that would otherwise be found between the sixth and seventh tones and the tonic. This produces what is called the "ascending melodic" minor scale. In the "descending melodic" minor scale, however, the sixth and seventh scale pitches are not raised, so that the descending melodic minor scale has the same pitches as the natural minor scale. The important point here is simply that these different forms of the minor scale make impossible any simple definition of distances for minor keys based on scale membership.

Another complication is that each minor key is considered closely related to two different major keys that are not themselves closely related to each other. First, a minor key is considered close to the major key that has the same scale pitches (but different tonic) as the natural minor scale, and the two are called the "relative" major and minor of each other. As was noted in the previous example, the C major scale and the natural A minor scale have the same pitches; A minor is the relative minor of C major, and C major is the relative major of A minor. Second, a minor key is considered closely related to the major key with which it shares a tonic. That is, A major and A minor are closely related by virtue of their shared tonic tone (A), a relationship that is reinforced by the fact that they also share the same fifth scale tone or dominant (E). This relationship between major and minor keys is called "parallel". For example, A minor is the parallel minor of A major, and A major is the parallel major of A minor. Thus, each minor key is closely related to two different major keys, but these major keys are not close to each other on the circle of fifths. For example, the key of A minor is closely related to both C major and A major, but these two major keys are three steps apart on the circle of fifths. As a consequence, the minor keys cannot easily be added to the circle-of-fifths representation of major keys. A more complicated description of key relationships must be used when both major and minor keys are considered; two music-theoretical descriptions will be shown later.

We (Krumhansl & Kessler, 1982) suggested that it might be possible to obtain a quantitative measure of the distances between keys from the profile ratings given in Table 2.1. Our argument was based on the idea that two keys are close to the extent that they impose a similar pattern of relative stability on the tones. If two keys have similar hierarchies, then it would seem that modulations between them would be able to be effected relatively easily. The probe tone ratings are taken to be a measure of stability; therefore keys that are close should have similar hierarchies. What would be needed, then, is a way of comparing two key profiles and obtaining a measure of their similarity. This measure of similarity would be construed as a measure of interkey distance.

Although the rating data shown in Table 2.1 are given as though the context key were either C major or C minor, it should be remembered that the results for any other major or minor key would be similar under transposition. For example, the rating profile for A minor would be the same as that for C minor, only shifted down three semitones. This means that the rating given to the tone C in the context of C minor should be the same as the tone A in the context of A minor; the rating given to the tone C♯(D♭) in the context of C minor should be the same as the tone A♯(B♭) in the context of A minor, and so on. [This procedure is supported by the Krumhansl and Kessler (1982) experiment, in which a number of different major and minor keys were used and the data were found to be similar under transposition.] By shifting the rating profiles the appropriate number of semitones, then, we have a rating profile for each of the 12 major keys and each of the 12 minor keys.

The top of Figure 2.5 shows the profiles for C major and A minor superimposed. Although there are differences, the patterns are generally the same. Other pairs of rating profiles are much less similar, for example, those for C major and F♯ major, which are shown at the bottom of Figure 2.5. One method for assessing the degree of similarity between profiles is the statistical measure called correlation. This statistic takes a value from −1 (for patterns that are exactly opposite) to 1 (for patterns that are exactly the same). Table 2.3 shows the formula for computing correlations and an application to the profiles for C major and A minor. The resulting value of .651 indicates a moderately high level of agreement between the two rating profiles. The corresponding value for C major and F♯ major profiles is −.683, the low value reflecting the mismatches between the profiles.

Other ways to measure the degree of similarity between profiles are possible. One alternative is, for each tone, to take the absolute value of the difference between the two ratings for the two keys in question. (The absolute value is simply the positive magnitude of the difference between the two numbers.) These absolute values can be added or averaged across the 12 probe tones to give a summary measure of the difference between the two profiles. Another alternative would be to take the sum of the squared differences between the corresponding ratings for the two keys, which also provides a summary measure of the differences between profiles but emphasizes the large differences relative to the small differences. These alternatives were, in fact, explored and they produced patterns of results almost identical to the analysis using correlations. We prefer the correlations because they have well-defined statistical properties.

The correlation between profiles was computed for each possible pair of major and minor keys (i.e., all major–major key combinations, all minor–minor key combinations, and all major–minor key combinations). The results are given in Table 2.4 for C major and C minor profiles correlated with the profiles for all other possible keys. The correlations for other pairs of keys are analogous. For example, the correlation between the rating profiles for D major and E major keys is the same as the cor-

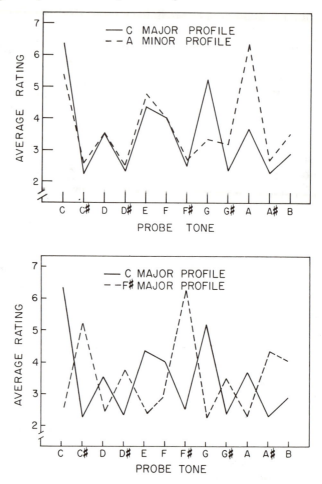

Fig. 2.5. Top figure compares the probe tone ratings for two closely related keys (C major and A minor). Bottom figure compares the probe tone ratings for two distantly related keys (C major and F♯ major). Similar patterns are seen in the ratings for closely related keys, but not for distantly related keys. The values are from the study by Krumhansl and Kessler (1982). Copyright 1982 by the American Psychological Association. Adapted by permission of the publisher.

relation between the rating profiles for C major and D major, because in both cases the tonics are separated by an interval of two semitones.

When the correlations are plotted as in Figure 2.6, certain interpretable patterns can be seen. The values plotted in the top left portion of the figure are the correlations between the profile for the key of C major and that of all other major keys. The major keys are ordered along the ab-

Table 2.3. Computation of correlations between key profiles

Tone	Context	
	C Major	A Minor
C	6.35	5.38
C♯/D♭	2.23	2.60
D	3.48	3.53
D♯/E♭	2.33	2.54
E	4.38	4.75
F	4.09	3.98
F♯/G♭	2.52	2.69
G	5.19	3.34
G♯/A♭	2.39	3.17
A	3.66	6.33
A♯/B♭	2.29	2.68
B	2.88	3.52
Average	3.48	3.71

$$r = \frac{\Sigma(x - \bar{x})(y - \bar{y})}{\sqrt{\Sigma(x - \bar{x})^2 \, \Sigma(y - \bar{y})^2}}$$

$$= \frac{(6.35 - 3.48)(5.38 - 3.71) + \cdots + (2.88 - 3.48)(3.52 - 3.71)}{\sqrt{[(6.35 - 3.48)^2 + \cdots + (2.88 - 3.48)^2]} \times \sqrt{[5.38 - 3.71)^2 + \cdots + (3.52 - 3.71)^2]}}$$

$$= .651$$

where

x = ratings in C major
$\bar{x}$ = average of ratings in C major
y = ratings in A minor
$\bar{y}$ = average of ratings in A minor

scissa (or horizontal axis) as they appear around the circle of fifths. It can be seen that the farther a major key is from C major on the circle of fifths, the lower is the correlation between its rating profile and that of C major. For example, they key of G major, which is next to C major on the circle of fifths, has a profile that correlates most highly with the profile of C major. The key of F♯ major, which is directly opposite C major on the circle of fifths, has the lowest correlation with C major. Then the correlations increase again as the keys move closer to C major around the circle of fifths. Thus the expected pattern, the distance around the circle of fifths, corresponds exactly to the order of the computed correlations.

The values plotted on the top right are the correlations between the profile for C major and the 12 minor keys, which are again ordered according to their positions on the circle of fifths (for minor keys). This plot

Table 2.4. Correlations between key profiles

	C Major	C Minor
C major	1.000	.511
C♯/D♭ major	−.500	−.158
D major	.040	−.402
D♯/E♭ major	−.105	.651
E major	−.185	−.508
F major	.591	.241
F♯/G♭ major	−.683	−.369
G major	.591	.215
G♯/A♭ major	−.185	.536
A major	−.105	−.654
A♯/B♭ major	.040	.237
B major	−.500	−.298
C minor	.511	1.000
C♯/D♭ minor	−.298	−.394
D minor	.237	−.160
D♯/E♭ minor	−.654	.055
E minor	.536	−.003
F minor	.215	.339
F♯/G♭ minor	−.369	−.673
G minor	.241	.339
G♯/A♭ minor	−.508	−.003
A minor	.651	.055
A♯/B♭ minor	−.402	−.160
B minor	−.158	−.394

contains two local peaks. The highest correlation is between C major and A minor, the relative minor of C major, and there is also a relatively high correlation between C major and C minor, the parallel minor of C major. Moving away from these two keys, the correlations generally decline. Thus, the correlations pick up on the dual (parallel and relative) associations between major and minor keys.

The values plotted on the lower left are the correlations between the profile for C minor and the 12 major keys. These are, in fact, the same values as plotted in the upper right graph, only here they are plotted in reference to a fixed minor key (C minor) rather than a fixed major key (C major). When they are considered in reference to C minor, the dual association between major and minor keys is again apparent. The profile for C minor is relatively similar to that of C major (its parallel major) and to that of E♭ major (its relative major); values decline from these local peaks.

The values plotted in the lower right are the correlations between the profile for C minor and the 12 minor keys ordered as around the circle of fifths. Generally, the correlations decline with distance around the circle.

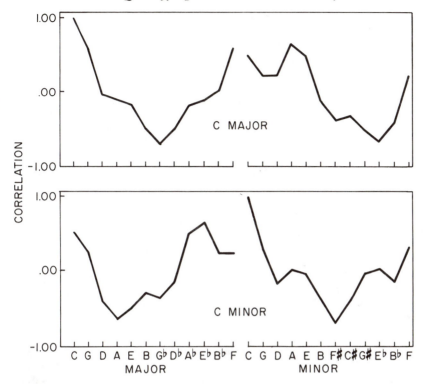

Fig. 2.6.   Correlations between probe tone ratings for C major and all other major and minor keys (top), and correlations between probe tone ratings for C minor and all other major and minor keys (bottom). These correlations are taken to be an indirect measure of interkey distance derived from the probe tone ratings of Krumhansl and Kessler (1982).

There is, however, a local peak at the key of A minor. This is accounted for by A minor's being the relative minor of C major, which in turn is the parallel major of C minor. There is also a local peak at E♭ minor; this is accounted for by E♭ minor's being the parallel minor of the relative major, E♭ major, of C minor. That is, the local peaks can be accounted for in terms of the parallel and relative major–minor relationships. Otherwise, the pattern conforms to distance around the circle of fifths for minor keys.

In summary, we see in these correlations substantial agreement with the patterns one would predict from music-theoretical descriptions of interkey distance. For major keys, the pattern of correlations corresponds to distances around the circle of fifths. For major and minor keys, we see the influence of both relative and parallel relationships between major and minor keys. Furthermore, for minor keys, we again see the influence of the circle of fifths, as well as the relative and parallel major–

minor relationships that produce associations between minor keys mediated through major keys. It is important to remember that the patterns arise from the tonal hierarchies and not direct perceptual judgments of key distances.

A spatial representation of interkey distance

Although the patterns as plotted in Figure 2.6 are quite clear, it is possible to take the analysis one step further. In this step, we use the correlations to produce a spatial representation of the distances between keys. This representation simultaneously summarizes the relationships between all major and minor keys in a form that is easily accessible visually. To obtain this spatial representation of interkey distance from the correlations, we (Krumhansl & Kessler, 1982) used a method called nonmetric multidimensional scaling. This method was originated by Shepard (1962 I, II) and Kruskal (1964); a good introduction can be found in Kruskal and Wish (1978). Although the algorithm for performing multidimensional scaling is fairly complicated, computer programs are widely available. What the method does, in general outline, is to transform a set of similarity values into a spatial representation of points.

The set of similarity values input to the multidimensional scaling program describes the degree of similarity or relatedness between all possible pairs of objects. Various kinds of data are possible, including direct ratings of similarity, measures of association or co-occurrence, probability of confusion, and measures that arise in other ways. It is assumed that a measure of similarity exists for each possible pair of objects in the domain under consideration (although algorithms exist for cases in which some measures are missing). In the present application, the objects were the 12 major and 12 minor keys. The correlations just described were used as the measure of interkey similarity. High values in this case corresponded to keys that have similar rating profiles.

What the multidimensional scaling program does is to place points in a coordinate space, with each point corresponding to one of the objects in the domain under consideration. The output of the program is a set of spatial coordinates for each of the points. These can then be plotted to get a visual representation. In this case, there will be 24 points, one for each of the major and minor keys. The rule that governs the placement of the points is that the order of distances between points in the spatial configuration should correspond as closely as possible to the order of similarity values (the values input to the program). If two objects have a high similarity value, then they should correspond to points close to each other in the coordinate space; conversely, if two objects have a low similarity value, then they should correspond to distant points. From the correlations, for example, we would expect the points for C major and A minor to be fairly close, but those for C major and F♯ major to be distant.

Only the relative order of the similarity values is used by the computer algorithm; it makes no stronger assumptions about arithmetic properties of the input data. In other words, the algorithm uses only the relative magnitudes of the similarity values, not their absolute magnitudes, arithmetic differences, or any other arithmetic combinations. For this reason, the method is called "nonmetric" multidimensional scaling. However, the distances between points (usually computed as Euclidean distance) are assumed to have metric properties such as the triangle inequality (that the third side of a triangle is shorter than the sum of the lengths of the other two sides). In addition to producing a spatial configuration, the scaling program gives a measure, called "stress," that specifies how well the resulting configuration fits the similarity values. Stress reflects how much the distances among the points in the spatial configuration deviate from the original order of similarity values. Different formulas are used to compute stress; a common one, called "stress formula 1", will be used here.

In application, various technical problems are encountered [which are covered in Kruskal and Wish (1978)]. Only one of these need concern us here: choosing the number of dimensions for the spatial configuration. The points can be located in a one-dimensional space, that is, required to fall on a single line. Or, the points can be plotted in two-dimensional space, as on a flat surface or plane. Or, the points can be located in three-dimensional space, or indeed a space of higher dimensions. The output of the program is a set of coordinates in a space of the number of dimensions specified in advance.

In principle, any number of dimensions can be specified. In practice, however, one wants a spatial representation that is visually accessible and that substantially reduces the amount of information contained in the original similarity values. These considerations suggest that a solution in a small number of dimensions is desirable because what we want is a convenient summary of the original ratings. On the other hand, the solution should not do too much violence to the data. That is, the distances should account for most of the ordering information in the similarity values. If the match is poor in a solution using a few dimensions, then this will be reflected in a high stress value. As the number of dimensions increases, the stress value will necessarily decrease, but at the expense of losing visual accessibility and having to estimate a larger number of parameters (spatial coordinates).

In the present application, it turns out that we need a four-dimensional solution. A solution in fewer dimensions fails to capture important aspects of the data. A glance at the correlation values plotted in Figure 2.6 suggests why. We need two dimensions to account for the circle of fifths that is reflected in the correlations among major keys and also in the correlations among minor keys. Two additional dimensions are required to account for the parallel and relative major–minor relationships that are reflected both in the correlations among major and minor keys, and less directly in the correlations among different minor keys.

Table 2.5 gives the coordinates of the 24 major and minor keys in the four-dimensional solution. This is the basic output of the multidimensional scaling analysis. The stress value, also given by the output, is .017 (stress formula 1), which reflects an excellent fit between the correlation data input to the program and the interpoint distances of the resulting configuration. That is, the solution obtained was able to account for virtually all the ordering information contained in the correlations of the musical key profiles.

In order to look at the obtained multidimensional scaling solution visually, the coordinates can be plotted. The configuration shown on the left of Figure 2.7 shows the 24 major and minor keys plotted in the first two dimensions (lower-case letters indicate minor keys). As can be seen,

Table 2.5. Coordinates of musical keys in multidimensional scaling solution

Key	Dimension			
	1	2	3	4
C major	.567	−.633	−.208	.480
C♯/D♭ major	−.175	.831	−.480	−.208
D major	−.265	−.807	.208	−.480
D♯/E♭ major	.633	.567	.480	.208
E major	−.832	−.175	−.208	.480
F major	.808	−.265	−.480	−.208
F♯/G♭ major	−.567	.633	.208	−.480
G major	.175	−.832	.481	.208
G♯/A♭ major	.265	.807	−.208	.480
A major	−.633	−.567	−.480	−.208
A♯/B♭ major	.831	.174	.208	−.480
B major	−.807	.265	.480	.208
C minor	.782	.206	.119	.580
C♯/D♭ minor	−.780	.212	−.580	.120
D minor	.570	−.574	−.120	−.580
D♯/E♭ minor	−.207	.782	.580	−.119
E minor	−.212	−.780	.119	.580
F minor	.574	.570	−.580	.120
F♯/G♭ minor	−.781	−.206	−.120	−.580
G minor	.780	−.212	.580	−.119
G♯/A♭ minor	−.569	.573	.119	.580
A minor	.206	−.781	−.580	.119
A♯/B♭ minor	.212	.780	−.120	−.580
B minor	−.574	−.570	.580	−.119

the 24 points in this two-dimensional projection fell essentially on a circle. Considering major keys only, the circular configuration is the circle of fifths. That is, going around the circle, the major keys are ordered as they are on the circle of fifths. The same pattern holds for minor keys.

Therefore, two dimensions contain one circle of fifths for major keys and one circle of fifths for minor keys. The alignment of these two circular components reflects a compromise between the relative and parallel relationship between major and minor keys. For example, C minor is located near B♭ major, although the profiles for these keys are not, in fact, highly correlated (.237). This can be understood, however, because C minor correlates relatively highly with both C major (.511) and E♭ major (.651), its parallel and relative major keys. Because these two major keys are not themselves close to each other on the circle of fifths, a compromise position is found, with the consequence that C minor is located between its parallel and relative major keys and close to B♭ major. If only two dimensions were used, then this would produce an unsatisfactory stress value. However, the other two dimensions compensate for this feature of the projection in the first two dimensions.

The configuration on the right of Figure 2.7 shows the spatial coordi-

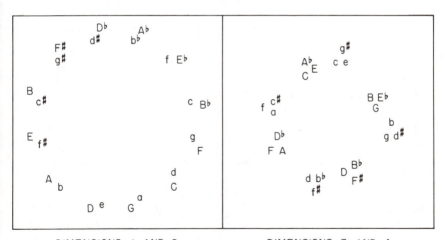

DIMENSIONS 1 AND 2   DIMENSIONS 3 AND 4

Fig. 2.7. The correlations between probe tone rating profiles (Krumhansl & Kessler, 1982) for all pairs of major and minor keys were analyzed using multidimensional scaling. The analysis produced a four-dimensional solution. The coordinates of the points in the first two dimensions are shown on the left; these two dimensions emphasize the circle of fifths. The coordinates in the last two dimensions are shown on the right; these two dimensions emphasize the relative and parallel major–minor relationships. Copyright 1982 by the American Psychological Association. Reprinted by permission of the publisher.

nates of the 24 major and minor keys in the third and fourth dimensions. Again, a circular pattern was found. On this circle, groups of three different keys cluster in eight compact regions. For example, the point for C, E, and A♭ major keys cluster together, as do the points for C, E, and G♯ minor keys. That is, in this projection, keys of the same mode (major or minor) with tonics separated by intervals of a major third are identified. The problem, then, is assigning an interpretation to this feature of the projection in the third and fourth dimensions.

The clustering of points into groups of three keys appears to be a consequence of the relative and parallel relationships between major and minor keys. When the clusters are ordered around the circular configuration in the third and fourth dimensions, each major key is flanked on one side by its relative minor key and on the other by its parallel minor key. For example, on one side of C major is A minor and on the other C minor, its relative and parallel minor keys. Similarly, each minor key is flanked on one side by its relative major key and on the other by its parallel major key. Therefore, on the one side of C minor is E♭ major and on the other C major, its relative and parallel major keys. The third and fourth dimensions, then, seem to be carrying information about the dual relationships between major and minor keys.

Note that major and minor keys that were located in proximal positions in the projection in the first two dimensions are separated in dimensions 3 and 4. For example, in the first two dimensions C major and D minor were located close together, a location that apparently represented a compromise between the pulls toward two relatively distant major keys. In the third and fourth dimensions, C major and D minor are widely separated. Therefore, a feature of the projection in the first two dimensions that is difficult to interpret is offset by features of the projection in dimensions 3 and 4. Similarly, the identification of clusters of three different keys with tonics separated by an interval of a major third in dimensions 3 and 4 was difficult to interpret. For example, C, E, and A♭ major all have virtually identical coordinates in dimensions 3 and 4. However, these three keys are maximally separated when the coordinates in dimensions 1 and 2 are considered. Here again we see a compensation for features in one two-dimensional projection in the other two-dimensional projection.

This discussion points to the importance of considering the coordinates in the full four-dimensional space. The multidimensional scaling method, it should be remembered, fits the similarity values (measured in this case as correlations between rating profiles) to distances in the spatial coordinate system (measured as Euclidean distance in four dimensions). Thus, it is really the distance in the spatial configuration in four dimensions that is the resulting representation of interkey distances. Unfortunately, however, because a satisfactory solution is found only in four dimensions, it is difficult to visualize the configuration.

However, another way of representing the resulting configuration brings out its structure more clearly. This alternative representation is possible because the points have the special property of falling on one circle in the first two dimensions and another circle in the other two dimensions. What this means is that the 24 points for the musical keys are located on the surface of a torus. Mathematically, a torus is defined as a circle in two dimensions crossed with a circle in two other dimensions. In other words, any point on a torus can be described by its angular position on each of the two circles. Thus, we can reduce the information about position in four dimensions to information about position measured on two circular dimensions of angle.

Figure 2.8 shows the angular values for the 24 major and minor keys. In this representation, the angle of a key around the first circle is given by the horizontal displacement, and the angle of a key around the second circle is given by the vertical displacement. (In order to have the key C major fall approximately in the center of the representation, zero degrees on the first circle was set to be the angle of D♭ major and D♯ minor, and zero degrees on the second circle was set to be the angle of F♯, D, and B♭ minor; compare Figure 2.7.) Because these are angular measures, opposite edges must be regarded as identical. That is, the left edge is considered the same as the right edge, and the top edge is considered the same as the bottom edge. (The reader may wish to think of cutting out the rectangle, folding it over to make a tube, and then bringing the two ends of the tube together.)

When viewed in this form, various features of the configuration are readily apparent. First, there is one circle of fifths for major keys, which wraps three times around the torus before joining back on itself. Similarly, there is another circle of fifths for minor keys, which also wraps three times around the torus before joining back on itself. The relative position of these two circles of fifths when drawn on the surface of the torus is such that they reflect the relative and parallel relationships between major and minor keys. That is, any major key is flanked by its relative and parallel minor keys, and any minor key is flanked by its relative and parallel major keys. In summary, the configuration exhibits expected properties governing interkey distance.

Although the form of the representation shown in Figure 2.8 is convenient visually, it should be remembered that the multidimensional scaling analysis really represents the distances between keys as the Euclidean distances in four dimensions, not as distances in the two-dimensional rectangular representation. Looking at the latter distances may lead to certain misperceptions about relative distances. For example, one apparent anomaly that has been noted is that C major looks closer to E minor than G major; in fact the opposite is true when one computes Euclidean distances from the coordinates in Table 2.5. Thus, to answer questions about precise differences in distances, it is necessary to go back to the four-

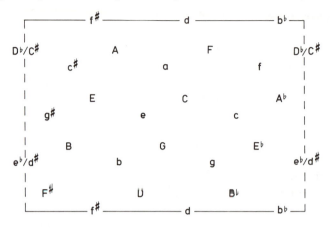

Fig. 2.8. Rectangular representation of the multidimensional scaling solution (Krumhansl & Kessler, 1982), in which the points for the 24 major and minor keys are located on the surface of a torus. The horizontal axis corresponds to the angle of each key on the circle in the first two dimensions; the vertical axis corresponds to the angle of each key on the circle in the last two dimensions. Because angle is a circular dimension, top and bottom edges are to be considered the same, and left and right edges are to be considered the same. Copyright 1982 by the American Psychological Association. Reprinted by permission of the publisher.

dimensional coordinates produced by the multidimensional scaling analysis.

To summarize, we found that it was possible to obtain a very regular and interpretable spatial representation of key distance from the probe tone ratings. The first step was to obtain a measure of interkey similarity by correlating the rating profiles for the 24 major and minor keys. These correlations were then subjected to multidimensional scaling to obtain a spatial configuration in four dimensions. This four-dimensional solution reflected both the circle of fifths and the relative and parallel major–minor relationships. This analysis demonstrates, then, that sufficient information is contained in the rating profiles to determine interkey distance. It may be possible to determine key distance by a combination of other variables, such as scale overlap or shared chords. Some of these possibilities are considered in later chapters. The analysis presented here, however, indicates that the patterns contained in the ratings of tones in tonal contexts are sufficient to arrive at a measure of key distance.

Theoretical maps of key relationships

Theoretical attempts to represent key distances geometrically have a long history, and have encountered many of the difficulties noted earlier when solutions were attempted in low-dimensional spaces. A summary of this history will not be attempted here, but two theoretical schemes will be described for comparison with the multidimensional scaling results.

Figure 2.9 shows the charts of key distance from Schoenberg (1954/1969, pp. 20 and 30). The figure at the top shows his chart of the key regions centered around the C major key; the figure at the bottom shows his chart of the key regions centered around the A minor key. It is readily apparent that his charts of key regions appear as local regions of the scaling solution. The configurations differ inasmuch as the scaling solution contains all 24 major and minor keys, whereas Schoenberg's representation is a subset of these, chosen to indicate those keys that are under the "control" of the key indicated at the center. A second difference is that his maps do not attempt to represent fine distinctions in key distances as, for instance, in the distance between a major key and its parallel and relative minor keys—despite his claim that the relative minor is closer.

Figure 2.10 shows three views of the model of key relationships proposed by Werts (1983). This representation is based on an extensive analysis of pro-

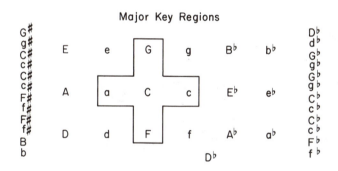

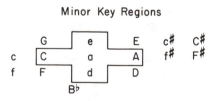

Fig. 2.9. Schoenberg's (1954/1969) charts of key regions for C major (top) and A minor (bottom), showing the relationship between the central key and other keys over which it exerts "control." These charts are contained within local regions of the multidimensional scaling analysis of interkey distances derived from the probe tone ratings (Krumhansl & Kessler, 1982). Adapted from Schoenberg (1954/1969) by permission of the publisher.

gressions between keys in a large number of compositions, both within movements and across movements. His model is such that virtually all key progressions found in the musical sample can be expressed as the movement from one key to its immediate neighbor in the configuration.

His solution is remarkably similar to that produced by the multidimen-

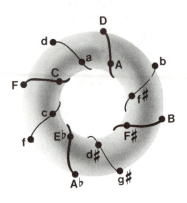

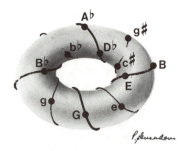

Fig. 2.10.   Three different views of Werts's toroidal model of key relationships (1983). This toroidal representation, based on an analysis of key relationships in a large corpus of tonal harmonic music, has many structural features in common with the multidimensional scaling analysis of interkey distances derived from the probe tone ratings (Krumhansl & Kessler, 1982). Adapted from Werts (1983).

sional scaling analysis. Although this convergence of approaches beginning with very different sets of observations is intriguing, three differences in detail between the two configurations should be noted. First, Werts's toroidal configuration (1983) shows the circles of fifths for major and minor keys wrapping four, rather than three, times around the torus before closing on themselves. Second, his model shows each major key and its relative and parallel minor keys as collinear, although these are offset somewhat in the scaling solution. At present, there appears to be no definitive criterion for deciding between these structural variants.

The third difference, however, warrants emphasis. The analysis on which his model is based forces the conclusion that progressions between keys are asymmetric. For example, the progression from a minor key to its relative major is stronger than the progression from a major key to its relative minor. There is also a preference for moving "upward" (clockwise) through the circle of fifths rather than in the opposite direction. Recently, Thompson (1986) found some psychological evidence for key progression asymmetries. His listeners judged the distance of modulations "upward" through the circle of fifths as smaller than modulations in the opposite direction. These considerations suggest that the assumption of symmetrical distances made by the multidimensional scaling analysis is incorrect, as noted also by Krumhansl and Kessler (1982), but no completely satisfactory account of asymmetries in key relations based on the probe tone data has yet been devised.

In general, however, the convergence between these theoretical models and the multidimensional scaling solution is striking. It suggests that the compositional practice summarized by the music-theoretical treatments has psychological reality in the degree to which the tonal hierarchies of different keys are similar. Additional evidence concerning the psychological effects of key distances is presented in later chapters. The next chapter, however, considers correlates of the quantified hierarchy of tonal stability that was the main focus of this chapter.

3. Musical correlates of perceived tonal hierarchies

The experiments reported in the previous chapter showed that tonal contexts in traditional Western music establish a perceptual hierarchy on the set of chromatic scale tones. The experimentally quantified hierarchy conforms to music-theoretical accounts of relative stability, with the tonic dominating in the hierarchy, followed by the third and fifth scale degrees, then by the remaining scale degrees, and finally by the nondiatonic tones. The experiments found essentially the same hierarchy when different contexts were used to establish a particular key. This suggests that the perceptual judgments reflect a highly structured and stable internal representation of tonal functions that can be evoked quite independently of the specific key-defining context. This chapter considers the question of how the tonal hierarchy becomes internalized.

The approach taken to this question is to determine what objective properties of music are correlated with the tonal hierarchies. These correlations, it should be emphasized, cannot be taken as unambiguous evidence that a particular objective property determines the nature of the tonal hierarchies, because correlations cannot be taken to imply causal relationships. However, strong correlations between objective and subjective properties of music can suggest mechanisms through which stable internal representations might become established. Two objective properties are considered in some detail. The first half of the chapter examines the correspondence between the perceptual hierarchies and the dimension of tonal consonance. This dimension has been explained in terms of, or at least associated with, acoustic properties of tones and how they are processed by the peripheral auditory system. The focus will be on quantitative treatments in the literature, which make possible precise comparisons to the experimental results. The correspondence between the perceptual hierarchies and the way tones are employed in tonal-harmonic music is examined in the second half of the chapter. In this section, the focus is also on quantifiable characteristics, specifically statistical summaries of tone distributions in various compositions.

If it is found that one, but not the other, of these objective musical properties correlates strongly with the experimental results, then this has important implications. If the tonal hierarchies correlate strongly only with tonal consonance, then it suggests that the hierarchies result from relatively peripheral perceptual processing. This would have the implica-

50

tion that they are largely fixed, invariant historically and cross-culturally, and do not necessarily require extensive experience to become internalized. If, however, the tonal hierarchies correlate strongly only with musical practice within the stylistic tradition, then it would suggest that they are products of culture, may vary historically and cross-culturally, and depend on (possibly extensive) musical experience to become internalized.

To anticipate the results somewhat, it turns out that the pattern of correlations is not so tidy; the tonal hierarchies correlate to some degree with both measures of tonal consonance and distributions of tones in traditional Western music. This outcome is not surprising given the extensive literature attempting to relate compositional practice (e.g., scalar and harmonic intervals) to acoustic facts. If the use of tones in music is constrained by acoustic considerations, and if the tonal hierarchies correlate with one kind of variable, then they will correlate with the other also. It is possible, however, to assess statistically their relative contributions, and the chapter closes with an analysis involving both tonal consonance and summaries of tone distributions in music.

Tonal consonance

It is important to distinguish at the outset between tonal consonance and musical consonance. Tonal consonance refers to the attribute of particular pairs of tones that, when sounded simultaneously in isolation, produce a harmonious or pleasing effect. Although the precise definition of this property varies in its many treatments in the literature, there is general consensus about the ordering of the intervals along a continuum of tonal consonance. Musical consonance, on the other hand, refers to intervals that are considered stable or free from tension, and constitute good resolutions. This kind of consonance depends strongly on the musical style and also the particular context in which the interval is sounded. Thus, musical consonance may bear only a rough correspondence to tonal consonance. The present discussion considers only tonal consonance.

In modern treatments (e.g., Piston, 1941/1978; Roederer, 1973) unisons, octaves, fifths, and fourths are classified as perfect consonances; major and minor thirds and sixths are classified as imperfect consonances. As will be discussed later, these intervals have special acoustic properties that have implications for how they are coded by the sensory system. Intervals considered consonant tend to predominate not only in Western music, but also in other musical cultures. For example, the octave is present in essentially all musical cultures—the only known exception being certain groups of Australian aborigines studied by C. J. Ellis (1965). The interval of a fifth plays an especially important role in tonal-harmonic music and in Indian classical music, and also appears in Eastern pentatonic scales. These kinds of observations have led many theorists to give a great deal of significance to consonance because it seems to offer a scientific explanation of musical structure. Reviews of the history of this idea, which will be outlined only briefly here, are given by Malmberg (1918), Plomp and Levelt (1965), and Hutchinson and Knopoff (1979).

Pythagoras is generally credited with the discovery that when a vibrating string is divided into two parts with lengths expressable in ratios of small integers, the resulting intervals have a pleasing, pure, smooth quality. The most consonant intervals are produced by ratios of the smallest integers (unison 1 : 1, octave 2 : 1, fifth 3 : 2, fourth 4 : 3). Less consonant intervals are produced by ratios of larger integers (major sixth 5 : 3, major third 5 : 4, minor third 6 : 5, minor sixth 8 : 5). Dissonant intervals are produced by ratios of even larger integers (major second 9 : 8, minor seventh 16 : 9, major seventh 15 : 8, minor second 16 : 15). Early theorists assumed that the listener somehow directly perceived the numerical ratios and preferred those expressable in simplest terms. With increased knowledge of acoustics, and an understanding of the relationship between the length of a vibrating string, its frequency of vibration, and the dependency of perceived pitch on frequency, came a variety of other explanations. These theories assumed that consonance of intervals with simple frequency ratios contained vibration patterns with a common periodicity, producing corresponding neural-firing patterns with a common periodicity (e.g., see Lipps, 1885; Boomsliter & Creel, 1961; Houtsma & Goldstein, 1972).

Additional explanatory concepts were derived from acoustic observations concerning complex tones. Complex musical tones, those produced by virtually all musical instruments, contain a number of frequency components. Under most circumstances, the frequency of the lowest of these components corresponds to the pitch heard. This component is called the fundamental frequency. When the waveform is periodic, as during the steady-state portion of many instrumental sounds, the other components will be integer multiples of the fundamental frequency. (Noninteger multiples may also occur as, for example, for bells and gongs.) These higher-frequency components are called overtones or harmonics. Because of the pattern of harmonics, when two complex tones are sounded, their component frequencies will coincide to the extent that their fundamental frequencies are related by simple integer ratios. For example, if two tones, one an octave higher than the other, are sounded simultaneously, all the harmonics of the higher tone will be present as harmonics of the lower tone. As the integers needed to express the ratios of the frequencies increase, the number of mismatches between the harmonics of the two tones will also increase.

In the interest of relating these observations to the perceptual effect of consonance, Helmholtz (1885/1954) noted that, when two tones that are close but not identical in frequency are sounded together, the listener has a sensation of beating or roughness. When complex tones with nonsimple frequency ratios are sounded simultaneously, a number of their harmonics will be in the range of frequency differences for which roughness occurs. This roughness, then, was assumed to produce the quality of dissonance. Modern formulations (e.g., Plomp & Levelt, 1965; Kameoka & Kuriyagawa, 1969; Hutchinson & Knopoff, 1978) have replaced Helmholtz's notion of beating or roughness with a more general concept of interference between component frequencies within what is known as the critical bandwidth (the frequency region over which sounds interact in producing sensations of loudness). Critical bandwidth is known to change with frequency, with larger critical bandwidths in lower frequencies. As a consequence, a given interval will be less consonant in lower registers. Explanations of consonance in terms of interference between harmonics falling within the same critical bands are now the most widely accepted.

One final theory based on acoustic properties of complex tones should be mentioned. Terhardt (1974, 1984; Terhardt, Stoll & Seewan, 1982a,b) has suggested that consonance is influenced not only by interference patterns as just described, but also by a second variable that he calls "tonal meaning." The basic idea is that through experience with complex tones (primarily speech), a pattern recognition system develops. This incorporates the primary pitch intervals (octave, fifth, fourth, thirds) found in complex tones. Then, when combinations of tones are heard, tonal meanings (virtual pitches) are evoked to the extent that the sounded frequencies match some part of the template of interval patterns. This kind of account could explain generalizations of consonance to successively sounded tones, and invariance of consonance over changes of timbre.

Attempts to relate the phenomenon of consonance, whatever its acoustic or psychological basis, to musical practice have been common. The standard combinations of simultaneously sounded tones in chords of Western harmony (fifths and thirds) are presumed to be selected at least in part because of their consonant effect. The spacing of chord components (with larger intervals typically found in the bass) is assumed to be a consequence of the greater consonance of chords with these spacings (e.g., see Hutchinson & Knopoff, 1979). In addition, numerous accounts of diatonic scale structure relate the selection of scale pitches to the overtones of single complex tones. Intervals (or their octave equivalents) that appear relatively early in the overtone series (fifth and major third) are taken to be the generative elements of the diatonic scale. Discussions about tuning systems have also relied extensively on the notion of consonance and its presumed basis in acoustics; representative samples of this approach are Backus (1969/1977), Roederer (1973), and Burns and Ward (1982).

Both psychologists and musicians, however, have recognized the limits of theories of acoustics for explaining musical practice. Theories of consonance do not adequately explain the status of certain musical entities: the seventh scale degree, the minor triad, and the construction of the minor scale. Cazden (1945), arguing for a cultural criterion for consonance, notes historical and cross-cultural differences in the employment of intervals. Moreover, in Western music open octaves and fifths (in which the interval is sounded without other pitches) produce a "thin" and unsatisfying effect because they are insufficiently rich harmonically. In addition, whether a fourth is dissonant or consonant depends on context. Studies of intonation in performance show deviations from small-integer ratios in accordance with the resolution tendencies of tones (Francès, 1958; Shackford 1961, 1962a,b). Shackford also found differences in intonation between tonal music and atonal music, in which dissonant intervals predominate and octaves are avoided. Equal-tempered tuning, in which the major third in particular deviates from a small-integer ratio, has been widely adopted. Moran and Pratt (1926) found that musicians even preferred equal-tempered tuning over "just intonation" (that preserves small-integer ratios), and L. Roberts and M. V. Mathews (1984) found that musicians preferred slightly mistuned intervals, possibly because of their greater "warmth." Judgments of consonance also show effects of training, experience, development, and the particular methodology employed. These findings and others in this extensive literature indicate that the psychological attribute of consonance is complex and, though related to acoustic properties, is also influenced by other variables, notably the listener's experience with the particular musical tradition.

Helmholtz (1885/1954, pp. 365–66) treats this problem as follows:

The construction of scales and of harmonic tissue is a product of artistic invention, and by no means furnished by the formation or natural function of our ear, as it has been hitherto most generally asserted. Of course the laws of the natural function of our ear play a great and influential part in this result; these laws are, as it were, the building stones with which the edifice of our musical system has been erected, and the necessity of accurately understanding the nature of these materials in order to understand the construction of the edifice itself, has been clearly shewn [sic] by the course of our investigation upon this very subject. But just as people with differently directed tastes can erect extremely different kinds of buildings with the same stones, so also the history of music shews [sic] us that the same properties of the human ear could serve as the foundation of very different musical systems.

Schenker (1906/1954, p. 44) also emphasizes the artistic contribution: "a considerable part of the system belongs to the artist as his original and inalienable property . . . ; the system is to be considered, accordingly, as a compromise between Nature and art, a combination of natural and artistic elements."

L. B. Meyer (1956, p. 230) points to the importance of psychological principles of perception and learning:

For consonance and dissonance are not primarily acoustical phenomena, rather they are human mental phenomena and as such they depend for their definition upon the psychological laws governing human perception, upon the context in which the perception arises, and upon the learned response patterns which are part of this context.

Cazden (1945, p. 10) concludes in a similar vein:

The neat and logical formulations of the natural sciences have little bearing on musical consonance and dissonance. The predictions of mathematical ratios, acoustic phenomena, beats and isolated perceptive qualities are consistently ignored and contradicted in musical practice. . . . Perceptions of interval qualities, though they do not arise on natural foundations, are neither arbitrary nor accidental. They are conditioned responses derived from the structural relations of a specific musical language and its history.

Tonal consonance and tonal hierarchies

Although acoustic observations can provide only a limited explanation of musical practice, it is still of interest to determine the extent to which something as basic as the tonal hierarchies reflect acoustic properties. After all, both the tonal hierarchies and measures of tonal consonance show influences of the structure of diatonic scales and triadic harmonies in traditional Western music. This section presents a number of analyses assessing the similarity between the tonal hierarchies from the study of Krumhansl and Kessler (1982, described in Chapter 2) and various measures of tonal consonance.

Before turning to the analyses, it should be noted that the experimental method for obtaining the tonal hierarchy is, in a number of respects, unlike the situation considered in treatments of consonance. In the latter, the situation typically considered is of two isolated, simultaneously sounded tones (usually complex tones). In our experiments, listeners judged single tones presented after a variety of key-defining contexts (and the tones contained frequency components only at octave intervals). Despite these differences, the key-defining contexts of the experiment strongly imply a tonal center (recall the high ratings given the tonic). If the listeners make their judgment of the probe tone with respect to the implied tonal center, then tonal consonance may enter into the rating judgments. This suggestion is compatible with Rameau's view (1722/1971, p. 141) that the source of harmony is a single tone, the harmonic center, from which all other tones can be derived (by mathematical operations) and to which all other tones should be related. It is also compatible with Terhardt's formulation (cited earlier) of virtual pitch, whereby listeners gain knowledge about harmonic pitch relations through experience with natural tones.

Malmberg (1918, p. 103) provided in his extensive study a useful table of rankings of consonance of musical intervals. The rankings came from 10 different treatments given the topic from the twelfth to twentieth century. These treatments used a wide variety of methods, some purely theoretical or mathematical, some involving perceptual judgments. A number of different instrumental timbres were employed in these studies (including pipe organ, violin, and tuning forks), and the criteria of consonance varied (pleasantness, smoothness, fusion, purity, rhythmic coincidences, and some purely mathematical and theoretical criteria). Despite these differences, the obtained rankings exhibited considerable convergence. The first set of values shown in Table 3.1 is the averaged ranks across the 10 different treatments considered by Malmberg.

The second set of values in Table 3.1 is from an experiment conducted by Malmberg (1918, Table II). The experiment presented musically experienced listeners with all possible pairs of two-tone intervals (spanning an octave range or less) and recorded for each pair which interval was preferred. The values shown are the total number of times that each interval was preferred to all the other intervals with which it was compared. The values were based on judgments of blending, smoothness, and purity, and the intervals were produced by either a piano or tuning forks. Malmberg found that preferred intervals are, in general, those that have low consonance ranks.

The third and fourth sets of values in Table 3.1 comes from Helmholtz's table of roughness (1885/1954, p. 332). The calculations of roughness are for equal-tempered and simple-ratio tunings. For the simple-ratio tuning, the following ratios were used: 16 : 15 (minor second [m2]), 9 : 8 (major second [M2]), 6 : 5 (minor third [m3]), 5 : 4 (major third [M3]), 4 : 3 (perfect fourth [P4]), 45 : 32 (tritone [TT]), 3 : 2 (perfect fifth [P5]), 8 : 5 (minor sixth [m6]), 5 : 3 (major sixth [M6]), 16 : 9 (minor seventh [m7]), 15 : 8 (major seventh [M7]), and 2 : 1 (octave).

The final two sets of values are based on the critical-bandwidth modification to Helmholtz's theory of consonance. Hutchinson and Knopoff (1978) computed the total dissonance of pairs of tones with the first 10 harmonics with relative amplitudes: one, one-half, one-third, and so on. They used equal-tempered tuning. For purposes of comparison, the values shown are those for a fixed reference tone of middle C (C4). Kameoka and Kuriyagawa (1969, Fig. 8) plotted dissonance values for pairs of tones with varying numbers of harmonics. The values in the table were estimated from their graph of the theoretical total dissonance values for tones with the first six harmonics of equal amplitude and a fixed reference pitch of A4 (the A above middle C). Local peaks in their graph were taken as measures for simple-ratio tuning.

Each one of these values was normalized (by subtracting from each value the average value and dividing by the standard deviation); the sign for all the sets of values (except for the Malberg data) was reversed so that higher values correspond to more consonant intervals. The results are plotted in Figure 3.1 together with the Krumhansl and Kessler (1982) major-key profile (top graph) and the minor-key profile (bottom graph).

Table 3.1. Consonance values from six studies

Musical Interval	Consonance Values	Consonance Values
	Malmberg Ranks	Malmberg Data
Unison/octave	1.00	11.00
m2	11.29	0.00
M2	9.50	1.50
m3	6.60	4.35
M3	4.65	6.85
P4	3.10	7.00
TT	8.28	3.85
P5	2.05	9.50
m6	6.45	6.15
M6	4.85	8.00
m7	8.83	3.30
M7	10.50	1.50
	Helmholtz Equal-Tempered	Helmholtz Simple-Ratio
Unison/octave	0	0
m2	76	70
M2	25	32
m3	24	20
M3	18	8
P4	3	2
TT	18	20
P5	1	0
m6	22	20
M6	22	3
m7	24	23
M7	48	42
	Hutchinson & Knopoff	Kameoka & Kuriyagawa
Unison/octave	.0019	190
m2	.4886	285
M2	.2690	275
m3	.1109	255
M3	.0551	250
P4	.0451	245
TT	.0930	265
P5	.0221	215
m6	.0843	260
M6	.0477	230
m7	.0998	250
M7	.2312	255

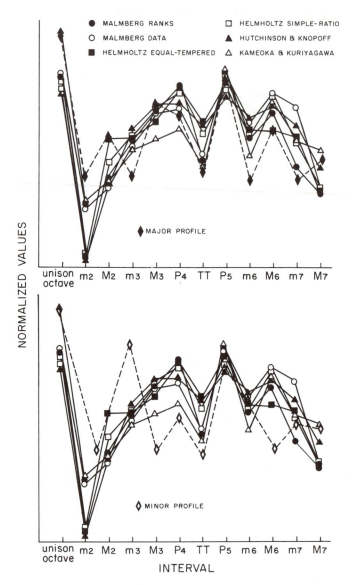

Fig. 3.1. Various theoretical and empirical measures of tonal consonance are compared with the major-key profile (top) and the minor-key profile (bottom). The key profiles are the perceived tonal hierarchies from the study by Krumhansl and Kessler (1982). The consonance values correlate quite strongly with the major-key profile, but not with the minor-key profile.

The tonic is set equal to the fixed reference tone for each set of consonance values.

Table 3.2 shows the correlations between all six sets of consonance values and between each of these and the major and minor key tonal hierarchies. The correlations that are statistically significant are indicated by asterisks in the table. Statistical significance refers to the probability that the result of a statistical analysis could have occurred by chance. What this means in the present context is whether the correlations could have occurred because of random variations or whether there is reason to conclude that there is a strong and reliable relationship between two sets of values. To assess this, the numerical values of the correlations are compared to a table of significance levels for correlations, which can be found in essentially any statistical textbook. The value of the correlation needed to conclude that an effect is reliable depends on the number of observations going into the correlation. The present case has 12 observations because there are 12 chromatic scale tones. The computed correlation estimates two parameters; therefore, the degrees of freedom of the correlation is $12 - 2$, or 10. (In general, the degrees of freedom for a correlation with n observations is $n - 2$.) The statistical table says that, for 10 degrees of freedom, a correlation of .576 or more would occur by chance only 5 percent of the time. Therefore, if the correlation is larger than this value, then it seems safe to conclude that there is a strong relationship, one that is unlikely to occur by chance.

Table 3.2 and Figure 3.1 show substantial agreement between the six sets of consonance values. This is true even though some of the sets of values are based purely on theoretical calculations and others are based on perceptual judgments. Somewhat weaker relationships can be seen between the consonance values and the major-key tonal hierarchy. The discrepancies can be characterized in the following way. In the tonal hierarchy, the major second is higher than the minor third, whereas the opposite relation obtains in the consonance curves. Similarly, the major seventh is higher in the tonal hierarchy than the minor seventh, and the opposite holds for the consonance curves. Both of these discrepancies reflect scale membership, one of the variables that is apparent in the experimentally measured major-key profile. One other small discrepancy should be noted, which is the different ordering of the major third and the perfect fourth; tonic-triad membership is another variable influencing the major-key profile, but the perfect fourth is more consonant than the major third. Despite these differences, the consonance values generally agree quite well with the major-key profile; five of the six correlations are significant.

The minor-key tonal hierarchy, however, shows large and systematic differences from the consonance values. In particular, the consonance values for the major third and the major sixth are considerably higher than

Table 3.2. Correlations between consonance values and tonal hierarchies

	Malmberg Ranks	Malmberg Data	Helmholtz Equal	Helmholtz Simple	Hutchinson & Knopoff	Kameoka & Kuriyagawa
Major key	.827*	.796*	.647*	.653*	.524	.839*
Minor key	.564	.528	.480	.387	.384	.645*
Malmberg ranks	—	.974*	.842*	.892*	.812*	.857*
Malmberg data	.974*	—	.820*	.897*	.847*	.895*
Helmholtz equal	.842*	.820*	—	.951*	.917*	.701*
Helmholtz simple	.892*	.897*	.951*	—	.963*	.761*
Hutchinson & Knopoff	.812*	.847*	.917*	.963*	—	.732*
Kameoka & Kuriyagawa	.857*	.895*	.701*	.761*	.732*	—

*Significant at $p < .05$.

the values in the minor-key profile, and the value for the minor third is considerably lower. Again, these discrepancies reflect that scale and tonic-triad membership are important determinants of the tonal hierarchy. These discrepancies result in considerably lower correlations between the minor-key profile and the consonance values; only one of the six correlations is significant.

One might also ask how strongly the consonance curves correlate with the tonal hierarchies of other keys. The analyses so far have identified the tonic with the fixed reference pitch used in the studies of consonance. To address this question, each of the six sets of consonance values was correlated with the tonal hierarchy of each of the 24 major and minor keys; by convention, the fixed reference pitch for the consonance values is taken now to be the tone C. The average correlations are plotted in Figure 3.2, which, for interest, might be compared with Figure 2.6.

Very similar patterns are contained in Figure 3.2 and the top graph of Figure 2.6; this would be expected given the high correlations between the consonance curves and the major profile. There is an interesting difference, however. The consonance curves generally correlate more strongly with major keys "downward" (counterclockwise) on the circle of fifths than major keys "upward" (clockwise) on the circle of fifths. For example, the correlation with F major is stronger than that with G major. This means that the system of consonances of the tone C fits better with the F major tonal hierarchy than the G major tonal hierarchy. This may, in part, serve to explain the asymmetric key distances discussed at the end of the last chapter. It is also interesting to note the relatively high

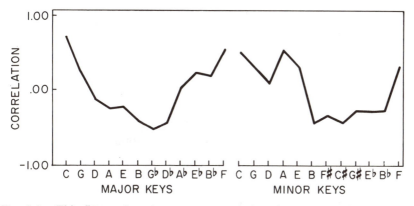

Fig. 3.2. This figure plots the average correlations between tonal consonance values and the 24 major and minor key profiles (the tonal hierarchies from Krumhansl and Kessler, 1982). Comparisons with the top of Figure 2.6 show similar patterns, because of the relatively strong correlations between the measures of tonal consonance and the major-key profile.

correlations with both C minor and A minor, which are approximately equal. The system of consonances of the tone C fits well with both these keys, again reflecting the dual relative and parallel major–minor relationship and the strong tonal function of the minor third in minor keys.

Before summarizing, one final result from Parncutt (1987) will be mentioned. He extended the algorithm of Terhardt, Stoll, and Seewann (1982b), which predicts pitch salience for complex tonal stimuli. Pitch salience is assumed to be a combination of the spectral-pitch pattern and the virtual-pitch pattern (based on the coincidence of subharmonics). Each of these patterns consists of a number of pitches with an associated value expressing its relative prominence. Parncutt considered how well an algorithm of this type could predict the tonal hierarchies of Krumhansl and Kessler (1982). He used a composite cadence consisting of six tonic triads (I), three dominants (V), a supertonic (II), a subdominant (IV), and a submediant (VI). The resulting profile of tone prominence correlated strongly with the major-key hierarchy ($r = .986$) and the minor-key hierarchy ($r = .941$).

These results are striking and suggest that acoustically based theories of tone perception incorporating effects of virtual pitches may account quite well for the tonal hierarchies. Three limitations of Parncutt's analysis (1987) should be noted, however. First, his composite cadence heavily weighted the tonic chord and does not, in fact, correspond to the distribution of chords used in the key-defining contexts of the Krumhansl and Kessler (1982) study. Second, his application of the algorithm does not show the predictions separately for the different contexts used in the experiment; therefore, it is unclear that it predicts the obtained invariance of judgments over the different contexts. Finally, it would be desirable to evaluate the relative contributions of the components of the model, and to compare its performance to alternative models.

In summary, the relationships found between the tonal hierarchies and various theoretical and psychological measures of consonance are best described as only moderately strong. Regular, and in some cases, large discrepancies are seen. These findings suggest that, although the tonal hierarchies may have a natural basis in acoustical properties of tones, it is also shaped by other influences. The rest of the chapter considers another possible influence, namely the way tones are used in tonal-harmonic music as summarized in statistical distributions of tone frequency.

Statistical analyses of tonal compositions

According to L. B. Meyer (1956, p. 54), "styles in music are basically complex systems of probability relationships in which the meaning of any term or series of terms depends upon its relationships with all other terms possible within the style system." These regularities are codified in music theory, which describes normative practice within the style system. Of greater psychological import, however, is Meyer's suggestion that through experience, listeners internalize the complex system of probability relationships, and, when listening to a particular piece of music, relate the sounded elements to this knowledge. This process gives rise to dynamically changing expectations about subsequent events, which may or may not be satisfied, or may be satisfied only partially, indirectly, or with some delay. In these expectations reside what to Meyer is the syntax, the meaning, and the aesthetic experience of music.

Hindemith (1952/1961, p. 20) describes the listener's experience as follows:

While listening to the musical structure, as it unfolds before his ears, he is mentally constructing parallel to it and simultaneously with it a mirrored image. Registering the composition's components as they reach him he tries to match them with their corresponding parts in his mental construction. Or he merely surmises the composition's presumable course and compares it with the image of a musical structure which after a former experience he had stored away in his memory.

What components enter into the listener's mental construction? In answer to this, Hindemith (p. 63) suggests that one basic aspect of the plan is tonality:

All harmonies . . . will by our analytic capacity be understood as in close relationship to tones which, by frequent recurrence, or by favorable position in the structure, or finally by support received from other tones, will be felt as tones superior to the others; tones that occupy the place of fundamentals, or tonics.

Thus, the hierarchical ordering of tones is assumed to be determined in part by the frequency with which the different tones are sounded.

To provide empirical support for these kinds of arguments, it is necessary to demonstrate that listeners have internalized something about regularities in music. This information need not be consciously identified as probabilities or likelihoods, but it must be reflected in some psychological measure of the way music is encoded, processed, and remembered. As an initial step toward this end, this section presents a number of analyses relating the quantified tonal hierarchies to the relative frequencies and durations of tones in tonal compositions. Later chapters consider whether other measured psychological quantities covary with distributions of elements in tonal music.

The impetus for statistical analysis of music derives from at least four sources. In the 1950s and 1960s, information theory (or communication theory) began to quantify the amount of information that could be transmitted (or received) by a communication channel in a given amount of time. This theory introduced a quantitative measure of the amount of uncertainty (information) in a message. If a message is highly unpredictable, it is said to convey a large amount of information; conversely, when the message is highly predictable or redundant, it is said to convey a small amount of information. The method for computing the information value of a message is somewhat technical and there is no need to go into it here—only to note that the calculation depends on knowing various statistics, including the frequencies (or probabilities) of each of the possible elements and the probability of their sequential orderings (the higher-order statistics).

Information theory rapidly extended beyond the engineering applications for which it was originally developed. It had considerable impact on psychology in particular, in which it was applied to both linguistic and perceptual information. The area of psychology now known as information-processing psychology has its roots in information theory. Information theory also had some influence in the area of music, in which music was compared to a transmitted message. In this context, the question was whether it would be possible to ascertain the level of uncertainty that is optimal. Music that is too simple, with too much redundancy, is perceived as uninteresting; however, very complex or random music is perceived as incomprehensible. How much information should a piece of music contain to reach the right balance between regularity and variation? Another question asked in this context was whether the measure of information would distinguish between different musical styles or different composers. Summaries of early applications of information theory to music are J. E. Cohen (1962) and Pinkerton (1956); studies concerned with musical style are Youngblood (1958), Fucks (1962), Hiller and Fuller (1967), and Knopoff and Hutchinson (1981, 1983).

A second area that has stimulated interest in statistical analysis of music is artificial intelligence. The problem in artificial intelligence is to create a machine (usually a computer) that will act in a human (i.e., intelligent) way. In the context of music, the question is whether it is possible to program a computer to write music of a particular style. In approaching this problem, it is necessary to begin with a description of the way music of that style is written. In certain early efforts, these descriptions took the form of statistical analyses of the music of the particular period or composer. This statistical information was then incorporated into the computer program, so that the music was "composed" by the computer in a way that accords with the statistical probabilities. Applications of this general approach are described by Pinkerton (1956), Brooks, Hopkins, Neumann, and Wright (1957), and Hiller and Isaacson (1959); other works are cited by J. E. Cohen (1962).

A third area in which statistical analyses of music have been employed is ethnomusicology. In this context, statistical analyses are used to summarize properties of music the structural characteristics of which may be poorly or incompletely understood. For example, the number of different tones used in a composition might be counted to determine the nature of the underlying scale. Or, the relative frequencies or durations of tones might be counted in an attempt to identify the musically important tones.

Like measurements of tuning systems, which are also found in this liter-ature, statistical treatments permit comparisons across diverse musical systems. A description of this approach is contained in Nettl (1964).

A fourth motivation for statistical treatments, offered by Budge (1943), is pedagogical. She undertook an extensive analysis of the relative fre-quencies of chords in representative composers of the eighteenth and nineteenth centuries. This work will be reviewed in more detail in a later chapter. The objective of her study was to provide an ordering of the relative importance (frequency of occurrence) of chords in Western tonal music so that the musical curriculum could be organized accordingly. In this, she followed the lead of Thorndike (1921), who compiled an exten-sive list of the most frequently occurring words in English, which resulted in the revision of school readers, spelling books, and other texts.

Despite the enthusiasm from various quarters for statistical treatments of music, the success of the approach is not clear. L. B. Meyer (1957, p. 421) noted that

many difficult problems involved in any statistical approach must be recognized if such studies are to have anything more than a curiosity value. The mere collec-tion and counting of phenomena do not lead to significant concepts. Behind any statistical investigation must be hypotheses that determine which facts shall be collected and counted.

J. E. Cohen (1962, p. 158) expressed a similar concern in the context of applications of information theory to music, and pointed out that infor-mation-theoretical measures are insensitive to characteristics specific to the composition: "What is required is a theory between the 'traditional' information theory and [a] modified form: one that accounts for the past experience of the listener in generalized, averaged terms, while measur-ing the current information flux of the present musical experience." He also noted that a number of more technical assumptions of the theory may not be supportable. Knopoff and Hutchinson (1983, p. 93), in evaluating the utility of information theory measures as a means of distinguishing between composers and compositions, concluded by saying, "There would seem to be much more efficient methods of pattern recognition, that is, the identification of one piece or another or of a group of pieces as belonging to a given style, than those presently applied in information theory."

From the psychological point of view, however, the basic question re-mains as to whether statistical properties of music are related in any way to how it is that we perceive music. Have we, as L. B. Meyer (1956) suggests, gained through our experience with music knowledge about the statistical regularities in the musical tradition we know best? In support of this idea, the literature on human and animal learning shows a high degree of sensitivity to frequency information, which is taken to be a fun-damental mechanism through which learning occurs (e.g., see Estes,

1950, 1972, 1976; Whitlow & Estes, 1979; Whitlow & Skarr, 1979; Hasher & Zacks, 1979, 1984; Hintzman, 1976, 1988).

As summarized by Hasher and Zacks (1979, p. 382), quite accurate judgments of frequency of occurrence can be made by many different populations of subjects, and these judgments are less susceptible to experimental manipulations—such as practice and instruction—than many other measures. Frequency information, together with other basic attributes such as spatial and temporal information, is assumed to be learned automatically and without intention, sometimes without awareness, and without interfering with other processes. Attributes learned in this way are presumed to be those that the organism is biologically "prepared" to encode and remember, leading to the suggestion of the "existence of a small set of basic cognitive processes that encode certain attributes of information directly into long-term memory throughout the life span and in spite of alterations in capacity" (p. 382).

Tonal distributions and tonal hierarchies

In considering measurable properties of compositions that might be correlated with the tonal hierarchies, two possibilities suggested themselves. One is the total frequency of occurrence of the 12 chromatic scale tones; the other is their total durations. These properties are readily quantifiable and can be correlated with the tonal hierarchies, and various published studies contain tabulated values. It should be emphasized, however, that these measures are severely limited in the extent to which they capture musical structure. For example, they take into account neither order information—a consideration of obvious musical and psychological importance that will be discussed in later chapters—nor the tone's position in the event hierarchy, for example its place in the rhythmic, melodic, or harmonic structure. Nonetheless, these measures are convenient starting points for an analysis of the question of the relationship between statistical properties of music and the experimentally quantified tonal hierarchies.

Youngblood (1958) and Knopoff and Hutchinson (1983) published studies applying information theory to vocal compositions in an attempt to distinguish between different composers. As noted earlier, the measures of information theory were not especially sensitive to stylistic differences. These studies did, however, contain useful tables giving the total frequencies of each tone of the chromatic scale in a variety of compositions. The study by Youngblood analyzed eight songs from *Die Schöne Müllerin* by Schubert, six arias from *St. Paul* by Mendelssohn, and six songs from *Frauenliebe und Leben* by Schumann. The Knopoff and Hutchinson study analyzed three complete song cycles (*Die Schöne Müllerin, Die Winterreise,* and *Schwanengesang*) by Schubert; songs in major keys were tabulated separately from songs in minor keys. They also analyzed a number of arias and songs by Mozart, cantatas by J. A. Hasse, and lieder by R. Strauss.

In both studies, all pitches were reduced to a single octave and transposed to a common key; these transpositions were always determined from the written key signature, taking no account of transitions or modulations. In the second study, explicit changes in key signature were taken into account. (The first study does not specify what is done in the case of a change of key signature, if relevant.) The published tables show the total number of times that each tone of the chromatic scale was sounded in the vocal lines of the pieces; the durations of the tones are not taken into account in the analysis. Table 3.3, which summarizes the two studies, gives the total frequencies of tones in the major key pieces combined and in the minor key pieces combined, with a reference tonic of C. The sample represents over 20,000 tones in major-key pieces and nearly 5000 in minor-key pieces.

Figure 3.3 plots the frequency distributions of the tones for the pieces analyzed by Youngblood (1958) and Knopoff and Hutchinson (1983). The top graph shows the distributions for the pieces in major keys; the bottom graph shows the distribution for the Schubert pieces in minor keys. For comparison, the major and minor key profiles (Krumhansl & Kessler, 1982) are also plotted; all values are normalized (shifted to a common mean and standard deviation). As can be seen, the distributions for pieces

Table 3.3. Tonal distributions[a]

Tone	Pieces in Major	Pieces in Minor
C	3,213	906
C♯/D♭	194	103
D	3,001	550
D♯/E♭	352	564
E	3,111	124
F	1,947	430
F♯/G♭	556	117
G	3,615	1,042
G♯/A♭	348	343
A	1,840	100
A♯/B♭	361	259
B	1,504	272
Total	20,042	4,810

[a]Frequencies are shown with reference to tonic C.
Source: Youngblood (1958) and Knopoff and Hutchinson (1983)

in major keys are virtually identical to one another, suggesting why this kind of statistical analysis or information measures based on it may not be able to distinguish between the musical styles.

The correspondence of these tone distributions to the quantified major and minor tonal hierarchies is also remarkably strong. Table 3.4 shows

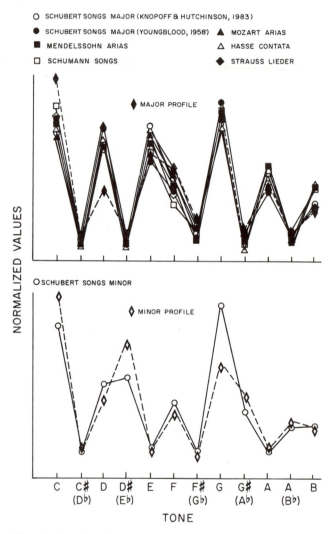

Fig. 3.3. The distribution of tones (the total frequency of occurrence) in tonal-harmonic compositions compared with the major-key profile (top) and minor-key profile (bottom). The key profiles are the perceived tonal hierarchies from the study by Krumhansl and Kessler (1982). Correlations between tone distributions and perceived tonal hierarchies are strong for both major and minor keys.

the correlations between the statistical distributions and the experimentally quantified tonal hierarchies. For pieces in major keys, the correlations are consistently high, with an average of .887; for the songs in minor keys, the correlation is .858. These correlations are on average considerably higher than those between measures of consonance and the tonal hierarchies, shown in Table 3.2. This is particularly the case for the minor key, for which the consonance values were found to deviate markedly from the quantified tonal hierarchy.

There are some small discrepancies, which may be instructive. When the normalized values are considered, the rating of the tonic for both major and minor is higher than the corresponding frequencies in the note count analyses, and the rating of the fifth scale degree is in both cases lower than the corresponding frequencies. This is consistent with the notion that, although the tonic occupies the highest position in the hierarchy of tonal functions, the dominant may play a more important role in establishing the key, and this is reflected in its greater frequency. There is also a consistent discrepancy for the second scale degree, which is sounded more frequently than would be expected based on its position in the tonal hierarchy. This result may reflect that the statistical analyses were done on the melodic lines only, with the second scale degree strongly related melodically to the tonic by virtue of its proximity in pitch (melodic relationships are discussed in a later chapter). For minor keys, the rating of the third scale degree is relatively higher than its frequency of occurrence; this would be accounted for if listeners are rating it highly because of its tonic function in the relative major of the minor-key context.

Despite these minor mismatches, the correspondence between the tone distribution functions and the rated values of the tonal hierarchies is strong. This supports the possibility, then, that the experimentally measured tonal hierarchies are based in part on internalized information about the distribution of tones in tonal compositions. It should be emphasized

Table 3.4. Correlations between tonal distributions and tonal hierarchies

Pieces	Correlation
Schubert songs in major (Youngblood, 1958)	.873*
Schubert songs in major (Knopoff & Hutchinson, 1983)	.888*
Mendelssohn arias	.900*
Schumann songs	.914*
Mozart arias and songs	.837*
Hasse cantatas	.875*
Strauss lieder	.925*
Schubert songs in minor	.858*

*Significant at $p < .05$.

that this correspondence holds even though the perceptually immediate contexts used in our experiments do not themselves have this distribution. This fact indicates that the distributional information is not drawn from the experimental context but has been abstracted and internalized by listeners from their broader musical experience.

Pinkerton (1956) performed a similar statistical analysis on 39 common nursery tunes. Although his sample is not nearly as extensive, it is included here for possible developmental interest. He first transposed all the tunes to the key of C, and then counted the frequency of the seven tones of the diatonic scale, identifying all notes with the same name. [Dowling (1988) has shown that nursery tunes are remarkable for their almost total lack of nondiatonic tones.] The distribution of tones is shown in Figure 3.4, plotted as a function of the scale degree (I = C, II = D, etc.). Pinkerton does not distinguish between the tunes in major and minor keys. The major-key profile shown in Figure 3.4 consists of the ratings given the seven tones of the major scale; the minor-key profile consists of the ratings given the seven tones of the natural minor scale. It is interesting to note that, when plotted in terms of the seven scale degrees, the major and minor profiles are quite similar, except for the relative orderings of the third and fifth scale degrees, as noted in the last chapter.

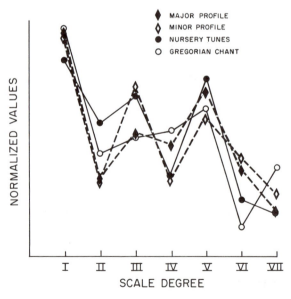

Fig. 3.4. Frequency of occurrence of the seven scale degrees in nursery tunes and Gregorian chants compared to the major and minor key profiles. The key profiles are the perceived tonal hierarchies from the study by Krumhansl and Kessler (1982).

All values in the figure have been shifted to a common mean and standard deviation.

The distribution of tones in Pinkerton's analysis correlates quite highly with the major and minor key profiles. The correlation with the major profile is .833, and the correlation with the minor profile .806. (Because seven observations, corresponding to the seven scale degrees, go into the correlations, the number of degrees of freedom is $7 - 2$, or 5. For this many degrees of freedom, a correlation of .754 is required to conclude that the correspondence is unlikely to have occurred by chance. Both correlations exceed this value; therefore, they are said to be statistically significant.) Again, the second scale degree is sounded more frequently than its position in the hierarchies would suggest, possibly reflecting its melodic relatedness to the tonic. Also, the tonic tone is sounded somewhat less frequently and the dominant sounded somewhat more frequently than would be expected from the rating data. These minor discrepancies are similar to those found in the analysis just described of the Youngblood (1958) and Knopoff and Hutchinson (1983) data. In general, however, the correspondence is again quite strong.

In addition to the analyses described earlier, Youngblood (1958) counted the frequency of tones in four selections of Gregorian chant in the Dorian mode, Mode 1 (the Gloria, Sanctus, and Agnus Dei from the first Mass for Solemn Feasts, and the Kyrie from the Mass *Orbis Factor,* all from the *Liber Usualis*). This sample consists of 658 tones. The distribution of tones in this sample is also shown in Figure 3.4 and the correlation, .846, with the major-key hierarchy is significant. However, the correlation, .714, with the minor-key hierarchy falls short of statistical significance. This is somewhat surprising, given the similar intervallic structure of the minor scale and the Dorian mode. The lack of correspondence is, in part, due to the mismatch at the third scale degree; this may be as a result of its function as tonic in the relative major, which is not applicable to Gregorian chant but influences the minor-key ratings. The relative frequency of the fourth and seventh scale degrees in the Gregorian chants are also notable compared to the major and minor key hierarchies. In this case, we may be seeing stylistic limits in the extent to which the tonal hierarchies correspond to tonal distributions, a question taken up again later.

The next analysis we turn to is one done by Hughes (1977) of the first of Schubert's *Moments Musicaux,* op. 94, no. 1, a short piece for piano. The analysis produces a result that, following Draeger (1967), is called "tonal orientation," which is contrasted with "tonal organization." Hughes (1977, pp. 144–45) describes the difference as follows:

Analysis of organization is an analysis of chords, progressions, measures, and periods in their mutual relationships. Orientation is at no time a chord-by-chord analysis but is a result of the total occurrence of each note and its durational value. This result is expressed in the statistically important notes . . . and is understood to be the overall tonality or tonal orientation of a composition. This condensation of important notes or tonal orientation could reveal that a composition in C major, for example, was in reality tonally oriented toward G major. . . .

Indeed, Hughes (1977) finds for this composition an overall orientation toward G major despite many features (such as harmonic progressions) indicating C major. The G major orientation is seen in Figure 3.5 as the predominance of diatonic tones from G major, especially G and D. Whatever the utility of statistical treatments such as this in music analysis, it is striking that the distribution of tones corresponds so well to the hierarchy of G major, which is also plotted in Figure 3.5. The correlation here is .969. That this relationship is stronger than any of those described earlier might be due to two differences in Hughes's method of analysis. First,

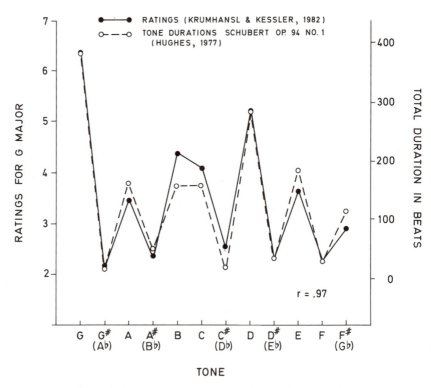

Fig. 3.5. Total duration of each of the chromatic scale tones in Schubert's op. 94, no. 1 compared to the profile of the G major key (from Krumhansl and Kessler, 1982). Hughes (1977) finds the tonal orientation of the piece to be G major. The correspondence between the two sets of values is strong. Reprinted from Krumhansl (1985) by permission of the publisher.

the analysis included all the tones, not just those in the melodic lines; consequently, the statistics reflect both melodic and harmonic structures. Second, Hughes takes tone duration into account (not just their frequency of occurrence), so his values may give a more precise account of the relative emphasis given the tones in the composition.

The final analysis is of an atonal composition. Out of curiosity, I totaled the tone durations in the third of Schoenberg's *Five Pieces for Orchestra,* op. 16, no. 3. This composition, called "Farben" [Colors], has been the subject of extensive analysis (e.g., see Forte, 1973; Rahn, 1980). My objective was to determine what global statistical regularities might be identified in this piece, to what extent the distribution of tones would match the tonal hierarchy of any key, and whether or not the mismatches would be interpretable. Figure 3.6 shows the total duration of each tone of the chromatic scale. For this analysis, the simplified score presented by Forte (1973, pp. 163–65) was used. The distribution of tones is by no means flat, showing a peak in the region of G♯(A♭) through C, and decreasing to a minimum at F♯(G♭).

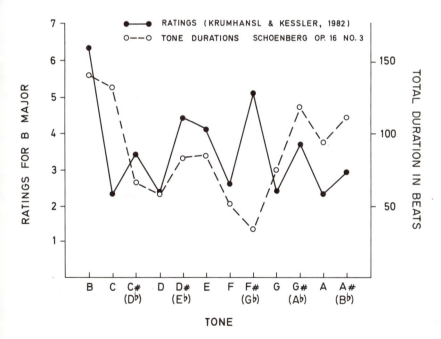

Fig. 3.6. Total duration of each of the chromatic scale tones in Schoenberg's op. 16, no. 3 ("Farben") compared with the profile of the major key whose tonic has the greatest total duration, B major. Large discrepancies can be seen, particularly at F♯(G♭), the tone a fifth above the tone with longest duration.

This distribution was correlated with the tonal hierarchies for all major and minor keys. All these correlations were low and statistically nonsignificant. Figure 3.6 shows for comparison the tonal hierarchy for the major key the tonic of which is the tone sounded for the longest total duration in the piece. As to interpreting the mismatches, only one possibly interesting feature brought out by the analysis is noted. The tone, F♯(G♭), that is a perfect fifth above the tone sounded for the longest total duration, B, is itself sounded for the shortest duration. This property contrasts sharply with both the tonal distributions of the experimentally quantified tonal hierarchies and the distributions in the tonal compositions just described. The latter all reflect the tonic–dominant relationship by corresponding peaks at the interval of a fifth, unlike the distribution of tones in "Farben." Thus, the global statistical properties of this piece differ markedly from those in tonal compositions. Implications of stylistic differences of this sort for perceived tonal hierarchies are considered in a later chapter.

Before leaving this section on tonal distributions in music, one final intriguing result should be mentioned. It comes from a case study conducted by L. K. Miller (1985, described briefly in L. K. Miller, 1987) of a boy whose development was severely delayed as a consequence of a case of rubella during his mother's pregnancy. For example, he began to walk at about age 4, and at 5½ years of age—the time at which the study was done—he spoke only isolated words. The boy, however, exhibited an exceptional ability to pick out melodies on a piano at first hearing despite having had no musical training. To investigate this ability, and the boy's sensitivity to tonal-harmonic structure in particular, Miller played 24 short preludes (one in each key from a graded series of music instruction books) twice each to the boy. He was asked to play them back and the performances were scored.

The renditions were by no means exact replications of the original preludes. On average, he played only about 75 percent of the correct notes in the correct temporal position. However, the renditions preserved almost exactly the distribution of tone frequencies in the original music. Figure 3.7 shows the probability distribution of notes heard and those played in the renditions of the preludes in major keys (left) and preludes in minor keys (right). The probabilities are plotted as a function of scale degree; the designation "N" refers to nondiatonic tones in the key of the prelude. As can be seen, the match between the distribution of tones in the original and the renditions is almost perfect; the only notable discrepancy is that nondiatonic tones were played more frequently in the original than in the renditions. Thus, the renditions exhibit a great deal of sensitivity to the statistical distributions of the music. It is also interesting to compare these results to Figure 3.4, which shows the major and minor tonal hierarchies plotted as a function of scale degree.

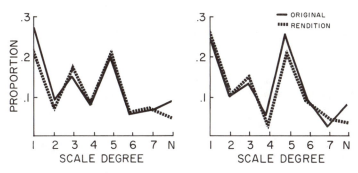

Fig. 3.7. The proportions of the seven scale degrees and nondiatonic tones (denoted N) in the original preludes and the renditions produced by L. K. Miller's (1985) developmentally delayed subject. Although the renditions contained only 75 percent of the correct tones, they preserved the relative frequencies of the scale tones. Also, compare with Fig. 3.4.

Tonal hierarchies, tonal consonance, and tonal distributions

The analyses presented to this point in the chapter have shown that the tonal hierarchies we measured experimentally are strongly correlated with statistical properties of tonal music. This, then, supports L. B. Meyer's view (1956) that through experience with music, listeners have abstracted and internalized certain probabilistic regularities underlying the musical tradition. In addition, the tonal hierarchies correspond more strongly to the distribution of tones in tonal compositions than they do to the dimension of tonal consonance, which is presumed to be rooted in acoustic properties of tones. However, both these variables correlate to some degree with the tonal hierarchies.

To look more closely at the relative contributions of consonance and distributions of the tones, it is possible to do a statistical test involving both these variables. For this, a multiple regression was used. In it, the tonal hierarchy was simultaneously compared with the consonance and frequencies of the tones, and the relative weights of these variables were determined. This analysis was done separately for the major and minor key tonal hierarchies. For the test, a composite profile of tonal consonance (the average of the values in Table 3.1 normalized to a common mean and standard deviation) and the tone frequencies (shown in Table 3.3) were used. For the major-key profile, the contribution made by the distribution of tones was far stronger than that made by the values of tonal consonance (the β value for tone frequencies was .669, $p = .001$, and that for tonal consonance was .376, $p = .027$). For the minor-key profile, the contribution made by the tone frequencies was again very strong (the β

value was .819, $p = .003$); tonal consonance did not make a significant contribution (its β value was .070, $p = .74$). What this means is that once the tone distributions were taken into account, there was no residual effect of tonal consonance on the minor-key hierarchy.

These tests show that the predominant correlate with the tonal hierarchies is the summary statistics of how tones are used in music, rather than tonal consonance. Although the acoustic properties associated with consonance may determine to some extent both the way tones are used in music and the quantified tonal hierarchies, the latter two variables are more strongly interdependent. These results point to learning as the dominant mechanism through which the tonal hierarchies are formed. Apparently, listeners are sensitive to the relative frequencies and durations with which tones are sounded, and this gives rise to an internal representation specifying varying degrees of tonal stability. This suggestion raises two important questions. The first is how much musical experience is required for the tonal hierarchy to become internalized. The second, related question is whether the tonal hierarchies, once acquired, are imposed on music with tonal organizations different from those in tonal-harmonic music. Both these questions can be addressed by directly measuring perceived tonal hierarchies using music outside the tonal-harmonic tradition and employing listeners with varying degrees of experience with the musical styles. These approaches are taken in studies to be reported in later chapters.

4.   A key-finding algorithm based on tonal hierarchies

The last chapter showed that the experimentally measured tonal hierarchies correlate strongly with the distribution of tones in tonal-harmonic music. This suggested that the tonal hierarchies might be acquired through experience with the musical style, particularly through internalizing the relative frequencies and durations with which tones are sounded. The question is turned around in this chapter. Here it is asked whether listeners could use the tonal hierarchies, once acquired, to determine the key of particular musical selections. The basic idea is that the tonal hierarchies function as a kind of template against which the tones of the musical selection are matched. This pattern-matching process is modeled by a computer algorithm—written in collaboration with Mark Schmuckler—which is applied to a variety of musical segments. To the extent that the key-finding algorithm produces correct results, it strengthens the case that pattern-matching to tonal hierarchies may be one mechanism through which listeners arrive at a sense of key.

A second motivation for developing and testing the algorithm was that determining key is prerequisite to successful automation of music analysis. The artificial-intelligence literature describes a number of attempts along these lines. These include harmonic analysis (Winograd, 1968; Winold & Bein, 1985) and Schenkerian analysis (Meehan, 1980; Smoliar, 1980) of tonal music, and set-class analysis of atonal music (Forte, 1970). For the automatic analysis of tonal music, the key needs to be determined in order for the structural roles of melodic and harmonic events to be coded meaningfully. For example, in connection with harmonic analysis, Winograd (1968) noted the inherent ambiguity of chords and the necessity to ascribe meaning to them in terms of their functions within the system of interrelated tonalities. Various approaches to the problem of determining the key of a piece are described in the artificial-intelligence literature.

Two algorithms, those of Longuet-Higgins and Steedman (1971) and Holtzman (1977), provide direct comparisons with the present algorithm, so they will be described in more detail later. Briefly, Longuet-Higgins and Steedman's algorithm (1971) successively eliminates keys on the basis of whether or not the tones in the musical sample are contained in the scale of each of the major and minor keys. Holtzman's algorithm (1977) examines the music for various key-defining features, such as the tonic triad (the major or minor chord built on the tonic), the tonic–fifth relationship (the interval between the tonic and the fifth scale tone, which is called the dominant), and the tonic–third relationship (the interval between the tonic and third scale tone, which is called the mediant and can be used to establish whether the key is major or minor). Both algorithms were quite successful when applied to the fugue subjects from Bach's *Well-Tempered Clavier.*

Sockut (described in Holtzman, 1977) devised a procedure for key-finding giving positive weights if the tonic, dominant, leading tone (seventh scale degree), and characteristic note sequences are contained in the music, and a negative weight if the tritone is present. Chafe, Mont-Reynaud, and Rush (1982) assigned key after previously finding points of rhythmic and melodic accent. Tones occurring at these points are searched for important pitch relations, and a list of possible tonics is formed. This list of tonics is weighted by frequency of occurrence and their own key implications, and from these statistics the best choice of key is found. Winold and Bein (1985), in their analysis of Bach chorales, used a somewhat similar approach by attaching weights to the tonics of all cadences, giving a double weight to the final cadence, and finding the most frequently occurring tonics. In their analysis, the cadences were determined externally to the algorithm by locating fermatas, which signal cadences in this style.

The algorithm described in this case differs from previous artificial-intelligence approaches to the problem of key-finding inasmuch as it is based directly on prior psychological results. An additional difference is that earlier approaches have taken as their objective the assignment of a single key, usually for the purpose of determining the appropriate key signature. As such, they treat musical key as a discrete, single-valued quality. In contrast, the present algorithm produces a vector of quantitative values. The key with the highest value might be taken as the main key; the extent to which it has been established is considered to be a matter of degree. In addition, the key assignment occurs within the context of other closely related, but subordinate keys. Thus, the algorithm produces a result that is consistent with the idea that at any point in time a listener may entertain multiple key hypotheses, which may or may not be made unambiguous by other features of the music. These hypotheses could serve to establish an appropriate tonal framework for encoding subsequent events and appreciating contrasts with other, more or less closely related keys.

The key-finding algorithm

As shown schematically in Figure 4.1, the input, $\mathbf{I}$, to the algorithm is a 12-dimensional vector $\mathbf{I} = (d_1, d_2, \ldots, d_{12})$, specifying the total durations of the 12 chromatic scale tones in the musical selection to which the key is to be assigned. Note that the input vector might be based on a selection of any length, from a few tones to an entire composition. By convention

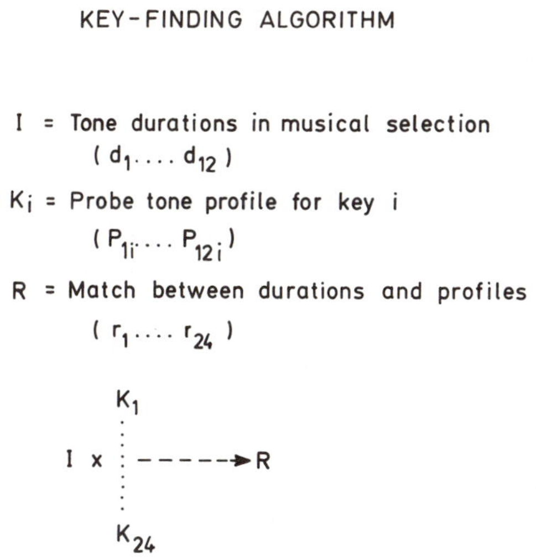

KEY-FINDING ALGORITHM

I = Tone durations in musical selection
($d_1 \ldots d_{12}$)

K_i = Probe tone profile for key i
($P_{1i} \ldots P_{12i}$)

R = Match between durations and profiles
($r_1 \ldots r_{24}$)

$$ I \times \begin{matrix} K_1 \\ \vdots \\ \vdots \\ \vdots \\ K_{24} \end{matrix} \; ----- \!\!\!\rightarrow R $$

Fig. 4.1. The key-finding algorithm takes as input the distribution of tone durations in the musical segment, **I**. It is correlated with the probe tone rating profile
(Krumhansl & Kessler, 1982) for each of the 24 major and minor keys, **K**$_i$. The
output is a vector of numerical values indicating the strength of each key, **R**.

d_1 will specify the total number of beats that the tone C is sounded, d_2
will specify the total number of beats that the tone C$\sharp$ (or its enharmonic
equivalent D$\flat$) is sounded, and so on.

In the present applications, the durations in the input vector are specified in terms of numbers of beats but other units of time would do equally
well. The input to the algorithm does not code the octave in which the
tones are sounded or their order; how order information might be incorporated in an algorithm of this sort is discussed later. Nor does the algorithm distinguish between enharmonic tones: that is, tones played the
same on fixed-pitch instruments but with different spellings in musical
notation, such as C$\sharp$ and D$\flat$. This means that the input to the algorithm
might potentially come from a musical score, from a fixed-pitch instrument such as a keyboard, or from an analysis of acoustic information.
However, once a key (or key region) has been determined, the correct
spellings of the tones will be able to be determined in most cases. For
example, if the predominant key contains a number of sharps, then the
C$\sharp$ spelling would be preferred over D$\flat$. If, on the other hand, the predominant key contains a number of flats, then the D$\flat$ spelling would be
preferred. Ambiguities would arise primarily in the region of F$\sharp$ or G$\flat$
major, which have six sharps and six flats, respectively.

The algorithm correlates the input vector, **I**, with 24 stored 12-dimen-
sional vectors, **K**$_1$, **K**$_2$, . . . , **K**$_{24}$. The 24 vectors represent the tonal hier-

archies of the 24 major and minor keys. Each vector contains 12 values, which are the ratings from the Krumhansl and Kessler (1982) study, described in Chapter 2, of the degree to which each of the 12 chromatic scale tones fit with the particular key. The vector for C major is (6.35, 2.23, 3.48, 2.33, 4.38, 4.09, 2.52, 5.19, 2.39, 3.66, 2.29, 2.88). By convention, the first number corresponds to the tone C, the second to C♯(D♭), and so on. The vector for D♭ major is found by shifting these values one place to the right and filling in the first value from the end of the C major vector, resulting in a D♭ major vector of (2.88, 6.35, 2.23, 3.48, 2.33, 4.38, 4.09, 2.52, 5.19, 2.39, 3.66, 2.29). The vectors for all other major keys are obtained by a similar procedure that is justified by the perceptual equivalence of major keys under transposition (Krumhansl & Kessler, 1982). The vector for C minor, again taken as the ratings from the probe tone experiment, is (6.33, 2.68, 3.52, 5.38, 2.60, 3.53, 2.54, 4.75, 3.98, 2.69, 3.34, 3.17). The vectors for all other minor keys, as for the major keys, are found by shifting the values the appropriate number of places to the right and filling in the resulting empty spaces by the values at the end of the C minor vector, which is justified by the perceptual equivalence of minor keys under transposition.

The input vector, I, is correlated with each of the vectors, K_1, K_2, . . . , K_{24}, producing an output vector of correlations, $R = (r_1, r_2, . . . , r_{24})$, in which r_i, is the correlation between the vectors, I and K_i, computed as described in Chapter 2. In this instance, it is a measure of the degree to which the durations of the tones in the input segment match the tonal hierarchy of each key. The correlation will be high to the extent that tones with the longest relative durations match tones dominating in the tonal hierarchy. Each correlation can be evaluated for statistical significance. Note that the number of degrees of freedom for the correlation is constant; it does not depend on the size of the musical selection on which the input vector is based. Nor is the correlation affected by the mean or standard deviation of the values of the input vector (which would vary with sample size). Hence, the algorithm can be applied to musical selections varying over a wide range of lengths, although sections containing only a few tones would probably produce unstable results.

Further analyses of the output vector, R, can be performed depending on the application. If the objective is to assign a key signature to a composition as a whole, then the input vector might be based on an initial segment of the piece, on a final segment, or even on the entire piece; in this case, the highest value in the output vector would determine the best choice of key signature based on the sample segment. If the objective is to detect possible changes of key within the composition, then the algorithm might use as input the durations of tones within significant subsections of the composition, or within initial or final segments of these subsections. In both of these applications, the magnitude of the highest correlation (or its level of significance) would be expected to be high and the key assignment relatively unambiguous. If the objective is to trace shifting tonal orientations or temporary modulations, then the algorithm might move through an entire piece using as input the tone durations for segments of only a measure or two in length. For some segments, it may be that no single correlation is very high and a number of keys have approximately equal values. This ambiguity might be represented as a point between keys in a spatial map; one method for doing this is employed here.

Three applications test this simple algorithm for determining key strengths. In the first, the algorithm is applied to the initial four-note segments of Bach's 48 preludes from the *Well-Tempered Clavier,* and the results are compared with those of a study by A. J. Cohen (1977) in which she asked listeners to identify the key of a subset of the preludes after hearing short initial and final segments. To investigate the robustness of the algorithm across musical styles, the same analysis is performed on the 24 preludes of Shostakovich and Chopin. In the second application, the algorithm is applied to the fugue subjects of Bach's 48 fugues in the *Well-Tempered Clavier.* In this application, the input sample is increased in length until it includes the entire subject. This application determines the first point at which the correct key is assigned, and the results are compared with those of Longuet-Higgins and Steedman (1971) and Holtzman (1977). The same kind of analysis is done of the Shostakovich fugues. In the final application, one of Bach's preludes containing an interesting pattern of shifting tonal centers is analyzed by the algorithm on a measure-by-measure basis. The results are compared to analyses made by two music theory experts who were asked to assign a most likely key interpretation to each measure and indicate other keys of lesser strengths.

Application I: initial segments of preludes of J. S. Bach, Shostakovich, and Chopin

The key-finding algorithm was first applied to the 48 preludes of Bach's *Well-Tempered Clavier.* This choice was made for two reasons. First, these preludes (and their accompanying fugues) move through the entire set of 24 major and minor keys and were written to demonstrate the utility of equal-tempered tuning, which allows any tonality to be played on fixed-pitch instruments like the piano. Each prelude begins quite unambiguously in the key of the key signature; therefore failures of the algorithm would suggest that it should be abandoned immediately. Second, A. J. Cohen (1977) described a study in which listeners, who were all university music majors, heard short segments of 12 of the preludes. They were then asked to sing the scale of the key in which they thought the piece was written. In one condition of her experiment, listeners heard just the first four sounded events and were quite accurate in their responses, choosing the correct key about 75 percent of the time. Applying the algorithm to the preludes allows us to compare its performance to these psychological data.

The input vectors were based on the first four notes of the preludes. Figure 4.2 gives as an illustration the initial segment of the C Minor Prelude, Book I, and indicates the four notes on which the input vector **I**, was based. The tone C is sounded for two sixteenth notes (giving a total of one half beat); the E♭ and G are each sounded for one sixteenth note (one quarter beat each); all other tones have zero duration in this sample. This results in an **I** vector of (.5, 0, 0, .25, 0, 0, 0, .25, 0, 0, 0, 0). For some of the preludes, the four-tone rule had to be modified slightly because two or more tones sounded simultaneously at the time when a fourth tone was sounded; all the simultaneously sounded tones were then included in the sample. The input vectors used the full notated temporal durations of the tones in the sample until the time at which either the fourth tone ended, or the fifth tone began.

The input vectors for each of the 48 preludes were correlated with the 24 tonal hierarchy vectors, K_i. Let d denote the designated (intended) key, and r_d the correlation of the input vector with the tonal hierarchy of the designated key. The value r_d is considered to be the strength of the in-

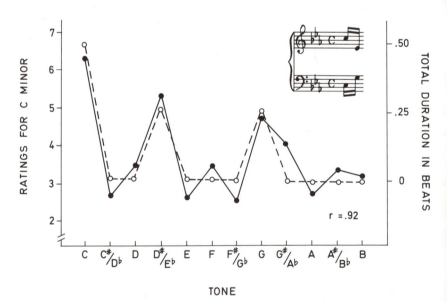

Fig. 4.2. The durations of the first four tones in J. S. Bach's C Minor Prelude, Book I, are plotted together with Krumhansl and Kessler's probe tone ratings for C minor (1982). The durations correlate significantly, $r = .92$, with the probe tone ratings for the intended key. The algorithm finds C minor to be the strongest key.

tended key as established by the input segment. A number of questions can be asked about the r_d value. First, we can ask if the value is statistically significant; if so, then the correspondence between the distribution of durations and the probe tone ratings for the intended key is unlikely to have occurred by chance. Second, we can ask if the r_d value is the largest in the output vector; if so, then we can say that the algorithm has found the correct key. Third, if the r_d value is not the largest, then we can ask how many other keys have higher r values and how far these other keys are from the correct key. Figure 4.2 plots, for the C Minor Prelude, the duration values of the first four tones superimposed on the tonal hierarchy of the intended key; the r_d value is .92, which is statistically significant and the highest value in the output vector, **R**.

Table 4.1 shows, for each of the 48 preludes, the r_d values based on the first four tones; each of these values was statistically significant, as indicated by the asterisks in the table. They averaged .83 and .79 for Books I and II, respectively, and .77 and .85 for major and minor preludes, respectively. The overall average was .81. In all but four cases, the r_d value was also the largest in the output vector. Table 4.1 indicates for the four exceptional cases the number of other keys with higher r values and their average distance from the intended key in Schoenberg's maps of key regions (1954/1969) shown in Figure 2.9. Distance is measured in terms of the number of keys along vertical and/or horizontal dimensions using a city-block metric. In the four cases in which some other key or keys had higher r values, these keys are closely related to the intended key with an average of 1.40 steps away. In two cases, the algorithm incorrectly assigns the parallel major of the designated key; in both, the third scale degree (which differentiates the modes) is missing from the input segment. Example 1 in Figure 4.3 illustrates this with the input segment of the C Minor Prelude (Book II), to which the algorithm assigns C major. In the remaining two cases, the algorithm assigns the relative minor of the key of the dominant. To illustrate this, Ex. 2 shows the input segment of the E♭ Major Prelude (Book II), to which the algorithm assigns G minor because of the relatively long G and B♭ with which the prelude begins. In general, however, the algorithm was quite accurate, finding the correct key in almost all cases and identifying the correct key region in the remainder.

Table 4.2 compares the results of our algorithm with those of the listeners in A. J. Cohen's experiment (1977) for the 12 Bach preludes used in her study. The stimuli used the first four events, or attack points, of the preludes, which meant (because of simultaneously sounded tones) that more than four tones were included in some cases. The r_d values shown in the table were computed in two different ways: first, using the tones actually sounded in Cohen's experiment and, second, using the first four tones, as before. Comparison of the last two columns shows substantial agreement between the r_d values, however. In all cases, they were significant and, for this sample of preludes, they were always the highest

Table 4.1. Application of the key-finding algorithm to the initial segments of the Bach preludes

Prelude	Book I r_d	Other Keys[a]	Book II r_d	Other Keys[a]
1 C major	.81*		.69*	
2 C minor	.92*		.73*	1 (1)
3 C♯ major	.83*		.82*	
4 C♯ minor	.87*		.89*	
5 D major	.73*		.69*	
6 D minor	.81*		.68*	
7 E♭ major	.87*		.60*	2 (1.5)
8 D♯/E♭ minor	.92*		.77*	
9 E major	.83*		.81*	
10 E minor	.92*		.78*	
11 F major	.83*		.66*	
12 F minor	.85*		.90*	
13 F♯ major	.67*	1 (2)	.90*	
14 F♯ minor	.93*		.89*	
15 G major	.83*		.83*	
16 G minor	.85*		.75*	1 (1)
17 A♭ major	.87*		.83*	
18 G♯ minor	.83*		.92*	
19 A major	.73*		.79*	
20 A minor	.82*		.84*	
21 B♭ major	.88*		.66*	
22 B♭ minor	.91*		.77*	
23 B major	.68*		.73*	
24 B minor	.83*		.92*	

[a]The first number shows the number of keys with higher r values than r_d; the number in parentheses indicates their average distance from the intended key in Schoenberg's maps of key regions (1954/1969).
*Significant at $p < .05$.

in the output vectors. If cases in which the r_d value is the largest are counted as correct responses, then our algorithm was correct 100 percent of the time, whereas Cohen's listeners were correct on average only 75 percent of the time.

A number of further analyses were performed to determine whether the algorithm modeled the variations in performance across preludes exhibited by A. J. Cohen's listeners (1977). In Cohen's study, listeners performed better on major than minor preludes, which may indicate a perceptual bias toward the more stable major mode. In contrast, the algorithm shows r_d values for minor keys as higher on average than those

DESIGNATED KEY   ASSIGNED KEY

BACH
Ex.1 C MINOR   C MAJOR
      (Book II)

Ex.2 E♭ MAJOR   G MINOR
      (Book II)

SHOSTAKOVICH
Ex.3 D♭ MAJOR   F MINOR

Ex.4 B MINOR   D MAJOR

CHOPIN
Ex.5 B MAJOR   F♯ MAJOR

Ex.6 C♯ MINOR   A MAJOR / MINOR

Ex.7 A MINOR   E MINOR

Fig. 4.3. Examples in which the present algorithm fails to find the correct key for four-tone initial segments of preludes by Bach, Shostakovich, and Chopin. The designated key and the key assigned by the algorithm are indicated in each case.

85

Table 4.2. Comparison of the key-finding algorithm with Cohen's listeners (1977) for preludes in Book I

Prelude	Percentage Correct	Computation of Strength of Intended Key[a]	
		r_d1	r_d2
1 C major	.89	.81*	.81*
3 C♯ major	.67	.79*	.83*
5 D major	.72	.73*	.73*
7 E♭ major	.89	.87*	.87*
9 E major	.94	.81*	.83*
11 F major	.89	.78*	.83*
Average	.83	.80*	.82*
Minor Preludes			
2 C minor	.56	.87*	.92*
4 C♯ minor	.83	.84*	.87*
6 D minor	.72	.83*	.81*
8 E♭ minor	.67	.92*	.92*
10 E minor	.56	.93*	.92*
12 F minor	.61	.88*	.85*
Average	.66	.88*	.88*

[a]r_d1 is based on durations of tones used in A. J. Cohen's stimuli (1977). r_d2 is based on durations of first four tones.
*Significant at $p < .05$.

for major keys. For the major and minor keys considered separately, no correspondence was found between the listeners' performance and the values of r_d. Nor was a correspondence found between the listeners' performance and the difference between this value and the next highest r value in the output vector, which might be taken as a measure of tonal ambiguity. Thus, the algorithm does not mirror in a detailed way the variations in level of performance across preludes, although it is unclear whether these differences are statistically reliable in Cohen's study. In addition, the lack of correspondence may be due to the algorithm performing at a ceiling level, whereas performance was lower in Cohen's study possibly because of limits in memory or response production.

In tribute to J. S. Bach, Shostakovich wrote a set of 24 preludes and fugues that were completed in 1951. Despite their relative recency, these works are highly tonal and, like the *Well-Tempered Clavier,* they move completely through the set of 24 major and minor keys. To determine the algorithm's success at finding the intended keys of these preludes, the same kind of analysis was carried out using as input samples the first four tones; the results are shown on the left of Table 4.3, where the preludes are reordered to correspond to the Bach preludes.

The analysis of the Shostakovich preludes found that in all but three cases the r_d value, measuring the strength of the intended key, was statistically significant and, in all but seven cases, it was the highest in the output vector, **R**. The r_d values averaged .71 and .75 for major and minor preludes, respectively, with an overall average of .73. The other keys with higher r values than r_d were, however, relatively close to the intended key, with an average distance of 1.42 steps. In four of the seven cases, the algorithm confuses parallel major and minor keys; in each case, the third scale degree is missing from the input segment. In two other cases, the input segment consists of only one or two different tones and the algo-

Table 4.3. Application of the key-finding algorithm to the initial segments of the Shostakovich and Chopin preludes

	Shostakovich		Chopin	
Prelude	r_d	Other Keys	r_d	Other Keys
1 C major	.80*		.81*	
20 C minor	.71*	1 (1)	.88*	
15 Db major	.46	2 (1.5)	.82*	
10 C♯ minor	.83*		.25	6 (1.67)
5 D major	.88*		.27	3 (1)
24 D minor	.87*		.76*	
19 Eb major	.72*		.59*	2 (1.5)
14 Eb minor	.27	4 (1.75)	.71*	1 (1)
9 E major	.67*		.88*	
4 E minor	.74*	1 (1)	.55	2 (1.5)
23 F major	.80*		.76*	
18 F minor	.89*		.00	11 (2.45)
13 F♯ major	.64*		.88*	
8 F♯ minor	.83*		.38	4 (1.25)
3 G major	.57	1 (1)	.79*	
22 G minor	.85*		.21	7 (2.71)
17 Ab major	.84*		.76*	
12 G♯ minor	.84*		.85*	
7 A major	.67*	1 (1)	.49	3 (1.67)
2 A minor	.74*		−.08	11 (2.55)
21 Bb major	.79*		.53	2 (1.5)
16 Bb minor	.89*		.18	6 (1.83)
11 B major	.72*		.38	3 (1.67)
6 B minor	.59*	2 (1.5)	.92*	

*Significant at $p < .05$.

rithm's assignments are reasonable given the inadequate information. Example 3 in Figure 4.3 shows the input segment for the D♭ Major Prelude to which the algorithm understandably assigns F minor (in which the two sounded tones are the tonic and third scale degree). The final case, the B Minor Prelude shown in Ex. 4, is more problematic. The initial segment contains the tonic triad of the key, but because of the long durations of the third and fifth scale degrees, the algorithm incorrectly assigns D major. Overall, however, the algorithm was quite accurate, determining the correct key in most cases and the correct key region in all cases.

The final analysis in this section is of the 24 Chopin preludes, also composed in homage to Bach. However, these preludes differ from those of Bach and Shostakovich in their more pronounced tonal ambiguity, the use of expanded diatonic and chromatic vocabulary, and the roles of dissonances and chromaticism. They are of interest, therefore, for exploring the range of musical styles to which the algorithm might be applied. The results of the analysis using input vectors based on the first four tones are shown on the right of Table 4.3. In 13 cases, the r_d value was statistically significant and in 11 cases the intended key had the highest value in the output vector. The average r_d values were .66 and .47 for major and minor preludes, respectively, with an overall average of .57

Thirteen Chopin preludes had one or more keys with r values higher than r_d; their average distance from the intended key was 2.02 steps. These values are considerably larger than in previous applications. The 13 cases can be classified into three groups. The first group contains eight preludes for which four or fewer keys had higher values than the intended key. These keys were an average of 1.40 steps away from the intended key, a distance comparable to that for the Bach and Shostakovich preludes. In one case the algorithm found the relative major of the designated key, in one case the key of the subdominant, and in six cases the key of the dominant. Example 5 in Figure 4.3 shows one of the latter cases, the Prelude in B Major. The input segment clearly emphasizes F♯ and as a consequence F♯ major was the assigned key. In all these cases, however, the algorithm is finding the correct key region.

The second group contains the three preludes in C♯ minor, G minor, and B♭ minor for which six or seven keys had higher values than the intended key, with an average distance of 2.11 steps. In none of these cases was an r value very large or significant (the highest value was .44). In all three cases, the tones in the input sample are contained in the scale of the intended key, but the tonic is absent and at most one of the tones of secondary importance (third and fifth scale degrees) appears. In the face of this, the algorithm determined that no key is very strongly indicated by the initial segments. Keys with higher r values than the intended key tended to be located in a diffuse region around the intended key. Example 6 shows the input segment for the Prelude in C♯ Minor to which the algorithm assigned weak A major and A minor keys (in which the tones are leading tone and tonic).

The two final cases, the Preludes in F Minor and A Minor, have strikingly low r_d values and 11 other keys with higher values the distances of which average 2.50 steps away from the intended key. Example 7 shows the input segment for the A Minor Prelude to which the algorithm assigned E minor. In this segment, the tonic of the designated key is raised by a semitone from A to A $\sharp$. This means that the input segment contains the tonic, third, and fifth scale degrees of E minor. The Prelude in F Minor is similar; it contains a chromatic alteration of the third scale degree, resulting in a better match to B♭ minor. Note that in both these cases, however, the key found to be strongest by the algorithm is an immediate neighbor of the correct key.

To summarize, these applications used as the input vector the first four tones of each prelude in the three sets. It was most successful in finding the keys of Bach's preludes. In the few exceptional cases, a key close to the intended key was selected instead. Comparison with A. J. Cohen's experiment (1977) showed that the algorithm was more accurate than her subjects; also, the algorithm did not mirror the specific pattern of errors across the subset of preludes used in the experiment. In the analysis of the Shostakovich preludes, the algorithm selected the intended key in somewhat fewer cases, but in these the correct key region was always determined. The algorithm had more difficulty with the Chopin preludes, but still performed far better than the chance level of 1 in 24. More important, in the large majority of cases it identified the correct key region, and errors could be traced directly to the input segments themselves. It should be emphasized that the segments consisted of just four tones, which in quite a few cases contained duplicated tones. Given this, it was encouraging that the results were as accurate as they were. This raises the question, however, of what would happen if the input segments were increased in length. The next application addresses this question.

Application II: fugue subjects of J. S. Bach and Shostakovich

Longuet-Higgins and Steedman (1971) proposed a computer algorithm for assigning key, which they applied to the fugue subjects from Bach's *Well-Tempered Clavier*. This algorithm matches the tones in the fugue subjects to box-shaped regions delimiting the scale tones of the key in a spatial array. This array, shown in Figure 4.4, is such that neighbors in the horizontal dimension are separated by an interval of a fifth and neighbors in the vertical dimension are separated by an interval of a major third (similar arrays can be found in Fokker, 1949; Helmholtz, 1885/1954). Each major and minor key corresponds to a set of diatonic scale tones forming a compact set in this array. The sets for C major and C minor are shown

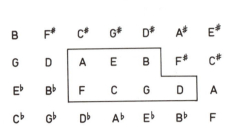

C Major

B	F#	C#	G#	D#	A#	E#
G	D	A	E	B	F#	C#
Eb	Bb	F	C	G	D	A
Cb	Gb	Db	Ab	Eb	Bb	F

C Minor

B	F#	C#	G#	D#	A#	E#
G	D	A	E	B	F#	C#
Eb	Bb	F	C	G	D	A
Cb	Gb	Db	Ab	Eb	Bb	F

Fig. 4.4. The arrays of scale tones for C major (top) and C minor (bottom) from Longuet-Higgins and Steedman's key-finding algorithm (1971). Their algorithm, applied to the fugue subjects of Bach's *Well-Tempered Clavier*, works by successively eliminating keys the arrays of which do not contain the tones of the fugue subject. Adapted by permission of the author and publisher.

in the figure; the set for any other major or minor key can be found by shifting the box-shaped region appropriately.

Their algorithm works by eliminating musical keys as the fugue subject progresses. The first note eliminates those keys in the box-shaped region of which the first tone is not contained. Then, the second tone eliminates from the remaining keys those in which the second tone is not contained. This process is continued until one single key remains, and the step (number of tones required) at which this occurs is recorded. Applied to the fugue subjects, the correct key is found in 26 of the 48 cases.

The remaining cases are of two types. In the first, a conflict arises at some step in the process so that all keys have been eliminated, that is, no single key contains all the tones. When this state of affairs occurs, an additional rule, the tonic–dominant preference rule, is invoked. The algorithm goes back to the point just before the conflict occurred, and first preference is given to the key the tonic of which is the first tone of the fugue subject if this was one of the candidate keys. If not, the rule gives second preference to the key the dominant (fifth scale tone) of which is

the first tone of the fugue subject. There were fives cases in which the
tonic–dominant preference rule was invoked when a conflict of this sort
arose, giving the correct key in all cases.

The second kind of case is one in which the end of the fugue subject is
reached and two or more possible keys remain. That is, the set of pitches
in the fugue subject is not unique to a single key. At this point, the tonic–
dominant rule is also invoked; there were 17 cases in which the correct
key was found in this way. Table 4.4 shows the step at which Longuet-
Higgins and Steedman's algorithm (1971) found the correct key, that is,

Table 4.4. Application of the key-finding algorithm to the fugue subjects
of the Bach fugues

	Book I			Book II		
Fugue	r_d	Step	L-H&S[a]	r_d	Step	L-H&S
1 C major	.51	2	16+	.79*	4	23+
2 C minor	.70*	5	5	.70*	5	9+
3 C♯ major	.82*	7	16	.67*	2	4+
4 C♯ minor	.74*	3	4	.59*	12	12
5 D major	.51	2	15+	.84*	10+	9+
6 D minor	.68*	3	8	.68*	3	15
7 E♭ major	.71*	6	11+	.83*	2	20+
8 D♯ minor	.69*	6	12+	.61*	15+ +[c]	9
9 E major	.63*	12+[b]	11	.64*	2	6+
10 E minor	.83*	2	7+	.73*	15	18
11 F major	.60*	10	6	.74*	4	17
12 F minor	.62*	15	4+	.77*	5	7
13 F♯ major	.81*	2	8	.55	5	12+
14 F♯ minor	.71*	18	5+	.89*	3	18+
15 G major	.64*	2	15	.76*	4	16
16 G minor	.66*	3	4	.33	18+	18+
17 A♭ major	.81*	2	7+	.69*	12	22+
18 G♯ minor	.75*	5	5	.68*	3	25+
19 A major	.64*	4	7	.51	2	20+
20 A minor	.72*	5	5	.64*	9	5
21 B♭ major	.68*	4	14	.51	2	9
22 B♭ minor	.72*	3	6+	.62*	3	5
23 B major	.71*	11	11	.67*	2	12+
24 B minor	.89*	3	7	.89*	3	6

[a]Longuet-Higgins and Steedman's algorithm.
[b]The symbol + indicates that the tonic–dominant preference rule was invoked
and selected the intended key.
[c]The symbol + + indicates that the tonic–dominant preference rule was invoked
and did not select the intended key.

the number of tones needed to find the key. The table also indicates those cases requiring the tonic–dominant preference rule.

To compare their algorithm with our own, we again used the fugue subjects. A duration profile was found for samples varying in length from one tone to the entire subject. This means that, for each of the fugues, there were n input vectors, $\mathbf{I}_1, \mathbf{I}_2, \ldots, \mathbf{I}_n$, where n is the number of tones in the fugue subject. Each of these was correlated with the tonal hierarchies of the 24 major and minor keys producing n output vectors, $\mathbf{R}_1, \mathbf{R}_2, \ldots, \mathbf{R}_n$. The first step (the number of tones in the input sample) for which r_d is the highest in the output vector was recorded. We say this is the step at which the algorithm finds the correct key.

Figure 4.5 illustrates the application of the algorithm to two fugues, in C major and F major, from Book I. For the C Major Fugue (Fugue I), the first input sample contains the tone C, the second C and D, the third C, D, and E, and so on. The first point at which the algorithm finds that C major has the highest r value in the output vector is after the first two tones. For the Fugue in F Major (Fugue XI), the correct key is not determined until after the tenth tone. Until that time, C major has consistently higher values despite the early sounding of the B♭ (which is the only tone distinguishing between F and C major). This can be understood because the tone C is emphasized more than the tone F at the beginning of the subject. Only after the second repetition of the B♭ is the algorithm able to find the correct key.

Table 4.4 shows, for comparison with the Longuet-Higgins and Steed-

Fig. 4.5. The fugue subjects from the C Major Fugue and the F Major Fugue from Bach's *Well-Tempered Clavier* (Book I). In the first case, the present algorithm (which matches tone durations to tonal hierarchies) determines the correct key after the first two tones; that is, C major is the strongest key in the output vector when two tones are included in the input vector. In the second case, 10 tones are required to find the correct key of F major.

man (1971) algorithm, the step at which our algorithm finds the designated key for each of the 48 fugues, together with the corresponding r_d values. In all but six cases, the r_d value, measuring the strength of the intended key, was statistically significant at the point when it was first maximum, averaging .69 across Books I and II. In four cases, the algorithm did not find the correct key by the end of the fugue subject. In three of these, the tonic–dominant preference rule would eliminate all keys having higher r values at the end of the fugue subject. For the remaining case, the Fugue in D♯ Minor, the parallel major of the intended key had a higher correlation at the end of the fugue subject. Because this key has the same tonic and dominant as the designated key, the rule cannot be used to find the correct key.

The number of tones required to determine the intended key is of primary interest for comparing the two algorithms. Figure 4.6 shows, for the two algorithms, the distribution of steps at which the correct key was found for those fugues to which the tonic–dominant preference rule was not applied. It is clear that the present algorithm found the correct key considerably faster, requiring only two or three tones in almost half the cases. The average number of tones needed was 5.11 for the present algorithm and 9.42 for that of Longuet-Higgins and Steedman (1971).

We believe the reason for the more efficient performance of the present algorithm is that it makes finer gradations among the tones by assigning them numerical values in a tonal hierarchy. Thus, the pattern-matching process is one in which the tones are weighted by their tonal significance. In contrast, the algorithm proposed by Longuet-Higgins and Steedman (1971) is based on the distinction between scale and nonscale tones without considering the relative importance of the scale tones in the key. In fairness, though, it should be noted that their approach has the advantage that the stopping rule is internal to the algorithm; the algorithm proceeds until all but one key has been eliminated or the end of the fugue subject has been reached. In our approach, we used prior knowledge of the intended key and examined the output of the algorithm for the point at which this was the key of maximal strength. At subsequent points in time, other keys will likely have higher values. This, however, reflects the common practice of shifting to related keys in tonal music, a point that is directly addressed in the application in the next section.

Holtzman (1977) also applied his algorithm to the Bach fugues, using Book I only. The entire fugue subject was employed in each case. First, the algorithm examines the subject for the presence of a tonic triad chord. If one is not present, then it searches for the tonic–fifth relationship and the tonic–third relationship (which can be used to establish whether the key is major or minor) at significant points in the music, such as the first two tones of the subject and the first and last tones. Failing this test, the music is examined at other points for these relationships. If the tests still yield ambiguous results, then the algorithm proceeds to a recursive pro-

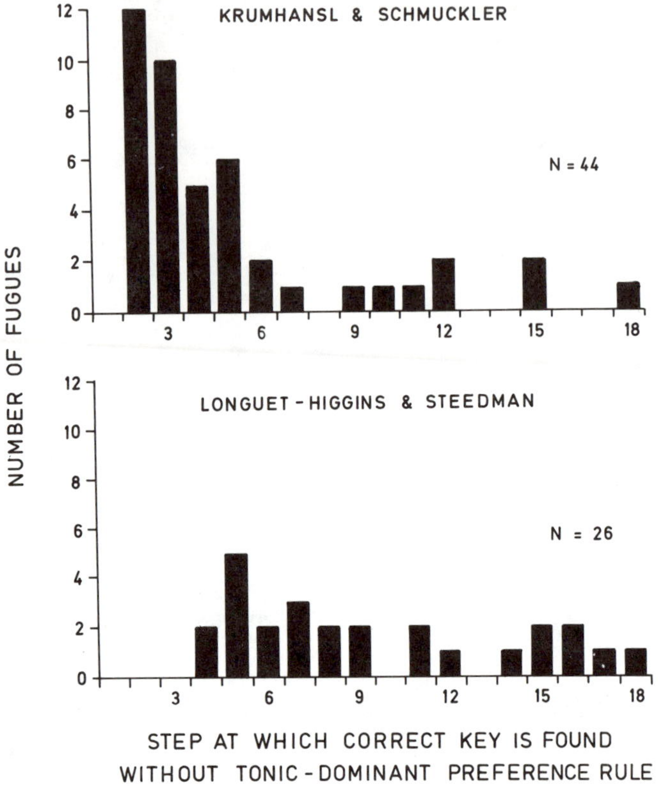

Fig. 4.6. The step (number of tones) at which the present algorithm (top) and the algorithm of Longuet-Higgins and Steedman (1971) find the correct key for the Bach fugues. These are all cases in which the tonic–dominant preference rule is not invoked. The average number of tones needed is 5.11 for the present algorithm and 9.42 for the earlier algorithm.

cedure. In this, all possible keys consistent with the tones are determined, weighted according to whether the tonic and dominant tones are present. If no conclusive decision can be reached with the whole input string, then the last tone is removed and the process repeated until a key is determined or fewer than six tones remain, in which case the algorithm concludes that the music is chromatic (i.e., not clearly in any key). Holtzman's algorithm differs from that of Longuet-Higgins and Steedman (1971) in that, whereas both look for scale tones, the former allows a small number of nondiatonic tones.

In Holtzman's application (1977) of this algorithm to the 24 fugues in Book I, it determined the correct key in all but one case. This performance rate is identical to that of the present algorithm (without the use of the tonic–dominant preference rule) for these fugues. In one case, the Fugue in F♯ Minor, Holtzman's algorithm was unable to find the key, and this is the fugue requiring the longest input segment for the present algorithm. The similarity between the results is probably due to both algorithms emphasizing the importance of the tonic, third, and fifth scale tones for defining the key. The present algorithm, however, is simpler computationally and determines the correct key with input segments considerably shorter than the entire fugue subjects used by Holtzman.

The final analysis presented here is of the subjects of the Shostakovich fugues, which, like the preludes, are written in a highly tonal style. Table 4.5 shows the r_d values and the step at which the intended key first had a maximal value. All but two of the correlations at these steps were statis-

Table 4.5. Application of the key-finding algorithm to the fugue subjects of the Shostakovich fugues

Fugue	r_d	Step[a]
1 C major	.75*	3
20 C minor	.59*	2
15 D♭ major	.21	21 +
10 C♯ minor	.72*	13 + +
5 D major	.71*	7
24 D minor	.75*	15
19 E♭ major	.74*	2
14 E♭ minor	.65*	22
9 E major	.68*	2
4 E minor	.84*	2
23 F major	.73*	3
18 F minor	.84*	2
13 F♯ major	.67*	2
8 F♯ minor	.66*	9
3 G major	.51	2
22 G minor	.68*	3
17 A♭ major	.81*	3
12 G♯ minor	.64*	2
7 A major	.80*	2
2 A minor	.67*	3
21 B♭ major	.83*	2
16 B♭ minor	.68*	2
11 B major	.67*	2
6 B minor	.78*	3

*Significant at $p < .05$.
[a]The symbol + indicates that the tonic–dominant preference rule was invoked and selected the intended key; the symbol + + indicates that the tonic–dominant preference rule was invoked and did not select the intended key.

tically significant, with an overall average of .69. Furthermore, in all but two cases, the algorithm found the correct key without invoking the tonic–dominant preference rule. Excluding these last two cases, the average number of tones needed was 4.32, and in 18 of the 24 cases the algorithm found the correct key with three tones or less. For one of the other two cases, the tonic–dominant preference rule would eliminate keys with higher correlations than the intended key. In the remaining case, the parallel major of the intended key, which has the same tonic and dominant, had a higher correlation at the end of the fugue subject; therefore the rule could not be used to find the correct key. In general, however, the algorithm proved efficient in finding the keys of the Shostakovich fugues, just as it had for the Bach fugues.

Application III: J. S. Bach's C Minor Prelude, Book II

In the third and final application of the key-finding algorithm, we examined the entire Prelude in C Minor from Book II of Bach's *Well-Tempered Clavier*. We selected this prelude because it contains an interesting pattern of shifting tonal centers, and we were interested in knowing whether the algorithm would be sensitive to this aspect of the piece. To have a basis for comparison, two music theorists were independently asked to provide an analysis of the prelude on a measure-by-measure basis in a form comparable to the output vector of the algorithm. We chose one-measure units because initial explorations of the algorithm showed that they provided the clearest pattern of shifting tonal centers while maintaining a fairly high degree of stability. The experts were asked to indicate the primary key for each measure and also any keys of lesser strengths. Thus, this application examines the extent to which the algorithm models experts' judgments about the keys suggested at a local level by this composition.

More specifically, the experts were asked to rate on a 10-point scale the strengths of any keys suggested by each of the 28 measures of the prelude. If a key was judged to be at maximal strength, then it was to be given a rating of 10; if, however, a key was only very weakly suggested, then it was to be given a rating of 1. It was understood that the majority of "no-mention" keys were implicitly given a rating of zero. Both of the experts had previous familiarity with the piece, had at their disposal the score and a piano so that they could play the prelude, and had a variety of analytical tools that they were free to employ. Each provided a detailed account of the structure of the piece in addition to the numerical ratings.

The first expert, Daniel Werts, was asked to consult on the project because his theory of scale reference (Werts, 1983) provides a framework that is especially congenial to the present approach. In the theory, a primary scale reference, or key, is normally established through some combination of the following means: emphasis of the tonic triad pitches in the outer voices, durational emphasis, presence of a cadence, and presence of a motif. A primary scale reference may be strong and unambiguous or it may be weak, such as during transitions, development sections, or other tonally unstable sections.

In addition, the theory allows for the possibility of secondary and tertiary scale references. Secondary scale references are described as projected by harmonic means, in which a chord borrowed from one scale can be injected into a context controlled by another, for example, an applied dominant. Tertiary scale references occur through nonharmonic means to three main ends: to foreshadow and echo primary and secondary references, to create melodic interest, or to avoid harmonically unacceptable phenomena. An example of a tertiary scale reference is the use of chromatic neighbors.

Basic to Werts's theory (1983) is the notion that keys are established to varying degrees that, in principle, would be possible to quantify and compare with the results of the key-finding algorithm described here. A second point of contact between the two approaches is the expression of key relations in the form of a toroidal configuration. Figure 2.10 shows his representation, which has the same basic structure as the multidimensional scaling of the correlations between the tonal hierarchies.

Werts (personal communication, June 1985) provided us with a graph, using a scale from 1 to 10, of the strength to which various keys are heard at each point throughout the prelude, and noted the advantages of construing modulatory strengths as points along a continuum:

> The flexibility of this method should be immediately apparent: one can depict not only differences in key-strengths, but also differences in the *rates* at which keys ebb and flow; moreover, the simultaneous presentation of several keys, which poses severe problems in most theories of modulation, submits readily to graphing.

The numerical values shown in the graph were justified by detailed observations concerning the use of chromatic tones, harmonic progressions, and adjacency in Werts's key scheme (1983). The graphed values were then integrated over units of one measure in length, the size of the unit of analysis for this application. These values are shown in Table 4.6 in rank order of their relative strengths. Because some keys were judged as exerting an influence for a period of less than one full measure, some of the values shown in the table are less than one. The number of keys receiving a nonzero value in a measure ranged from one to four, with an average of 1.93, indicating that more than one key was judged to be heard simultaneously in many measures of the piece.

The second expert, Gregory Sandell, was asked to assess key strengths independently on a measure-by-measure basis for the same Bach prelude. After graduate training in music theory at the Eastman School of Music, he came to Cornell University where he was involved in a number of

Table 4.6. Judgments of key strengths (Expert 1)[a] for Bach's C Minor Prelude (Book II)

Measure	Key 1		Key 2		Key 3		Key 4	
1	c	7.58						
2	c	10.00						
3	c	10.00						
4	c	9.42	B♭	3.81				
5	c	9.76	B♭	.36				
6	c	8.07	E♭	4.67	A♭	.59		
7	E♭	7.78	c	4.33	A♭	.89		
8	F♭	9.25						
9	E♭	10.00						
10	E♭	10.00						
11	E♭	10.00						
12	E♭	10.00						
13	E♭	10.00	B♭	1.63				
14	E♭	8.39	c	5.49				
15	c	8.11	E♭	4.67	A♭	1.17		
16	f	5.00	A♭	2.89	c	1.78		
17	f	8.50						
18	f	9.50	b♭	.15				
19	f	10.00						
20	f	8.44	A♭	5.72	E♭	.33		
21	f	8.77	b♭	2.25	A♭	1.29		
22	f	9.96						
23	f	9.11	E♭	3.50				
24	E♭	7.89	c	3.00	f	.67		
25	c	8.04	E♭	3.92				
26	c	9.65	E♭	1.67				
27	c	9.46	f	1.61	E♭	1.50	G	.43
28	c	10.00	G	.46				

[a]Lower-case letters indicate minor keys.

ongoing music perception projects. He was, however, unfamiliar with the nature of the key-finding algorithm. In addition to the numerical ratings requested, he provided a set of criteria for determining key strengths, and ranked them in terms of their importance (G. Sandell, personal communication, June 1985).

The first and most important criterion examines the music for the presence of a number of common-practice harmonic progressions: three-chord (or longer) expansions of the tonic, two-chord (or longer) expansions of the dominant or subdominant, cadential formulas ending on the tonic triad, metrically and durationally prominent half-cadences, and sequential contrapuntal or harmonic patterns. Such stylistically common progressions are considered to create expectations for specific continuations, thereby establishing specific keys. The second most important criterion, analogous to the key-finding algorithm of Longuet-Higgins and Steedman (1971), is that a key is a candidate if its set of scale tones is in operation over three successive harmonies. The third criterion concerns residual key effects, and asserts that the home key has an influence throughout the entire piece and that any other key established by a cadence has a continuing presence until approximately one measure beyond a subsequent cadence in a new key. The final criterion says that the simple presence of a major or minor triad makes the key of which it is the tonic a possible candidate, albeit a weak one on that basis alone. Its candidacy is more strongly supported if the triad is in root position or appears in a metrically strong position within a measure or larger musical unit.

The ratings given by Sandell are shown in Table 4.7 in rank order of their relative strengths. Although the values are based on a somewhat different set of considerations and exhibit a somewhat different use of the numerical rating scale, comparison with Table 4.6 shows good agreement between the two expert judges. For all but two measures (24 and 27), the judges agreed on the identity of the strongest key, and often on keys of lesser strengths. The second judge indicated an average of 3.29 different keys per measure, a value substantially greater than that found by the first judge. This difference is due in part to the second judge's criterion that the home key, C minor, is always present to some degree, a view held by Schenker (1906/1954).

Because both judges found that multiple keys were simultaneously present in many of the measures of the prelude, it is desirable to find a method for summarizing their judgments in a form that takes this feature into account. For this purpose, and for the purpose of comparing their judgments to the key-finding algorithm, we used the toroidal representation of musical keys shown in Figure 2.8. The objective is to find a point that best represents the relative weighting of the various keys in the experts' judgments and the algorithm's output.

First, however, some rather technical background is needed. Howard Kaplan (personal communication, November 1981) observed that if the toroidal multidimensional scaling solution is correct, the original probe tone rating profiles should contain two periodic components. This would give rise to the two circular projections found in the solution. Therefore, if a Fourier analysis were performed, then it should find two components with relatively large amplitudes. In particular, there should be one periodic component with five cycles per octave giving the horizontal dimension of Figure 2.8. This is because the circle of fifths is produced by taking the chroma circle (one cycle per octave) and wrapping it around five times. There should be another periodic component with three cycles per octave giving the vertical dimension of Figure 2.8. This dimension, which will be called the circle of thirds here, is such that keys the tonics of which

Table 4.7. Judgments of key strengths (Expert 2)[a] for Bach's C Minor Prelude (Book II)

Measure	Key 1		Key 2		Key 3		Key 4		Key 5	
1	c	8.70	f	1.32						
2	c	8.70	f	.66						
3	c	7.26	G	1.32						
4	c	6.66	B♭	3.18	A♭	1.32				
5	c	6.81	E♭	2.58	A♭	1.32	f	.99		
6	c	5.16	E♭	4.65	A♭	1.86	f	.66		
7	E♭	7.26	c	5.16	A♭	1.32	f	.66		
8	E♭	5.52	c	4.08						
9	E♭	8.62	c	5.07	A♭	3.57	B♭	.99		
10	E♭	6.84	c	4.08	f	.66				
11	E♭	7.71	c	4.08	f	.66	B♭	.66		
12	E♭	8.26	c	5.07						
13	E♭	9.75	c	4.08	B♭	.99				
14	E♭	7.20	c	7.02	A♭	.99				
15	c	6.48	E♭	3.21	A♭	1.86				
16	f	5.52	A♭	4.98	E♭	2.22	c	1.50	D♭	.99
17	f	9.75	Eb	2.22	c	2.16	C	.99	D♭	.66
18	f	5.10	E♭	2.22	c	1.50	C	1.32	b♭	.66
19	f	5.65	A♭	2.58	E♭	2.22	c	1.50	b♭	.99
20	f	5.88	A♭	4.98	c	1.50	E♭	1.32		
21	f	7.74	b♭	4.23	c	1.50				
22	f	7.54	c	1.50						
23	f	7.87	E♭	4.44	c	1.50				
24	c	5.16	E♭	4.65	f	2.22	A♭	1.32		
25	c	9.96	f	2.22						
26	c	7.62	E♭	4.44	f	2.22	A♭	.99		
27	f	5.76	E♭	5.31	c	4.38	G	1.86		
28	c	10.00								

[a]Lower-case letters indicate minor keys.

are separated by a major third have the same vertical displacements, which results if the chroma circle is wrapped around three times. Thus, the two circular dimensions of the scaling solution should be reflected in the third and fifth harmonics of the Fourier expression. (It is entirely co-incidental that the third and fifth harmonics correspond to the musical intervals called thirds and fifths; the harmonics refer to the number of periods per octave, whereas the musical intervals refer to the positions of the tones in the musical scale.)

Krumhansl (1982) obtained estimates of the constants in the Fourier expression, which is shown at the top of Table 4.8; the method used was that outlined in Jenkins and Watts (1968, pp. 17–21). Before computing the constants, the mean rating was subtracted from the data, so that the zeroth harmonic, which corresponds to the additive constant, had zero amplitude. The table shows the amplitudes, phases, and the proportion of variance accounted for by each of the other harmonics for the C major and C minor profiles. As expected, the third and fifth harmonics had the largest amplitudes for both profiles. The third harmonic was somewhat stronger for the minor key profile than the major key profile, whereas the fifth harmonic was stronger for the major-key profile than the minor-key profile. Profiles were resynthesized using only the third and fifth harmonics. These profiles correlated reasonably highly with the original data; the correlations were .91 and .89 for major and minor key profiles, respectively.

To substantiate the toroidal configuration, each of the 24 major and minor probe tone profiles was subjected to a Fourier analysis. This made it possible to generate a spatial representation of the full set of keys from the estimated phases. The spatial representation, with two angular dimensions corresponding to the phases of the third and fifth harmonics, was virtually identical to the scaling solution. Given that only the third and fifth harmonics were used, the configuration determined by the phases necessarily contained the circle of thirds and the circle of fifths, but it also placed the major and minor keys in the same relative positions as in the multidimensional scaling solution.

For the present application, Fourier analysis provided an efficient method for determining points in the toroidal configuration, where the points reflect the relative weights of different keys. Another method for accomplishing the same objective, multidimensional unfolding, was used by Krumhansl and Kessler (1982) (see Chapter 9), but it was not employed in this case because of its greater computational demands. (In

Table 4.8. Fourier analysis of major and minor profiles

$$f(x) = \sum_{m=1}^{6} R_m \cos(mx - \phi_m)$$

	Major Profile			Minor Profile		
Harmonic	R_m	ϕ_m	Percentage of Variance	R_m	ϕ_m	Percentage of Variance
1	.051	242.9	.003	.166	336.4	.041
2	.318	184.6	.127	.191	120.0	.055
3	.404	5.0	.205	.469	51.4	.330
4	.147	142.2	.027	.270	192.8	.109
5	.711	35.5	.634	.557	334.5	.465
6	.086	180.0	.005	.009	180.0	.000

cases when we have applied the two methods to the same data, we have found similar results.)

The following procedure was used to obtain a point for each measure of the prelude for each of the two judges. For each key receiving a non-zero value, the probe tone rating profile was multiplied by the judges' estimates of key strengths and the sum of the resulting vectors was computed. For example, the first judge gave for measure number 4 a value of 9.42 to C minor, so the 12-dimensional vector for C minor (the probe tone ratings) was multiplied by this value. To this vector was added the vector obtained by multiplying the 12-dimensional vector for Bb major (its probe tone ratings) by the value 3.81. The weighted sum of the vectors was then subjected to a Fourier analysis and the phases found for the fifth and third harmonics were taken as the coordinates in the toroidal configuration. For this example, the procedure produced a point between C minor and Bb major. A point was found in this way for each measure for each of the two judges; they are plotted in Figures 4.7–4.12 as the dashed lines.

We tried various schemes for modeling the experts' judgments using the distributions of tone durations in the piece. In one, we used the distributions for each measure separately; this distribution was then subjected to Fourier analysis to obtain a point in the torus representation.

MEASURES 1-4

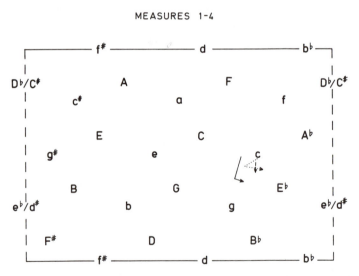

Fig. 4.7. The points obtained from the experts' judgments of key strengths (broken lines) and the model's analysis of tone durations (solid line) for measures 1–4 of Bach's C Minor Prelude, Book II. The model uses the tone durations in each measure weighted twice and the tone durations in preceding and subsequent measures each weighted once.

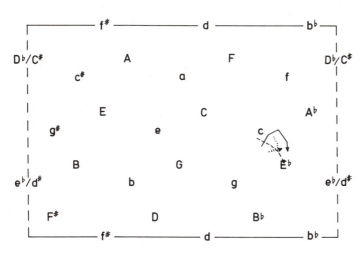

Fig. 4.8. The points obtained from the experts' judgments of key strengths (broken lines) and the model's analysis of tone durations (solid line) for measures 5–9 of Bach's C Minor Prelude, Book II.

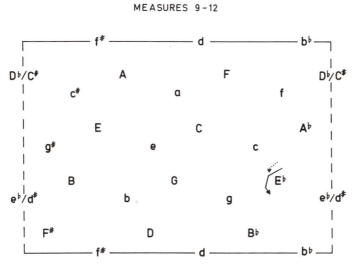

Fig. 4.9. The points obtained from the experts' judgments of key strengths (broken lines) and the model's analysis of tone durations (solid line) for measures 9–12 of Bach's C Minor Prelude, Book II.

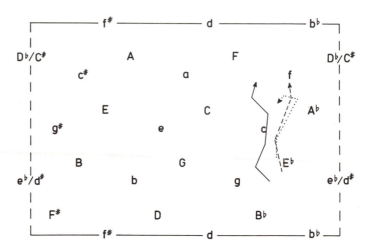

Fig. 4.10. The points obtained from the experts' judgments of key strengths (broken lines) and the model's analysis of tone durations (solid line) for measures 13–18 of Bach's C Minor Prelude, Book II.

MEASURES 19-22

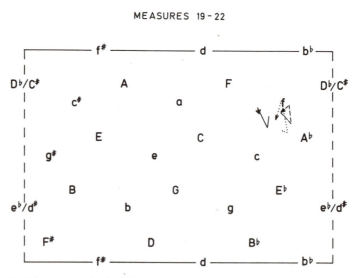

Fig. 4.11. The points obtained from the experts' judgments of key strengths (broken lines) and the model's analysis of tone durations (solid line) for measures 19–22 of Bach's C Minor Prelude, Book II.

MEASURES 23-28

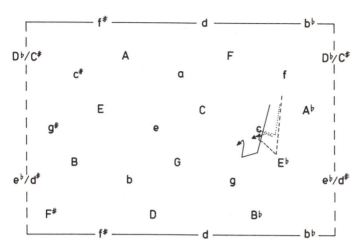

Fig. 4.12. The points obtained from the experts' judgments of key strengths (broken lines) and the model's analysis of tone durations (solid line) for measures 23–28 of Bach's C Minor Prelude, Book II.

Because this did not provide a completely satisfactory fit to the experts' judgments, we used various weighted sums of the duration distributions that included preceding and/or subsequent measures of the prelude. In no case did the input vector exceed three measures. The weighted sums of the duration distributions were then subjected to Fourier analysis. Of the various weighted models tried, the best match to the experts' judgments was obtained when the preceding measure had a weight of one, the current measure had a weight of two, and the subsequent measure had a weight of one. That this model provided a better fit to the experts' judgments than the other models suggests that their ratings of key strengths were based on information both preceding and following the measure in question. The points obtained using this model are shown in Figures 4.7–4.12 as the solid line.

In general, the weighted model agreed well with the experts' judgments. The first phrase of the prelude, measures 1–4 corresponds to points in the region of C minor (Fig. 4.7). The second phrase, measures 5–9, shows a shift from the C minor to the E♭ major region (Figure 4.8), where the points remain until the end of the next phrase in measure 12 (Figure 4.9). The next phrase, in measures 13–18, contains a pattern of shifting tonal orientations moving from E♭ major to the region around F minor (Figure 4.10). The following phrase, measures 19–22, remains in the F minor region (Figure 4.11), followed by a shift back to the original key of C minor in the final phrase in measures 23–28 (Figure 4.12). This pattern is apparent not only in the points for the two experts, but is also followed quite closely by the points found by the Fourier analysis of the weighted duration distributions.

To quantify the discrepancies between the three sets of points (for the model and the two experts), the square root of the sum of the deviations squared was computed for each measure. This corresponds to the distance between the points in the rectangular configuration shown in Figures 4.7–4.12. For the two experts, this value averaged 14.3 degrees. For the model and the first expert, this value averaged 23.3 degrees; for the model and the second expert, this value averaged 25.0 degrees. Therefore, there was somewhat greater agreement between the two experts than between the model and either one. For the unweighted model using only the duration distributions for each measure separately, the deviations of the model from the two experts averaged 33.6 and 35.5, respectively. Therefore, the weighted model clearly provided an improvement over the single-measure model.

A better fit to the experts' judgments might have been obtained if the analysis were based on longer segments of the prelude, rather than on input samples consisting of a maximum of three measures as used here. However, this probably would have resulted in a loss of sensitivity to the shifting tonal centers contained in this prelude, which is modeled quite well in this application. Clearly, the computer analysis lacks some of the precision found in the experts' judgments, which are based on examination of specific chromatic and harmonic features of the music. However, the extent to which the model is successful suggests, at a minimum, that it is able to identify those sections containing tonal ambiguity and modulations, relatively subtle features of the music, found by our expert judges.

Limitations and possible extensions of the algorithm

The present algorithm uses input vectors containing only information about tone durations, which are matched to the tonal hierarchies of major and minor keys. This is not to imply, however, that other features could not be used instead or in addition. The success of the algorithm demonstrates that this information would be sufficient in many cases to determine the correct key region, if not precisely the correct key. Other kinds of information might be used in conjunction with the tone durations to sharpen the key judgments. Various possibilities include the order of tones, melodic patterns, chords and chord sequences, and points of metrical and rhythmic stress. In what follows, we make some suggestions concerning the potential role of these variables and how they might be incorporated into a computer algorithm.

The importance of tone order was demonstrated by Krumhansl (1979) in both relatedness judgments of pairs of tones and memory confusions (this and related studies are described in the next chapter). These studies found that, for two tones differing in structural significance in a tonal context, the less stable tone was judged as more related to the more stable tone than the reverse. For example, the ordered pair of tones B C received a higher rating in a C major context than did the ordered pair C B. Similarly, less stable tones were confused relatively often with more stable tones compared to the reverse order. Moreover, the relatedness of tones depends on context. Although B and C, for example, are perceived as quite strongly related in C major, they are not perceived as strongly related in B major. These effects are also reflected in statistics of two-tone sequences in tonal melodies (Youngblood, 1958; see also Table 5.3).

This suggests it would be possible to supplement the present algorithm by a matrix specifying the perceived degree of relatedness between successive tones in each of the 24 keys. For a particular input segment, the average of the ratings for successive tones would reflect the likelihood that the sequence would appear in each possible key context. As will be seen, one influence determining perceived relations between tones is their position in the tonal hierarchy. Therefore, the results based on relatedness judgments and the tonal hierarchy would be expected to converge on the same key. The two sources of information in combination, however, would probably sharpen the key-finding process. These intuitions were supported by initial explorations in which we augmented the basic algorithm described here with perceptual judgments of melodic intervals in tonal contexts. We decided not to include order information in the algorithm described here primarily because the short input segments used in the applications contain many simultaneous tones, making the coding of order difficult; order is coded easily only for single-voiced melodies. In addition, an empirical assessment is presently lacking of the relative perceptual salience of the tonal hierarchies and order information, which would be needed in such an extension.

The series of experiments reported by Bharucha (1984a) also emphasizes the importance of order information. Briefly, his principle of melodic anchoring states that a tone will become anchored to a following tone if the first approaches the second by stepwise motion along a chromatic or diatonic scale. Under these conditions, the first tone becomes assimilated to the tonal framework of the second tone or, in other words, the second tone contributes more to the sense of key. The melodic-anchoring principle, supported empirically by experiments using a variety of tasks and stimulus materials, could be implemented in a key-finding algorithm in the following way. Each sequence of tones could be evaluated according to whether it satisfies the conditions of melodic anchoring; if so, greater weight would be given to the tones that serve as anchors. Additional experimentation and modeling would be needed to assign appropriate weights and determine how these interact with other variables such as tone duration and rhythm. In addition, plausible diatonic scales need to be determined before evaluating whether a sequence of tones satisfies melodic anchoring. The present algorithm might be used for this purpose. We suggest, then, that the two approaches might usefully be combined.

Brown and Butler (1981; Butler, 1982; Butler & Brown, 1984; Brown, 1988) have also stressed the importance of order information. Their focus, however, has been on the "rare" intervals, minor second and tritone (Browne, 1981). These are called rare because the minor second appears just twice in the diatonic scale (between the third and fourth scale degrees, and between the seventh scale degree and the tonic), and the tritone appears just once (between the fourth and seventh scale degrees). Because of this, these intervals are distinctive features of each key and could serve as important cues for finding the tonality, a hypothesis supported by their experimental results. This suggests that a key-finding algorithm might be devised that gives special weight to the rare intervals. In conjunction with other distributional information, this might yield highly accurate results.

Another source of information that is clearly important for determining key is harmonic structure, particularly the presence of structurally significant chords and conventional chord cadences. Winograd's artificial-intelligence model (1968) probably remains the single most comprehensive and successful contribution to the computer analysis of tonal harmony. At each point in the parsing process, each chord (or group of chords) is described by its function within the nested structure of tonalities in which it operates. However, because of the inherent ambiguity of harmonic functions, multiple parsings are possible. To deal with this problem, Winograd invokes two "semantic" measures: a tonality hierarchy and a system of plausibility values for selecting among possible parsings.

The first is a measure of the likelihood of various possible keys, and the algorithm proposed here might provide a simple method for determining these values. Other information, possibly derived from perceptual judgments of chords (e.g., Krumhansl, Bharucha, & Kessler, 1982; Bharucha & Krumhansl, 1983; Krumhansl, Bharucha, & Castellano, 1982; these studies are reviewed in a later chapter) or statistical summaries of harmonic music, might then be employed as plausibility values to guide the search for the most likely parsing. The extent to which the guided search finds expected progressions, cadential formulas, and other harmonic conventions might in turn provide feedback to sharpen the key assignments in an interactive fashion. Thus, in this kind of artificial-intelligence context, the present algorithm might serve as a preprocessing stage for more detailed computer analysis of tonal music.

A final source of information that may contribute to the sense of key is rhythmic or metrical structure. In general, one would expect structurally significant pitch events to fall at points of stress or accent. This suggests that assigning greater weight to these events would improve the key-finding algorithm. The choice of stress values might be guided by theoretical treatments (e.g., Cooper & Meyer, 1960; Lerdahl & Jackendoff, 1983; Benjamin, 1984; Longuet-Higgins & Lee, 1984) or empirical measures. The studies by Palmer and Krumhansl (1987a,b) introduced two methodologies for assessing rhythmic structure in a form that might be useful in such an algorithm (these studies are described briefly in Chapter 6).

For several reasons, this approach might encounter difficulties, however. At least, attempts to incorporate rhythm into a model such as that proposed here may be premature. Many theoretical treatments of rhythm are based, at least in part, on pitch information and more particularly on the structural significance of pitch events (e.g., as in harmonic rhythm), which requires prior knowledge of the tonality. Second, theoretical treatments presently lack detailed empirical evaluation and quantification. An exception to this is the partial confirmation found by Palmer and Krumhansl (1987a,b) of the metrical stress hierarchies of the theory of Lerdahl and Jackendoff (1983). What is more important for the present discussion is that these studies found that judgments of temporal patterns were independent from judgments of pitch patterns. For the particular musical selections employed, tonally strong events did not consistently occur at points of rhythmic stress.

The possibility of this kind of independence between pitch and rhythmic organizations was also suggested by a study of Knopoff and Hutchinson (1981). In a series of analysis of 14 Bach chorales (with a total of 1263 chords), chords on strong beats were not more consonant than chords on weak beats. Presumably, consonance correlates with stability or finality; therefore this again suggests that pitch and metrical patterns may be independent. A final reason for supposing that rhythmic stress is not necessary for determining key is that A. J. Cohen's listeners (1977) were quite accurate when they heard segments so brief that it is unlikely that a rhythmic organization would have had time to become established. These considerations suggest that further investigation of the relationship between rhythmic and pitch structures is needed before attempting to introduce rhythm into models of key-finding.

To conclude, the algorithm suggests one kind of process that may contribute to the listener's sense of key. The sounded events, matched against internalized tonal hierarchies, could yield useful hypotheses about possible keys. This could then set up a framework that would serve to guide expectations about ordered events, melodic patterns, harmonies, and metrical structure and phrasing. These other variables, in turn, may reinforce or contradict the sense of key to varying degrees. Some combination of variables and their interactions would be expected to yield higher accuracy rates than the present algorithm. However, it is important to bear in mind that music is, in some cases, intentionally structured to place various structural properties in opposition, creating perceptual ambiguity and tension that is resolved only when the separate components finally come into correspondence.

5.   Perceived relations between musical tones

The problem of quantifying perceived relations between tones is the issue of this chapter. Intuitively, certain pairs of tones seem psychologically more proximal or similar than other pairs of tones. Naturally, tones close in pitch tend to be heard as closer together than tones more separated in pitch. However, other effects may force us to reject a simple, unidimensional model based on pitch proximity. For example, tones forming musically significant intervals, such as octaves, fifths, and thirds, might be heard as strongly related. Additionally, how a given interval is perceived may depend strongly on the tonal context in which it is embedded. These considerations suggest that a full psychological description of pitch structure will need to be both multidimensional and context-sensitive.

The experiment central to this chapter is a replication and extension of an earlier study (Krumhansl, 1979). It uses a variant of the probe tone method described in Chapter 2. Each trial begins with a strong key-defining unit that is followed by two tones (rather than one as in the original method). The two tones are presented as melodic intervals, that is, in succession. The listener's judgment is to rate how well the second of the two tones follows the first in the context provided, which is taken as a measure of perceived relatedness or similarity. The experimental design gives a measure for each possible ordered pair of tones. The present experiment differs from that reported earlier in a number of respects. The most important difference is that the present experiment includes minor key contexts in addition to major key contexts. Other methodological differences include the particular choice of key-defining contexts, the precise instructions to the listeners, and the harmonic content of the tones. The data for major key contexts can be compared across the two experiments. The similar results suggest that the methodological differences have only minimal effects.

The data are then analyzed to uncover influences determining the listeners' judgments. One influence that will be considered is the functions of the tones within the tonal organization of the context, in particular their places in the tonal hierarchy. If two tones are understood as playing structurally significant roles in the key, this may strengthen the degree to which they are heard as related to one another. Another possibility is that the data may reflect the special status in tonal-harmonic music of intervals such as fifths and major thirds. Tones forming such intervals may have strong perceived relations by virtue of their tonal consonance or their roles in compositional practice. If the latter is important, then we would also expect the data to mirror the frequency with which tone combinations are sounded in tonal music. Two tones may be judged closely related if they co-occur relatively frequently in the musical style. Before turning to the experiment itself, I review previous treatments of the problem of representing pitch relations, many of which take a geometric approach.

Geometric representations of musical pitch

Attempts to represent musical pitch structure, particularly in spatial terms, have a long history that will not be comprehensively reviewed here. Shepard's work (1982) contains a summary of many of these models. Instead, a number of variables on which various representations have been based will be described as a way of motivating the analysis of the experimental data to be presented later. Certain limitations of the geometric approach will be discussed in the next section.

Geometric representations of musical pitch have a number of appeals. First, the quality of a musical pitch depends critically on its relations to other musical pitches. Both musically and psychologically, the meaning of a pitch depends on its configural properties with other pitches. Geometric representations provide one mechanism for expressing these dependencies. Second, when the geometric representation is of low dimensionality, it provides a concise summary of tonal relations in a form that is easy to visualize and understand. Evident in this tradition is a tendency to seek representations in a few dimensions, typically two or three. This has been true even though, musically speaking, it would be desirable to incorporate more features than can be accommodated in a small number of dimensions. Finally, spatial terms seem particularly apt when speaking of musical attributes. For example, a tone is described as low or high, an interval as ascending or descending, and so on. Sloboda (1981) presents an interesting historical review of spatial devices in music notation.

The simplest component of geometric representations is the rectilinear scale, the single dimension, of pitch height. Increases in physical frequency correspond to increases in the subjective dimension of pitch height. Musical pitch is a logarithmic function of physical frequency. This means that what is relevant for psychological relations between pitches is the ratios of their physical frequencies, not their arithmetic differences (see C. J. Ellis, 1965, for a possible exception to this generalization). Subjectively, for example, the distance between a 200-Hz tone and a 300-Hz tone is equal to the distance between a 400-Hz tone and a 600-Hz tone, because both pairs form a 2 : 3 ratio. The logarithmic character of musical pitch is also evident in the selection of corresponding scale pitches in different octaves, and the production of transposed melodies (Attneave & Olson, 1971).

Pitches close on this logarithmic scale are generally heard as more closely related than pitches far apart on this scale. Experimentally, this is reflected in ratings of relatedness or similarity between pitches (Levelt, Van de Geer, & Plomp, 1966; Krumhansl, 1979), naming and memory confusions between pitches (Lockhead & Byrd, 1981; Deutsch, 1978), and the tendency for tones far apart in frequency to segregate into distinct subgroups (G. A. Miller & G. Heise, 1950; Bregman & Campbell, 1971; Dowling, 1973; Van Noorden, 1975). Moreover, melodic lines tend to be constructed from successive pitches close on the log frequency scale. This has been documented in a number of statistical studies of Western musical compositions (e.g., Zipf, 1949/1965; Knopoff & Hutchinson, 1978), although Fucks (1962) found increases in interval size in some twentieth-century Western compositions. The prevalence of small melodic intervals also appears to generalize cross-culturally (Watt, 1923–1924; Dowling & Harwood, 1986, p. 155). These experimental effects and statistical analyses suggest that one strong determinant of the relatedness between pitches is their proximity on the unidimensional log frequency scale.

However, this unidimensional scale is inadequate to account for other influences governing the degree to which tones are heard as related to one another. One effect clearly inconsistent with it is the sense of identity between tones separated by octaves. This effect is apparent in a variety of experimental measures, including similarity ratings of intervals (Allen, 1967), recognition of musical intervals (Thurlow & Erchul, 1977), and confusion errors made by individuals with absolute pitch (Lockhead & Byrd, 1981; Ward & Burns, 1982, who also noted related methodological issues). Octave equivalence is also evident musically in the use of the same name for tones differing by octave multiples. For example, the name C is assigned to the corresponding tone in the different octaves. Dowling and Harwood (1986, p. 93) found this to be true in virtually all cultures for which multiple octaves have been documented. It should be noted, however, that Deutsch's listeners (1972b) had difficulty recognizing octave-scrambled melodies, indicating that at some level of processing octave-equivalent tones are not fully identical.

The octave effect has led to a number of modifications of the simple unidimensional scale model of musical pitch. Generally, this modification takes the form of an ascending spiral, shown in Figure 5.1. In this representation, height corresponds to pitch height and tones at octave intervals are located one above the other as the spiral wraps around (see Ruckmick, 1929; Bachem, 1950; Revesz, 1954; Shepard, 1964; Pikler, 1966). The circular projection on the plane perpendicular to the axis of the spiral is sometimes called the chroma circle (Bachem, 1950). On the chroma circle, tones separated by semitones are adjacent, and all octave-equivalent tones are identified as a single point. In other words, the chroma circle represents the relative positions of tones within octaves regardless of the octave in which they are placed. Variants of the basic spiral are found. Hahn and Jones (1981) proposed a planar spiral. Bachem (1950) suggested that only the pitch height dimension (not chroma) is effective at the low and high ends of the pitch range. Ruckmick (1929) proposed a tonal bell to account for the absence of a sense of tone chroma at the high end of the scale, and to represent the sense of volume or "breadth" of low tones. In it, the spiral is expanded at the low end of the pitch range and contracted at the high end.

Introducing the chroma circle component entails other complications. For those who emphasize consonance, the chroma circle is problematic because the most dissonant interval, the minor second, appears as adjacent tones in the representation. Moreover, the next most consonant in-

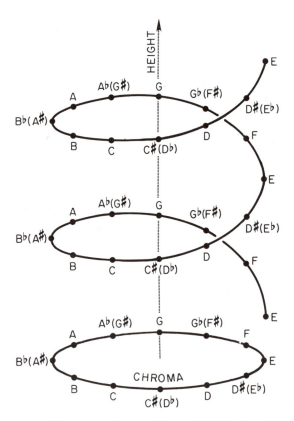

Fig. 5.1. Helical configuration of tones (Shepard, 1982) with pitch height as the vertical dimension and the chroma circle as the projection onto the horizontal plane. This kind of representation of pitch relations has been proposed by Ruckmick (1929), Bachem (1950), Revesz (1954), Shepard (1964, 1982), and Pikler (1966). Copyright 1982 by the American Psychological Association. Adapted by permission of the author and publisher.

terval after the octave, the fifth, is represented by points relatively far from one another. Also, the representation does not confer special status on the major and minor thirds, which, together with the fifth, are fundamental to tonal-harmonic structure. These considerations have motivated other representations of pitch that reflect the special musical roles of the intervals of fifths and/or thirds. Various grid and spatial representations fall into this category.

One such spatial representation is shown in Figure 5.2. This configuration is such that the coordinate of a tone along the horizontal dimension is determined by its position on the chroma circle, so that the projection onto the horizontal dimension is the chroma circle. The coordinate of a tone along the vertical dimension is determined by its position on the circle of fifths, so that the projection onto the vertical dimension is the circle of fifths. Because the configuration is generated by two orthogonal circular dimensions, it forms a toroidal surface in four dimensions. One

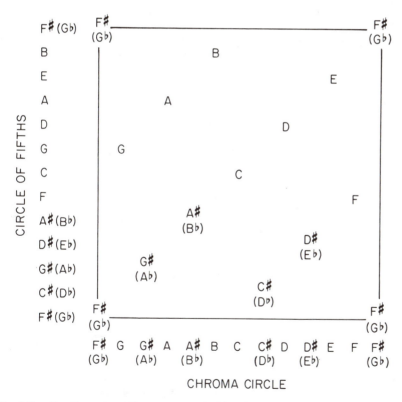

Fig. 5.2. Configuration of tones generated by the chroma circle (horizontal dimension) and the circle of fifths (vertical dimension). This forms a torus when opposite edges are identified. This kind of representation has been proposed by Lakner (1960) and is called the "melodic map" by Shepard (1982).

diagonal contains major seconds, the other minor thirds. Thus, this configuration emphasizes four musical entities: the chroma circle, the circle of fifths, the major seconds, and the minor thirds. Notice, also, that the diatonic scale tones are contained within a relatively compact subregion. However, major thirds are not well represented in this model. This representation was proposed by Lakner (1960), who used it to express various tonal relations, and is called the "melodic map" by Shepard (1982).

The final model, shown in Figure 5.3, emphasizes the major thirds and fifths; it derives primarily from concerns with tuning. The grid representation is such that any tone is flanked on the left and right by its neighbors on the circle of fifths, and above and below by tones at major thirds. The diagonals correspond to the chroma circle and minor thirds. Thus, tones constituting major and minor triads are proximal, and the diatonic set is contained in a compact subregion. This basic grid representation, or minor variants of it, appears in numerous discussions of tuning (e.g., Helmholtz, 1885/1954, p. 461; Fokker, 1949, who attributes it originally to Leonhard Euler; Longuet-Higgins, 1962a,b). Because of this concern with tuning, these authors have argued against identifying tones that are enharmonically equivalent (e.g., F♯ and G♭) or that have the same name but are located in different regions of the grid (e.g., the D a fifth above G and the D a fifth below A). Thus, it does not fold over to form a torus.

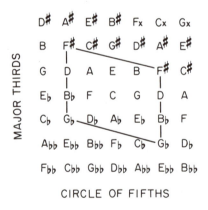

CIRCLE OF FIFTHS

Fig. 5.3. Configuration of tones generated by the circle of fifths (horizontal dimension) and major thirds (vertical dimension); the diagonals correspond to the chroma circle and the minor thirds. This kind of grid representation appears in discussions of tuning systems by Helmholtz (1885/1954), Fokker (1949, who attributes it to Leonhard Euler), and Longuet-Higgins (1962a,b). If enharmonically equivalent tones are identified, then a toroidal configuration results (indicated by the edges that would be identified). With this identification, the configuration is essentially that of Hall (1973, 1974), Balzano (1980), and Shepard (1982, "harmonic map").

If one accepts equal-tempered tuning, and identifies enharmonically equivalent tones and tones with the same name in different regions of the grid, then a toroidal configuration results (see rectangular region depicting torus in Figure 5.3). Shepard's "harmonic map" (1982) is essentially this configuration after making this identification. Balzano's grid model (1980) also resembles Figure 5.3, except the horizontal and vertical axes correspond to major and minor thirds, and the diagonals to the circle of fifths and the chroma circle; furthermore, his notation reflects acceptance of equal-tempered tuning. Hall's pitch model (1973, 1974) is also very similar, but to address the tuning problem he proposed a quantitative method for minimizing deviations from just-tuned intervals, which can be tailored to a particular composition or stylistic period.

Despite the advantages of reducing the number of distinct pitch categories and the general acceptance of equal-tempered tuning, one feature of the more complex representation of Figure 5.3 should be noted. Longuet-Higgins (1962a) superimposed on this grid a region corresponding to major keys and a region corresponding to minor keys. Similar regions were used in Longuet-Higgins and Steedman's key-finding algorithm (1971) described in Chapter 4 (except it used the minor scale with the raised seventh degree). In the original (1962a) paper, however, Longuet-Higgins described the region for the natural minor scale (with the lowered seventh degree); regions for C major and A minor are shown in Figure 5.4. He suggested that the overlap of the regions for different keys could be used as a metric for key distances.

SCALE REGIONS

C Major Key

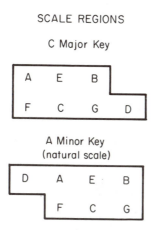

A Minor Key
(natural scale)

Fig. 5.4. Longuet-Higgins (1962a) superimposed these arrays of scale tones on the configuration shown in Fig. 5.3. The arrays shown are for C major and A minor (with the natural form of the minor scale). He suggested that key distance could be measured as the number of tones shared by the arrays of different keys. Adapted by permission of the author and publisher.

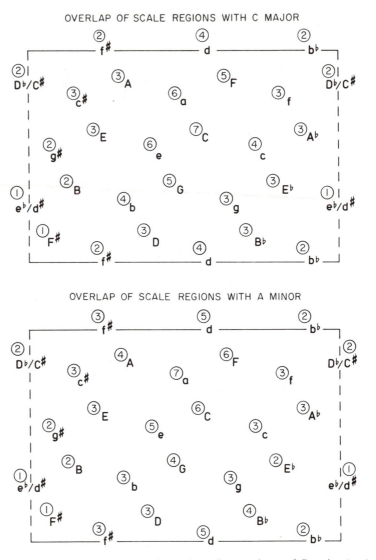

Fig. 5.5. Key distance measured from the reference keys of C major (top) and A minor (bottom). The values show the number of tones shared by Longuet-Higgins' key arrays for each key and the reference key (1962a, Fig. 5.4). They are superimposed on the multidimensional scaling solution of correlations of major and minor key profiles (Krumhansl & Kessler, 1982). The two measures of inter-key distance correspond well.

This suggestion was followed in computing the overlap of all possible major and minor key regions using C major and A minor as reference keys. When ambiguities occurred (when regions overlapped in more than one way), the arrangement that produced the maximal value was always taken. This resulted in a metric that corresponds almost perfectly to the measure of interkey distance derived from the tonal hierarchies. Figure 5.5 shows the number of tones in the overlap of the scale regions for all major and minor keys and the regions for C major and A minor. These values are superimposed on the key map derived from the tonal hierarchies as described in Chapter 2. As can be seen, the number of shared tones in the scale regions systematically declines with distance from the reference keys. Thus, distinguishing between enharmonically equivalent tones and between like-named tones in different regions does appear to have the advantage of generating a more interpretable measure of key distance than a simple measure of scale overlap in equal-tempered tuning.

Although the various models have features that appeal to intuitions concerning pitch relations, the psychological literature lacks a comprehensive empirical test. Experimental results support one or another of the variables incorporated into these models, but no single experiment evaluates their relative importance or their interdependencies. The study (Ueda & Ohgushi, 1987) that comes closest to this is a multidimensional scaling analysis of 18 circular tones synthesized according to the general method described by Shepard (1964). Their scaling results were similar to the helical representation of Figure 5.1; individuals differed somewhat in the weights given tone height and tone chroma. The literature has also not explicitly addressed the more general issue of whether geometric models are suitable for representing musical pitch relations, although the results obtained by Krumhansl (1979) raised questions about their ability to characterize hierarchical and context-sensitive properties. Therefore, before turning to the experiment, some comments will be made about possible limitations of geometric approaches.

Limitations of geometric models

Geometric models make strong implicit assumptions about the nature of the relations that are being modeled. For example, they assume that the metric axioms are satisfied, the Euclidean distance metric (or other similar metric such as city-block) is appropriate, and (for practical reasons) only a few dimensions are required. An influential paper by Tversky (1977) questioned the applicability of spatial models to similarity data, by noting violations of the metric axioms in particular, and proposed an alternative feature-matching model. Some of the difficulties with spatial models are addressed by generalizations of the basic model (Gower, 1977; Harshman, 1978; Krumhansl, 1978; Nosofsky, 1986; Mullen & Ennis,

1987; Ennis & Mullen, 1986; Ashby & Perrin, 1988). Alternative models also exist that take the form of hierarchical trees (Johnson, 1967), non-hierarchical trees (Cunningham, 1978; Sattath & Tversky, 1977), and hybrid spatial–tree models (Carroll, 1976; Krumhansl, 1983). A few attempts have been made (Pruzansky, Tversky, & Carroll, 1982; Tversky & Hutchinson, 1986) to determine the appropriate model on the basis of characteristics of the data. For the present purposes, it is important only to note the difficulties involved. In my view, it seems unlikely that a satisfactory solution to the problem will be one that exclusively considers properties of the data. The choice of representation also ought to depend on characteristics of the domain of application and how they enter into the representation. For this reason, the following discussion is limited to issues directly related to musical pitch structure.

Certain assumptions inherent in the pitch models just described are not supported by the data to be presented. Noting these now will serve to motivate the analyses to be presented later. One assumption is that geometrically regular representations are appropriate. Geometric regularity means that the distance between any two tones forming a fixed interval (e.g., C and G) is the same as the distance between any other tones forming the same interval (e.g., C♯ and G♯). This property is assumed by almost all of the models just discussed. Shepard (1982) justified this assumption with two arguments. The first is that geometric regularity follows from the observation that relations between corresponding tones in different keys are perceived as analogous (e.g., that C to G in C major is the same as C♯ to G♯ in C♯ major). The second is that it is needed to make modulations between keys possible.

However, the data from the earlier study (Krumhansl, 1979) and the experiment to be presented here indicate that all intervals of equal size are not perceived as equal when the tones are heard in tonal contexts. Instead, the degree to which listeners judge tones to be related depends on their functions in the key. These context effects mean that the rating for a pair of tones forming a certain interval is different from another pair of tones forming the same interval. For example, the rating for the pair of tones C and G in a C major context is different from the pair of tones C♯ and G♯ in the same context, even though both intervals are perfect fifths.

One variable underlying these context effects may be the position of the individual tones in the tonal hierarchy of the key. This possibility suggests a reply to Shepard's arguments (1982) for geometrically regular models. His first concern was with why it is that corresponding intervals in different keys have the same effect. For example, why does the interval C to G sound the same in C major as the interval C♯ to G♯ in C♯ major? The answer to this is simply that the tonal hierarchies of different keys of the same mode are identical under transposition. For example, the position of C in the tonal hierarchy of C major is the same as the position of

C♯ in C♯ major (and, similarly, the position of G in the tonal hierarchy of C major is the same as the position of G♯ in C♯ major). His second concern was with how modulations between different keys can be assimilated by the listener if the pitch representation is not geometrically regular. To this, it can be answered that most modulations are between closely related keys, and the analyses of Chapter 2 showed that these have similar tonal hierarchies. This means that, even if the context changes the representation in accordance with the tonal hierarchies, a minimum of restructuring would be required for most modulations. Moreover, this kind of perceptual restructuring of pitch relations, when of a moderate degree, may add richness and variety to sequences that move through related tonal areas.

Just as this discussion has suggested that intervals of equal size are not treated equivalently in perception, statistical studies of tonal music indicate that they are not treated equivalently in composition, either. The probability that two tones occur together, simultaneously or successively, depends on their functions within the key. That is, the relative frequency of intervals depends not only on the interval size per se, but also on the roles of the tones in the key context. For example, Knopoff and Hutchinson (1978) noted that in the fugue subjects of J. S. Bach's *Well-Tempered Clavier,* the majority of ascending fourths are leaps to the dominant or tonic, and that most descending fifths are returns to the tonic.

Similar dependencies are found in transition probability matrices, which give the probability that each tone is followed by each other tone. [Statistical summaries by Youngblood (1958) of melodies by Schubert, Mendelssohn, and Schumann will be described at the end of this chapter.] Watt (1923–1924) and Knopoff and Hutchinson (1978) also found that the probability of occurrence of intervals in Schubert's songs and Bach's fugues depends on whether the predominant key is major or minor. Finally, Fucks (1962) estimates that of all the possible successive combinations of two tones, only 23 percent of them *ever* occur in a sampling of compositions by Bach. The corresponding figures for Beethoven and Webern are 16 percent and 24 percent, respectively. These statistics suggest that composition is carried out in the context of a variety of constraints that depend on much more than interval size.

A second difficulty with geometric pitch models is the observation that perceived relations between musical tones depend on the order in which they are sounded. When two successive tones are considered, the sense of relatedness between them depends on the order of presentation. Consider, for example, the two tones C and B. When B is followed by C, the resulting sequence is heard as more coherent and final than when the same two tones are presented in the opposite order, that is, when C is followed by B. This kind of order dependency reflects the temporal nature of music, with auditory events occurring along the asymmetric dimension of time going forward in one direction. Such temporal effects are clearly inconsistent with geometric models in which distance is necessarily symmetrical. Temporal-order dependencies have been known for some time. They were treated experimentally by a number of early investigators (e.g., M. Meyer, 1903; Bingham, 1910; Farnsworth, 1925, 1926a,b), who demonstrated regular differences in judgments of pairs of tones as a function of the order in which they are heard. These studies find temporal asymmetries even for isolated melodic intervals, that is, when no musical key is explicitly invoked by the context. More recent studies (Krumhansl, 1979; Brown & Butler, 1981; Butler, 1982; Butler & Brown, 1984; Brown, 1988; Bharucha, 1984a) have found temporal-order effects in somewhat more complex tonal sequences.

Various theoretical explanations have been advanced for temporal asymmetries in two-tone melodic intervals. One explanation, known as the Lipps–Meyer law, is based on the ratios of the frequencies of tones. M. Meyer (1900) states this law as: "one of the tones being a pure power of 2, we wish to have this tone at the end of our succession of related tones." Consider again the pair of tones in which G is followed by C; these stand in a 3 : 2 ratio. According to the Lipps–Meyer law, this ordering will be preferred to the opposite because the final number is a pure power of 2. To take another example, consider the minor second formed by the tones B and C, which stand in a ratio of 15 : 16. According to the law, this ordering is preferred to the opposite because the final number is a pure power of 2. This explanation requires that the auditory system be sensitive to these frequency ratios, but how this might occur physiologically is not discussed.

Another explanation favored by Bingham (1910) and Farnsworth (1925, 1926a,b) is that listeners attempt to match sequences of tones to tonal relationships with which they are familiar. This is assumed to be the case even when two tones are sounded in isolation. Whenever possible, the listener will interpret one of the tones as a tonic. Because the tonic more often appears in the final position, the listener will prefer sequences ending on a tone that could, in some tonal framework, serve as a tonic. Bingham (1910, p. 34) extends this explanation to the fifth and third scale degrees, in addition to the tonic: "Even with these simple two-tone sequences it was necessary to recognize the operation of some such law as the following: *Two melodically 'related' tones tend to establish a tonality,* and the melody is judged to end only when the final tone is one of the members of the tonic triad—preferably the tonic itself" (italics in original). In support of this learning-based view, Farnsworth (1926a) demonstrated that experience with different melodic endings increases the listener's preference for simple two-tone sequences that could be interpreted as analogous to the melodic endings the listener had heard.

The asymmetric ratings found in the earlier scaling study (Krumhansl, 1979) were interpreted in a somewhat different but related way. In that case, the difference in judgments of pairs of tones as a function of their order of presentation was attributed to the explicit establishment of a tonal hierarchy by the key context. Two-tone sequences ending on a stable tone in the hierarchy were preferred to sequences ending on an unstable tone. In support of this, the largest temporal-order effects were generally found when one of the test tones was a component of the tonic triad chord—that is, one of the most stable tones—and the other test tone was chromatic in the established key and hence least stable. The magnitudes of the asymmetries were smaller when tones occupied more similar positions in the quantified hierarchy. Whatever the final account of temporal-order effects for musical tones, they raise problems for geometric models of musical pitch. The distance between two points in a geometric configuration is necessarily symmetrical and hence such models are unable to account for asymmetric psychological data.

Before turning to the experiment itself, it would be advisable to summarize the discussion so far. A variety of geometric models for musical pitch have been proposed. These emphasize a number of different variables that are presumed to affect the psychological relations between musical tones: pitch height differences, distance on the chroma circle, and relatedness by forming such musically significant intervals as octaves, fifths, and thirds. Two general limitations of the geometric models were noted. First, they are unable to account for the possibility that a fixed interval may be heard differently depending on the context. Second, they cannot represent the temporal-order effects just described. These considerations suggest, first, that no simple, low-dimensional geometric model will be adequate and, second, a nongeometric model, or a model with a nongeometric component, will be required to account for context effects and temporal asymmetries.

Experimental measures of tonal relations

Each trial of the experiment began with a strong key-defining unit in a major or minor key. All together, four different context types were used: (1) a C major key context, consisting of an ascending and descending major scale (the sequence: C D E F G A B C B A G F E D C); (2) a C minor key context, consisting of an ascending melodic and descending melodic (natural) scale (the sequence: C D Eb F G A B C Bb Ab G F Eb D C); (3) an F♯ major context, consisting of the chord cadence I IV V I; and (4) an F♯ minor context, consisting of the chord cadence i iv V i (lower-case numerals indicate minor triads; the seventh scale degree was raised as in the harmonic minor). Both scale and chord cadence contexts were used because they are quite distinct, but each unambiguous, indicators of musical key. The tones and chords consisted of circular tones produced as described in Chapter 2 (see Figure 2.2).

Two successive tones followed the key-defining context. All possible pairs of 12 tones appeared, giving 132 ordered combinations of tones. For each context, the 132 two-tone combinations were randomly ordered and divided into two blocks of 66 trials. Within each block, the context was held constant. Six musically trained listeners heard the blocks of trials in different random orders, each time preceded by a number of practice trials to orient them to the particular context. For the pair of tones on each trial, the listeners' task was to rate on a seven-point scale how well the second tone followed the first in the context provided.

The data for the F♯ major and minor contexts were first transposed to a reference tonic of C. The transposed data were similar to those for C major and minor (showing that the unit used to establish the key did not have a strong effect), so the corresponding values were averaged. Listeners also showed strong agreement with one another. Table 5.1 shows the average ratings for all possible pairs of tones presented after the major and minor key-defining contexts. The rows correspond to the first test tone, and the columns to the second. For example, the value in the first row and second column in the top matrix corresponds to the rating of C followed by C♯ (in the reference key of C major). The diagonal is missing because the experiment did not use repeated test tones; that is, only pairs of distinct test tones were used. The following analyses were undertaken to understand the variables underlying these judgments.

Table 5.1 also gives the average of the rows and columns, that is, the average rating for all pairs of tones beginning and ending on each of the 12 tones of the chromatic scale. For example, the first row average is the average rating for pairs of tones in which C is the first tone; the first column average is the average rating for all pairs of tones in which the C is the second tone. These averages were found in order to assess the possibility that tonal functions affect the degree to which a tone is heard as related to all other possible tones. Figure 5.6 plots these row and column averages, together with the probe tone ratings (Krumhansl & Kessler, 1982).

The average ratings for pairs of tones ending on a fixed tone (the column averages) showed considerable variation, indicating that the identity of the second tone had a strong effect. For the major-key contexts, highest ratings were given to melodic intervals ending on the tonic, C. This was followed by intervals ending on G, then E, and so on. A similar kind of pattern was contained in the data for the minor-key contexts. The column averages strongly resembled the tonal hierarchies of major and minor keys. The correlation between the column averages and the probe tone ratings (Krumhansl & Kessler, 1982) was .97 for major contexts and .92 for minor contexts. These highly significant correlations mean that, independently of the identity of the first tone, listeners preferred intervals ending on tones high in the tonal hierarchy. This reinforces the interpretation of the tonal hierarchy as a measure of stability or finality. A similar, but reduced effect was found for the average ratings for pairs of tones beginning on a fixed tone (the row averages, which are also plotted in

Table 5.1. Relatedness ratings of ordered pairs of tones (with C as reference tonic)

First Tone	Second Tone												
	C	C♯/D♭	D	D♯/E♭	E	F	F♯/G♭	G	G♯/A♭	A	A♯/B♭	B	Average
Major Key Context													
C		2.25	5.75	2.42	5.00	4.17	1.75	5.83	2.33	3.42	3.17	3.67	3.61
C♯/D♭	3.83		3.08	3.58	1.92	2.33	3.75	2.25	4.33	3.25	2.50	3.25	3.10
D	6.17	3.25		2.83	5.25	2.92	4.00	6.08	1.92	3.75	3.08	3.08	3.85
D♯/E♭	3.67	2.67	3.58		3.58	4.50	2.17	3.50	3.67	1.92	5.08	2.33	3.33
E	6.25	2.75	4.58	3.00		4.50	3.67	4.83	2.83	4.67	2.00	3.33	3.86
F	5.33	2.50	4.58	3.75	5.25		3.42	5.67	2.33	3.33	4.42	2.08	3.88
F♯/G♭	3.08	3.00	3.58	2.67	3.58	3.58		5.08	2.75	1.83	2.08	3.83	3.19
G	6.92	2.08	4.25	3.00	4.83	4.58	3.00		2.92	5.00	1.83	3.17	3.78
G♯/A♭	3.08	4.67	2.58	3.42	2.50	2.33	3.50	3.43		3.08	2.83	2.08	3.05
A	4.92	2.00	4.67	1.83	3.92	4.33	2.92	5.42	2.83		3.50	4.42	3.71
A♯/B♭	4.75	2.25	2.58	4.25	2.33	4.83	2.33	3.75	3.58	4.08		3.25	3.45
B	6.42	2.83	3.00	2.25	4.08	2.00	3.50	4.33	2.75	3.17	2.17		3.32
Average	4.95	2.75	3.84	3.00	3.84	3.64	3.09	4.56	2.93	3.41	2.97	3.14	
Minor Key Context													
C		4.08	5.00	5.25	2.67	3.83	2.50	4.92	3.75	3.33	4.42	5.00	4.07
C♯/D♭	5.08		3.58	3.58	3.83	2.25	3.33	2.08	4.17	3.67	3.75	4.33	3.61
D	6.00	4.08		5.17	3.25	4.67	2.67	5.42	2.58	3.58	3.33	4.17	4.08
D♯/E♭	4.83	3.75	5.08		3.50	4.42	3.50	3.83	4.25	2.33	4.00	3.42	3.90
E	4.42	3.67	3.17	4.33		4.92	3.50	4.75	2.00	4.17	2.67	3.67	3.80
F	4.50	3.83	4.75	4.50	4.00		4.08	5.33	3.42	2.33	5.17	2.42	4.04
F♯/G♭	4.33	3.75	4.08	3.50	3.33	4.33		5.83	3.92	3.17	2.17	3.08	3.77
G	6.33	2.17	4.83	5.17	2.92	3.58	3.83		5.58	3.83	3.50	2.75	4.05
G♯/A♭	3.50	3.92	3.42	4.50	4.50	3.83	3.25	5.42		3.67	4.42	4.25	4.06
A	4.33	2.17	4.08	2.67	3.58	3.83	3.50	4.42	4.08		4.33	4.00	3.73
A♯/B♭	5.33	3.42	3.00	5.17	3.00	3.67	3.42	4.33	4.42	4.08		4.50	4.03
B	6.42	4.00	4.58	2.50	3.08	2.58	2.75	3.83	2.58	3.83	4.25		3.67
Average	5.01	3.53	4.14	4.21	3.42	3.81	3.36	4.56	3.71	3.46	3.82	3.78	

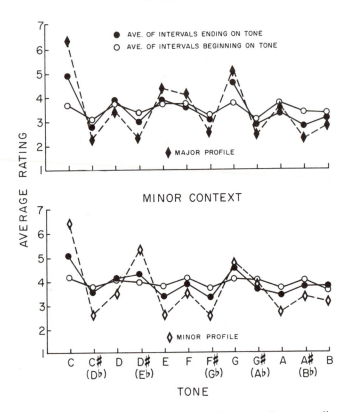

Fig. 5.6. Average ratings from the experiment for pairs of tones ending on each chromatic scale tone (column averages of Table 5.1) and beginning on each chromatic scale tone (row averages of Table 5.1). The average ratings are compared with the major-key profile (top) and the minor-key profile (bottom), using the values from Krumhansl and Kessler (1982).

Figure 5.6). Although these averages were less variable, they quite consistently related to the first tone's position in the tonal hierarchy. The correlation between the row averages and the probe tone ratings was .68 for major contexts and .60 for minor contexts; both values are statistically significant.

The differential weighting of the first and second tones predicts effects of the order in which the tones are presented. It predicts, for example, that the pair B C should receive a higher rating than C B, because C is more stable and more weight is given to the second tone. Computing the difference between the average rating for all intervals involving the same first tone (row averages) and the average rating for all intervals involving the same second tone (column averages) gives a measure of the degree to which a tone is preferred in the second rather than the first position. These measures were then correlated with the probe tone ratings. For major key contexts, this correlation was .87; for minor key contexts, it was .86. These highly significant correlations confirm the prediction that the temporal-order preferences depend on the tonal hierarchy.

These preliminary analyses uncovered two results. First, the rating for a pair of tones increases to the extent that the tones occupy high positions in the tonal hierarchy, but the influence of the second tone is stronger than that of the first. Second, the temporal-order effects also depend on the tonal hierarchy. These results suggest that a geometric representation of the data will reflect variables specific to the key context and, in particular, that it will be irregular with intervals of equal size represented by unequal distances.

Before applying multidimensional scaling to the data to see whether they can be modeled by a low-dimensional configuration, the data were first averaged across the diagonal. For example, the value for C followed by C♯ was averaged with the value for C♯ followed by C. This averaging ignores temporal-order differences, but such differences cannot be modeled geometrically because distances are necessarily symmetrical. The scaling analysis found a moderately good fit to the data in a three-dimensional solution. The stress value (using stress formula 1) was .15 for the major key data and .13 for the minor key data. The scaling solutions are quite well approximated by the two conical configurations shown in Figure 5.7. These theoretical configurations are shown rather than the actual three-dimensional solutions because they are easier to depict graphically.

In the configurations, the tones are located around a cone in order of their positions on the chroma circle. Distance from the vertex of the cone is inversely related to the probe tone ratings from the study by Krumhansl and Kessler (1982). For both major and minor contexts, the tonic tone, C, is placed at the vertex, and tones are distant from the vertex as an inverse linear function of their rating in the previous study. To assess the degree to which these theoretical configurations conform to the actual multidimensional scaling solutions, a second computer program (CMH2; Cliff, 1966) was used. This program rotates, shifts, and expands or contracts the actual multidimensional scaling solution to find the best match to a theoretical or a priori configuration, in this case, the theoretical configurations shown in Figure 5.7. The results showed that they are quite faithful representations of the actual scaling results; the goodness-of-fit measures were .89 and .86 for the major and minor key data, respectively.

These scaling results reflect that an interval is given a high rating to the extent that its component tones are relatively stable in the tonality. The conical configuration produced by the scaling analysis is such that tones in relatively high positions in the tonal hierarchy are located close to the vertex of the cone, drawing these close together. Tones low in the hier-

C Major Key Context   C Minor Key Context

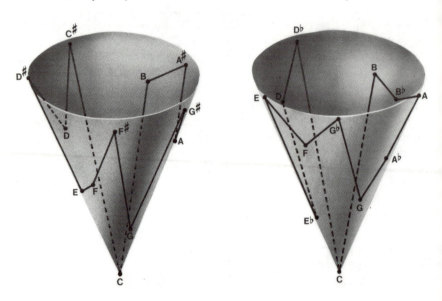

Fig. 5.7. Idealized configuration showing multidimensional scaling solution of judgments of pairs of tones in a C major key context (left) and a C minor key context (right) from the experiment. The tonic is located at the vertex of the cone. For other tones, the distance from the vertex is an inverse function of its position in the quantified tonal hierarchy (Krumhansl & Kessler, 1982). Around the cone, tones are arranged as on the chroma circle.

archy, far from the vertex, are distant both from one another and from tones higher in the hierarchy. These effects were also evident in the analysis of the row and column averages just described. This scaling analysis, however, uncovered an additional variable governing the relatedness judgments. Tones close on the chroma circle are located relatively close to one another on the conical surface. Thus, proximity on the chroma circle also contributes to perceived tonal relations.

Two considerations suggest that the spatial configurations shown in Figure 5.7 are not entirely adequate models of pitch relationships. First, the moderately high stress values for both major and minor key data indicate that a certain amount of variance in the data is not being accounted for by the spatial distances. Second, the analysis using the row and column averages indicate that there are regular temporal-order effects in the data. That is, the rating for a pair of tones depends on their order. These asymmetries in the data cannot be accounted for by spatial models in which distances are necessarily symmetrical.

One suggestion concerning the problem of reconciling asymmetric data with spatial representations is the distance–density model (Krumhansl,

1978). In that case, my argument was that psychological measures of similarity might be a weighted combination of two variables: the distance in a spatial representation (which is symmetrical), and the density of points in local regions of the space. The analysis of a number of data sets indicated a tendency for points in less dense regions to be judged more similar to points in more dense regions than the reverse. The present application also finds this effect of the relative density of points in regions. Tones far from the vertex (with lower density) tend to be rated as more similar to tones near the vertex (with higher density) than the opposite order. This pattern was also found in the original scaling study of musical tones (Krumhansl, 1979). In that case, however, I noted that the greater weight given the second tone (found here also) is inconsistent with the direction of asymmetries given the way the model was originally formulated. (The argument is too tedious to repeat here.) Moreover, the asymmetries in both studies are better accounted for in terms of the tonal hierarchy—a more meaningful musical and psychological construct—than density, a measure derived from a scaling analysis.

Before turning to the final analysis, which retains the tonal hierarchy as an explicit variable, an analysis of the data from the earlier scaling experiment (Krumhansl, 1979) will be described briefly. Tversky and Hutchinson (1986) undertook an impressive study of "nearest-neighbor" relations in 100 sets of similarity data. An object i is said to be the nearest neighbor of the object j if no other object is closer to object j. Note that this nearest-neighbor relation need not be symmetrical; i might be the nearest neighbor of j, but not vice versa. Reciprocity is defined as the rank, *R,* of an object in the proximity order of its nearest neighbor. If this value is low, then the nearest-neighbor relationship is symmetrical; however, if high, it is asymmetric. An object is called a focus if it is the nearest neighbor of more than one element; an object is called an outlier if it is farthest away from all other elements.

Figure 5.8 shows the Tversky and Hutchinson (1986) analysis of the Krumhansl (1979) scaling data of musical tones. That study presented all possible pairs of tones following a C major context. The tones were drawn from the set of 13 chromatic tones from middle C (denoted C) to C an octave above (denoted C'). The tones were not produced using the circular-tone method used in the experiment described in this chapter, but varied in overall pitch height. The figure shows the 13 tones as points in a two-dimensional scaling solution (although Krumhansl, 1979, found that three dimensions were needed). An effect of pitch height is apparent in that low tones are generally located on the right and high tones on the left. However, the influence of the tonal hierarchy is also evident, because the tones higher in the tonal hierarchy tend to cluster together at the top of the figure.

The arrows show the results of Tversky and Hutchinson's nearest-neighbor analysis (1986). For example, C is the nearest neighbor of D, G

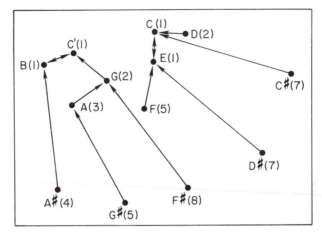

Fig. 5.8. Tversky and Hutchinson's nearest-neighbor analysis (1986) of the Krumhansl (1979) scaling data of musical tones. The arrow shows, for each tone, its nearest neighbor. The values given in parentheses are the reciprocity values. Small values indicate symmetrical relationships; large values indicate asymmetric relationships. Copyright 1982 by the American Psychological Association. Reprinted by permission of the author and publisher.

is the nearest neighbor of F♯, C and E are nearest neighbors of each other, and so on. The number in parentheses beside each tone is the reciprocity value, *R*. The reciprocity value of C, for example, is 1, which means that it ranks first in the proximity order of its nearest neighbor, E. In contrast, although C is the nearest neighbor of C♯, C♯ ranks only seventh in the proximity order of tones with C. The analysis finds two sets of focal tones, (C, E) and (G, B, C′), and a set of outliers, (C♯, D♯, F♯, G♯, A♯).

This method of analysis highlights features of the data not apparent in the scaling solution, namely, the relatedness of tones to particular tones at successively higher levels in a hierarchy. For example, G♯ is most related to A at the next level of the hierarchy, A is most related to G at a higher level of the hierarchy, and G is most related to C′ at the highest level. This analysis fits nicely with Bharucha's melodic-anchoring principle (1984a), whereby a tone is anchored to a following tone if it approaches it stepwise on either the chromatic or diatonic scale. It suggests, however, a third level of anchoring for tonic triad tones (with E and G anchored to C). It is also striking that the nearest-neighbor analysis yields a description virtually identical to Lerdahl's basic tonal space (1988). He proposed a five-leveled hierarchy: chromatic, diatonic, tonic triad, tonic–dominant, and tonic. All but one of these levels (tonic–dominant) is apparent in the nearest-neighbor analysis. For example, we see the following pattern of nearest-neighbor relations at different levels: G♯ (chromatic) to A (diatonic) to G (tonic triad) to C (tonic). (One might argue that the tonic–dominant level does not appear simply because E and G are most related to different C's in this analysis; thus, their relative proximity to an abstract C—which would differentiate between tonic triad and tonic–dominant levels—is not taken into account.)

The final analysis of the data shown in Table 5.1 used multiple regression to assess the relative importance of various variables suggested by the analyses presented so far and by the geometric models described earlier. This method, which was described at the end of Chapter 3, assesses how well the data can be modeled as a linear combination of the various variables. It gives a quantitative measure of each variable's strength (the β coefficient), which can be evaluated for the significance of that variable's contribution (by a t-statistic). The various variables considered in the analysis are the position of the two tones in the tonal hierarchy (Krumhansl & Kessler, 1982) and three measures of intertone distance. The three measures are indicated in Figure 5.9. The first distance is the number of steps around the chroma circle. For example, on this circle the distance between C and C♯ is one, the distance between C and D is two, and so on, until the maximal distance of six between C and F♯ is reached. The second distance is the number of steps around the circle of fifths, computed in a similar way. The third and final distance is computed from what might be called the circle of major thirds, which identifies tones separated by major thirds.

Table 5.2 summarizes the results of the multiple regression using these variables to predict the relatedness ratings of pairs of tones. Only four of the five variables had a consistent relationship to the data. For neither the major nor the minor key context did the distance on the circle of major thirds contribute significantly. The highly significant multiple correlations ($R = .78$ and $.72$ for major and minor key data, respectively) indicate that the data are well fit, however, by a linear function of the remaining four variables: distance on the chroma circle, distance on the circle of fifths, the position of the first tone in the tonal hierarchy, and the position of the second tone in the tonal hierarchy. As shown by the statistics in the table, each variable made a strong contribution to the fit of the data.

Looking first at the analysis of the major-context data, distance on the chroma circle was consistently related to the ratings given pairs of tones. The farther apart two tones on the chroma circle, the lower the rating (as is indicated by the negative sign of the β coefficient). This effect was less strong, however, than distance on the circle of fifths. For major contexts, this variable strongly influenced the ratings, as is seen by the relatively large negative coefficient. The position of the first tone in the tonal hierarchy also had a significant effect, but, as would be anticipated from previous analyses, the position of the second tone had a considerably stronger effect and, in fact, this was the strongest of all four variables.

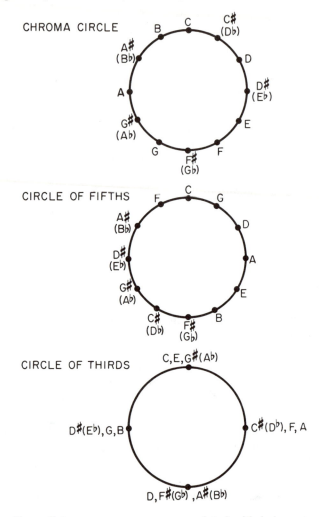

Fig. 5.9. Three distance measures were correlated with judgments of pairs of tones in the experiment. The first is distance on the chroma circle (top). The second is distance on the circle of fifths (middle), and the third is distance on the circle of major thirds (bottom). Only the first two contributed to the judgments of pairs of tones.

The positive sign of the coefficients indicates that intervals with tones higher in the hierarchy are generally given higher ratings, and the difference in the β weights accounts for the temporal-order effects.

The same four variables also contributed to the fit of the data from the minor context. Here, however, the chroma circle distance was stronger than distance on the circle of fifths. The position of both tones in the

Table 5.2. Summary of multiple-regression analysis

Factor	Normalized Coefficient	t-Statistic $df = 127$
Major Context Data $R = .78**$		
Distance on chroma circle	−.139	3.49**
Distance on circle of fifths	−.349	8.77**
Tonal hierarchy of first tone	.207	4.13**
Tonal hierarchy of second tone	.527	10.50**
Minor Context Data $R = .72**$		
Distance on chroma circle	−.266	7.47**
Distance on circle of fifths	−.167	4.67**
Tonal hierarchy of first tone	.122	2.49**
Tonal hierarchy of second tone	.393	8.00**

**Significant at $p < .01$.

minor-key tonal hierarchy had a consistent effect, which means that two tones are perceived as more related when they occupy relatively high positions in the tonal hierarchy. As with the major-context data, the influence of the second tone's position was stronger than that of the first. The strongest effect of all four variables was again the position of the second tone in the tonal hierarchy. The main difference from the major-context data was the reversal in the relative weight of the chroma circle and the circle of fifths.

To summarize, a number of variables influenced listeners' judgments of the degree of relatedness between two successively sounded tones. Two geometrically regular components emerged: the chroma circle and the circle of fifths. On these circular dimensions, tones fall at regular intervals, and the pattern is invariant across musical contexts. Independently of context, then, two variables contribute to perceived pitch relations: chroma distance and circle-of-fifths distance. These context-independent variables can be represented by the configuration shown in Figure 5.2. It should be noted, however, that the relative weights of the two variables depend on whether the context key is major or minor; therefore, the relative magnitude of the vertical and horizontal dimensions would need to be adjusted to reflect these weights.

In addition, a context-dependent variable emerged: the tonal hierarchy. Tones are heard as more or less related depending on their functions in the tonal framework. This effect cannot be represented by a geometrically regular configuration. Moreover, the temporal-order effects found to be so prevalent argue against geometric models in general. The present analyses suggest, however, that the contextual effects can be attributed largely to the tonal hierarchy. The resulting picture, then, is a complex one. Perceived pitch relations are a joint function of certain invariant structural features that can be summarized in geometric terms, and a contextually dependent component—the tonal hierarchy—that relates the individual tones to a prevailing tonal organization. The problem of formalizing contextual variables is treated more theoretically in the next chapter.

Correlations with tonal consonance and tonal distributions

Chapter 3 examined the question of whether the tonal hierarchies correlate with tonal consonance and tonal distributions in traditional Western music. The same question can be asked about relatedness judgments of two-tone intervals. The first analysis looked for effects of tonal consonance. The ratings were correlated with the dissonance values in the paper by Hutchinson and Knopoff (1978). Their values are based on the Helmholtz–Plomp and Levelt model, and were shown in Chapter 3 to correlate quite strongly with a number of other theoretical and empirical measures. The particular values used were for intervals formed with a fixed tone of middle C (C4). Shepard (1964) showed that intervals between tones produced by the circular-tone method, as in this experiment, tend to be heard as the smaller of the two possible intervals. For example, C to F is heard as a perfect fourth, rather than a perfect fifth. Consequently, the dissonance values used in the analysis were those for intervals ranging from a minor second to a tritone, using C4 as the reference pitch. Thus, for example, for all semitone intervals, the dissonance value used was that for C4 to C♯4, and, for all whole-tone intervals, the dissonance value used was that for C4 to D4.

This matrix of dissonance values was then correlated with the ratings for melodic intervals in major and minor key contexts. For the major context, the correlation was not significant ($r = .09$), indicating no consistent relationship between dissonance and the relatedness ratings. (This correlation is based on 132 observations—12 first tones times 11 second tones. Consequently, the degrees of freedom for the correlation is 130, which is $132 - 2$. A correlation of .17 or larger is considered significant.) For the minor context, the correlation was significant and of the opposite sign from what one would expect ($r = .39$). More dissonant intervals were quite consistently given higher ratings. This counterintuitive pattern can be understood, however, because of the relationship between dissonance and pitch proximity. Tones close in pitch tend to be more dissonant, and also tend to be rated as more closely related, particularly for the minor-key context. Moreover, tonal consonance is primarily a phenomenon of simultaneous intervals, whereas melodic intervals were used in the experiment. However, it is interesting to note that pitch proximity predominates to the extent of eliminating any positive effect of tonal consonance.

Do the judgments of melodic intervals correspond to the relative frequencies of melodic intervals in Western music? The statistical summaries in studies by Youngblood (1958) and Pinkerton (1956) were used to assess this possibility. Youngblood (1958) tabulated the frequencies of all possible successive two-tone combinations in 20 songs by Schubert, Mendelssohn, and Schumann (these are summarized in Table 5.3). His analysis considered only songs in major keys and, once the key was determined, the whole piece was analyzed in that key. The values in the table are shown with respect to a reference tonic of C. The analysis ignored the octave in which the tones are sounded. This gives a 12-by-12 matrix of the frequency of occurrence of each possible melodic interval in these songs. [Incidentally, the frequencies of the "rare" intervals—minor seconds and tritones—are of interest for the importance ascribed them for establishing tonality in treatments by Browne (1981), Brown and Butler (1981), Butler (1982), Butler and Brown (1984), and Brown (1988). As would be expected given their emphasis, the diatonic minor seconds—E and F, and B and C—are the most frequently sounded minor seconds, and are relatively frequent intervals in the sample as a whole. However, the tritone—F and B—occurs a total of only six times in this entire sample of melodic intervals, suggesting that this "rare" interval is indeed rare.] These frequencies were then correlated with the ratings for pairs of tones following a major-key context. The resulting correlation of .67 indicates a very strong relationship between the frequency distribution of intervals in these compositions and the rating data from the experiment. Higher ratings were given to pairs of tones that appear more frequently in this sample.

Youngblood (1958) also tabulated the frequencies of melodic intervals in four selections of Gregorian chant. These selections are assigned to Mode 1, the Dorian. Its scale differs from the major diatonic scale in that it begins and ends on the second scale degree of the major scale. This means that, in the Dorian scale, half steps occur between the second and third scale degrees and between the sixth and seventh scale degrees. The frequency of each interval in the scale is tabulated; tones not in the scale are omitted. Pinkerton (1956) presented a similar table, based on the seven scale degrees of 39 nursery songs. He does not specify whether the songs are in major, minor, or some other mode. He gave the probability that each tone is followed by each other tone. To convert these transition probabilities into probabilities of occurrence, the values were multiplied by the total probability of each first tone.

For purposes of comparison, the ratings for pairs of scale degrees for major and minor contexts were extracted from Table 5.1; for the minor context, the natural minor scale was used. Again, the listeners' ratings consistently related to the distributions of melodic intervals in these pieces. (The number of degrees of freedom for this analysis is reduced to

Table 5.3. Frequency of occurrence of melodic intervals

First Tone	Second Tone											
	C	C#/Db	D	D#/Eb	E	F	F#/Gb	G	G#/Ab	A	A#/Bb	B
C		6	111	3	70	4	2	84	5	18	3	66
C#/Db	1		7	2	1	4	0	2	0	2	1	0
D	72	10		14	103	29	0	25	0	20	2	14
D#/Eb	6	0	9		1	8	0	11	1	0	2	1
E	63	3	54	11		82	5	44	3	7	0	15
F	18	0	22	0	25		4	67	0	19	1	4
F#/Gb	3	0	2	0	7	0		21	0	3	0	1
G	55	0	28	4	59	20	19		12	80	2	37
G#/Ab	5	0	0	2	1	1	0	8		8	11	0
A	20	1	22	1	19	11	2	35	10		15	52
A#/Bb	20	0	1	1	0	0	0	2	6	5		4
B	93	1	32	0	2	2	2	28	0	28	1	

Source: Youngblood (1958).

Table 5.4. Summary of correlation analysis using distributions of seven scale tones

	Major Context Ratings	Minor Context Ratings	Youngblood (1958) Gregorian Chant
Minor context ratings	.61*	—	—
Youngblood (1958) Gregorian chant	.45*	.37*	—
Pinkerton (1956) nursery songs	.62*	.56*	.64*

*Significant at $p < .05$.

40; a correlation of .30 or larger is statistically significant.) Table 5.4 shows the correlations between the four sets of values: the data from the major and minor key context in the present experiment, the frequency of occurrence of intervals in Youngblood's sample of Gregorian chant, and the probability of occurrence in Pinkerton's sample of nursery songs. Each of the correlations was statistically significant, indicating the seven scale tones in the various modes are treated somewhat analogously. However, stylistic limits may be suggested by the finding that the correlations for the nursery songs were considerably larger than those for the Gregorian chants.

To summarize, in this chapter we found that a number of variables underlie the degree to which successively presented tones are perceived as related to one another. Tones close on the chroma circle and the circle of fifths tended to be heard as more related than tones distant in these geometric configurations. The tonal hierarchies of the contexts strongly affected the ratings, enhancing the degree to which tones stable in the tonality are heard as related and inducing preferences for intervals ending on stable tones. These effects cannot be expressed easily in geometric terms, indicating that a nongeometric, hierarchical component is needed. Finally, the ratings showed no correspondence to tonal consonance, but correlated strongly with the frequencies with which the intervals occur in Western tonal compositions. This latter result suggests that listeners have internalized higher-order statistical properties of music, and base their judgments of melodic intervals, in part, on this knowledge. The next chapter turns to other experimental results that converge on these conclusions, and takes a more general view of the patterns that emerge from these studies.

6. Perceptual organization and pitch memory

The first chapter began with the observation that listeners do not hear the sounded events in music as isolated units. Rather, listeners perceive the events functioning in larger pitch and rhythmic organizations. The experimental work summarized to this point has been concerned with the abstract relations that exist between musical tones, and between musical tones and keys. The approach has been to obtain quantitative measures of the degree to which the elements are perceived as related. Various techniques were applied to the data to uncover contributing influences and highlight regular patterns. In this chapter, we turn away from these specific results to consider some principles that emerge from the empirical findings. The focus will be on three principles that describe the way tonal contexts affect perceived relations between tones. These principles will be presented in the context of Gestalt theory, which provides a congenial framework for some of the phenomena to be discussed.

Gestalt theory

According to Wertheimer (1938, p. 2), "The fundamental 'formula' of the Gestalt theory might be expressed in this way: There are wholes, the behavior of which is not determined by that of their individual elements, but where the part-processes are themselves determined by the intrinsic nature of the whole. It is the hope of Gestalt theory to determine the nature of such wholes." In other words, "holistic" attributes emerge from configurations, significantly altering the way the individual elements are perceived, remembered, and understood. This view holds it is impossible to account for psychological phenomena solely in terms of the response to elementary parts of the stimulus, studied in isolation. Once they are reassembled other influences come into operation, and these in turn change the perception of the component parts.

In this, the Gestalt psychologists are criticizing the assumption that "has appeared obviously sound that scientific comprehension of a mental phenomenon required the discovery of its 'elements' and then, by laws applicable to those elements, a reconstruction of the phenomenon" (Wertheimer, 1938, p. 12). This approach, they argued, would be futile because it ignores the possibility that isolating elements from their larger context loses significant, configural properties in the process. Despite this

138

warning, and the numerous demonstrations of configural effects provided by psychologists working in this tradition, contemporary psychology generally subscribes to the reductionistic approach. Current psychological theory assumes that internal representations and processes can be understood as conjunctions of elementary units and mental operations.

Even contemporary psychologists influenced by the Gestalt tradition are sympathetic with explanations in terms of underlying elementary units. Garner (1981, p. 119), for example, says, "I consider the essence of scientific behavior to be that of analysis. When we want to understand a phenomenon, we must somehow analyze it, take it apart, see what its components are, and otherwise subdue the holistic percept into analyzed components." He continues: "A configuration has properties that have to be expressed as some form of interaction or interrelation between the components, be they features or dimensions . . . the configural properties can only be described as relations between component properties" (p. 126). Thus, even though the perceptual experience may be holistic and unanalytical, the scientist's approach is necessarily analytical, seeking to decompose the phenomenon into its elementary components.

By current standards, the Gestalt psychologists failed to establish a rigorous scientific methodology for investigating holistic properties independently of more elementary components. Of their various contributions, the laws of perceptual organization continue to be most influential. These laws specify why certain configural properties, rather than others, emerge from a complex perceptual stimulus. Elementary units tend to group together if, for example, they are close in space or time or similar in such properties as form, color, or pitch. In this way, the entire stimulus is organized into a unified whole with specifiable subwholes. These principles are congenial with current theorizing because, although they acknowledge the existence of configural properties, the properties of the whole are explained in terms of the properties of the elementary parts. The configural properties, the properties of the whole, are derived from the parts, "the creation of emergent features via interaction of parts in the perceptual process" (Pomerantz, 1981, p. 141). Emphasizing this aspect of Gestalt theory, however, ignores its fundamental premise. To repeat, "there are wholes, the behaviour of which is not determined by that of their individual elements" (Wertheimer, 1938, p. 2). Thus, the appropriate unit of study is the whole perceptual object, with the understanding that it may have characteristics independent of its parts.

Wertheimer (1938, p. 4) claims that the most important impulse for the development of Gestalt theory came from the following problem posed by Ehrenfels. How is it that when we hear a melody, for example, one consisting of six tones, and then the same melody transposed to a new key, that we recognize it as the same, even though the sum of the elements is different? The solution proposed is that there must be something more than the sum of the six tones. In particular, there must be an emergent feature, a Gestaltqualität (a property of the whole), that allows the melody to be recognized.

Wertheimer rejects two alternatives to this additional-element hypothesis. The first is that, although the tones in the transposed melody are different, the intervals (or relations) are constant. This is rejected because the precise intervals may also be altered to some degree without destroying the similarity to the original melody. (One such case is described later in this chapter.) The second alternative account assumes that certain "higher processes" operate on the given material to "produce" unity. In other words, some additional, entirely mental property ("ideal") is imposed on the stimulus. Wertheimer argues, instead, that a property of the *stimulus* is being preserved under transposition without, however, specifying its exact nature.

Wertheimer (1938, p. 5) stresses the importance of each element's function in the whole:

What is given me by the melody does not arise (through the agency of any auxiliary factor) as a secondary process from the sum of the pieces as such. Instead, what takes place in each single part already depends upon what the whole is. The flesh and blood of a tone depends from the start upon its role in the melody: a B as leading tone to C is something radically different from the B as tonic. It belongs to the flesh and blood of the things given in experience, how, in what role, in what function they are in their whole.

Thus, tonality (a kind of Gestaltqualität) governs the perceptual effects of the component tones. The perceived quality of each tone is determined by its role in the key. The experimental findings summarized in previous chapters strongly support this proposition. The tonality of the context affected the perceived stability (or structural significance) of individual tones and the degree of relatedness of pairs of tones.

Three principles of tonal stability

In the spirit of Wertheimer's analysis (1938), let us consider tonality as a holistic property or Gestaltqualität. Identifying constructs in this way, can we systematically categorize the effects of tonality? This section describes a variety of results in the psychological literature on pitch perception and memory. It will be argued that these effects can be summarized in terms of three general principles. They were first stated in a somewhat different form in two studies of harmonic relations (Bharucha & Krumhansl, 1983; Krumhansl, Bharucha, & Castellano, 1982). However, they apply equally well to musical tones (a later chapter considers their application to chords).

The three principles, given in Table 6.1, correspond to the three logically independent components of recognition accuracy and similarity (or relatedness) measures. Because the effects are assumed to depend on context, the principles are called "contextual." Suppose the elements (musical tones) under consideration are denoted by the letters: a, b, c. . . . The principles will be stated in terms of the psychological distance between any two elements, say a and b, denoted as $d(a,b)$. The notion of psychological distance can be thought of as the degree to which the elements are discriminable, distinct or dissimilar. It is assumed that the elements are presented in a tonal context that induces a hierarchy of tonal stability; this hierarchy affects psychological distance according to the three principles. The first principle, contextual identity, governs the sense of identity between instances of the same tone. The second principle, contextual distance, governs the average psychological distance between two distinct tones. The third principle, contextual asymmetry, governs asymmetric distances between two distinct tones that depend on the order in which they are sounded. They will each be described in more detail later.

The experiments that support these principles employ both direct rating methods, such as in the experiments so far, and measures of memory accuracy. To substantiate any theoretical construct—particularly one concerning an internal, psychological system—it is highly desirable to have evidence from experiments using different methods. This strategy is known as "converging operations" (Garner, Hake, & Eriksen, 1956). Each method may impose its distinctive characteristics on the data; therefore, the results may reflect, in part, the experimental task rather than the operation of the internal system. For example, the patterns of data in the rating tasks may partially reflect how rating scales tend to be used, rather than the perceptual effects of the stimulus materials. For this reason, it is important to reproduce the pattern of results using another experimental method. Accuracy in memory tasks has proved to be a useful

Table 6.1. Three contextual principles of tonal relations[a]

Principle	Definition
Contextual identity	$d(a,a)$ decreases as the stability of a increases.
Contextual distance	$\frac{1}{2}[d(a,b) + d(b,a)]$ decreases as the stability of a increases and the stability of b increases.
Contextual asymmetry	$d(a,b) - d(b,a)$ increases as the stability of a increases and as the stability of b decreases.

[a] $d(a,b)$ denotes the psychological distance between tone a and tone b.

source of converging evidence for the rating tasks, and simultaneously elucidates how musical pitch is encoded and retained in memory.

Studies of musical memory most commonly use a short-term recognition paradigm. In it, the listener first hears one tone or group of tones; this is called the "standard" stimulus—it is the one to be remembered. At a later time, a second tone or group of tones is sounded; this is called the "comparison" stimulus. The listeners' task is to judge whether or not the standard and comparison stimuli are the same. On some trials they are, in fact, the same, but on other trials they are different. Listeners give a "same" or "different" response, and the accuracy of their response is recorded (and sometimes also the reaction time, although this measure is not used in musical memory studies as frequently as in other memory studies). Because the second, comparison stimulus is matched to the standard, the task is one of recognition. This is in contrast to recall tasks in which participants are required to reproduce the to-be-remembered material.

The recognition method is advantageous because it does not require the listener to have any special skill, such as the ability to produce or transcribe the music. Thus, the method can be used with listeners with varied musical backgrounds. The temporal interval between the standard and comparison stimuli is short, typically well under a minute. Therefore, the task is called short-term recognition; conversely, delays of more than a few minutes are considered long-term. In some cases a sequence of tones is interpolated between the standard stimulus and the comparison stimulus. This sequence is sometimes called an "intervening" sequence, and its purpose is to assess the effect of the intervening material on memory for the standard stimulus. Even with intervening sequences, the temporal interval between standard and comparison stimuli is still usually in the range of short-term memory. This general method has uncovered a variety of influences affecting memory for tones and sequences of tones; however, only those concerned with tonal organization will be discussed here.

Tones occupying high positions in the tonal hierarchy have been described as stable. This carries the implication that stable tones in a tonal context should be remembered better than unstable tones. Moreover, one would expect that sequences conforming to familiar conventions of tonal composition should be remembered better than sequences not conforming to these conventions. These predictions follow from the Gestalt description of the memory trace. My reliance in this case is primarily on Goldmeier's recent treatment of the concept (1982), although related theoretical and empirical contributions can be found, for example, in Koffka (1935), Köhler (1947), and the collection of essays edited and translated by W. D. Ellis (1938). The memory trace, according to Goldmeier (1982, p. 10), "consists of coded phenomenal parts, including their functions in the whole." An element in a configuration or a configuration as a whole will be remembered to the extent that it is "singular," where singularity is defined as resistance to change. The notion of singularity is variously associated with normativeness, regularity, symmetry, and "goodness." Singularity is a property of individual phenomenal parts within the whole and of the whole configuration.

The memory trace, moreover, affects the coding of new information. "Once singularities are established . . . , they form the matrix, the schema, the framework, the filing system within which new information is assimilated" (Goldmeier, 1982, p. 43). A nonsingular element that does not fit with, or is not consistent with, the configuration as a whole will be subject to distortion. This follows from the law of *Prägnanz,* whereby perceptual and memory systems seek the simplest possible organization. To achieve this, nonsingular elements will be normalized so the resulting configuration has a higher singularity value. Thus, the Gestalt approach implicates a kind of dynamic quality of psychological processes in which the quality of individual elements is determined, and sometimes distorted, by the organizational processes operating on the configuration. When the configuration as a whole cannot be organized simply, the phenomenal parts cannot be coded accurately, and the memory trace of the component elements and the whole configuration will be unstable.

Taking tonal organization to be a kind of norm or singularity, Goldmeier's account predicts that the accuracy of memory for individual tones and sequences of tones will depend on tonality. In particular, nonsingular or unstable elements within the prevailing key will be poorly recognized and frequently confused with more stable elements, and melodies not conforming to tonal conventions familiar to the listener will be difficult to organize into a simple whole, and thus produce an unstable memory trace. Meyer (1956, pp. 86–91) provides essentially the same analysis of Gestalt theory applied to music. The following formalizes the predictions concerning individual musical tones in three principles and describes supporting evidence from pitch memory and rating studies.

The first principle, *contextual identity,* governs the degree to which two instances of a musical tone are perceived as identical. Elsewhere (Krumhansl, 1978), I have called this self-similarity and assumed that the degree of perceived self-similarity or identity is inversely related to psychological distance. For two instances of the same tone, a, the psychological distance is denoted $d(a,a)$. The principle says that this distance is less for more stable tones.

(1) Contextual identity: $d(a,a)$ decreases as the stability of a increases.

This is to say that the psychological distance between two instances of the tone is smaller (or the sense of identity stronger) for tones more stable in the tonal system than for tones less stable. That this would not be the same for all elements may seem counterintuitive at first. However, the foregoing discussion has characterized certain elements in configurations as more stable with higher singularity values; they are more normative or consistent with the whole, and more resistant to change in the memory trace.

Various empirical measures can be used to evaluate this principle: the probability that an element is correctly named, reproduced, or recognized, direct ratings of the likeness of two instances of the same element, or judgments of how well an element fits or is consistent with the whole. The measures considered here are ratings of how well individual tones fit with a key-defining context, and the probability that a tone is correctly recognized when it is presented in a tonal context. The first measure comes from the probe tone experiments discussed in Chapter 2 and will not be described again here, only to note that it corresponds well to musical intuitions concerning stability. The second measure comes from two memory studies reported in Krumhansl (1979).

In the first of the memory studies (experiment 2 of Krumhansl, 1979), the standard tone was one of the following: C, C♯, D, D♯, E, F, F♯, G, G♯, or A. This to-be-remembered tone was sounded immediately preceding a sequence of eight tones; this can be considered an intervening sequence, but phenomenologically the standard tone was heard as the first tone of the sequence. This was then followed by a final comparison tone, which either was identical to the standard or differed by a semitone. The listeners' task was to rate whether the very first and last tones were the same or different using a six-point scale (1 = "very sure same"; 6 = "very sure different"). The participants had a moderate level of musical training.

The sequence intervening between the standard and comparison tones was designed to suggest either the key of C major or no key at all. The sequences in C major, which are shown at the left in Figure 6.1, included all seven tones of the diatonic scale, with either the tonic or the dominant repeated. Two of these sequences were used with the standard tones: F, F♯, G, G♯, and A. The other two sequences were used with the standard tones: C, C♯, D, D♯, and E. The other sequences, shown at the right of Figure 6.1, were constructed from a set of tones not contained in any diatonic scale; this was accomplished by raising two of the tones of the C major sequences by semitones. (In a subsidiary experiment conducted to check the perceived degree of tonality of the sequences, listeners judged the sequences intended to suggest C major as more musical than those intended to suggest no key.)

The left-hand side of Table 6.2 shows the average responses on the rating scale for the 10 standard tones when the 8-tone sequences suggested the key of C major. The tones are separated into three subcategories: the components of the tonic triad (C, E, and G), other diatonic scale tones (D, F, and A), and nondiatonic tones (C♯, D♯, F♯, and G♯). Repeated tones that are components of the tonic triad were judged as the "same" with the greatest confidence, followed by other diatonic tones.

DIATONIC   NOT DIATONIC

Standard Tones F, F♯, G, G♯, A

Sequence

1

2

Standard Tones C, C♯, D, D♯, E

3

4

Fig. 6.1. Sequences used in the first tone recognition memory experiment (Krumhansl, 1979, experiment 2); sequences on left suggest C major and sequences on the right suggest no key. The sequences at the top were preceded by a standard (to-be-remembered) tone of F, F♯, G, G♯, or A; the sequences at the bottom were preceded by a standard tone of C, C♯, D, D♯, or E. The comparison tone, which followed the sequence, was either identical to the standard or differed by a semitone. The data for the sequences on the left are presented in Tables 6.2 and 6.3. Adapted by permission of the publisher.

Listeners were least sure of their judgments for nondiatonic tones. This pattern generally confirms the prediction that recognition memory for a tone depends on its position in the tonal hierarchy, with more stable tones in the tonal hierarchy more stable in the memory trace.

It should be noted, however, that a potential artifact might be contributing to these results. When the standard tone was in the diatonic scale of C major, the tone was also contained in the sequence. This was not true for nondiatonic tones. This may, in part, explain the results because Deutsch (1972a) showed better memory for standard tones that are included in an intervening sequence than standard tones not included in an intervening sequence. There are three reasons this cannot account entirely for the results obtained, however. First, this potential artifact could

Table 6.2. Memory judgments on "Same" trials[a]

Pair	Experiment 2	Experiment 3
Tonic triad tones		
C C	1.531	1.475
E E	1.669	—
G G	1.444	1.469
Average	1.548	1.472
Other diatonic tones		
D D	2.100	—
F F	2.707	—
A A	1.694	—
Average	2.167	—
Nondiatonic tones		
C♯ C♯	3.156	2.213
D♯ D♯	4.232	—
F♯ F♯	3.263	2.581
G♯ G♯	3.238	2.413
Average	3.472	2.402

[a]Data are from Krumhansl (1979). Ratings are on a scale from 1 = "very sure same" to 6 = "very sure different," so that correct responses correspond to low ratings.

not explain the difference between the tonic triad components (C, E, and G) and the other diatonic scale members (D, F, and A), because both are contained in the C major sequences. Second, the difference between diatonic tones (C, D, E, F, G, and A) and nondiatonic tones (C♯, D♯, F♯, and G♯) in C major was larger when the intervening sequences were in C major than when they suggested no key. This was true even though the latter sequences also contained the standard tones from C major. Third, an additional experiment (reported as experiment 3 in Krumhansl, 1979) had intervening sequences that did not contain any of the standard tones, and a difference between diatonic and nondiatonic tones was again found.

The standard tone in this second experiment was one of the following: B, C, C♯, F♯, G, or G♯. The sequences used with these standard tones are shown in Figure 6.2. Again, the sequences shown on the left were constructed to imply the key of C major. The results for these sequences are shown on the right-hand side of Table 6.2. Again, the effect of tonal stability is apparent in the recognition memory accuracy of the tones. The C and G, which are diatonic in C major, were recognized with more confidence than the nondiatonic tones, C♯, F♯, and G♯. That this difference was reduced in magnitude compared to the first experiment suggests that the inclusion of the diatonic standard tones in the interpolated sequences of the first experiment was having an effect, but the other findings just described establish that tonality was also influencing the recognition memory judgments. To summarize, the identification accuracy data converge nicely with judgments in the probe tone studies described in an earlier chapter. Both support the notion that there is a quality of individual musical tones—tonal stability—that depends on the context in which the tones are embedded. This quality has the consequence that certain tones are more accurately recognized and are heard as fitting better with the tonal context.

The second principle, *contextual distance,* governs the average psychological distance between two distinct tones. Consider the two tones a and b; let $d(a,b)$ denote the distance between a and b, and let $d(b,a)$ de-

Fig. 6.2. Sequences used in the second tone recognition memory experiment (Krumhansl, 1979, experiment 3); sequences on left suggest C major and sequences on the right suggest no key. The sequences at the top were preceded by a standard tone of F♯, G, or G♯; the sequences at the bottom were preceded by a standard tone of B, C, or C♯. Note that the standard tones are never contained in the sequences. The comparison tone, which followed the sequence, either was identical to the standard or differed by a semitone. The data for the sequences on the left are presented in Tables 6.2 and 6.3. Adapted by permission of the publisher.

note the distance between b and a. As psychological distance—as opposed to geometric distance—these values may be different (as considered later in connection with the third principle). The contextual-distance property, however, concerns the average distance, which can be written as ½[d(a,b) + d(b,a)]. It is assumed that this average distance depends on the tonal stability of the two tones, a and b.

(2)   Contextual distance: ½[d(a,b) + d(b,a)] decreases as the stability of a increases and as the stability of b increases.

This is to say that two tones will be heard as more related when they occupy relatively high positions in the tonal hierarchy; conversely, tones occupying lower positions in the hierarchy will be heard as less related to one another.

The experiment described in the last chapter provides empirical support for this principle. Recall that, in the experiment, listeners heard all possible pairs of distinct tones from the chromatic scale following a key-defining context. They were required to judge how well the second tone followed the first in the context. This can be considered as inversely related to psychological distance and positively related to psychological similarity. Support for this identification comes from the agreement between the major-key context data presented in the last chapter and the earlier study (Krumhansl, 1979, experiment 1) in which listeners rated similarity. Thus, both kinds of instructions produce judgments that can be considered as inversely related to psychological dissimilarity or distance.

The analysis of the data in the last chapter found a strong effect of the tonal hierarchy. This effect was such that higher ratings were given to pairs of tones that are stable in the key. In particular, the analysis showed that the ratings correlated significantly with the probe tone ratings (Krumhansl & Kessler, 1982) of both the first and the second tones. This is precisely what is stated in the contextual-distance principle: stable tones are heard as more related. Other variables, in particular distance on the chroma circle and circle of fifths, also contributed, but the ratings were systematically related to the tonal hierarchy in addition.

The memory study of Cuddy, Cohen, and Miller (1979) provides additional evidence for the contextual-distance principle. Their experiment included a number of short melodic sequences written to indicate clearly a particular musical key. Listeners first heard the to-be-remembered melodic sequence played in one key, and then compared the sequence to two test sequences. One of the test sequences was an exact transposition of the first melody; the other test sequence was also a transposition of the first melody except that one tone was shifted by a semitone. The listener's task was to indicate which of the two test sequences was an exact transposition of the first, to-be-remembered sequence. Relevant to the present discussion are the differences they found as a function of whether or not the changed tone was a member of the diatonic scale of the key of the transposed sequence. In some cases, the incorrect comparison sequence was such that the changed tone was nondiatonic; in other cases the changed tone was diatonic.

These two kinds of trials produced large differences in memory accuracy. When the change was to a tone contained in the scale, listeners had difficulty discriminating between the correct and incorrect transpositions. That is, they made frequent errors when choosing between an exact transposition and one that contained a tone changed to another diatonic scale tone. Another way of stating this result is that listeners had difficulty discriminating between two different diatonic scale tones. When, however, the changed tone was outside the key, far fewer errors occurred; listeners were able to discriminate with relatively high accuracy between the exact transposition and the transposition in which one of the tones was changed to a nondiatonic tone. Thus, the incorrect nondiatonic tone is infrequently confused with the correct diatonic tone. Stated in more general terms, these results can be summarized as follows: the psychological distance between different diatonic tones is less than the distance between diatonic and nondiatonic tones. The tonality of the melodic sequences induces greater similarity, and thus more frequent memory confusions, between the diatonic tones. Because diatonic scale membership is one variable reflected in measures of tonal stability, these findings support the contextual-distance principle stated earlier. Thus, evidence for this principle comes from both direct scaling and memory accuracy measures.

The third and final principle, *contextual asymmetry,* governs differences in psychological distance between tones when the tones are placed in somewhat different roles. Consider the pair of tones, a and b. In a tonal context, if a is followed by b, then the psychological effect may be different than if b is followed by a. Therefore, in a task in which listeners give ratings to pairs of tones sounded sequentially, the degree to which the tones are heard as related may depend on their order of presentation. Or, consider the typical memory experiment in which one tone is presented first and compared with a tone presented later. If a is the tone presented first and b is the tone presented second, then the probability of a confusion error may be different than if b is the tone presented first and a is the tone presented second. These are the kinds of results that will be considered here, but other situations producing asymmetries have been described elsewhere (Rosch, 1975; Tversky, 1977; Krumhansl, 1978).

The contextual-asymmetry principle concerns the difference between psychological distances depending on which tone is in which temporal position; the order of tones denoted in the distance expression corresponds to their temporal order. This difference, for tones a and b, can be written as $d(a,b) - d(b,a)$. The principle states that this difference will increase as the tonal stability of tone a increases and the tonal stability of tone b decreases.

(3)   Contextual asymmetry: $d(a,b) - d(b,a)$ increases as the stability of a increases and as the stability of b decreases.

What this means is that if a is relatively stable in the tonal system, and b is relatively unstable, then the psychological distance between a and b will be greater than the psychological distance between b and a.

In the experiment described in the last chapter, listeners rated how well the second of two tones followed the first in a tonal context. The contextual-asymmetry principle predicts that there should be temporal-order effects when one of the two tones is more stable in the tonal system than the other tone. In particular, the principle says that an unstable tone followed by a stable tone should receive a higher rating than when the same two tones are presented in the opposite order, and the magnitude of the difference should increase with the difference of the tonal stabilities. Again, this assumes that psychological distance is inversely related to the ratings of the experiment. In support of this prediction, the analysis of the data presented in the last chapter found the tonal stability of the second tone contributed much more strongly to the rating data then the tonal stability of the first tone. This means that for a fixed pair of tones with different tonal stabilities, there was a preference for the order that ends on the more stable tone, and the magnitude of the temporal-order effect increases with the differences of the stabilities of the two tones.

Additional support comes from the two memory studies of Krumhansl (1979, experiments 2 and 3), the designs of which were described earlier. Briefly, a first standard tone was followed by an intervening sequence and then a final comparison tone, and the listeners' task was to rate whether or not the standard and comparison tones were the same and to indicate the confidence of their judgment. When the standard and comparison tones were different, they differed by a semitone. Table 6.3 shows the results from the two experiments for the intervening sequences designed to suggest the key of C major. The first column shows for experiment 2 the average judgments for cases in which the standard tone was diatonic in the key of the melody and the comparison tone was nondiatonic. As can be seen, listeners were able to judge these tones as different with a high degree of confidence. The second column shows the results for the same tones taking the opposite roles. When a nondiatonic standard tone was changed to a diatonic comparison tone, listeners were much less confident that the tones were different. Analogous results can be seen in the third and fourth columns for experiment 3. The direction of the differences in both experiments is predicted by the contextual-asymmetry principle; the less stable nondiatonic tones are more often confused with the more stable diatonic tones than the reverse.

Finally, a series of experiments by Dowling and Bartlett (1981; Bartlett & Dowling, 1988) provides additional support for the contextual-asymmetry principle. Their study presented pairs of melodies; some listeners

Table 6.3. Memory judgments on "Different" trials[a]

Experiment 2				Experiment 3			
Diatonic–Nondiatonic		Nondiatonic–Diatonic		Diatonic–Nondiatonic		Nondiatonic–Diatonic	
C C♯	5.550	C♯ C	4.000	C C♯	5.617	C♯ C	4.759
D C♯	5.480	C♯ D	4.030				
D D♯	5.680	D♯ D	4.080				
E D♯	5.820	D♯ E	4.350				
F F♯	5.630	F♯ F	4.900				
G F♯	5.560	F♯ G	3.510	G F♯	5.500	F♯ G	4.692
G G♯	5.860	G♯ G	4.370	G G♯	5.808	G♯ G	4.917
A G♯	5.610	G♯ A	4.110				
Average	5.649	Average	4.168	Average	5.642	Average	4.789

[a]Data are from Krumhansl (1979). Ratings are on a scale from 1 = "very sure same" to 6 = "very sure different," so that correct responses correspond to high ratings.

rated how similar they sounded, while other listeners rated how confident they were that the pair was "same" (versus "different"). In fact, all pairs of melodies differed in terms of a single tone, which was changed by a semitone. Melodies were of two types: scalar (in which all the tones were diatonic in C major), and nonscalar (which contained the same pitches as its scalar counterpart except one tone that was changed to a nondiatonic tone). In both response measures, large asymmetries were found depending on the order in which the scalar and nonscalar melodies were presented. When the scalar version was sounded first, it was judged as relatively dissimilar from the nonscalar version and listeners were more confident that the two sequences were different. When they occurred in the opposite order, they were judged as more similar and listeners were less confident that they were different. Bartlett and Dowling (1988) demonstrated that these asymmetries did not depend on a variety of variables: greater overall memorability of scalar melodies, task-specific strategies, or the greater number of semitone intervals in nonscalar melodies. Rather, the consistent structure of the first-presented scalar melody is violated by introducing a nondiatonic tone in the second melody, an explanation that is consistent with the contextual-asymmetry principle, which states that a change from a diatonic to a nondiatonic tone is larger than the reverse.

In summary, the findings reviewed in this section fit nicely with the Gestalt notion of singularity of elements within a whole. Individual tones within tonal contexts are perceived as more or less stable, normative, or consistent with the tonality. This has the consequence that certain elements are better remembered, are less often confused with other—less stable—elements, and are preferred in final positions. More precisely, three logically independent contextual principles can be stated for musical tones. These principles are supported by both rating and memory data, despite differences between the two paradigms. The rating studies generally produce somewhat more consistent and interpretable results than the memory studies. It seems likely that this derives in part from the difficulty of unambiguously establishing a context key with the kinds of short melodic sequences used in the memory studies. For this reason, studies of context effects to be summarized in later chapters employ harmonic sequences. The results so far, however, show regular effects of context that can be understood well in terms of Gestalt theory. The next section turns to variables that apply to whole musical sequences, particularly those governing perceptual grouping and perceived similarity of melodic sequences.

As a final comment here, however, it may be worth mentioning some implications these principles have for psychological measurement and scaling. Axiomatic measurement (Krantz, Luce, Suppes, & Tversky, 1971; F. S. Roberts, 1979; Luce & Krumhansl, 1988) treats the problem of how a set of quantitative scale values might be assigned to quasi-quantitative, empirical observations. The kinds of scale values that can be assigned depend on the properties of the empirical observations. The three principles stated in this section express certain regularities observed in a variety of empirical measures. They constitute a case that has not been considered in this literature. In particular, axiomatic measurement has not, with one exception, considered cases in which there are asymmetries in measures of psychological distances or differences in the strength of identity between an object and itself. The exception is the model proposed by Tversky (1977), which assumes that objects can be decomposed into discrete features—an assumption that cannot be made for the case of musical tones considered here. Moreover, the axiomatic measurement tradition has not considered the possibility that context may have systematic effects on measures of psychological distance. These contextual effects may provide a rich source of information concerning the nature of the underlying scale, and may be a fruitful avenue for theoretical development. If the principles uncovered here do represent a fairly general case, then it would also be desirable to devise scaling methods for the analysis of such data.

Perceptual organization in music: Segmentation and melodic similarity

Musical phenomena that are consistent with other aspects of Gestalt theory, particularly the principles of perceptual organization, are considered briefly in this final section. A sequence of musical tones tends to be heard, not as a succession of unrelated events, but as organized into metrical, rhythmic, melodic, and harmonic units. Smaller units are joined together to form larger units in an embedded, hierarchical fashion. The individual musical tones are perceptually grouped together, not only according to their functions in the abstract tonal framework as has been discussed, but also by other kinds of attributes. The psychological literature describes certain grouping principles. Some of these are of a strictly musical character, others apply to auditory perception more generally. Indeed, many treatments draw parallels between grouping in music and visual perception, suggesting that these principles operate cross-modally.

Support for Gestalt laws of perceptual organization comes primarily from visual examples. However, certain laws, such as those of proximity, similarity, and good continuation, have been extended to music. A number of heuristics have been proposed for translating between visual and musical cases (e.g., Kubovy, 1981; Julesz & Hirsh, 1972), although this approach encounters certain difficulties. In some cases, the Gestaltists provided only visual examples, rather than general statements of the principle, so it is sometimes difficult to know how to make the appropriate translation. Moreover, the various translation schemes differ from one another and may yield inconsistent results when applied. For these reasons, it seems preferable to state the principles for music in terms of physical, acoustic attributes as has generally been done in the literature.

Comprehensive reviews of various grouping influences, and supporting empirical studies, are provided by Deutsch (1982a,b; 1986b), McAdams (1984), and Bregman (1978, 1981), so they will be noted only briefly here. Each of the influences contributes to the tendency to group sounded events together, although it should be understood that the relative psychological importance of the various influences needs to be taken into account. For example, two influences may simultaneously operate to converge on the same grouping. In other cases, two influences may tend toward different groupings, and one will predominate over the other. Thus, as with the principles for visual configurations, there may be trade-offs between different influences in a particular situation.

Two simultaneously sounded tones will tend to be heard in the same perceptual group to the extent that they are close in frequency, harmonically related, emanate from the same spatial location, have temporally synchronous onsets or offsets, or undergo synchronized amplitude of frequency modulation (such as vibrato). Two successively presented tones will, with other conditions being equal, tend to group together to the extent that they are sounded close in time. Spatial location, frequency proximity, timbral similarity, and the formation of simple contours (patterns of increasing and decreasing pitch) also contribute to the probability that successively sounded tones are perceived as part of the same unit; moreover, in some cases, these variables may override temporal proximity, producing two or more interleaved streams. The formation of simple, repeated metrical or rhythmic units may also promote grouping. All these variables presumably operate in complex ways to give rise to the perception of coherent sequences of auditory events. Attempts to formalize the influence of these principles and relate them to music have been described, for example, by Simon and Sumner (1968), Tenney and Polansky (1980), Deutsch and Feroe (1981), and Lerdahl and Jackendoff (1983). These theoretical treatments also suggest that representing musical structure requires multiple levels of description.

In support of the need for multiple levels of description, Palmer and Krumhansl (1987a,b) found in a study of perceived musical phrasing that temporal and pitch components make independent contributions. Two basic paradigms were used in these studies to separate temporal and pitch components of short musical selections (the fugue subject of Bach's Fugue XX in A Minor from the *Well-Tempered Clavier,* Book I, and the first eight measures of Mozart's A Major Piano Sonata, K. 331). In one paradigm, illustrated in Figure 6.3 for the Bach fugue subject, one condition retained just the temporal pattern of the music (the same pitch was used throughout), a second condition retained just the pitch pattern of the

Fig. 6.3.   The first paradigm used in Palmer and Krumhansl (1987a,b) to separate temporal and pitch structures applied to the fugue subject of Bach's Fugue XX in A Minor from the *Well-Tempered Clavier,* Book I. Sequence A retains only the original temporal pattern; sequence B retains only the original pitch pattern; sequence C retains the original temporal and pitch patterns. Trials of different lengths are played and listeners rated how good or complete a phrase the sounded segment formed. Copyright 1987 by the American Psychological Association. Reprinted by permission of the publisher.

music (the same duration was used throughout), and a third condition retained both temporal and pitch patterns (as in the original music). Trials of different lengths were played and listeners rated how good or complete a phrase the sounded segment formed. In the second paradigm, one condition retained the original pitch pattern but shifted the temporal pattern to varying degrees. A second condition retained the original temporal pattern but shifted the pitch pattern to varying degrees; a third condition shifted both temporal and pitch patterns together to varying degrees. Figure 6.4 illustrates this for the Bach fugue subject for shifts of one position to the right. Again, listeners rated how good or complete a phrase the sounded segment formed.

A number of results were found for the two pieces and for the two experimental paradigms. First, the position of the last sounded event in

Fig. 6.4. The second paradigm used in Palmer and Krumhansl (1987a,b) to separate temporal and pitch structures applied to the same fugue subject. Sequence A retains the pitch pattern of the original, but shifts the temporal pattern one position to the right; sequence B retains the temporal pattern of the original, but shifts the pitch pattern one position to the right; sequence C shifts both temporal and pitch patterns together one position to the right. All possible shifts were used, and listeners rated how good or complete a phrase the sounded segment formed. Copyright 1987 by the American Psychological Association. Reprinted by permission of the publisher.

the metrical hierarchy (using the values predicted by Lerdahl & Jackendoff, 1983) correlated with the ratings in the conditions varying the temporal pattern only. Second, the position of the last sounded event in the tonal hierarchy (using the values for the appropriate key from Krumhansl & Kessler, 1982) correlated with the ratings in the conditions varying the pitch pattern only. Third, ratings in the conditions varying only temporal patterns and varying only pitch patterns did not correlate strongly with each other, indicating that the two components make independent contributions to defining the phrase structure. Finally, the ratings in the conditions varying both temporal and pitch patterns simultaneously could be modeled very well as an additive combination of the conditions separately varying temporal and pitch patterns. Thus, this study identifies two independent components contributing to phrasing, which combine additively in music with both temporal and pitch variations. In a similar vein, Schmuckler (1988) showed that melodic and harmonic processes make independent and additive contributions to expectations generated for continuations of musical passages taken from Schumann's "Du Ring an meinen Finger" from the song cycle *Frauenliebe und Leben.*

A study by Deliège (1987) considered other influences that may contribute to musical segmentation. In particular, her study tested empirically the grouping preference rules from Lerdahl and Jackendoff (1983). Their rules divide into two categories. In the first category, groups are defined by temporal characteristics, with segmentation occurring after slurs or rests, or after a prolonged sound among shorter sounds. In the second category, the groups are defined by changes in musical parameters, such as register, dynamics, articulation, duration, and timbre. In Deliège's first experiment, listeners heard short excerpts from Baroque, Classical, Romantic, and early twentieth-century music. The material to be segmented was symbolized by a horizontal row of dots (with one dot corresponding to each event in the upper voice); listeners indicated the perceived segmentation by drawing a vertical line at the corresponding position in the row of dots. Segmentations in accordance with the rules occurred significantly more frequently than chance. Musicians' responses conformed with the rules somewhat more frequently than those of nonmusicians. In addition, some rules produced more consistent responses than others, although these differences may depend on the particular excerpts chosen to test each rule. Her second experiment pitted the rules against one another using artificially constructed sequences. Again, certain rules were found to predominate over others. The relative importance of the rules, however, differed between the two experiments, which, again, might be traced to the specifics of the test excerpts employed. Though generally providing support for the grouping rules of Lerdahl and Jackendoff's theory (1983), the results also suggested that additional rules might be needed.

Recent experiments by E. F. Clarke and C. L. Krumhansl (1990) investigated segmentation of extended musical passages as part of a study of the perception of large-scale musical form. We chose two pieces written in very different styles, Stockhausen's *Klavierstück IX* and Mozart's Fantasie in C Minor (K. 475). The pieces, however, share certain general characteristics. They are both written for solo piano, are about 10 minutes in length, contain a variety of musical ideas and contrasting tempi. Both pieces were recorded by professional musicians from their current concert repertoire. We were interested in determining where listeners locate major boundaries in these two pieces, and assessing properties of the music contributing to boundary formation. For this, we used the following procedure. Listeners, who all had extensive musical training, first heard the piece in the study played from beginning to end. On the second hearing, they were asked to push a foot pedal after hearing what they thought was a major boundary. On the third hearing, they were given a copy of the score that indicated the approximate locations of the boundaries they had indicated on the second hearing. The piece was played just beyond each boundary and stopped. Listeners were asked to indicate on the score the precise point at which the boundary occurred, and on a separate answer form the strength of the boundary (on a scale from 1 to 7) and characteristics in the music they felt contributed to establishing the boundary. During this third phase, they were free to eliminate any boundaries that they had indicated earlier but about which they had changed their minds.

For both pieces, listeners agreed well with one another on boundary locations. Figure 6.5 summarizes the results for the Stockhausen *Klavierstück IX*. Ten boundaries were agreed on by the majority of listeners and also had the greatest judged boundary strengths. Two strong boundaries (at measures 17 and 117) divide the piece into three main sections, which are, in turn, subdivided by weaker boundaries. A variety of musical characteristics were described as contributing to forming these boundaries. However, they fall into four general categories. The first (comprising 9 percent of all responses) includes silences and long pauses. The second (36 percent of all responses) includes changes of musical parameters such as dynamics, register, texture, and rhythm. The third (30 percent of all responses) includes changes of pitch organization, content, or contour. The final category (25 percent of all responses) includes restatement or repetition of previously heard material. It should be emphasized that most boundaries were defined by a combination of more than one characteristic, often four or more.

Figure 6.6 summarizes the results for the Mozart Fantasie in C Minor. Again, a majority of the listeners agreed on 10 boundary locations, which also had the greatest judged boundary strengths. The main difference from the Stockhausen results is that a number of strong boundaries are

STOCKHAUSEN'S KLAVIERSTÜCK IX

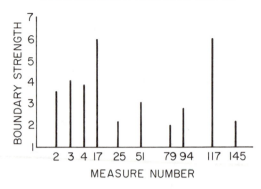

Fig. 6.5. Graphic illustration of the boundaries agreed on by the majority of listeners for Stockhausen's Klavierstück IX (Clarke & Krumhansl, 1990). These boundaries also had the greatest judged boundary strengths. A variety of factors were cited as contributing to boundary formation; most boundaries were marked by a convergence of multiple factors as described in the text.

located throughout the piece, whereas the Stockhausen piece contains a long central section containing only weakly marked boundaries. Of the musical features cited as defining the boundaries in the Mozart piece, the majority (60 percent) were changes of musical parameters such as dynamics, register, texture, and rhythm. The pitch characteristics included changes of organization, content, or contour (17 percent of all responses), as well as characteristics specific to tonal music, such as change of harmony or key (16 percent of all responses). Return of material was not a predominant segmentation characteristic (7 percent all responses) for this piece, nor were silences or long pauses (no responses).

To summarize, listeners in these experiments showed considerable agreement on the locations of major boundaries within these two extended musical selections. The kinds of features identified as contributing to boundary formation varied somewhat between the pieces. For both, however, the predominant feature was contrasts of surface characteristics of the music. In a related study, Deliège (1989) also found considerable agreement between listeners on the judged locations of boundaries in two pieces, Berio's *Sequenza VI* and Boulez's *Eclat,* despite different levels of musical training of the listeners in her experiments. Generally similar characteristics were identified by Deliège as contributing to establishing boundaries (the listeners themselves were not asked to indicate the characteristics on which their judgments were based). These results offer some initial suggestions as to how extended musical passages are segmented; moreover, similar principles appear to operate on both brief and extended time scales.

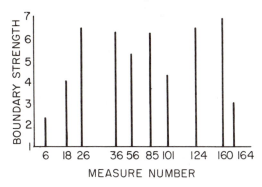

Fig. 6.6. Graphic illustration of the boundaries agreed on by the majority of listeners for Mozart's Fantasie in C Minor (K. 475) (Clarke & Krumhansl, 1990). These boundaries also had the greatest judged boundary strengths. As in the Stockhausen piece, most boundaries were marked by a convergence of multiple factors as described in the text.

One final result concerning perceived segmentation in music will be mentioned briefly. It comes from a developmental study (Krumhansl & Jusczyk, 1990) using 6-month-old infants. The question addressed in the experiment was whether infants are sensitive to phrase structure in music. This question was stimulated by the earlier finding of Hirsh-Pasek, Kemler Nelson, Jusczyk, Cassidy, Druss, and Kennedy (1987), showing that young infants are sensitive to clause structure in speech. For our stimulus materials, we chose 16 Mozart minuets (from *Thirty Easy Pieces for Piano*) having simple and regular melodic, harmonic, and rhythmic structures. We played the initial section of each (with the repeat sign) in two versions. In the "natural" version, two-beat pauses (duration approximately 1 second) were inserted at the end of each phrase. The "unnatural" version had the same pattern of pauses, except the segments began after one, three, five, seven, or nine measures of the music with the consequence that the pauses did not occur at natural phrase endings. Figure 6.7 shows the natural and unnatural versions of one of the minuets.

We adopted a "looking-time procedure" from previous studies investigating speech perception by infants (Fernald, 1985; Hirsh-Pasek et al., 1987). The infant was seated on its parent's lap in the center of a three-sided test booth. After the infant looked straight ahead at a flashing light, that light was extinguished. Then, a light on either the left or the right side began to flash and, as soon as the infant oriented in that direction, the musical selection was played from a loudspeaker on that side. It continued until completion or until the infant looked away. Natural versions were always played from one side, and unnatural versions from the other

Natural

Unnatural

Fig. 6.7. The natural and unnatural versions of one of the stimulus sequences used by Krumhansl and Jusczyk (1990). The sequence is based on one of Mozart's minuets from *Thirty Easy Pieces for Piano*. Two-beat pauses (of duration approximately 1 second) were inserted at the end of phrases in the natural version. The pattern of pauses in the unnatural version was identical, only the music began after five measures of the original music, so that the pauses did not correspond with phrase endings.

side (the side was counterbalanced between subjects). The result was that on average infants looked longer in the direction of the speaker playing the natural versions (10.23 seconds) than in the direction of the speaker playing the unnatural versions (8.03 seconds). Although this difference may not seem large, it was extremely reliable. This pattern was shown by 22 of the 24 infants, and the natural version of each minuet had a longer looking time on average than its unnatural counterpart. Thus, infants do seem to be able to distinguish between appropriate and inappropriate segmentations of these pieces.

Three musical variables correlated with the looking-time measures: drops in pitch contour, lengthening of durations (in the melody), and presence of octave simultaneities (between the melody and accompaniment) before the pauses. The top of Figure 6.8 shows the average pitch height as a function of position relative to the pauses for natural and unnatural versions; the bottom of Figure 6.8 shows the average durations of melody tones. Octave simultaneities occurred considerably more frequently just before the pauses in the natural versions (58 percent of the time) than in the unnatural versions (11 percent of the time). Together, these variables accounted for more than 70 percent of the variance in the looking-time data, which is remarkable given the inherent variability of infant response measures and the number of specific differences between the selections that might influence infants' attention. However, other previous studies have suggested that infants are sensitive to these general kinds of acoustic variables. Trehub (1987) showed that infants respond to changes in melodic contour and rhythm, and Demany and Armand (1984) demonstrated

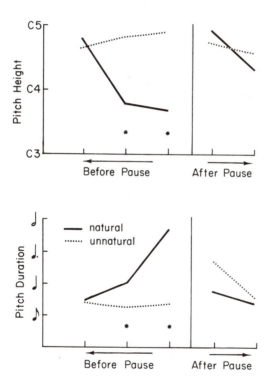

Fig. 6.8. The top graph shows, for the stimulus sequences used by Krumhansl and Jusczyk (1990), the average pitch height of the last three tones before the pauses (including the end of the piece) and the first two tones after the pauses (including the beginning of the piece). The bottom graph shows the average pitch duration of the melody tones for the same positions. Values for the last two positions before the pauses correlated significantly with the times 6-month-old infants looked in the direction of the speaker playing the excerpt. Looking times also correlated with the number of octave simultaneities between the melody and accompaniment preceding the pauses.

octave equivalence in infants. Moreover, segmental organization in speech is thought to be signaled by falling intonational contour and syllable lengthening, suggesting possible segmentation principles common to the two domains.

In summary, the literature on segmentation in music shows considerable convergence between theoretical and experimental approaches. Gestalt principles of grouping on the basis of such characteristics as proximity and similarity have been incorporated into theories about music and have been found to have explanatory power in the analysis of music. Grouping principles predict the way listeners segment auditory patterns and, when musical materials are employed, they can in part account for segmentation on both local and global time scales. Finally, at least some principles appear to operate quite independently of the musical training of the listeners, and parallels with language and visual perception suggest that these kinds of principles are quite general.

At this point, less is known about structural characteristics that contribute to the coherence of melodic sequences and that govern the perceived similarity between sequences. Tonality, as has already been suggested, is one such characteristic. Sequences conforming to tonal principles would be expected to be heard as better organized, self-consistent, and regular than sequences not conforming to tonal principles. A number of studies confirm this prediction (e.g., Francès, 1958; Dewar, Cuddy, & Mewhort, 1977; Krumhansl, 1979; Cuddy & Lyons, 1981). Melodic sequences, particularly those that are well structured by stylistic conventions, have an integrity that is maintained under various kinds of transformation. One such transformation is transposition, a shift in pitch range that preserves the relative interval sizes. The ease of recognizing a transposed melody, however, depends on the key distance between the original and transposed versions (e.g., Bartlett & Dowling, 1980; Cuddy, Cohen, & Miller, 1979). Transpositions between closely related keys are easier to recognize, suggesting that structure at the level of musical keys is important for perceiving the similarity between the two melodies.

Dowling (1978) showed, in addition, that listeners tend to base melodic-recognition judgments on the maintenance of a scale framework. The listeners found it difficult to distinguish between an exact transposition (in which the relative sizes of the intervals are kept constant) and a transposition up or down the scale of the original melody (which results in altered intervals). Despite the changed intervals in the latter kind of transposed melody, such melodies were perceived as very similar to the original because the underlying scale is maintained. Dowling's study also demonstrated that contour has an important influence on melodic similarity. White (1960) and Welker (1982) have demonstrated that melodic similarity is also preserved under other transformations of meter, rhythm, and interval size.

A variety of studies have investigated the perception of mirror forms of pitch sequences that arise in dodecaphonic or 12-tone serial music.

There are three mirror forms: inversion (which reverses the pitch direction of each interval in the sequence), retrograde (which reverses the temporal order of the tones in the sequence), and retrograde inversion (which is the reverse temporal order of the inversion). These are called mirror forms because they are symmetrical transformations in pitch direction (inversion), time (retrograde), or both (retrograde inversion). For relatively simple sequences in which the tones were presented in a musically neutral fashion, studies (Dowling, 1972; Francès, 1958; Balch, 1981; Krumhansl, Sandell, & Sergeant, 1987) have generally shown that listeners recognize some invariant characteristics of the original sequence under the various mirror transformations, especially inversion and retrograde.

However, recognition of invariances under the mirror transformations becomes more difficult as rhythmic patterns, octave substitutions, and other variations are introduced (Francès, 1958; Pederson, 1975; Krumhansl, Sandell, & Sergeant, 1987). It should be noted, however, that the latter study (unlike the other two) found above-chance performance for all three mirror forms despite extremely diverse presentations of the original sequence and its mirror forms. Excerpts were drawn from Schoenberg's Wind Quintet and String Quartet No. 4 (other parts of this series of experiments will be discussed in a later chapter). The study used a classification task employing just two original pitch sequences (the tone rows of the two pieces) with which the listeners had considerable experience. The result suggests that, under some circumstances, the relationship between the original sequences and its mirror forms can be perceived despite quite radical variations of surface characteristics of the music.

Pollard-Gott (1983) used similarity and classification tasks to study whether listeners perceive the relationship between a theme and its variations. She used as stimulus materials the two themes from Liszt's Sonata in B Minor and a number of variations of these themes. Care was taken to ensure that the variations of the themes could not be discriminated simply by superficial characteristics of the music. Both similarity judgments and classification accuracy showed that the excerpts tended to be grouped more strongly on the basis of theme after repeated listenings. At earlier stages of learning, other characteristics were influential: general pitch height, dynamics, complexity, tempo, and sonority, among others. In the experiment, listeners heard only the first part of the piece. Despite this, they generalized the distinction between the two themes to excerpts from the second part of the piece that they had not heard. Grouping on the basis of theme varied with expertise, as one would expect. In summary, the study found quite strong evidence that listeners perceive theme and variation structure. Although other characteristics influenced the similarity judgments, a theme dimension was extracted by most listeners despite the absence of explicit instructions concerning the presence of two themes and their function in determining the form of the composition.

Rosner and Meyer (1982, 1986), also using classification and similarity measures, investigated whether listeners relate musical excerpts to underlying melodic "archetypes" or processes. L. B. Meyer (1973) proposed that melodies in Western tonal music can be classified according to a small number of underlying processes, specifying the means through which a melody moves from its starting point to its point of closure. A changing-note process, for example, begins on the tonic, may then move down to the seventh, then up to the second, and finally return to the tonic. The kinds of processes identified can be characterized as a combination of Gestalt principles, such as good continuation and closure, and characteristics specific to the musical style, such as scalar structure and the employment of special intervals.

Their experiments presented excerpts classifiable in terms of two different melodic processes that varied across experiments. The classification task of Rosner and Meyer (1982) demonstrated an ability to learn to classify excerpts according to their underlying melodic process and generalize this knowledge to new excerpts. The similarity ratings of Rosner and Meyer (1986) less strongly supported the perception of underlying melodic processes. Grouping on the basis of process would have to be described, on balance, as weak and inconsistent. Other characteristics tended to predominate, including rhythmic structure, contour, initial intervals, and form. An influence of melodic process was apparent in some cases, but it was often obscured by other musical characteristics. It may be that listeners, when making similarity judgments, found it difficult to remember the relatively complex sequences, and to abstract and compare the underlying melodic processes. In support of the possibility that task difficulty may have affected their results, Schmuckler's findings (1988) confirmed Meyer's melodic processes in a simpler task assessing listeners' expectations for melodic continuations. Tones consistent with melodic processes were generally preferred as continuations to tones inconsistent with them; the tonal hierarchy of the key and contour also influenced the judgments.

Together, these results on the perception of melodies suggest that melodic organization depends on much more than grouping principles based on acoustic properties. These principles undoubtedly influence the initial parsing or grouping of the sounded events. However, listeners are sensitive to underlying structural properties that are preserved under a variety of transformations. At present, we are far from having a full account of the exact features that promote the perception of invariance under transformation, the processes by which they are apprehended, and their contribution to the sense of form on a larger scale. The literature has uncovered a large number of variables influencing melodic similarity suggesting, in addition, that melody is a highly dimensional aspect of perceived musical organization.

7. Quantifying harmonic hierarchies and key distances

A number of perceptual studies of harmonic structure in traditional Western music are presented in this and the next chapter. The music of the eighteenth and nineteenth centuries, called the common-practice period, is marked by the consolidation of a system of harmony. The sounding of tones in certain intervallic relations came to be considered, both theoretically and compositionally, as an organizational principle that was distinguishable from melodic considerations. The vertical (harmonic) organization came into balance with the horizontal (melodic) organization as a force shaping musical structure. The system of tonal harmony permitted extremely precise control over the pitch materials and generated a rich musical and theoretical literature. The harmonic practice became so conventionalized during this period that it has been possible to codify it precisely (e.g., see Rameau, 1722/1971; Schoenberg, 1922/1978; Piston, 1941/1978). Despite other more recent developments in music composition, the tonal-harmonic system continues to represent the dominant organizational scheme underlying most Western music.

The objective of the experiments summarized in this and the following chapter is to describe, from the listener's point of view, the structure that applies to the level of chords and the interdependencies between the level of chords and the levels of single tones and musical keys. Presented in this chapter are two experiments directed at measuring the hierarchy of structural stability that a tonal context induces on the set of chords of different types built on all chromatic scale steps. The method employed is similar to that used to quantify the tonal hierarchy described in Chapter 2. The data are analyzed to uncover characteristics that may contribute to the perceived hierarchy. These include the chord type, tonal consonance, whether or not the chord is diatonic in the context key, and the frequency with which the chords are sounded in tonal-harmonic music. In addition, various analyses are directed at determining whether the harmonic hierarchy can be accounted for in terms of the structural stability of the tones that are contained within the chords. The chapter concludes by deriving from the harmonic hierarchy a description of interkey distance, which can be compared to that derived from the tonal hierarchy. In the next chapter are summarized experiments on perceived harmonic relations and how these are influenced by tonal context using similarity rating and memory measures.

Music-theoretical descriptions of harmony

In the so-called common-practice period, certain chords were treated as structurally significant; these chords function, in one way or another, to establish the tonality. Most central to the system are the triads built on the first and fifth degrees of the scale, commonly denoted by the Roman numerals I and V, respectively, to indicate the position of the roots of the chords in the scale. In some treatments, the chord built on the fourth scale degree, denoted IV, is considered to be a member of this central set. The harmonic functions of the II and VI chords are generally considered to be somewhat weaker, although the II may take a stronger role if it functions as a substitute for IV, and VI has a stronger role if it substitutes for I (as in a deceptive cadence). The least harmonically significant are the III and VII chords, although again this needs to be qualified because the VII chord can, under certain circumstances, function as a dominant seventh. The basic form that these chords take are triads built from diatonic scale tones, with the second tone of the chord a third above the root (the first tone), and the third tone of the chord a fifth above the root. Thus, the tone above the root is called the third of the chord and the next tone above the root is called the fifth of the chord. Table 7.1 indicates the component tones in each triad in this basic set for C major and C minor keys.

Because of the intervallic structure of the major and minor diatonic scales, these chords do not all have the same component intervals. Chords are classified as major, minor, diminished, or augmented as a function of their intervals. Chords in which the third is a major third above the root and the fifth a minor third above the third are called major chords. For example, in the C major chord, the E is a major third above the root, C, and the G is a minor third above the third of the chord, E. Chords in which the lower interval is a minor third and the higher interval a major third are called minor chords. An example is the D minor chord, in which

Table 7.1. Diatonic triads in C major and C minor keys

C Major Key			C Minor Key		
Chord	Components	Type	Chord	Components	Type
I	C E G	Major	i	C E♭ G	Minor
ii	D F A	Minor	ii°	D F A♭	Diminished
iii	E G B	Minor	III	E♭ G B♭	Major
IV	F A C	Major	iv	F A♭ C	Minor
V	G B D	Major	V	G B D	Major
vi	A C E	Minor	VI	A♭ C E♭	Major
vii°	B D F	Diminished	vii°	B D F	Diminished

the interval between D and F is a minor third, and the interval between F and A is a major third. Chords in which both intervals are minor thirds are called diminished because the interval between the root and fifth is a semitone less than a perfect fifth. An example is the B diminished chord, with minor thirds between B and D, and between D and F. Finally, an augmented chord is one in which both the lower and upper intervals are major thirds. The term augmented reflects that the interval between the root and the fifth of the chord is a semitone larger than a perfect fifth. For example, the E♭ augmented chord consists of an interval of a major third between E♭ and G, and another major third between G and B. This chord appears in C minor (when the seventh scale degree is raised from B♭ to B). However, this chord most often employs the lowered seventh scale degree, producing the E♭ major chord in Table 7.1. In contrast, the seventh scale degree appears in the raised form in the triads built on the fifth and seventh scale degrees.

Note that the corresponding chords in major and minor keys are often of different types. For example, the I of a major key is a major chord, but the I of a minor key is a minor chord. The different chord types in the two modes—major and minor—may have different perceptual effects, but in harmonic practice corresponding chords of the two modes are generally treated analogously as is implied by the Roman numeral notation. This, and other considerations, suggest that compositionally the chords function in a way that is somewhat abstract from their component tones and their intervallic content.

Tonal-harmonic music established certain conventions concerning the use of these chords. The structurally significant chords, particularly the I and V, serve as the primary mechanism for establishing the tonal framework; they tend to be used more frequently, particularly near the beginnings and endings of sections of compositions. The IV chord is also considered important for establishing the tonality. Together, the I, IV, and V chords contain the entire set of diatonic scale tones. Certain sequences of chords, called cadences, have come to be used in tonal-harmonic music to establish a tonic, and signal periodic returns to the tonic. For example, the strong IV V I cadence is an unambiguous indicator of the key and produces a feeling of stability or finality. Other regularities in harmonic practice can also be identified, with certain successive combinations of chords appearing more frequently than others. In part, these regularities derive from considerations of voice leading, with the components of the successive chords entering into melodic relationships.

Another feature characterizing tonal-harmonic music is modulation, that is, changes between keys. The well-defined harmonic functions provided a mechanism for marking departures from and returns to the original key, which became a major principle governing form in music of this style. Modulation is frequently effected by the use of a pivot chord, a chord that is common to the initial key and the new key. Closely related

Table 7.2. Triads of C major and C minor keys shared with closely related keys

Chord	C Major	C Minor	A Minor	F Major	G Major
C Major	I		III	V	IV
D Minor	ii		iv	vi	
E Minor	iii				VI
F Major	IV		VI	I	
G Major	V	V			I
A Minor	vi		i	iii	ii
B Diminished	vii°	vii°	ii°		

Chord	C Minor	C Major	E♭ Major	F Minor	G Minor
C Minor	i		vi		iv
D Diminished	ii°		vii°		
E♭ Major	III		I		VI
F Minor	iv		ii	i	
G Major	V	V			
A♭ Major	VI		IV	III	
B Diminished	vii°	vii°			

keys share a number of diatonic triads that can function as pivot chords. Table 7.2 shows the diatonic triads of C major and C minor keys and indicates their functions in four closely related keys: the parallel and relative major or minor keys, and the neighboring keys on the circle of fifths. Modulation to a wider range of keys can be achieved through the use of chromatically altered chords and chords with enharmonic equivalents (different spelling of the same tones). Detailed expositions of modulatory procedures can be found in Reger (1903) and Schoenberg (1954/1969).

Quantifying the harmonic hierarchy

Music-theoretical treatments of harmony, the elementary aspects of which were just summarized, suggest that a tonal context establishes a hierarchy of structural significance on the set of chords, just as a tonal context establishes a hierarchy on the set of single tones. By analogy to the experimental results for single tones described in earlier chapters, certain chords should be heard as more normative or stable within an established tonal framework. The analogy predicts that these chords should be heard as conforming better to the tonal context. Moreover, they should be heard as more closely related to one another and preferred as endings of sequences. It would also be expected that the perceived hierarchy of harmonic stability should mirror the distribution of chords in tonal-harmonic compositions just as the tonal hierarchy was found to correspond to the distributions of tones. To the extent that the experiments validate each of these predictions, it would suggest similar abstract psychological principles operating for both tones and chords.

To begin the empirical test of these predictions, the two experiments described in this chapter measured the perceived relative structural significance of chords in tonal contexts; they were patterned after the probe tone experiments reported in Chapter 2. Each trial began with a strong key-defining context followed by a single chord. The key of the context was either major or minor. The trials were presented in blocks during which the context was held constant. The listeners' task was to rate how well the final chord fit, in a musical sense, with the preceding key-defining context. For this purpose, they used a rating scale on which 1 was designated "fits poorly" and 7 was designated as "fits well." This open-ended instruction produced consistent and interpretable patterns in previous studies without explicitly instructing listeners as to which attributes or features were to be considered in making their judgments. The data, however, can be analyzed to extract perceptually important features.

In the first experiment, the context was either a major or minor scale, played first in ascending form and then in descending form. Two different major and minor keys were used with tonics of C and F♯. The C major and C minor scale contexts are shown at the top of Figure 7.1. The minor-key scale contexts used the ascending melodic form and the descending melodic (natural) form. This meant that the sixth and seventh scale degrees were presented in both lowered and raised positions. The scale contexts for F♯ major and minor keys were similar, only beginning and ending on the tonic, F♯. The tones of the scale contexts were generated with sine wave components sounded over a five-octave range. In the second experiment, the contexts used were those shown at the bottom of Figure 7.1. They consisted of a sequence that contained all diatonic triads of the two keys of C major and C minor played in their order on the circle of fifths for chords. The voicings indicated in the figure were used. If similar results are obtained for these two very different kinds of contexts, this would indicate that the perceptual judgments are made with reference to an abstract structure invoked by the context and that they do not depend on particular features of the key-defining contexts.

On each trial, the context was followed by a single chord. In the first experiment, 48 chords were paired with each context. This set consisted of the major, minor, diminished, and augmented chords with roots on all 12 chromatic scale tones. An analysis of these data showed that the ratings for augmented chords were generally low and showed little variation. For this reason (and because the III in minor only rarely appears as an augmented chord), the second experiment eliminated the augmented chords. Thus, the basic data of these two experiments consist of the ratings for the 36 major, minor, and diminished chords.

For reasons of practicality, the stimulus materials were limited in vari-

C MAJOR SCALE CONTEXT

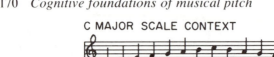

C MINOR SCALE CONTEXT

C MAJOR CHORD CONTEXT

C MINOR CHORD CONTEXT

Fig. 7.1. The top shows the major and minor scale contexts used in the first harmonic-hierarchy experiment; bottom shows the major and minor chord contexts (in which chords are presented in their order on the circle of fifths for chords) used in the second harmonic-hierarchy experiment. The contexts were followed by major, minor, and diminished chords built on all 12 pitches of the chromatic scale.

ous ways. The chords presented following the key-defining contexts were all triads, consisting of three different pitch classes. Other chords, such as seventh and ninth chords, were not included, nor were various altered, chromatic, or borrowed chords. In addition, the chord tones were sounded simultaneously, even though in many musical circumstances the harmonic content is expressed by successively sounded tones (arpeggiated chords). Finally, in order to minimize the effects of melodic motion, the chords were built from "circular" tones (Shepard, 1964; Krumhansl, Bharucha, & Kessler, 1982) with sine wave components sounded over a five-octave range with loudness determined according to the scheme shown in Figure 2.2. Consequently, the experiments do not address possible perceptual effects of different chord inversions (with tones other than the root in the bass), a variable of musical interest given that inversion is theoretically assumed to influence stability. [L. A. Roberts and M. L. Shaw (1984), however, showed that trained musicians judged chords similarly independently of their inversion and whether the chord tones were presented simultaneously or in arpeggiated form.]

Ten listeners participated in the first experiment and 12 in the second experiment. They had a moderate level of training in instrumental or vocal music, with an average of approximately 11 years of study, but little formal instruction in music theory. In terms of the responses given, the listeners in each experiment agreed well with one another, with highly significant average intersubject correlations. In addition, similar ratings were given in the first experiment for the two major and two minor scale contexts when the ratings were shifted to compensate for the different tonics. However, responses for the two major-scale contexts were somewhat more consistent than those for the two minor-scale contexts. Finally, the results of the two experiments were highly correlated. The correlations between experiments were .90 and .81 for major- and minor-key contexts, respectively, which were both highly significant ($p < .01$), though again showing somewhat more consistency for major contexts than for minor contexts. In general, however, the pattern of responding did not depend on the particular context used to establish the key; therefore, features specific to each context were not influential. The values shown in Table 7.3 are the average ratings across the two experiments.

Table 7.3. Ratings of chords in harmonic-hierarchy experiments

Chord	C Major Context	C Minor Context
C Major	6.66 (I)	5.30
C♯/D♭ Major	4.71	4.11
D Major	4.60	3.83
D♯/E♭ Major	4.31	4.14 (III)
E Major	4.64	3.99
F Major	5.59 (IV)	4.41
F♯/G♭ Major	4.36	3.92
G Major	5.33 (V)	4.38 (V)
G♯/A♭ Major	5.01	4.45 (VI)
A Major	4.64	3.69
A♯/B♭ Major	4.73	4.22
B Major	4.67	3.85
C Minor	3.75	5.90 (i)
C♯/D♭ Minor	2.59	3.08
D Minor	3.12 (ii)	3.25
D♯/E♭ Minor	2.18	3.50
E Minor	2.76 (iii)	3.33

Table 7.3. (Continued)

Chord	C Major Context	C Minor Context
F Minor	3.19	4.60 (iv)
F♯/G♭ Minor	2.13	2.98
G Minor	2.68	3.48
G♯/A♭ Minor	2.61	3.53
A Minor	3.62 (vi)	3.78
A♯/B♭ Minor	2.56	3.13
B Minor	2.76	3.14
C Diminished	3.27	3.93
C♯/D♭ Diminished	2.70	2.84
D Diminished	2.59	3.43 (ii°)
D♯/E♭ Diminished	2.79	3.42
E Diminished	2.64	3.51
F Diminished	2.54	3.41
F♯/G♭ Diminished	3.25	3.91
G Diminished	2.58	3.16
G♯/A♭ Diminished	2.36	3.17
A Diminished	3.35	4.10
A♯/B♭ Diminished	2.38	3.10
B Diminished	2.64 (vii°)	3.18 (vii°)

A number of analyses were performed on these data to determine the variables governing the listeners' responses. The first analysis considered the effect of chord type. For both major- and minor-key contexts, different ratings were on average given to the different chord types. The average ratings are shown in Table 7.4. In a major-key context, listeners strongly preferred major chords over minor and diminished chords, which were given approximately the same ratings. The preference for major chords over the other chord types was reduced considerably in the minor-key contexts. Although the ordering was the same as for the major context, the differences were consistently smaller. Thus, the minor context produced a weaker effect of chord type.

The chord type effect just described generally corresponds to intuitions concerning their relative degree of consonance, with major chords considered most consonant and diminished chords most dissonant. Roberts (reported in L. A. Roberts and M. L. Shaw, 1984) obtained a similar ordering in an experiment in which listeners judged the consonance of various chord types, and this ordering can account, in part, for the relative discriminability of different chord types found in their experiments. However, as discussed in Chapter 3, it is important to distinguish between musical consonance (which depends on stylistic and contextual charac-

Table 7.4. Effect of chord type in harmonic-hierarchy experiments

Context	Chord Type		
	Major	Minor	Diminished
Major Key	4.94	2.83	2.76
Minor Key	4.19	3.64	3.43
Average	4.57	3.24	3.10

teristics) and tonal consonance (which depends only on acoustic characteristics).

To investigate whether tonal consonance per se could account for the effect of chord type found in the present experiments, I used the tabulated values for triads from Hutchinson and Knopoff (1979). These values were based on their previous calculations for dyads (Hutchinson & Knopoff, 1978), computed using Helmholtz's original model with the modifications suggested by Plomp and Levelt (1965). They calculated the dissonance of triads with the three component tones sounded in an octave range. The dissonance value was found for each of the possible inversions of each chord type, where inversion refers to the spacing of the components of the triads in the octave range. In order to remove an effect due to the change of critical bandwidth with register, the triads were required to be centered around C4 (middle C). Their tabulated values of the dissonance of major, minor, and diminished triads in the three possible inversions are shown in Table 7.5, where higher numbers correspond to more dissonant

Table 7.5. Theoretical dissonance values

Position*	Chord Type		
	Major	Minor	Diminished
$\frac{5}{3}$ (root position)	.1390	.1479	.2303
$\frac{6}{3}$ (first inversion)	.1873	.1254	.2024
$\frac{6}{4}$ (second inversion)	.1190	.1712	.1834
Average	.1484	.1482	.2054

Source: Hutchinson and Knopoff (1979).

*The position of a chord is determined by the note that appears in the bass. If the root is in the bass, the chord is in root position. If the third is in the bass, the chord is in first inversion. The fifth in the bass results in second inversion.

triads. As can be seen in the table, the dissonance of major, minor, and diminished chords depends strongly on the inversion. For example, when a major triad is sounded in root position, the theoretical dissonance value is .1390; when it is sounded in first inversion, the dissonance value is considerably higher, .1873.

In the present experiment, it should be remembered, the components of the chords were repeated over a five-octave range with no clearly defined bass note. Consequently, the chords in the experiment are not strictly comparable to any of the cases considered by Hutchinson and Knopoff (1979). For the purpose of comparing their dissonance values to the present results, the averages over the different inversions for each chord type were first computed; these average values are shown in the last row of Table 7.5. When the values were averaged in this way, major and minor had approximately equal dissonance values, and diminished chords had a higher value. These values do not conform well to the effects of chord type found in the experiments. For example, although the average dissonance values for major and minor chords were approximately equal, listeners generally gave higher ratings to major chords than to minor chords; this was particularly true in the major-key contexts. When the different inversions were considered separately, the best fit to the chord ratings was with the dissonance values for the second inversion— shown in the third row of Table 7.5—although why this should be so is unclear. Moreover, the dissonance values cannot account for the interaction between chord type and the mode of the context (whether major or minor). Thus, the results were not well explained in terms of dissonance, at least the theoretical values computed by Hutchinson and Knopoff (1979).

Terhardt (1974) has suggested that the consonance of chords depends in part on the degree to which they evoke salient, harmonically related virtual pitches. Terhardt, Stoll, and Seewan (1982a) showed, however, that pitch salience weights depend strongly on the inversion in which chords are sounded. For example, a major triad in root position or first inversion produces a strong virtual pitch coincident with its root; however, this is not true for the second inversion. A similar dependency on inversion was also found for minor chords, which, in general, were more ambiguous in terms of their root. Because of the inversion effect, it is difficult to compare their theoretical predictions with the effects of chord type found in the present study. Parncutt (1987), however, applied Terhardt's general model to chords constructed in a similar fashion to those employed here: with sine wave components spaced at octave intervals across the musical range. The obtained tonal saliency profiles showed the major chord to have the least ambiguous root, followed by the minor chord, and then the diminished chord (see also Parncutt, 1988). This pattern corresponds to the ordering of chord types found here, suggesting that this kind of model holds promise for explaining perceptual differences between chords. However, the values of root salience do not relate linearly to the experimental effects, nor do they explain the differences between major- and minor-key contexts. Clearly, more precise modeling and more extensive perceptual investigations are needed relating theories of consonance to chord perception.

The next analysis considered another characteristic that may influence listeners' ratings in the experiments. Did chords that are in the basic set of harmonies of the key tend to be given higher ratings than chords outside the set? For this purpose, the basic set of harmonies was taken to be the seven triads built on the diatonic scale, denoted I–VII and shown in Table 7.1. A variable coding whether a chord is in this diatonic set or not was constructed (assigning 1 if it is in the set and 0 if it is not) and correlated with the set of 36 ratings shown in Table 7.3. The correlations are shown in Table 7.6. The correlation for minor-key contexts (.41) was significant and somewhat greater than that for major-key contexts (.32), which narrowly missed being significant (a value of .33 is needed). Thus, the relationship between the ratings and membership in the diatonic set is only moderately strong, which may be due to two variables. First, the quantified harmonic hierarchy may be more finely differentiated than simply distinguishing between whether or not a chord is diatonic. Second, the large effect of chord type may have masked a relationship between the ratings and the variable coding chords as diatonic.

To eliminate the chord type effect entirely, the data were normalized by chord type. That is, the average rating for a given chord type in a given key context was subtracted from the rating for each chord of that type in that context. For example, the average rating for major chords was sub-

Table 7.6. Correlations of harmonic-hierarchy data with various variables

	Context	
	Major	Minor
Membership in diatonic set	.32	.41*
Tonal hierarchy of component tones	.38*	.71*
Frequency of occurrence of component tones	.30	.64*
Multiple correlation with three variables	.61*	.80*
Data Normalized for Chord Type		
Membership in diatonic set	.52*	.42*
Tonal hierarchy of component tones	.87*	.82*
Frequency of occurrence of component tones	.68*	.74*
Multiple correlation with three variables	.88*	.82*

*Significant at $p < .05$.

tracted from each major-chord rating; this was done separately for major- and minor-key contexts. The normalized values express the relative rating of each chord within the set of chords of the same type. The normalized values were then correlated with the variable coding diatonic set membership as just described. The resulting correlations are shown at the bottom of Table 7.6. The correlations for both major and minor contexts were significant for the normalized data (.52 and .42, respectively), supporting the idea that the chord type effect was partially masking the relationship in the nonnormalized data. This analysis found a tendency for chords that function in the basic set of harmonies of the key to receive higher ratings than other chords of the same type.

The next analysis asked whether the ratings of the 36 chords could be predicted by the positions of the component tones in the tonal hierarchy of the context key. It explores the degree to which the tonal and harmonic hierarchies are independent. Were higher ratings given to chords the component tones of which are relatively stable in the context key? The data from the probe tone study of Krumhansl and Kessler (1982; Table 2.1) were used to assess this. For each chord, the average of the ratings of the three component tones was taken. For example, for a C major chord in a C major context, the value was the average of the ratings given the tones C, E, and G in the C major key context of the earlier experiment. These values were computed for all chords in both major- and minor-key contexts and correlated with the chord rating data. The correlations are shown in Table 7.6.

For both major and minor contexts, the correlations between the nonnormalized chord rating data and the chord components' position in the tonal hierarchy of the context key was significant. However, the value for the minor-key context (.71) was considerably higher than that for the major-key context (.38). The large overall effect of chord type in the major-key context might have obscured a relationship between the tonal hierarchy and the major-context data. Consequently, the same analysis was done for the data normalized for chord type as just described. The correlations with the normalized data were both very high (.87 and .82 for major- and minor-key contexts, respectively). Thus, high ratings were given consistently to chords the component tones of which occupy high positions in the tonal hierarchy as quantified in the earlier experiment.

The final analysis was similar except, instead of using the probe tone ratings from the previous experiment, it used the frequency distribution of tones in tonal compositions (Youngblood, 1958; Knopoff & Hutchinson, 1983; Table 3.3). As discussed in Chapter 3, the frequency with which the tones occur in tonal compositions correlates strongly with the probe tone ratings. Thus, the two variables should have similar effects on the chord ratings. This is substantiated by the correlations shown in Table 7.6. With the nonnormalized data, the correlation for minor-key contexts (.64) was considerably higher than that for major-key contexts (.30).

However, both values were high for the normalized data (.68 and .74 for major- and minor-key contexts, respectively).

Summarizing the results for the entire set of 36 chords, there was an overall effect of chord type, with highest ratings given to major chords, intermediate ratings to minor chords, and lowest ratings to diminished chords. These differences were stronger for major-key contexts than for minor-key contexts. This ordering corresponds to intuitions concerning the relative musical consonance of chords, but does not consistently correspond to theoretical estimates of tonal consonance of the three triad types. Three other variables, however, were found to contribute to the chord ratings of the present experiments, especially once the data were normalized to compensate for overall effects of chord type.

The first variable was whether or not the chord is contained in the set of diatonic triads of the context key. Listeners gave higher ratings to chords functioning as basic harmonic elements of the key. The second variable was the position of the chord's component tones in the tonal hierarchy of the key. Higher ratings were given to chords the components of which are perceived as structurally significant in the context key. The final variable was the distribution of tones in tonal music. Higher ratings were given to chords the component tones of which appear more frequently in tonal music. Thus, these last two variables influenced the chord ratings in a similar way, as would be expected given the strong correspondence between tonal distributions and perceived tonal hierarchies. To assess the relative predictive power of these variables, all three were entered into a multiple regression with the nonnormalized and with the normalized data. The multiple correlations, shown in Table 7.6, were all highly significant. More importantly, the strongest predictor by far was the chord tones' positions (the average of the root, third, and fifth) in the tonal hierarchy of the context key. This suggests a strong interdependency between tonal and harmonic hierarchies, which will be examined again in the following sections.

Harmonic hierarchy of diatonic triads I–VII

These preliminary analyses identified a number of variables influencing the chord ratings in these two experiments. They suggest that listeners made the judgments based, in part, on knowledge of diatonic scale structure as it determines the construction of triads, tonal hierarchies, and distributions of tones in tonal-harmonic music. Although these patterns are systematic and musically interpretable, additional regularities may be found when the data for the diatonic triads are extracted from the full set of major, minor, and diminished chords. This section focuses on the results for the diatonic triads.

There were a number of motivations for examining this subset of the data. First, music theory makes well-defined predictions concerning the relative structural significance of the chords in this set. A second motivation was to facilitate comparisons between corresponding chords in major and minor keys. Theoretically, corresponding chords in the different modes are considered as serving analogous harmonic functions despite their different chord types. This raises the psychological question of whether they are perceived as playing similar roles, at least as reflected in the rating data of these experiments. Finally, the frequencies of these chords in compositions from the common-practice period have been tabulated; this information about the statistical distribution of chords in music can be compared to this subset of the results.

Table 7.7 shows the ratings given the diatonic triads (the chords shown in Table 7.1) in major- and minor-key contexts. For the major-key context, the chord that received the highest rating was the I chord. This was followed by the IV and V chords, then the ii and vi chords, and finally the iii and vii° chords. The ordering of the chords agrees quite well with music-theoretical predictions. The tonic triad is considered the most stable harmony of the system. The IV and V chords are described as functioning in important secondary harmonic roles, although most treatments would predict that the V chord would have predominated over the IV chord (a possible experimental artifact contributing to the high rating of the IV will be noted later). The ii and vi chords are considered less structurally important, and the iii and vii° chords to have the weakest harmonic functions. Thus, a musically interpretable hierarchy of chord functions was found in the rating data for major-key contexts.

For the minor-key contexts, the tonic triad again received the highest ratings, and relatively high ratings were given to the iv and V chords. In this case, however, the ratings for the III and VI chords were also quite high. This finding can be accounted for by these chords being major chords, which were, on average, given higher ratings than minor and diminished chords. The ii° and vii° chords, both diminished chords, re-

Table 7.7. Ratings of diatonic triads I–VII in harmonic-hierarchy experiments

Chord	Context	
	Major	Minor
I	6.66	5.90
II	3.12	3.43
III	2.76	4.14
IV	5.59	4.60
V	5.33	4.38
VI	3.62	4.45
VII	2.64	3.18

ceived the lowest ratings consistent with the lowest ratings received by diminished chords generally. Thus, the ratings for the diatonic triads in minor-key contexts showed influences of chord type, but despite this the results conform reasonably well to music-theoretical predications.

Moreover, the ordering of the diatonic triads was very similar for major- and minor-key contexts. This was substantiated by a correlation between the corresponding values; the resulting value of .86 was significant ($p < .05$). This result is in accord with music-theoretical descriptions of closely analogous harmonic functions of corresponding chords in the two modes. Despite the similarity of the patterns, it was also clear that listeners were making finer discriminations in the major-key contexts than in the minor-key contexts. The ratings for chords in major-key contexts ranged from 2.64 to 6.66, whereas the ratings for chords in minor key contexts ranged from 3.18 to 5.90. This result and others showing differences between major- and minor-key contexts suggest that listeners may have been somewhat less certain about the harmonic functions of chords in minor keys.

A number of additional analyses were performed on the data for the diatonic triads; the results are summarized in Table 7.8. The first two analyses were analogous to those described earlier for the full set of 36 chords, and the results were, for the most part, similar. The first considered the effect of the position of the chord components in the tonal hierarchy of the context key. Higher ratings tended to be given to triads the three component tones of which occupy high positions in the tonal hierarchy, and this trend was found whether or not the data were normalized for chord type. Similarly, the chord ratings were influenced by the frequency of occurrence of the component tones in tonal music. Because of the reduced number of degrees of freedom for these correlations, a value

Table 7.8. Correlations of harmonic-hierarchy data for diatonic triads I–VII with various variables

	Context	
	Major	Minor
Tonal hierarchy of component tones	.69	.86*
Frequency of occurrence of component tones	.60	.89*
Percentage of chord count	.84*	.74
Data Normalized for Chord Type		
Tonal hierarchy of component tones	.88*	.73
Frequency of occurrence of component tones	.75*	.82*
Percentage of chord count	.74	.74

*Significant at $p < .05$.

of .75 is required to reach statistical significance. Despite this, both these variables approached this value, especially for the normalized data. Therefore, even restricting the analysis to this subset, these two variables had systematic effects on the chord ratings.

The final analysis considered whether the ratings for the diatonic triads corresponded to their frequency of use in tonal-harmonic music. Budge (1943) compiled an extensive frequency count of chords in representative compositions of the eighteenth century and the first 75 years of the nineteenth century. This count was based on a wide variety of compositions, divided into five classes: orchestral music, chamber music, piano music, choral works, and solo songs. The total frequencies of diatonic and chromatic chords in these pieces were tabulated. The sample consisted of a total of nearly 66,000 chords, with somewhat more chords from compositions in major keys than in minor keys. The diatonic chords were classified according to their root, that is, as I–VII, and their inversion. Seventh and ninth chords (with additional thirds added above the triad tones) were included in the count. The analysis of these results showed some differences across the various time spans within the period covered, and some differences between composers. However, there were strong consistencies in the relative frequencies of the chords across the sample as a whole.

For the present purpose of comparing the chord frequencies with the chord rating data, the percentages of all diatonic chords with each root, including all inversions and seventh and ninth chords, were summed. These values were taken from Budge's Tables IX and X (1943), which presented the results for compositions in major and minor keys separately; they are shown in Table 7.9. In compositions in both major and minor keys, the I chord was the most frequent, followed by the V chord, then the IV, II, VI, VII, and, finally, the III chord. The percentage of chords analyzed as I–VII in the two modes agreed almost perfectly with a correlation of .997 between the corresponding values in the table! Thus, at least in terms of frequency of occurrence, the tabulated results support the view that corresponding chords in the different modes are treated as equivalent in compositions of this period.

The ratings of the chords in the experiments also agreed quite well, although not perfectly, with the distributions of chord frequencies. The correlations between the chord rating data and the percentages of chord roots in Budge's sample (1943) are shown in Table 7.8. Whether or not the data were normalized for overall effects of chord type, the correlations were quite strong despite the small number of observations going into the analyses. One of the correlations was significant, and the remaining three just narrowly missed significance (a value of .75 is required). These results indicate a systematic relationship between the chord frequencies in these compositions and the ratings given to the chords in the experiment.

Table 7.9. Percentage of chords on each root in
Budge's chord count analysis (1943)

Chord	Key	
	Major	Minor
I	41.79	40.37
II	8.35	6.90
III	1.35	1.25
IV	8.45	10.59
V	31.68	31.76
VI	5.27	4.89
VII	2.76	3.73

However, a notable anomaly can be seen for the IV chord, which appears considerably less frequently than the V chord in the chord count analysis, but ranks with the V chord in the rating data. This anomaly may be due, in part, to the preponderance of seventh and ninth chords based on the root V in the chord count analysis, which raises its frequency considerably above the frequency of the IV chord. More likely, however, it may be that the contexts of the present experiments artificially elevated the rating of the IV chords, especially the circle-of-fifths chord context. The IV chord would be heard as the natural continuation of the sequence and, with the last chord of the sequence, would form the strong V–I progression in the key of the subdominant. With the exception of the IV chord, the relative rankings in the experiment of the seven chords agreed quite well with their frequency of occurrence in the sample of compositions. This suggests that the ratings given by the listeners to the chords reflect their structural significance in tonal music as measured in global statistical distributions. Moreover, the agreement suggests the relative frequencies of chords in the listeners' musical experience may have initially shaped the form of the perceived harmonic hierarchy.

Before summarizing, one final result will be mentioned. It concerns the relationship between the relative frequencies of the chords in the analysis of Budge (1943) and the tone frequencies in tonal melodies in the analyses of Youngblood (1958) and Knopoff and Hutchinson (1983). The question is whether the frequencies of chords, as analyzed by Budge, can be predicted by the frequencies of their component tones in the two note count studies that used melodic lines only. To assess this, the total frequencies of the components of the diatonic triads were computed for each of the seven chords based on the two note count studies. These values were computed separately for pieces in major and minor keys, and were then correlated with the frequencies of the chords in major and minor keys.

The resulting correlations were .72 and .74 for major and minor keys, respectively. These nearly significant values again reflect the interdependency between melodic and harmonic processes in music of this style.

Taken together, the results for the diatonic triads in major and minor keys showed a hierarchical ordering of harmonic functions that is generally consistent with music-theoretical predictions. Moreover, the hierarchies of the major and minor keys were quite similar despite differences in chord types across the two modes. As with the full set of chords, influences were found of the positions in the tonal hierarchy of the chord's components and their frequency of occurrence in tonal compositions. In addition, the ratings corresponded quite well to the relative frequencies with which the different chords appear in compositions in the common-practice period. These results suggest that listeners have abstracted a harmonic hierarchy through sensitivity to stylistic regularities in tonal-harmonic music and that, psychologically, the harmonic hierarchy is strongly tied to the tonal hierarchy of this same musical style.

Deriving key distances from harmonic hierarchies

This final section examines the question of whether an interpretable measure of interkey distance can be recovered from the experimentally quantified harmonic hierarchies. The basic idea is that a key context imposes a hierarchy on the set of chords, and these hierarchies should be similar for closely related keys. Support for this idea comes from two results already discussed. First, closely related keys share a number of basic harmonies, as indicated in Table 7.2, and membership in the set of diatonic triads was one variable found to influence the chord rating data. Thus, the interlocking pattern of chord functions in closely related keys should support the derivation of key distances from the chord ratings. Second, the chord ratings were also influenced by the position of their components in the tonal hierarchy. In Chapter 2, a very regular and interpretable map of musical keys was derived from the experimentally quantified tonal hierarchies. To the extent that the tonal hierarchies are mirrored in the chord ratings, a similar map should be obtained from the quantified harmonic hierarchies.

The steps in the present analysis are analogous to those in Chapter 2 where a key map was derived from the tonal hierarchies. The first step was to generate a harmonic hierarchy for each of the 24 major and minor keys. This was done by shifting the ratings to correspond to the different tonics (a procedure that is justified by equivalence of chord functions in the different keys under transposition). For example, the rating assigned to the D♭ major chord in a D♭ major key is taken to be the rating given a C major chord in the C major context; the rating assigned to a D major chord in a D♭ major key context is taken to be the rating given a D♭ major chord in the C major context, and so on. This method generated a complete set of chord rating data for each major and each minor key context. In this analysis, the data were normalized for chord type, as described earlier, because otherwise the stronger effect of chord type for major-key contexts would have artificially elevated the similarity of the harmonic hierarchies for major keys.

The second step in the analysis was to intercorrelate the normalized harmonic hierarchies for all major and minor keys. That is, a correlation was computed for each possible pair of major keys, of minor keys, and of major and minor keys. The correlations of all keys with C major and C minor keys are shown in Table 7.10 (compare Table 2.3); the results for any other major or minor key are analogous. The values are plotted in Figure 7.2 (compare Figure 2.6), where the keys are arranged on the horizontal axis according to their position on the circle of fifths.

The values plotted in the upper left of Figure 7.2 are the correlations between the normalized chord ratings for C major and those for all other

Table 7.10. Correlations between harmonic hierarchies

	Key	
Key	C Major	C Minor
C Major	1.000	.738
C♯/D♭ Major	− .301	− .224
D Major	− .141	− .320
D♯/E♭ Major	− .013	.405
E Major	− .139	− .256
F Major	.297	.194
F♯/G♭ Major	− .407	− .281
G Major	.297	.175
G♯/A♭ Major	− .139	.123
A Major	− .013	− .286
A♯/B♭ Major	− .141	.031
B Major	− .301	− .298
C Minor	.738	1.000
C♯/D♭ Minor	− .298	− .373
D Minor	.031	− .189
D♯/E♭ Minor	− .286	.072
E Minor	.123	− .096
F Minor	.175	.245
F♯/G♭ Minor	− .281	− .321
G Minor	.194	.245
G♯/A♭ Minor	− .256	− .096
A Minor	.405	.072
A♯/B♭ Minor	− .320	− .189
B Minor	− .224	− .373

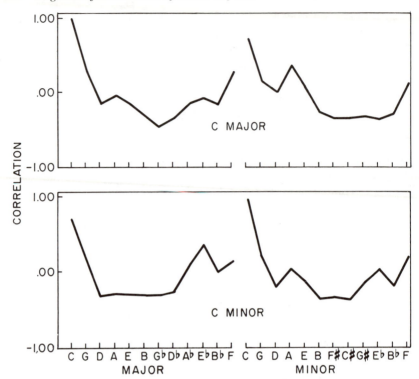

Fig. 7.2. Correlations between the harmonic-hierarchy ratings in a C major key context and those of all other major and minor keys (top), and correlations between the harmonic-hierarchy ratings in a C minor key context and those of all other major and minor keys (bottom). These correlations are taken to be an indirect measure of interkey distance derived from the harmonic-hierarchy ratings (compare Figure 2.6).

major keys. As can be seen, the pattern of correlations conforms almost exactly to the distance on the circle of fifths. For example, relatively high values were found for G and F major keys, which neighbor the C major key on the circle of fifths, and the lowest correlation corresponds to the F♯ major key, which is directly opposite the C major key—and hence maximally distant—on the circle of fifths. Local peaks for A major and E♭ major can be understood as deriving from the parallel and relative major–minor key relationships. (A major is the parallel major of A minor, which is the relative minor of C major; E♭ major is the relative major of C minor, which is the parallel minor of C major.)

The values plotted in the upper right are the correlations between the normalized chord ratings for C major and those for all minor keys. This plot shows two distinct peaks, one at C minor—the parallel minor of C major—and the other at A minor—the relative minor of C major. Thus, these peaks reflect the dual major–minor relations of parallel and relative. The correlations generally decline as the minor keys move away from these two minor keys on the circle of fifths. The values plotted in the lower left are the correlations between the normalized chord ratings for C minor and those for all major keys; moreover, these values are, in fact, the same as those in the upper right graph, only now shown for a reference key of C minor. Again, the dual major–minor relations are apparent in the local peaks for C major (the parallel major of C minor) and E♭ major (the relative major of C minor).

Finally, the values on the lower right are the correlations between the normalized chord ratings for C minor and all the other minor keys. Generally, the correlations decline with distance from C minor on the circle of fifths for minor keys. However, two local peaks appear at A minor and E♭ minor. As with the correlations for pairs of major keys, these can be understood as deriving from the parallel and relative major–minor relations. (A minor is the relative minor of C major, which is the parallel major of C minor; E♭ minor is the parallel minor of E♭ major, which is the relative major of C minor.) Thus, two variables govern the correlations plotted in Figure 7.2: the circle of fifths, and the parallel and relative major–minor relations.

The final step was to enter the correlations of the normalized harmonic hierarchies into a multidimensional scaling analysis. This analysis found a spatial configuration of points for the 24 major and minor keys such that keys with similar harmonic hierarchies were represented by proximal points, and keys with dissimilar harmonic hierarchies were represented by distant points. (More details of this method can be found in Chapter 2.) A very good fit to the data was obtained with a four-dimensional solution. The stress value, indicating the degree of fit between distances in the configuration and the correlations, was .042 (stress formula 1).

The configuration was such that the points for the 24 major and minor keys fell on the surface of a torus in four dimensions. A torus is generated by two circular components. The first circular component was the circle of fifths, which is seen in the projection in the first two dimensions on the left of Figure 7.3 (compare Figure 2.7). There was one circle of fifths for major keys and another circle of fifths for minor keys; furthermore, these circles had the same centers and essentially the same radii. They were aligned to reflect a compromise between parallel and relative major–minor key relations, although the relative relation exhibited a somewhat stronger pull. On the second circular component, which is the projection in the last two dimensions shown on the right of Figure 7.3, groups of three different keys occupied the same position. These were keys of the same mode (major or minor) the tonics of which are separated by major thirds. Each cluster of major keys had the corresponding parallel minor keys on one side and the corresponding relative minor keys on the other

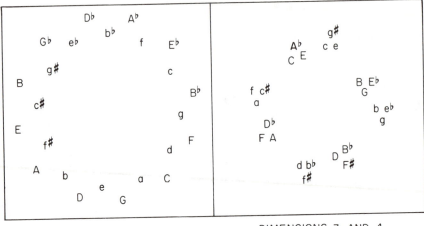

DIMENSIONS I AND 2   DIMENSIONS 3 AND 4

Fig. 7.3. The correlations between the harmonic-hierarchy ratings for all pairs of major and minor keys were analyzed using multidimensional scaling. The analysis produced a four-dimensional solution. The coordinates of the points in the first two dimensions are shown on the left; these two dimensions emphasize the circle of fifths and relative major–minor relationships. The coordinates in the last two dimensions are shown on the right; these two dimensions emphasize the parallel major–minor relationship and, to a lesser degree, the relative major–minor relationship (compare Figure 2.7).

side. Similarly, each cluster of minor keys had the corresponding parallel major keys on one side, and the corresponding relative major keys on the other side. Here, the parallel major–minor relation exhibited a somewhat stronger pull than the relative major–minor relation.

To facilitate visualizing this four-dimensional configuration, it is shown in Figure 7.4 on the rectangular representation of a torus in which it is understood that opposite edges are really the same (compare Figure 2.8). The positions of the points are determined by their angular coordinates on the two circular dimensions generating the torus. As can be seen, there are two circles of fifths, one for major keys and one for minor keys; moreover, these each wrap three times around the torus before joining with themselves again. In addition, each major key is flanked by its relative minor on one side and its parallel minor on the other. Similarly, each minor key is flanked by its relative and parallel major keys. It is striking that the results obtained in the present analysis for the harmonic hierarchies are virtually identical to those obtained earlier for the tonal hierarchies. Both kinds of hierarchies generate essentially the same conception of the degree to which different abstract tonal centers are related to one another. The degree of relatedness, moreover, is highly consistent with music-theoretical descriptions.

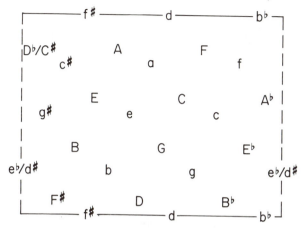

Fig. 7.4. Rectangular representation of the multidimensional scaling solution (in which opposite edges are to be considered the same) shows the locations of the points for the 24 major and minor keys on the surface of a torus. The horizontal axis corresponds to the angle of each key on the circle in the first two dimensions; the vertical axis corresponds to the angle of each key on the circle in the last two dimensions (compare Figure 2.8).

The convergence between the two maps of key distance derived from the tonal and harmonic hierarchies is of considerable interest for a number of reasons. First, it substantiates the earlier results for tonal hierarchies, suggesting that the obtained description of key structure is not a consequence of some property that is special to the probe tone data. The same conception of key distance arises from two completely independent sets of data using different probe elements (chromatic scale tones in one case, and major, minor, and diminished chords in the other). Second, the convergence reinforces the notion that, psychologically, tonal and harmonic hierarchies are strongly interdependent. Chord ratings were found to depend on the position of their component tones in the tonal hierarchy of the context key. Thus, although single tones and chords may have distinctive perceptual effects, their hierarchical orderings contain sufficient underlying commonalities to yield the same measure of key distance. Finally, theoretical treatments have found it useful to analyze tonal-harmonic music in terms of harmonic elements considered as units rather than in terms of their component tones. However, the psychological interdependencies between tones and chords suggest that these levels generally function together to produce an extremely stable internal representation of key structure. The next chapter summarizes other experiments demonstrating common psychological principles operating at the levels of tones and chords, thus further tying together the two levels of structure in tonal-harmonic music.

8. Perceived harmonic relations

Having considered in the last chapter the hierarchy of harmonic functions of single chords in tonal contexts, we now turn to experiments investigating the perceived relations between chords. A number of experiments in which listeners gave relatedness ratings to successively presented chords is summarized in the first half of this chapter. Three different questions were addressed by these studies. The first question was whether relatedness measures reflect structure at the level of musical keys. In other words, do listeners judge chords that function in the same key as more related than those that function in different keys? The second question was how to characterize the relations among diatonic triads of a single key. In particular, can the judgments be accounted for in terms of such variables as the chords' positions in the harmonic hierarchy and the frequency of successive chord combinations in tonal-harmonic music? The third question was whether perceived harmonic relations can be systematically manipulated by varying the tonal context in which the chords are presented. Can changes in the responses be explained by changes of the harmonic hierarchies of the context?

Recognition memory studies provide an alternative methodology for investigating the psychological representation of harmonic relations, and the experiments summarized in the remainder of the chapter address some of the same questions: Does the pattern of memory confusions also support the idea that harmonic elements are coded in terms of their functions in musical keys? Does the tonality of the context alter the pattern of errors in a way that is consistent with the hierarchical differentiation of chords associated with the tonality? What role do harmonic functions play in coding relations between successive elements when remembering chord sequences? These results are presented with an eye toward identifying general psychological principles applicable to both tones and chords. The chapter concludes with a compilation of structural principles that appear common to the two kinds of elements in music and supporting empirical evidence.

Perceived harmonic relations and key structure

The question considered in the first scaling study of chords was whether key structure affects the judged degree of relatedness between chords. The experiment, which is described in more detail in the article by Krumhansl, Bharucha, and Kessler (1982), employed the diatonic triads, I–VII, of three closely related keys: C major, A minor, and G major. The diatonic triads of A minor were based on the harmonic minor scale with a raised seventh, G♯. The triads are shown in Table 8.1; as can be seen, a number of chords play multiple functions in the three keys. All possible pairs of chords were presented following an ascending scale in one of the three keys. Chord tones and tones in the scale contexts consisted of sine wave components sounded over a five-octave range with loudness determined by the envelope shown in Figure 2.2. Listeners were asked to rate how well the second chord followed the first in the context of the scale sounded at the beginning of each trial. As in other experiments, listeners had moderate levels of practical musical experience, but little formal training in music theory.

This procedure generated a matrix of ratings for all possible pairs of diatonic triads in these three keys. The ratings did not depend in a regular way on whether the chords were sounded following a scale in C major, G major, or A minor. Consequently, the values were averaged over these three contexts. The average data were then analyzed using multidimensional scaling to produce a spatial configuration in which chords judged as closely related were represented by nearby points and chords judged as less related were represented by more distant points. The scaling solution in two dimensions is shown at the top of Figure 8.1; it is repeated three times below to show the functions of the chords in G major (left), C major (middle), and A minor (right). As is apparent, the chords of G major tended to occupy positions in the left half of the spatial representation, chords of C major in the center, and chords of A minor in the right half.

Table 8.1. Chords in scaling experiment

Chord	Components	C Major	G Major	A Minor
C Major	C E G	I	IV	
D Minor	D F A	ii		iv
E Minor	E G B	iii	vi	
F Major	F A C	IV		VI
G Major	G B D	V	I	
A Minor	A C E	vi	ii	i
B Diminished	B D F	vii°		ii°
D Major	D F♯ A		V	
F♯ Diminished	F♯ A C		vii°	
B Minor	B D F♯		iii	
E Major	E G♯ B			V
G♯ Diminished	G♯ B D			vii°
C Augmented	C E G♯			III⁺

Source: Krumhansl, Bharucha, and Kessler (1982).

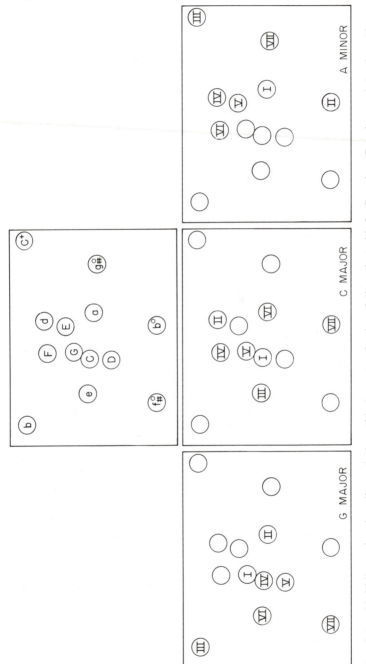

Fig. 8.1. Multidimensional scaling solution of judgments of pairs of diatonic traids in G major, C major, and A minor (from Krumhansl, Bharucha, & Kessler, 1982). The figure at the top shows the points labeled by the chord name. The same solution is repeated three times on the bottom with the points labeled by their functions in G major (left), C major (middle), and A minor (right). Copyright 1982 by the American Psychological Association. Adapted by permission of the publisher.

Despite the multiple functions that many of the chords play in these three closely related keys, the results of the scaling analysis showed influences of key distance. Chords of A minor and G major were farther apart in the solution than chords of A minor and C major or chords of C major and G major, as would be predicted given the relative distances between these keys. Chords in the diatonic set of a single key were located even closer together, especially the most harmonically significant I, IV, and V chords. Thus, the scaling solution accommodates the interlocking pattern of chord functions in the three closely related keys, and at the same time separates chords according to their distinctive roles in the different keys. At least for closely related keys, then, the results support the idea that perceived harmonic relations reflect structure at the level of musical keys.

The second experiment, reported by Bharucha and Krumhansl (1983), employed the diatonic triads, I–VII, of two musically distant major keys, C major and F♯ major. The sets of diatonic triads of these two keys do not overlap. All possible pairs of these chords were presented in the experiment, and again listeners rated how well the second chord followed the first. Included in this experiment was a condition in which the pairs of chords were presented in the absence of any context. The reason for including this condition was to evaluate whether the chords of this set would separate according to their functions in the two keys even when no context was provided. If so, this would argue strongly for effects of key structure on perceived harmonic relations.

The results of the multidimensional scaling analysis of the data are shown in Figure 8.2. As can be seen, listeners judged the diatonic triads of C major as generally more related to one another than they were to the diatonic triads of F♯ major; the complementary pattern for the chords of F♯ major was, of course, also found. The chords of C major occupied positions on the left side of the scaling solution and the chords of F♯ major positions on the right. Again, chords that play central roles in the two keys (I, IV, and V) formed relatively compact subsets for each of the two keys.

To summarize, these two experiments confirmed the prediction that key structure influences perceived harmonic relations. The experiments showed chords that function in the same key were perceived as more related, in general, than chords that function in different keys. This was the case even for the diatonic triads of the three very closely related keys used in the first experiment. Thus, listeners made fine discriminations between chords according to the keys in which they function. At the same time, the results also showed that listeners have knowledge of the multiple functions that chords play in nearby keys. The second experiment demonstrated listeners' sensitivity to key structure in a different way. Even in the absence of any context at all, chords of two different keys were judged as less related than chords of the same key. These findings argue

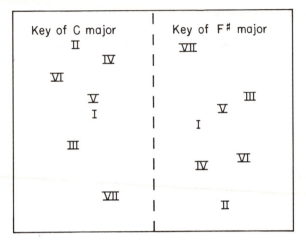

Fig. 8.2. Multidimensional scaling solution of judgments of pairs of diatonic triads in C and F♯ major (from Bharucha & Krumhansl, 1983). Listeners judged all possible pairs of these chords in the absence of any key-defining context. Chords separate according to key; chords in C major are located on the left, and chords in F♯ major are located on the right. Reprinted by permission of the publisher.

for strong psychological connections between harmony and key, which will be considered again in various ways in later sections.

Perceived harmonic relations of diatonic triads I–VII

This section presents a more detailed analysis of the perceived relations between chords in the set of diatonic triads. Specifically, the concern is to understand how the quantified harmonic hierarchy described in the last chapter influences perceived harmonic relations. The data considered here were taken from the scaling experiment reported by Bharucha and Krumhansl (1983) in which all possible pairs of diatonic triads of C and F♯ major were judged in terms of how well they sounded in succession. In two conditions of the experiment, the chords were presented following a IV–V–I cadence in C major or F♯ major. The analyses here consider only the set of I–VII chords of C major in the C major context, and the I–VII chords of F♯ major in the F♯ major context. Table 8.2 shows the ratings given by listeners to pairs of these triads, which were averaged over the two different major-key contexts because the results were very similar. The relatively high ratings of these chord pairs can be understood because the experiment also included pairs of chords of different keys that were given substantially lower ratings. The table also gives the row and column averages.

Table 8.2. Ratings of pairs of chords in major-key context

First Chord	Second Chord							
	I	ii	iii	IV	V	vi	vii°	Average
I		5.10	4.78	5.91	5.94	5.26	4.57	5.26
ii	5.69		4.00	4.76	6.10	4.97	5.41	5.16
iii	5.38	4.47		4.63	5.03	4.60	4.47	4.76
IV	5.94	5.00	4.22		6.00	4.35	4.79	5.05
V	6.19	4.79	4.47	5.51		5.19	4.85	5.17
vi	5.04	5.44	4.72	5.07	5.56		4.50	5.06
vii°	5.85	4.16	4.16	4.53	5.16	4.19		4.68
Average	5.68	4.83	4.39	5.07	5.63	4.76	4.76	

Source: Bharucha and Krumhansl (1983).

Considering the column averages first, there was a definite preference overall for two-chord sequences ending on the I chord and the V chord; these sequences were followed by the sequences ending on the IV, II, VI, VII, and III chords. This ordering was quite close to that of the ratings given single chords in major contexts in the harmonic-hierarchy experiments described in the last chapter. Indeed, the correlation between the column averages from this study and the chord ratings in the earlier experiments was .88 ($p < .01$). This means that higher ratings were on average given to pairs of chords ending on a chord that was judged as fitting well with the context key. A somewhat higher correlation, .94 ($p < .01$), was found between the column averages and the frequencies of the seven chords in tonal compositions (Budge, 1943). Both these results indicate that the ratings of pairs of chords depended quite strongly on the position of the second chord of the pair in the hierarchy of harmonic functions as measured by either ratings of single chords in tonal contexts or their frequency of occurrence in compositions in the tonal-harmonic style.

A similar, but reduced effect was found for pairs of chords beginning on a fixed first chord, as can be seen in the row averages. Listeners tended to prefer pairs of chords beginning on a chord that is structurally significant in the key context. The correlation between the row averages and the ratings of the first chord of the pairs in the harmonic-hierarchy experiments was .73, and the correlation between the row averages and the frequencies of the first chords of the pairs on the chord count analysis (Budge, 1943) was also .73. These values closely approached significance. Thus, in general, there was a preference for pairs of chords in which the first is a central harmony in the tonal system. Together, these results for row and column averages demonstrated that the harmonic significance of the chords affected their perceived relations to one another, and greater weight was given to the second chord than to the first chord.

A multiple correlation assessed whether the harmonic hierarchy predicts the individual cells within the data matrix of Table 8.2. In particular, could the ratings of pairs of chords be predicted by the rating of the first and the second chords of the pair using the data from the harmonic-hierarchy experiments? This analysis showed a highly significant relation between the ratings of the pairs of chords and the ratings of each of the separate chords. The multiple correlation was .75, which, with 39 degrees of freedom, is highly significant ($p < .01$). Both the first and second chords contributed significantly to the multiple correlation but, as would be expected given the just-mentioned analyses on the row and column averages, greater weight was given to the second chord. The weight of the second chord was, in fact, approximately twice that of the first chord.

A second multiple correlation assessed whether the ratings of pairs of chords could be predicted by the frequency of occurrence of the individual chords in the chord count analysis (Budge, 1943). Again, a highly significant multiple correlation, .80 ($p < .01$), was found, indicating that pairs of chords receiving the highest ratings were those that occur most frequently in the sampling of tonal compositions. As in the just-mentioned analysis, the weight given the second chord was greater than (in fact, again approximately twice) the weight given the first chord.

These analyses showed that ratings of sequentially presented pairs of chords were strongly affected by their positions in the harmonic hierarchy. Chords were judged as more related to the extent that they have strong harmonic functions. Consider the I, IV, and V chords, which are considered most important for establishing the tonality. Highest ratings tended to be given to pairs of chords involving these three structurally significant chords. Lower ratings tended to be given to pairs of chords in which one or both is outside this central set. The analyses also found that greater weight was given to the second chord of the pair. This means the ratings depended on the order in which the chords were presented; for a fixed pair of chords, the rating tends to be higher when the more harmonically significant chord was sounded in the second position. Consider, for example, the pair of chords ii and V of which the V is the more central chord of the pair. Higher ratings were given to the ordered pair in which ii is followed by V than the opposite order; this is a consequence of the greater weight given the harmonic function of the second chord. Thus, the harmonic hierarchy predicts not only average ratings for chord pairs, but also differences that depend on the order in which they were sounded.

One final result will be mentioned, which concerns the relationship between the rating data of Table 8.2 and the frequency with which the various sequential pairs of chords are sounded in Western tonal-harmonic music. Do the ratings correspond to the statistical distribution of pairs of successive chords in music (the first-order statistics)? Although no suitable tabulation was found in the literature containing quantitative values, Piston (1941/1978, p. 21) presents a table of usual root progressions expressed in qualitative terms. For each of the seven chords, the table lists those chords by which it is typically followed, sometimes followed, or less often followed. This table, based on observation of harmonic practice, is reproduced in Table 8.3. Although not in a quantitative form, this table is, according to Meyer (1956, p. 54), "actually nothing more than a statement of the system of probability which we know as tonal harmony."

In order to perform a statistical test of the degree to which this table of root progressions corresponds to the ratings of pairs of chords from the experiment, the following numerical values were assigned: 3 to "followed by," 2 to "sometimes followed by," 1 to "less often followed by," and 0 otherwise. With this assignment, a matrix of values was constructed and correlated with the rating data of Table 8.2. The result was a correlation of .53, which, with 40 degrees of freedom, is highly significant statistically ($p < .01$). This correlation indicates a systematic preference for chord progressions considered by Piston (1941/1978) to be most common. This was true even though the analysis used rough categorical estimates of the relative frequency of occurrence of pairs of chords; presumably a higher correlation would be found with appropriate summary statistics of the frequencies of pairs of chords.

Key context effects on perceived harmonic relations

The two experiments summarized in this section tested the idea that the degree to which chords are heard as related depends on the tonal context in which they are embedded. If varying context systematically changes perceived harmonic relations, then it supports the idea, already suggested by other findings, that harmony and key are strongly interdependent. The two experiments, described in the articles by Bharucha and Krumhansl (1983) and Krumhansl, Bharucha, and Castellano (1982), employed the diatonic triads of C and F♯ major keys. Pairs of these triads were pre-

Table 8.3. Table of usual root progressions

First-Sounded Chord	Followed by:	Sometimes Followed by:	Less Often Followed by:
I	IV V	VI	II III
II	V	IV VI	I III
III	VI	IV	I II V
IV	V	I II	III VI
V	I	IV VI	II III
VI	II V	III IV	I
VII	III	I	

Source: Piston (1941/1978).

sented in the context of five different major keys: C, G, A, B, and F♯. In each case, the context key was established by sounding a IV–V–I cadence in the key prior to the two test chords. The context keys were selected to vary in terms of their distance from C major and F♯ major. G major is one step from C major on the circle of fifths and five steps from F♯ major; A major is three steps from both C major and F♯ major keys; finally, B major is one step from F♯ major and five from C major. Thus, the context keys move around the circle of fifths from C major to F♯ major. Listeners rated how well the second chord followed the first in the context of the chord cadence sounded at the beginning of each trial. As in other studies, the listeners had a moderate level of practical musical experience, and the chords consisted of components sounded over a five-octave range.

The different contexts had two systematic effects on the judgments listeners gave to pairs of diatonic triads from the set I–VII of C and F♯ major keys. The first of these effects can be seen in Figure 8.3, which shows the results of the multidimensional scaling analysis of the data for the five context conditions. There were regular distortions in the spatial configurations when different keys were established by the context. These distortions were such that the diatonic triads of C major were drawn closer together when the context key is C major or G major, a key that is closely related to C major. Similarly, the diatonic triads of F♯ major were drawn closer together when the context key was F♯ major or B major, a key that is closely related to F♯ major. The intermediate key of A major was neutral in this regard. The top of Figure 8.4 shows the same effect in another way. The average ratings for pairs of chords in C major decreased as the context key moved away from C major. In a complementary fashion, the average ratings for pairs of chords in F♯ major increased.

Thus, the perceived relations between chords were strengthened when they appeared in a context key in which they are diatonic or in a closely related key. This effect is described by the contextual-distance principle defined in Chapter 6. This principle states that the average distance between any two elements varies inversely with the extent that the elements are stable or play significant functions in the context key. When chords are diatonic triads of the context key, they are stable; however, as the context key moves away on the circle of fifths, the degree of chord stability decreases and interchord distance increases. That this effect was a regular function of key distance further supports the view that the perceptual effects of chords are determined by their harmonic roles in a system of interrelated keys.

The second contextual effect was seen in the ratings for pairs of chords in which one was diatonic in C major and the other was diatonic in F♯ major. The ratings depended on the order in which the two chords were

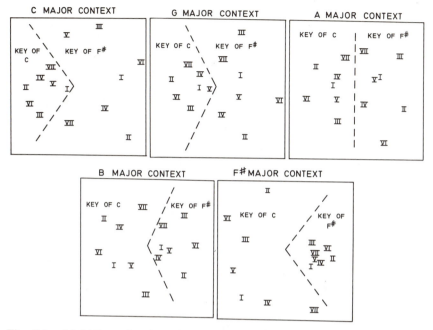

Fig. 8.3. Multidimensional scaling solution of judgments of pairs of diatonic traids in C and F♯ major presented in the context of C major, G major, A major, B major, or F♯ major (from Bharucha & Krumhansl, 1983, and Krumhansl, Bharucha, & Castellano, 1982). The key context enhances the perceived relatedness of chords that function in that key and in closely related keys, an example of the contextual-distance principle. Adapted by permission of the publishers.

presented. Because the multidimensional scaling representation cannot capture order differences, the effect is described with respect to the average ratings for diatonic triads in different keys. These values are shown in the lower graph of Figure 8.4. For pairs in which the first is a diatonic triad in F♯ major and the second in C major, the ratings generally declined as the context key moves from C major to F♯ major. For pairs in which the first is a diatonic triad in C major and the second in F♯ major, the ratings generally increased as the context key moves from C major to F♯ major. Small deviations from increasing or decreasing functions can be understood because the data for C and F♯ major contexts came from a different experiment, in which ratings were lower on average than the experiment with the G, A, and B major contexts. Thus, listeners generally preferred two-chord sequences in which the final chord of the pair was a diatonic triad of the context key or a closely related key. This effect is described by the contextual-asymmetry principle defined in Chapter 6. It

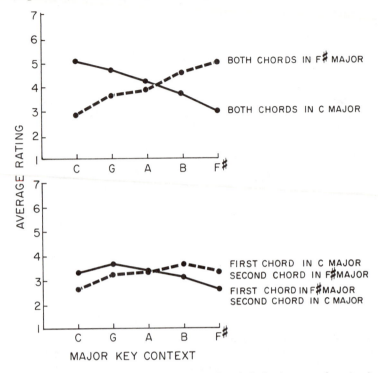

Fig. 8.4. Average ratings for pairs of diatonic triads in the same key (top) or in different keys (bottom) presented in the context of C major, G major, A major, B major, or F♯ major (from Bharucha & Krumhansl, 1983, and Krumhansl, Bharucha, & Castellano, 1982). The top effect is an example of the contextual-distance principle; the bottom effect is an example of the contextual-asymmetry principle.

states that the psychological distance between a less stable first element and a more stable second element will be less than the distance between a more stable first element and a less stable second element.

The effects of the context key on the chord ratings in these experiments were so regular, in fact, that it was possible to recover the circle of fifths for major keys from the data. In this analysis, the matrix of chord ratings for each of the five contexts was correlated with the matrix of chord ratings for each of the other contexts. This produced a measure of interkey distance for each possible pair of the five keys. When these correlations were analyzed using multidimensional scaling, the circle-of-fifths dimension expressing the relations among these keys was recovered (details of this analysis can be found in Krumhansl, Bharucha, and Castellano, 1982). This provides additional evidence for the description of key distance that has emerged from other experimental findings.

The two contextual effects described in this section reinforce the view that chords are perceived in terms of their functions in a system of musical keys. These studies showed regular effects of key distance on the judgments of a fixed set of chords, the diatonic triads of two maximally distant major keys. The chords also tended to separate according to their functions in the two keys, and this was independent of context. Chords in C major were heard as more related to one another than they were to chords in F♯ major, and the complementary pattern was found for chords in F♯ major. Also independently of context, the most structurally significant chords within each key—the I, IV, and V chords—tended to be heard as most related to one another. These effects were similar to those described in earlier sections of this chapter.

Key structure and memory for chord sequences

A number of recognition memory experiments have been conducted in parallel with the rating studies of chords. The initial motivation for studying memory for chord sequences was to determine whether the effects would be analogous to those for memory of melodies. Of particular interest were those effects concerning tonal structure: more accurate memory for sequences conforming to tonal structure, the difficulty of remembering unstable elements inconsistent with the tonality, the tendency to confuse unstable elements with more stable elements, and the relatively frequent confusions between elements in the tonality. In addition, as evidence accumulated from the chord ratings studies concerning perceived harmonic relations, the memory studies became more important for confirming the emerging patterns with a different methodology. A final, subsidiary reason for employing sequences of chords in the memory tasks was that they afforded somewhat better control over the tonal interpretation of the stimulus sequences than melodic sequences. The stimulus materials of these experiments made use of various harmonic conventions to establish unambiguously a predominant tonality, as will be described later.

The three experiments reviewed here were originally published in the articles by Bharucha and Krumhansl (1983), Krumhansl, Bharucha, and Castellano (1982), and Krumhansl and Castellano (1983). Because the three studies employed similar methodologies, the commonalities will be described first, with more specific details of the individual experiments given later. All the studies employed a recognition memory paradigm in which two sequences of chords were presented in succession. Each sequence consisted of seven or eight chords. In some cases, the listeners were required to judge whether the two sequences were identical, chord for chord, or whether the two sequences were different. When the sequences were different, they differed only in terms of one chord. In other cases, the two sequences always contained one different chord and the listeners' task was to judge its serial position.

A computer algorithm was written to construct chord sequences that would quite unambiguously establish a single major key. To this end, the chords were selected from the set of diatonic triads: I, ii, IV, V, and vi chords; in some cases the iii chord was also included. The vii° was excluded because, in major keys, it is of a different type (diminished) than the others, and consequently might induce effects extraneous to the central concern, which was the effect of tonal structure on memory. In the sequences, the chords were additionally constrained to conform to the common chord progressions listed by Piston (1941/1978, p. 21; Table 8.3). Any chord in the sequence could only be followed by a chord designated as forming a common progression under the heading "is followed by" or "is sometimes followed by." Also, the final chord was required to be the tonic (I) chord. In addition to these constraints based on harmonic practice, the sequences were controlled for the number of chord repetitions in the sequences as a whole. The chords of the sequences were produced using the same method as in the scaling studies, with the components of the chords sounded over a five-octave range (see Figure 2.2).

The various conditions of the first memory experiment (Bharucha & Krumhansl, 1983) can best be understood with reference to Table 8.4. The experiment included sequences designed to establish quite unambiguously a single key; these sequences were constructed according to the just-mentioned constraints and are labeled as "tonal" in the table. In some of these sequences a single, randomly selected nondiatonic chord was substituted for a diatonic chord. In addition, the experiment contained a number of sequences in which the chords were selected randomly subject to the constraint that they match the others in terms of the number of repetitions and the types of chords (whether major or minor); these are labeled "random." On each trial, two sequences were sounded. The first sequence is called the standard sequence; it is the one to be remembered. The second is called the comparison sequence because it is to be compared with the first sequence.

On some trials, the sequences were identical, chord for chord. On other trials, they different in terms of a single chord. The listeners judged whether the two sequences were the same or different. As can be seen, there were a total of five kinds of trials in which a single chord, called the target chord, was changed between the standard and comparison sequences. These are labeled "different" in the table. When the sequence was tonal, a diatonic chord in the standard sequence was changed either to another diatonic chord in the comparison sequence or to a randomly selected nondiatonic chord. When a nondiatonic chord was contained in the standard sequence, it was changed either to a diatonic or a nondiatonic chord in the comparison sequence. For the random sequences, chords cannot be classified as diatonic or nondiatonic. In these cases, one chord was simply chosen randomly as a substitute chord so that the resulting sequence would match the others in terms of variables such as the

Table 8.4. Conditions of memory experiment for chord sequences

Trial Type	Context Sequence	Target Chord in Standard	Target Chord in Comparison	Proportion Correct
Different	Tonal	Diatonic (Ex. C a d a F G C	Diatonic C F d a F G C)	.569
Different	Tonal	Diatonic (Ex. F C a F d G C)	Nondiatonic F C g♯ F d G C)	.868
Different	Tonal	Nondiatonic (Ex. C F d G♯ G F C	Diatonic C F d a G F C)	.613
Different	Tonal	Nondiatonic (Ex. a F G F d♯ G C	Nondiatonic a F G F f♯ G C)	.776
Different	Random	— (Ex. C a D♯ a♯ D♯ F C	— C a D♯ a♯ D♯ D C)	.667
Same	Tonal	All Diatonic (Ex. a G C F d G C	a G C F d G C)	.693
Same	Tonal	One Nondiatonic (Ex. d C♯ d G C F C	d C♯ d G C F C)	.550
Same	Random	(Ex. A♯ C f♯ C♯ e A♯ C	A♯ C f♯ C♯ e A♯ C)	.550

Source: Bharucha and Krumhansl (1983).

number of repetitions and distribution of chord types. Finally, three different kinds of trials had identical standard and comparison sequences: tonal sequences in which all chords were diatonic, tonal sequences containing a single nondiatonic chord, and random sequences. On these trials, the two sequences matched exactly so that no chord is designated as the target chord; these trials are labeled "same" in the table. For ease of comparison, the examples shown in the table all have a final chord of C major; actually, the chord sequences were transposed so that the final chord might be any major chord.

This experiment produced a rather complex pattern of results, and the discussion here will emphasize those that bear most directly on the effects of tonal organization on memory. The last column of Table 8.4 shows, for each trial type, the proportion of trials on which the correct response was given. Before considering the results for the various trial types, it is interesting to note that performance in this task was far from perfect. Even though the listeners were all at least moderately experienced musically—with an average of almost 9 years of musical instruction—their recognition of short chord sequences showed frequent errors. Thus, the memory representation of the sequences is not a veridical recoding of the sounded events.

Rather, the pattern of responses showed that listeners depended strongly on tonal organization in making their judgments, resulting in large differences in accuracy across the various conditions. Among the different trials, performance was best when the first sequence consisted only of diatonic chords, one of which was changed to a nondiatonic chord in the comparison sequence. The first sequence in this case would be expected to establish unambiguously the tonality, so that the nondiatonic chord in the second sequence was readily apparent. Somewhat lower performance was found when a nondiatonic chord was changed to another nondiatonic chord, suggesting that the memory encoding of the first, nondiatonic chord was unstable and, thus, sometimes confused with the different nondiatonic chord in the second sequence. More errors occurred for the random sequences, consistent with the idea that it is difficult to remember the chords in the absence of a tonal framework. Still lower performance was found when the first target chord was nondiatonic and the second target chord was diatonic, which can be accounted for in terms of the tendency to assimilate unstable elements to more stable elements. The large temporal-order effect—with nondiatonic chords much more frequently confused with diatonic chords than the reverse—is another example of the contextual-asymmetry principle, according to which a less stable element is more similar to, or less distant from, a more stable element than the reverse. Lowest performance was found in the condition in which the first target chord was diatonic and it was changed to another diatonic chord in the comparison sequence. Very frequent confusions occurred between the two diatonic target chords, an effect accounted for by the contextual-distance principle, according to which a tonal context increases the similarity, or decreases the distance, between elements that are stable within the tonality.

The three final conditions of the experiment had identical standard and comparison sequences. Of these, highest performance was found when each chord was diatonic in a tonal sequence, presumably because the tonality provided a framework for encoding the chords. Substantially more errors were made when a single nondiatonic chord was included in an otherwise tonal sequence, or the sequences consisted of randomly selected chords. The large number of errors on trials with a single nondiatonic chord derives from the instability of its memory encoding (another experiment showing this same effect will be described later). When the sequence consisted of randomly selected chords, errors resulted because of the absence of a tonal framework with respect to which the sounded chords could be encoded.

This initial study showed that musically trained listeners made relatively frequent errors in recognizing short chord sequences. The large differences between conditions indicated that they relied heavily on tonal organization in making their judgments. In some conditions, this strategy facilitated noticing the changed chords, but in others it led to low accuracy. Various effects were analogous to those documented in studies of melodic memory summarized in Chapter 6. For both, tonal sequences were better remembered, in general, than sequences not conforming to tonal structure. Moreover, nondiatonic elements in otherwise tonal sequences were difficult to recognize and tended to be confused with more stable, diatonic elements. Finally, stable elements were frequently confused with one another. In addition, the results provided convergent evidence for the findings of the chord rating studies discussed at the beginning of this chapter. In particular, the memory data mirrored the rating data in terms of the enhanced psychological relatedness of elements that were stable within the tonal framework, and the asymmetries between stable and unstable elements depending on their roles in the experimental situation. The next experiment also finds parallels between chord memory performance and chord ratings.

Key context effects on memory for chord sequences

The second experiment, reported in the article by Krumhansl, Bharucha, and Castellano (1982), explored memory for individual chords in tonal sequences when the key of the sequence was systematically varied. We chose a fixed set of 12 target chords: the diatonic triads I–VI of the keys of C major and F♯ major. Again, the vii° was eliminated, being of a different chord type from the others. Target chords always appeared in the fourth serial position in an otherwise diatonic sequence in one of the following four keys: C major, G major, A major, or B major. To ensure that the tonality of the context was clear, all sequences began with the I and ended with the V–I chords in the context key. For each of these context keys, there were six conditions, listed in Table 8.5. In the first two, the standard and comparison sequences were identical, with the repeated target chords a diatonic triad in C or F♯ major. In the next two, the standard and comparison sequences differed, with the two target chords both diatonic triads of C major or both diatonic triads of F♯ major. In the final two conditions, the standard and comparison sequences also differed, but one target chord was a diatonic triad in C major and the other in F♯ major. On each trial, listeners were required to judge whether the standard and comparison sequences were same or different.

The results for the six target chord conditions are plotted in Figure 8.5. The top graph shows the probability of a correct response for the first two trial types in which the standard and comparison sequences were the same. The probability that a repeated target chord in C major was correctly identified was highest when the rest of the sequence was in C major and declined as the context key moved away from C major on the circle of fifths. A complementary increase was found in the probability that a repeated target chord in F♯ major was correctly identified. That is, chord recognition performance varied systematically with the context key such that greatest recognition accuracy was found in the context in which the target chord would be most stable. This effect is an example of the contextual-identity principle, according to which two instances of an element will have greater self-similarity, or smaller psychological distance, when they are more stable in the tonal system. In terms of memory performance, this means that the number of correct recognition judgments

Table 8.5. Conditions in memory experiment for chord sequences

Trial Type	Target Chord in Standard	Target Chord in Comparison
Same	I–VI of C Major	I–VI of C Major
(Ex. G major)	G C a d a D G	G C a d a D G)
Same	I–VI of F♯ Major	I–VI of F♯ Major
(Ex. C major)	C F d F♯ F G C	C F d F♯ F G C)
Different	I–VI of C Major	I–VI of C Major
(Ex. A major)	A E D d f♯ E A	A E D F f♯ E A)
Different	I–VI of F♯ Major	I–VI of F♯ Major
(Ex. B major)	B E f♯ a♯ c♯ F♯ B	B E f♯ g♯ c♯ F♯ B)
Different	I–VI of C Major	I–VI of F♯ Major
(Ex. G major)	G e a F C D G	G e a F♯ C D G)
Different	I–VI of F♯ Major	I–VI of C Major
(Ex. A major)	A f♯ E g♯ b E A	A f♯ E d b E A)

Source: Krumhansl, Bharucha, and Castellano (1982).

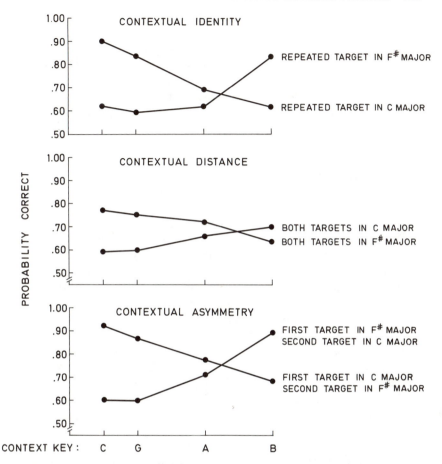

Fig. 8.5. Probability of a correct response for repeated diatonic triads (top), for different diatonic triads from the same key (middle), and for different diatonic triads from different keys (lower); values are shown as a function of the prevailing tonality of the sequence, which was C major, G major, A major, or B major. The results, from Krumhansl, Bharucha, and Castellano (1982), are examples of the contextual-identity, contextual-distance, and contextual-asymmetry principles, respectively. Reprinted by permission of the publisher.

should covary with the stability of the target element in the predominant tonality, and this was the pattern found.

The central graph of Figure 8.5 shows the performance for trials in which the target chords in the standard and comparison sequences were different, but they were both diatonic triads in either C or F♯ major. The greatest number of confusions occurred between these target chords when they were relatively stable in the predominant key of the sequence.

For example, two different diatonic triads of C major were most frequently confused, showing the greatest number of errors, when the key of the sequence was C major. As the key of the sequence moved away from C major, the number of errors of this type decreased. The complementary pattern was again found for diatonic triads in F♯ major. This is an example of what has been called the contextual-distance principle, according to which the psychological similarity between two elements is enhanced to the extent that they are stable in the tonal framework, resulting in this case in the greater number of confusions.

The lower graph of Figure 8.5 shows the performance for trials in which the target chords in the standard and comparison sequences were diatonic triads in different keys. The results show large effects of the context key on the probability of confusing these target chords. If the first target chord is a diatonic triad of F♯, then it is very frequently confused with a diatonic triad of C when the key of the sequence is C major or a closely related key. The confusion errors decrease as the context key moves away from C major, accompanied by an increase in the probability that a diatonic triad in C major is confused with a diatonic triad in F♯ major. This effect can be described by the contextual-asymmetry principle, according to which an unstable element is more similar to, or less distant from, a more stable element than the reverse. Thus, more confusion errors should occur when the first chord is unstable in the context key and the second target chord more stable than when the two chords play opposite roles. The results showed this to be a strong effect.

The final analysis focused on the confusions among the set of I–VI diatonic triads of C major in the C major context. The pattern of confusions among these chords did not systematically relate to either the ratings of successive pairs of chords from the earlier experiment (Bharucha & Krumhansl, 1983; Table 8.2), or Piston's table of usual root progressions (1941/1978, p. 21; Table 8.3). This can be understood because the latter two govern ordered pairs of successive chords, whereas the recognition memory task assessed confusions between chords when they substituted for one another in otherwise identical chord sequences. However, there was one commonality between the memory confusions and the ratings of successive chords. Both measures showed greater psychological proximity between chords when the second is relatively harmonically stable; the correlation between the recognition memory data and the rating of the second target chord in the harmonic-hierarchy experiments described in the last chapter was $-.57$ ($p < .01$). This highly significant correlation means that more confusions occurred when the substituted target chord was relatively harmonically significant in C major. This effect, analogous to the preference for two-chord sequences ending on relatively stable chords, fits with the contextual-asymmetry principle.

To summarize, this experiment demonstrated that the key of the context had a marked and regular effect on the recognition of target chords.

Variations in the context key produced systematic changes in the three independent aspects of the data: the probability of correctly recognizing a repeated target chord, the probability of confusing two different target chords that are in the same key, and the probability of confusing two different target chords that are in different keys. In each case, these effects were regular functions of key distance, providing very strong support for the interdependency between the perceived harmonic functions of chords and structure at the level of musical keys. Moreover, these findings are described by the contextual principles of contextual identity, contextual distance, and contextual asymmetry.

Relational effects on memory for chord sequences

The next experiment reviewed here considered a somewhat different question, even though it employed a similar methodology to the two experiments just described. The study was an initial exploration into the dynamic processes involved in the formation of a memory code for a sequence of chords. As a sequence of musical events is sounded, the interpretation of each successive event is presumably affected by previous events. In addition, a new event may cause previous events to be reinterpreted. Thus, the interpretation of any event shows influences of both prior and subsequent events. The objective of this experiment—described in more detail in the article by Krumhansl and Castellano (1983)—was to investigate whether these effects could be demonstrated in memory performance and, if so, to determine the nature and the temporal extent of their influence.

The experimental design again used two successively sounded chord sequences, a standard and a comparison, consisting of eight chords each. They were constructed to indicate quite unambiguously a particular key. In this study, the two sequences always differed in terms of one chord, in the third, fourth, fifth, or sixth serial position of the sequence. Listeners were required to judge which serial position contained the changed chord. The various trial types are indicated in Table 8.6. On some trials, the sequence consisted only of diatonic triads. On other trials, the sequence contained a single nondiatonic triad in one of the serial positions: 3, 4, 5, or 6. When a nondiatonic chord was included, it was never the changed chord on the trial. That is, the same nondiatonic chord appeared in the standard and comparison sequences, and the changed chord was always in one of the other serial positions.

If, as suggested, chords are encoded in relation to preceding and subsequent events, then listeners should make systematic errors in this task. Previous experiments have shown that a nondiatonic chord is poorly encoded when it is embedded in an otherwise tonal sequence; therefore, it may disrupt memory for other chords, particularly those that occur close to it in time. In addition, any chord, whether diatonic or nondiatonic, is

Table 8.6. Conditions in memory experiment for chord sequences

Sequence Type	Serial Position of Changed Chord
All diatonic	3, 4, 5, or 6
(Ex. C a d G C a F C	C a d G C G F C)
One nondiatonic chord in serial position 3	4, 5, or 6
(Ex. C a d♯ G C F G C	C a d♯ G a F G C)
One nondiatonic chord in serial position 4	3, 5, or 6
(Ex. C G a E d a F C	C G a E d G F C)
One nondiatonic chord in serial position 5	3, 4, or 6
(Ex. C G F d A d G C	C G F C A d G C)
One nondiatonic chord in serial position 6	3, 4, or 5
(Ex. C F d a d g♯ F C	C F C a d g♯ F C)

Source: Krumhansl and Castellano (1983).

presumably encoded with respect to preceding and subsequent events, so that when a chord is changed it would be expected to affect the encoding of these other events, both proactively and retroactively.

These predictions were tested in the experiment. Each trial was scored according to whether the listener correctly identified the serial position containing the changed chord. When an error was made, the trial was scored in terms of the distance of the error from the correct position and the distance of the error from the nondiatonic chord (when one was included in the sequence). In general, far more errors occurred when the sequence contained a single nondiatonic chord than when the sequence was completely diatonic. The majority of these errors were such that the nondiatonic chord was incorrectly judged to be the changed chord, which was consistent with previous results suggesting that the memory encoding of nondiatonic chords is unstable. The data were then normalized to compare the errors made for sequences containing all diatonic chords and sequences containing one nondiatonic chord. That is, the errors were considered as a percentage of the total number of errors for each sequence type. These normalized values are shown in Figure 8.6.

The left panel shows the relative number of errors as a function of distance from the chord actually changed on the trial, where negative values designate positions before the changed chord and positive values designate positions after the changed chord. Four different error types are considered: total errors in completely diatonic sequences, total errors in sequences containing one nondiatonic chord, errors in which the nondiatonic chord is incorrectly judged as changed in a sequence containing one

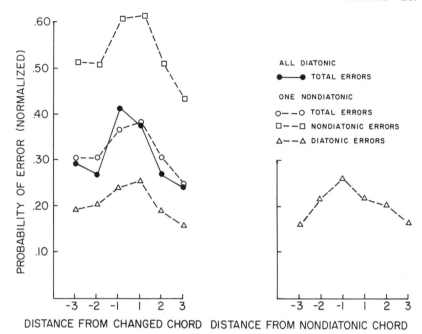

Fig. 8.6. The normalized probability of errors at positions surrounding the chord actually changed (left) and surrounding the nondiatonic chord (right). The data are from Krumhansl and Castellano (1983). Trials on which nondiatonic chords are incorrectly judged as changed ("nondiatonic errors") were much more frequent than trials on which diatonic chords were incorrectly judged as changed ("diatonic errors"). All error types decreased in frequency as a function of the distance from the chord actually changed (left panel), and as a function of the nondiatonic chord when one was included in the sequence (right panel). Reprinted by permission of the publisher.

nondiatonic chord (called "nondiatonic errors"), and errors in which a diatonic chord is incorrectly judged as changed in a sequence containing one nondiatonic chord (called "diatonic errors"). Comparison of the latter two error types show the much greater frequency of nondiatonic than diatonic errors.

Independent of this effect reflecting the instability of nondiatonic chords, a systematic pattern can be seen in these four graphs. Errors occurred most frequently in serial positions immediately preceding and following the chord that was actually changed, and decreased quite symmetrically with distance from the changed chord. As predicted, then, changing a chord in the sequence had consequences for encoding both prior and subsequent events. The figure on the right shows the number of errors as a function of distance from the nondiatonic chord for those trials in which the sequence contained a single nondiatonic chord. Errors in positions neighboring the nondiatonic chord were more frequent than errors in more distant positions. Thus, as expected, the inclusion of a nondiatonic chord disrupted memory for other chords, particularly those in a temporally adjacent position. Furthermore, the effect was again quite symmetrical.

The results of this final memory study supported the view that the individual chords in the sequences are encoded with respect to both preceding and subsequent events. The number of errors around the position containing both the changed chord and the nondiatonic chord—when one was included—showed a generally symmetrical pattern, indicating that the disruption caused by both kinds of chords have effects that are equally proactive and retroactive. Thus, the process by which musical events are encoded relies not just on preceding events, but also on subsequent events, and these dependencies decrease with temporal separation. These results support the view that music perception is a dynamic process in which each event is encoded in terms of its relations to other events in its temporal context.

Parallels between perceived tonal and harmonic structures

Standing back from the results summarized in this and preceding chapters, some rather striking parallels emerge between the way tones and chords enter into perceptual relations. These parallels are listed in Table 8.7. Consider first the results presented in Chapters 2 and 3 on tonal hierarchies and those presented in Chapter 7 on harmonic hierarchies. For both tones and chords, tonal contexts establish well-defined hierarchies of stability or structural significance. The experimentally quantified hierarchies are generally consistent with music-theoretical predictions. These hierarchies are multileveled including, but not limited to, the distinction between diatonic and nondiatonic elements. The hierarchical differential of tones and chords seems to reflect a general tendency in perception and cognition to encode, name, and remember elements in terms of their relations to a few stable, psychologically central reference points.

The tonal and harmonic hierarchies measured in the experiments mirror the distributions of the elements (their frequency of occurrence) in tonal-harmonic compositions. This correspondence suggests that sensitivity to frequency information is a mechanism through which the hierarchies might be internalized initially. Once acquired, they can be invoked with relatively schematic key-defining contexts, such as the scales, tonic triads, and chord cadences used in the experiments. Compared with statistical summaries of tone and chord distributions, tonal consonance proved to be a relatively poor predictor of the hierarchies. Although consonance may have played a role in shaping musical practice, the psychological hierarchies themselves seem to depend more strongly on regular-

Table 8.7. Summary of parallels between tones and chords

Hierarchies of Structural Significance for both Tones and Chords

Hierarchies Mirror Distribution of Tones and Chords in Music

Relationships between Tonal and Harmonic Hierarchies:

    Harmonic hierarchy depends on position of components in tonal hierarchy
    Tonal and harmonic hierarchies generate same measure of interkey distance

Relationships between Tones and between Chords:

Rating Studies
    Enhanced relatedness between structurally significant elements
        (contextual-distance principle)
    Preferences for sequences ending on structurally significant elements
        (contextual-asymmetry principle)
    Ratings mirror distribution of successive tones and chords in music

Memory Studies
    More accurate memory for structurally significant elements
        (contextual-identity principle)
    More confusions between structurally significant elements
        (contextual-distance principle)
    Less structurally significant elements confused with more structurally
        significant elements (contextual-asymmetry principle)

ities learned through experience with the musical style. The following chapters return to this issue.

The results also suggest strong interdependencies between the three levels of musical structure: tones, chords, and keys. The harmonic hierarchy could be accounted for quite well by the chord components' positions in the tonal hierarchy. That is, the ratings of triads in key-defining contexts were predicted by the ratings of their three component tones in the tonal hierarchy. Moreover, virtually identical measures of interkey distance were derived from the tonal and harmonic hierarchies. These measures were based on the idea that keys are close to the extent that their hierarchies are similar. That tonal and harmonic hierarchies, coming from completely independent perceptual judgments, yielded the same interkey distances further argues that structures applicable to tones, chords, and keys are strongly tied to one another. In this connection, it is interesting to consider the recent theoretical contributions of Bharucha (1987) and Lerdahl (1988).

Bharucha (1987) proposed a connectionist model for tonal-harmonic music in which activation spreads in a network of nodes representing tones, chords, and keys. Initially, nodes corresponding to individual tones are activated, and then activation spreads to chord nodes, and to key nodes. Because of excitatory and inhibitory connections between nodes, the network settles into a state of equilibrium over time. He finds that a model of this sort predicts precisely a variety of empirical results, including facilitation in priming studies (Bharucha & Stoeckig, 1986, 1987). These studies demonstrate faster processing of chords harmonically closely related to a preceding context than chords distant from the context. In addition, this kind of model predicts the pattern of results in the chord rating and recognition memory studies summarized in this chapter. Finally, the approach appears to have the potential to model how the sense of key develops over time (a question already considered in Chapter 4, which will be considered again in the next chapter), and how stylistic regularities are learned. It should be noted that this model assumes very simple connections between levels, reflecting tone membership in chords, and chord membership in keys.

Lerdahl's model (1988), which was mentioned briefly in Chapter 5, was proposed from a music-theoretical point of view. It begins with a pitch space containing multiple levels: chromatic scale, diatonic scale, tonic triad, tonic–dominant, and tonic. This hierarchy is similar to the experimentally quantified tonal hierarchy. From this starting point, he derived a number of measures, including tone, chord, and key proximities that were highly consistent with the empirical measures presented here. Moreover, the model's emphasis on contextual effects would seem to make it well suited to account for the effects of key context on chord proximity measures summarized in this chapter, and the perception of modulations between keys, which is examined experimentally in the next chapter. In short, empirical studies and theoretical treatments both converge on a conception of tonal-harmonic music in terms of three strongly interconnected levels of structure.

The final way in which the empirical results suggest strong commonalities between tones and chords is that similar principles of organization have been found to apply to both. Consider the parallels between the material on pitch relations presented in Chapters 5 and 6 and the material on harmonic relations presented in this chapter. It was possible to formulate three general principles characterizing how elements of one type (tones or chords) are perceived in relation to one another. These three principles—contextual identity, contextual distance, and contextual asymmetry—provide detailed accounts of how interelement associations depend on the key context in which they are embedded. Specifically, they suggest that the essential variable governing both tonal and harmonic relations is the hierarchical differentiation of elements. Supporting evidence comes from both relatedness ratings and memory accuracy measures. In addition, that the internal representation of tonal and harmonic relations is acquired through experience is suggested by the correspondence between the psychological data and the distribution of successive combinations of tones and chords in tonal-harmonic music.

9. Perceiving multiple keys: Modulation and polytonality

A number of detailed case studies are presented in this and the following chapter, in which the basic probe tone technique (Krumhansl & Shepard, 1979; Krumhansl & Kessler, 1982; Chapter 2) is applied to more complex contexts than in the original studies. The basic studies used schematic key-defining contexts, such as scales, tonic triads, and short chord cadences. These contexts were used as unambiguous indicators of key so the resulting probe tone ratings, or key profiles, can be considered a psychological marker or indicator of a key having been established. These profiles can then be used as a standard against which to compare the results for contexts that may not so clearly define a key. That the tonal hierarchies are functional in more complex sequences has been suggested by other experimental studies. As was mentioned in Chapter 6, Palmer and Krumhansl (1987a,b) showed that tonal hierarchies influence judgments of what constitutes a good or complete phrase. Schmuckler (1988) found that tonal hierarchies, together with contour and melodic processes, determine expectations for melodic continuations. Thompson (1986; experiment 4) used the probe tone technique to investigate modulation distance in Bach chorales in a way somewhat similar to the first experiment reported here.

The two experiments summarized in this chapter investigate how listeners perceive successive and simultaneous tonalities. The focus of the first experiment is on how listeners initially develop a sense of key, and how they assimilate modulations to new keys. For this purpose, chord sequences are used as contexts and probe tone ratings are obtained at each successive point in the sequence. The experiment asks: Is the sense of key stronger than local chord effects, that is, does it depend on integrating information about chord functions over time? When a modulation occurs, how quickly does a sense of the new key develop and is a sense of the initial key maintained after the modulation? How do these effects depend on the distance between the initial and final keys? The second experiment investigates the capacity to perceive more than one tonal organization simultaneously. The probe tone technique is applied to a bitonal passage in which materials from two distantly related keys are employed in parallel. Do the probe tone ratings contain patterns attributable to the two component keys? Are the two tonalities perceived as functionally separate or fused into one complex organization? Can listeners attend to the two tonalities separately and, if not, what attributes of the passage make selective attention difficult?

Tracing the developing and changing sense of key

Tonality, the sense of key that emerges from music, is a complex attribute. On the one hand, it is based on the succession of tones but, on the other hand, it evokes a rich system of knowledge about tonal and harmonic relations. The sense of key may be more or less strong. At some times it may be ambiguous or changing, at other times definite and stable. These alterations are important to the psychological experience of the listener, facilitating the comprehension of the larger plan of the composition. The feeling of tension and resolution as the sounded events play against this background is held to be fundamental to tonal music. The listener appreciates the attributes of instability and stability, ambiguity and clarity; these attributes, according to L. B. Meyer (1956), largely determine the affective response of the listener. This view of music as continually unfolding process raises the question of how to examine empirically the changing perception over time. The experiment reported in this section employed a technique specially designed for this purpose.

The experiment, originally described in the article by Krumhansl and Kessler (1982), used 10 different chord sequences consisting of nine chords each. Some of the sequences were constructed to suggest modulations, or changes, between keys; some of the modulations were to more distant keys than other modulations. The design of the experiment is illustrated in Figure 9.1. The first chord of each sequence was followed by each of the 12 probe tones from the chromatic scale. That is, the first chord was sounded, then followed by a single tone; then the first chord was sounded again, followed by another tone. This process continued until all 12 probe tones had been sampled. The listeners' task was to rate how well the probe tone fit with the preceding chord. This generated a rating profile for the sequences after the first chord of the sequences. Then, the first two chords were sounded, followed by all possible probe tones, each of which was rated in terms of how well it fit with the two-chord sequences. This generated a rating profile for the sequences after the first two chords. Probe tone ratings were then given following each of the remaining chords in an analogous manner, generating ratings profiles for sequences of lengths three through nine. Notice that the listener never heard the sequence beyond the point at which it was being probed. All the chords and the probe tones were generated with components sounded over a five-octave range (see Figure 2.2).

Table 9.1 shows the chords, which were all triads, used in the 10 sequences. The first 2 sequences consisted entirely of diatonic triads in C major and C minor, respectively. These are considered nonmodulating sequences in the intended C major and C minor keys. Notice that these

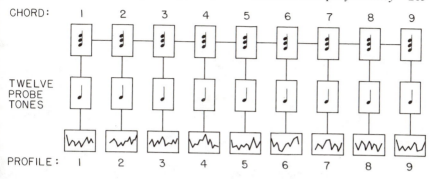

Fig. 9.1. The design of the probe tone experiment using chord sequences (Krumhansl & Kessler, 1982). The first chord was followed by all possible probe tones; then the first two chords were followed by all possible probe tones; this process was continued until rating profiles had been generated for all sequence lengths up through nine chords. Copyright 1982 by the American Psychological Association. Reprinted by permission of the publisher.

two sequences have the same structure when analyzed in Roman numeral notation designating chord functions within a key. That is, although the chords in the two sequences are of different types, the roots of the triads are corresponding tones of the scales of the two modes. In both these sequences, the tonic triad, I, is not sounded until the fifth position, the rationale for which was to determine whether the sense of the intended key becomes established before the tonic triad is sounded. In addition to selecting from among the diatonic triads of the intended key, various other structural constraints were imposed to promote the key interpretation. Throughout the sequence, the succession of chords conformed to the table of usual root progressions from Piston (1941/1978, p. 21; Table 8.3), and the sequences ended with a strong V–I cadence.

The eight remaining chord sequences were constructed to suggest a modulation, or shift between two different keys. Some of these pairs of keys are closely related, others more distant. For example, Schoenberg (1954/1969) classifies C major and G major as "direct and close"; at the other end of the extreme are C minor and C♯ minor, which are classified as "distant." His classifications consider not only key distances, but also the means through which the modulation is effected, whether "direct" or "indirect." All these sequences were constructed according to the same general plan. In them, the first chord was either II or IV, the second always V, and the third I, so that the first three chords constituted a cadence in the first intended key. The fourth chord and fifth chords were also diatonic triads in the first key, except that the fifth chord was also a diatonic triad in the second intended key (and so was a pivot chord). Then, the sixth chord in each case is a diatonic triad in the second key only. The

Table 9.1. Chord sequences used in probe tone experiment*

Modulation	First Key	Second Key	Chord 1	Chord 2	Chord 3	Chord 4	Chord 5	Chord 6	Chord 7	Chord 8	Chord 9
No	C major	C major	F major, C: IV	G major, V	A minor, vi	F major, IV	C major, I	A minor, vi	D minor, ii	G major, V	C major, I
No	C minor	C minor	F minor, c: iv	G major, V	Ab major, VI	F minor, iv	C minor, i	Ab major, VI	D diminished, ii°	G major, V	C minor, i
Yes: Direct and close	C major	G major	F major, C: IV / G:	G major, V (I)	C major, I (IV)	A minor, vi (ii)	E minor, iii (vi)	B minor, iii	E minor, vi	D major, V	G major, (V) I
Yes: Direct and close	C major	A minor	F major, C: IV / a: (VI)	G major, V	C major, I	F major, IV (VI)	D minor, ii (iv)	E major, V	B diminished, (vii°) ii°	E major, V	A minor, (vi) (i)
Yes: Close	C minor	F minor	D diminished, c: ii° / f:	G major, V	C minor, i	Ab major, VI	F minor, iv (i)	Db major, VI	Bb minor, iv	C major, V	F minor, (iv) i
Yes: Close	C minor	C major	D diminished, c: ii° / C:	G major, V (V)	C minor, i (iii)	Ab major, VI	G major, V (vi)	A minor, VI	F major, IV	G major, V	C major, I
Yes: Indirect but close	C minor	Ab major	D diminished, c: ii° / Ab:	G major, V	C minor, i (iii)	Ab major, VI (I)	F minor, iv (vi)	Eb major, V	Bb minor, ii	Eb major, V	Ab major, (VI) I
Yes: Indirect and remote	C major	D minor	F major, C: IV / d:	G major, V	C major, I	A minor, vi	D minor, ii (i)	Bb major, VI	E diminished, ii°	A major, V	D minor, (ii) i
Yes: Indirect and remote	C major	Bb major	F major, C: IV / Bb: (V)	G major, V	C major, I	A minor, vi	F major, IV (V)	G minor, vi	Eb major, IV	F major, (IV) V	Bb major, I
Yes: Distant	C minor	C# minor	D diminished, c: ii° / c#:	G major, V	C minor, i	G major, V	Ab major, VI (V)	A major, VI	F# minor, iv	G# minor, (VI) V	C# minor, i

*Minor keys and chords are indicated by lower-case letters.

final three chords constitute a cadence in the second key, ending with a V–I progression in the last two serial positions. Again, the ordering of the chords generally conformed to Piston's table of common root progressions.

Listeners, who all had at least a moderate level of musical training, showed strong agreement with one another; therefore their data were averaged. These average rating profiles were then compared to the rating profiles from the earlier experiment using unambiguous key-defining contexts (Krumhansl & Kessler, 1982; Table 2.1). For this purpose, each of the nine rating profiles for each sequence was correlated with the earlier rating profiles for each of the 24 major and minor keys. For example, the rating profile after the first chord was correlated with that for C major, D♭ major, and so on. The same correlations were computed for the rating profile after the second chord, and similarly for the third through ninth rating profiles. This gives a measure of the strength of each possible key interpretation at each point in time (see Chapter 4 for more discussion of the rationale for considering key strength to be a matter of degree). Various analyses were then undertaken to find patterns contained in the data, particularly as they reflected the listeners' abstraction of a sense of key from the chord sequences.

The series of analyses will be described in detail with respect to the nonmodulating sequence in C major. Then, the results for the other sequences will be presented more briefly. In the first analysis, each of the nine rating profiles for the nonmodulating sequence in C major was correlated with the rating profiles for all possible major and minor keys. If listeners were, in fact, interpreting the sequence in terms of the intended key of C major, then the correlations between the rating data for this sequence and that for unambiguous C major contexts should be high. These correlations with the C major profile are shown as the solid line in the left-hand graph of Figure 9.2 for each of the nine serial positions of the sequence. As expected, the correlations were generally quite high, and tended to increase throughout the sequence. Peaks in the correlations occurred for the fifth and ninth positions in the sequence at which a tonic, I, chord was sounded. However, after the first couple of chords, the correlations with the C major key profile were already quite high, indicating that the key was quite well established even before the tonic chord was heard.

The second analysis tested whether these correlations could be accounted for in terms of local effects of the individual chords of the sequence. In other words, can the correlations with the intended key be attributed to the separate chords, or were the listeners integrating information over multiple chords and abstracting from them a sense of key? For this purpose, we needed some measure of the degree to which each individual chord would produce the same results. In a subsidiary experiment—described in more detail in Krumhansl and Kessler (1982)—other

SEQUENCE: C MAJOR

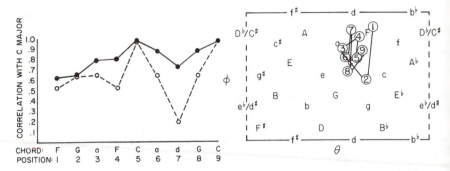

Fig. 9.2. The results for the sequence intended to suggest C major (Krumhansl & Kessler, 1982). The diagram on the left shows the correlations between the probe tone ratings at each serial position and the C major key profile (solid line) compared with the correlations between the probe tone ratings for isolated chords and the C major key profile (dashed lines). The diagram on the right shows the results of the multidimensional unfolding analysis. The sense of C major is strong and increases throughout the sequence.

listeners were presented with single major, minor, and diminished chords, followed by all possible probe tones. This gave a rating profile for each of these chord types. Various roots were used for each of the chord types, but the results were similar when the profiles were shifted to compensate for the different roots of the chords. Therefore, the values were averaged to produce a maximally stable rating profile for major, minor, and diminished chords.

These chord rating profiles were then used in the present analysis in the following way. For each chord of the sequence, its rating profile was correlated with that of the intended key. These correlations are shown in the left-hand graph of Figure 9.2 as the dashed line. The value for the first position in the sequence shows the correlation between the rating profile for a single F major chord and the rating profile for a C major key; in other words, it shows the degree to which a single F major chord would be expected to establish the C major key. The value for the second position in the sequence shows the correlation between the rating profile for a single G major chord and the rating profile for the C major key; in other words it shows the degree to which a single G major chord would be expected to establish the C major key. For each of the remaining nine chords, the correlations were computed in a similar way, and the resulting values are plotted in the figure.

As would be expected, the two graphs were close together in the initial positions of the sequence. Listeners have only heard a few chords of the sequence and therefore the values for the experiment would be expected to resemble closely the values for the isolated chords. However, by the third serial position, the two graphs began to diverge, with the sense of key stronger than would be implied by the individual chords in isolation. The coincidence of the graphs at the fifth and ninth serial positions can be understood because at these points the tonic triad, I, was sounded, which strongly suggests the key even in isolation. However, at other positions after the initial chords, the correlations with the intended key were higher than predicted by the single chords. Thus, listeners were integrating information about the possible functions of the chords across multiple chords, and arriving at a sense of the intended key that was stronger than each individual chord would predict.

The results of the final analysis are shown in the plot on the right-hand side of Figure 9.2. This analysis finds a point on the torus representation of keys that expresses the relative strength of each possible key interpretation for each position in the chord sequence. The particular method used is called multidimensional unfolding, which is described in detail by Carroll (1972). It determines a point or vector in a spatial configuration that reflects the psychological distance between an object and a set of other objects. In this case, the method finds a point on the torus representation of musical keys that expresses the distance between the listeners' sense of key (after each successive chord) and each of the 24 major and minor keys. The values entered into the analysis were the correlations between each of the nine profiles and each of the 24 major and minor keys. The resulting points are labeled in the figure according to the position in the sequence at which the rating profile was generated.

The point found on the torus following the first chord was close to the key of F major, which would be expected given that listeners had only heard an isolated F major chord. Following the second, G major chord, the point moved toward the keys of C major, C minor, and G major, in which the G major chord plays important harmonic functions. After this, however, the points clustered fairly tightly around the intended key of C major. Some local effects of the individual chords are evident. For example, the point for the seventh position in the sequence reflected the sounding of the D minor chord in that position. Despite these local variations, the sense of the key of C major was apparently quite firmly established following the initial chords of the sequence. This method of representation provides a depiction of the developing sense of key, which in this case was found to settle quite quickly in the region around the key of C major.

Figure 9.3 shows the corresponding results for the nonmodulating sequence in C minor. The sense of the key of C minor was quite strong, particularly after the sounding of the tonic triad in the fifth serial position. The correlations with the intended key from the experiment exceeded those for single chords in all positions exclusive of those containing the

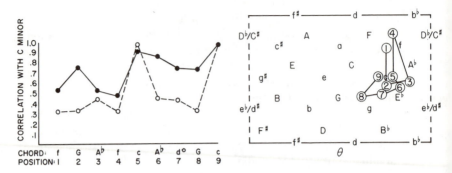

Fig. 9.3. The results for the sequence intended to suggest C minor (Krumhansl & Kessler, 1982). The sense of C minor is quite strong throughout, although there is more variability early in the sequence than late in the sequence.

tonic triad itself, in which both values were high. However, in the initial position, this finding is anomalous given that only a single chord had been sounded. It can be attributed only to the tendency of the rating profiles to show more variability early in the sequences, particularly when the initial chord was minor or diminished and the intended key was minor (other examples of this will be seen later). As is apparent in the right-hand plot, the points for the sequence on the torus representation tended to cluster around C minor, although this sequence showed more variation than the nonmodulating sequence in C major. In other words, even though the two nonmodulating sequences had parallel constructions in terms of the roots of the chords, the sense of key was more firmly established by the sequence in the major key than by the sequence in the minor key.

Figure 9.4 shows the results for the sequence intended to suggest a modulation between C major and G major. The plot on the upper left shows the correlations with the C major key profile; the plot on the right, those with the G major key profile. The sense of the C major key was quite firmly established following the third chord, and continued to exceed the local effects of the chords until the final position with the conclusion of the cadence in the key of G major. The sense of the G major key increased throughout the sequence and exceeded the effects of the component chords from the fourth position through the remainder of the sequence. These effects were mirrored in the torus representation at the bottom of the figure, where the points shifted from the C major to the G major region. Figure 9.5 shows a similar pattern for the sequence intended to modulate between C major and its relative minor, A minor. Again, there was a relatively early shift to the second key, and some sense of the first key was maintained throughout most of the sequence. The

SEQUENCE: C MAJOR – G MAJOR

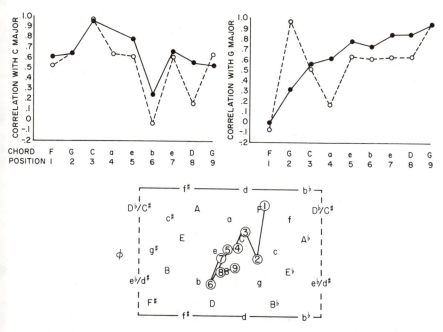

Fig. 9.4. The results for the sequence intended to suggest a modulation from C major to G major (Krumhansl & Kessler, 1982). The diagram on the left shows the correlations between the probe tone ratings at each serial position and the C major key profile (solid line) compared with the correlations between the probe tone ratings for isolated chords and the C major key profile (dashed lines). The diagram on the right shows the same correlations with the G major key profile. The lower diagram shows the results of the multidimensional unfolding analysis. The sense of C major was quite strong and remained so until the final chord; the sense of G major increased throughout the sequence.

results for these two sequences suggest that the sense of key shifts easily between closely related keys, maintaining some sense of both until the second key was firmly established by the conclusion of the cadence.

Figures 9.6, 9.7, and 9.8 show the results for the three sequences beginning in C minor and modulating to keys that are considered by Schoenberg (1954/1969) to be relatively closely related to C minor, although none of these modulations is classified as "direct." The instability of the rating profiles in the first position of these sequences, which contained a diminished II chord in the intended minor key, was again apparent in the graphs on the upper left. However, the C minor key was quite firmly established by the third serial position. For the sequences that modulate to the key of F minor and Ab major, some sense of the initial key was maintained

SEQUENCE: C MAJOR - A MINOR

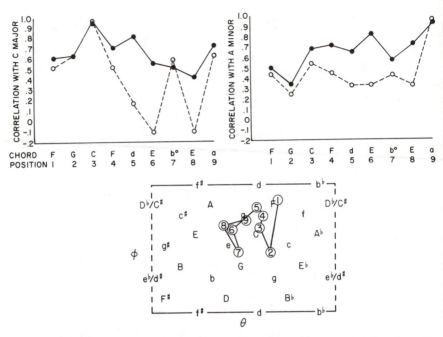

Fig. 9.5.   The results for the sequence intended to suggest a modulation from C major to A minor (Krumhansl & Kessler, 1982). The sense of C major was quite strong and remained so until the final chord; the sense of A minor generally increased throughout the sequence.

throughout the sequence. For the sequence that modulates to C major, the sense of the initial key declined more after the modulation, perhaps because the parallel major dominates over its parallel minor. In all three cases, the second key did not become perceptually established until the sixth or seventh serial position, developing somewhat later than in the sequences just described. The points on the torus representation generally confirmed these conclusions. It is interesting to note the path outlined by the points for the sequence modulating between C minor and A♭ major keys. Schoenberg classified them as "indirect but close," and the path taken between these two keys passed through the region of E♭ major (the relative major of the initial key and the key of the dominant of the second key). Thus, this mode of representation expresses not just the distance between the initial and final keys, but also something about the path distance traversed by the particular sequences.

SEQUENCE: C MINOR – F MINOR

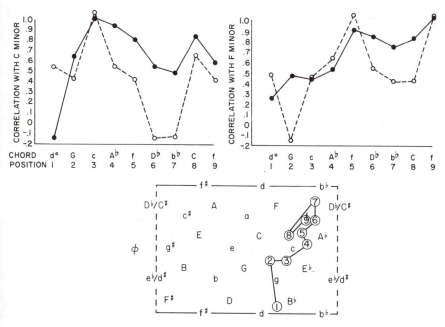

Fig. 9.6. The results for the sequence intended to suggest a modulation from C minor to F minor (Krumhansl & Kessler, 1982). The sense of C minor was quite strong and remained so until the final chord; the sense of F minor developed after the sixth chord.

Figures 9.9 and 9.10 show the analyses of the two sequences beginning in C major and modulating to keys considered as "indirect and remote." Of these two sequences, the sequence modulating to D minor appeared to be less remote. Some sense of the initial key was maintained until the end of the sequence, and the sense of the second key was established by the sixth serial position. The path between these two keys traversed through the region of A minor (the relative minor of the initial key) and F major (the relative major of the final key). In contrast, the results for the sequence that modulates between C major and B♭ major shows a sudden shift between the two keys in the seventh serial position, where the sense of the first key dropped markedly. This drop was accompanied by a rapid rise in the strength of the second key. Thus, this modulation was heard as an abrupt shift between the two keys.

Finally, Figure 9.11 shows the results for the modulation between C minor and C♯ minor, which Schoenberg described as "distant." This

SEQUENCE: C MINOR – C MAJOR

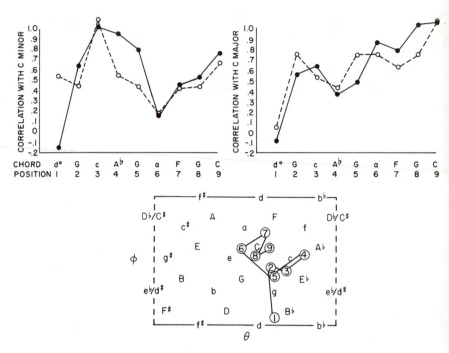

Fig. 9.7. The results for the sequence intended to suggest a modulation from C minor to C major (Krumhansl & Kessler, 1982). The sense of C minor was quite strong until after the sixth chord, where it was suppressed by the stronger sense of C major.

modulation is effected by the enharmonically equivalent A♭ major chord (the VI of C minor) and G♯ major chord (the V of C♯ major), which appeared as the pivot chord in the fifth serial position. As can be seen, the sense of the first key was established by the third serial position, and was maintained in the fourth serial position and the fifth serial position, which contained the pivot chord. As the sense of the first key was quite strong at this point, the pivot chord was clearly interpreted in terms of the initial key of C minor. When the A major chord is sounded in the sixth serial position, the sense of neither the first nor the second key was very strong. The corresponding point on the torus representation was located close to the key of A major (in which the sixth cord of the sequence is I) and D minor (in which it is V). Thus, this point reflects the dominance of local chord effects. By the seventh chord, however, the sense of key has shifted to the region of the new key, suppressing the sense of the initial

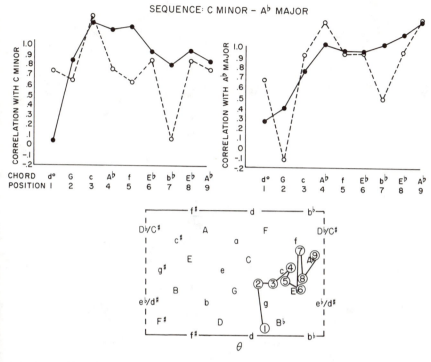

Fig. 9.8. The results for the sequence intended to suggest a modulation from C minor to A♭ major (Krumhansl & Kessler, 1982). The sense of C minor was quite strong and remained so until the final chord; the sense of A♭ major developed after the seventh chord.

key entirely. It is interesting to note that, as the torus representation wraps around, the two keys of C minor and C♯ minor are not so distantly related. However, the path taken by the modulation was the long way around the torus, reflecting the particular means used to bring about the modulation.

To summarize, the probe tone method, in conjunction with the spatial representation of musical keys, provides an approach to understanding continually unfolding processes in music perception. In this application, the question addressed was how the sense of key develops and changes over time. The results showed that listeners develop a sense of key by integrating the possible harmonic functions of the individual chords over time. This sense of key, however, changes as subsequent events occur that suggest another key. This process is ideally served by the strong interconnection between chord functions and key structure, which has been demonstrated in numerous ways in the two preceding chapters. Chords

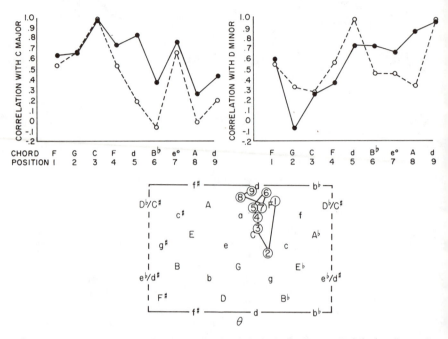

Fig. 9.9. The results for the sequence intended to suggest a modulation from C major to D minor (Krumhansl & Kessler, 1982). Some sense of the key of C major was maintained until the end of the sequence; the sense of D minor developed after the sixth chord.

play multiple roles in closely related keys, which permits listeners to entertain alternative tonal interpretations and thus easily assimilate modulations to nearby keys. When the keys are more distantly related, listeners tend to resist the change to the new key longer, and then suddenly jump to the new key, suppressing the sense of the initial key. The probe tone technique has, in this experiment, proved useful for investigating the process through which the sense of tonality arises from musical events as they are sounded over time. In the next experiment, the technique is applied to investigate whether listeners can perceive the tonal organizations of two simultaneous keys.

Tonal hierarchies and polytonality

This study looked at the perceptual effects of a polytonal passage simultaneously using materials from two distantly related keys. The series of experiments was described in the article by Krumhansl and Schmuckler

SEQUENCE: C MAJOR – B♭ MAJOR

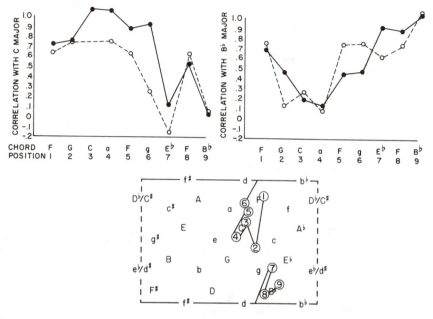

Fig. 9.10. The results for the sequence intended to suggest a modulation from C major to B♭ major (Krumhansl & Kessler, 1982). The initial sense of C major dropped sharply in the seventh serial position, accompanied by a rapid rise in the sense of B♭ major.

(1986) and will be outlined only briefly here, with emphasis given to results bearing on issues raised to this point. Western composers in the twentieth century have often found traditional tonal-harmonic resources too confining and have developed other techniques for organizing pitch materials. One of these techniques—an extension of tonality—is polytonality, in which materials from more than one key are used simultaneously. The experiment employed one of the most well-known and striking examples of polytonal writing from Stravinsky's *Petroushka* (the passage, from the beginning of the second tableau, is shown in Figure 9.12). It presents what has come to be known as the "Petroushka chord" and consists basically of arpeggiated C and F♯ major chords, with the C major chord sounded in root position and the F♯ major chord sounded in first inversion. The two chords are played simultaneously in the same pitch range (initially by the first and second clarinets and then by the piano), and with the same rhythmic patterns and contours.

Traditionally, the passage has been considered to be bitonal with tonal centers of C and F♯; indeed, this was how Stravinsky himself described

SEQUENCE: C MINOR – C# MINOR

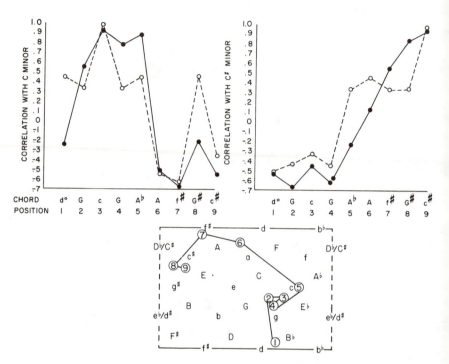

Fig. 9.11. The results for the sequence intended to suggest a modulation from C minor to C# minor (Krumhansl & Kessler, 1982). The initial sense of C minor drops sharply after the sixth chord; the sense of C# minor appears after the seventh chord; no sense of either key is apparent after the sixth chord.

it (Stravinsky & Craft, 1962, p. 56). However, because the passage contains only the tonic triads, it might more appropriately be called "bichordal." Either interpretation raises the question of whether listeners perceive the two implied tonalities and, if so, whether they hear them as separate and independent entities or whether they hear them as perceptually fused together. To address these questions, the probe tone technique was employed with the passage serving as context. The rating data were then analyzed to determine whether the results could be accounted for in terms of the tonal hierarchies of the two component keys. Following this, divided and selective attention tasks—in which listeners were instructed to attend to one of the two components of the passage—examined the question of whether the two tonalities were heard as independent or as fused together.

Recently, the bitonal interpretation of the passage has been questioned

SECTION ONE

SECTION TWO

Fig. 9.12. Passage from Stravinsky's *Petroushka,* taken from the beginning of the second tableau, used in probe tone experiment (Krumhansl & Schmuckler, 1986). In the first experiment, listeners heard section one and sections one and two followed by all possible probe tones. The two voices in C and F♯ major were presented both separately and combined. Copyright 1986 by the Regents of the University of California. Adapted by permission of the publisher.

and, instead, the passage and much of Stravinsky's other music has been related to the octatonic collection (e.g., Berger, 1968; Van den Toorn, 1975, 1977, 1983). The octatonic collection consists of the eight tones: C, C♯/D♭, D♯/E♭, E, F♯/G♭, G, A, and A♯/B♭. This scale, containing an alternating pattern of whole and half steps, can also be described as the combination of two diminished triads: C, D♯/E♭, F♯/G♭, A; and C♯/D♭, E, G, A♯/B♭. (For this reason, it is called the diminished scale in jazz.) Notice that the set contains the tones of the C and F♯ major triads; these triads, according to Van den Toorn (1983, p. 53), constitute one of the main partitionings of the collection as employed by Stravinsky. Various approaches, which will be described later, were taken to evaluate this alternative theoretical interpretation.

In the first experiment, the passage shown in Figure 9.12 was played with the single-key voices presented both separately and simultaneously. These contexts were followed by each of the 12 tones of the chromatic scale, which the listeners rated in terms of how well it fit with the preceding context. The listeners in this experiment were all unfamiliar with the particular passage and probably with polytonal music more generally. The single-voice conditions were included to ensure that the two separate components established the expected keys. For this purpose, the ratings were correlated with the C and F♯ major key profiles from Krumhansl and Kessler (1982; Table 2.1). As expected, the probe tone ratings made following the single-voice contexts correlated strongly with the corresponding major-key profiles from the earlier experiment; the value for the C major voice was .88, and the value for the F♯ major voice was .94 ($p < .01$, for both). Thus, the two components, when played separately, clearly established the expected keys.

The C and F♯ major voices, when played simultaneously, produced the average rating data shown as the dashed line in Figure 9.13. Some influence of the two keys was evident; notice the relatively high ratings for C and G (the first and fifth scale degrees of the key of C major) and F♯ and C♯ (the first and fifth scale degrees of the key of F♯ major). The multiple-regression technique was applied to the ratings to see whether they could be modeled as a weighted additive combination of the tonal hierarchies of the two keys of C and F♯ major. The resulting multiple correlation ($R = .80$, $p < .01$) showed that this model provided a good fit to the data and the tonal hierarchies of both keys contributed significantly to the fit. (The solid line in Figure 9.13 shows the predictions of the regression equation.) This first analysis, then, supported the notion that listeners were rating the probe tones according to their positions in the tonal hierarchies of the keys of C and F♯ major.

However, the same result would have been obtained if some listeners were emphasizing one key while other listeners were emphasizing the other key because the analysis just described was done on the ratings averaged over listeners. To test this alternative account, the multiple-regression analysis was done for individual subjects separately. Figure 9.14 shows the regression weights for individual subjects for C major (horizontal axis) and F♯ major (vertical axis). If different listeners were emphasizing different keys, then there should be a negative trade-off between the regression weights for the two keys over listeners. Instead, the opposite pattern was found; listeners with relatively large weights for one key also tended to have relatively large weights for the other key. The

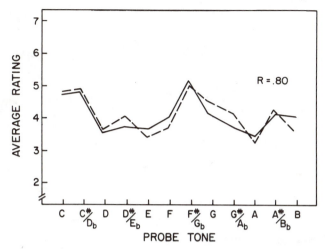

Fig. 9.13. Probe tone ratings (Krumhansl & Schmuckler, 1986) given to combined C and F♯ major passage (dashed line) compared to solution of regression equation using C and F♯ major key profiles (solid line). The significant multiple correlation showed that both C and F♯ major key profiles contributed to the fit of the probe tone ratings. Copyright 1986 by the Regents of the University of California. Reprinted by permission of the publisher.

positive relationship between the strengths of the two keys was reflected in a significant correlation, .67, between the regression weights for the two keys. This indicates that the contribution made by the tonal hierarchies of the two keys to the average ratings was not a consequence of averaging over listeners who focused on different keys. Thus, one viable account of the data appears to be as bitonal with both keys functional in perception.

Another possibility, suggested by the general correspondence between tonal hierarchies and tonal distributions discussed in Chapter 3, is that listeners were basing their responses on the distribution of tones in the musical passage. To test this, the frequency of occurrence (number of attacks) of each of the 12 tones of the chromatic scale was tabulated for the C major passage, the F♯ major passage, and the combined C and F♯ major passage. Using the frequency of occurrence of tones was preferable to using their durations because of the inclusion of a few very long tones (and, indeed, analyses using the durations produced less clear results). The effect of the distribution of tones was then evaluated by correlating the frequency of occurrence of the tones in the passage with the probe tone ratings. For all three passages, the correlations were highly significant, with a value of .95 for the C major context, .93 for the F♯ major contexts, and .88 for the combined C and F♯ major context. Thus, for

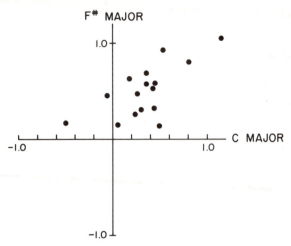

Fig. 9.14. Results of multiple-regression analysis predicting probe tone ratings for combined C and F ♯ major passage from C and F ♯ major key profiles for individual listeners (Krumhansl & Schmuckler, 1986). The horizontal axis corresponds to weight of C major key profile and vertical axis corresponds to weight of F ♯ major key profile. There is no evidence of a trade-off between the keys; instead, listeners whose responses showed influences of C major also showed influences of F ♯ major. Copyright 1986 by the Regents of the University of California. Reprinted by permission of the publisher.

all contexts, the probe tone ratings were systematically related to the frequency of occurrence of the 12 tones in the contexts sounded in the experiment.

A further analysis was performed to determine whether the tonal hierarchies contributed significantly to the ratings in addition to the distribution of tones. In this analysis, the probe tone ratings were entered into a multiple regression with the frequencies of occurrence of the tones in the passage and the quantified tonal hierarchies (Krumhansl & Kessler, 1982; Table 2.1). For example, the probe tone ratings made following the passage in C major were regressed against the frequency of occurrence of the tones in the C major passage and the quantified tonal hierarchy for C major. If effects of the tonal hierarchies are found over and above the effects of tone distributions, then this indicates that listeners were relating the musical passages to their internalized tonal hierarchies.

For the C major passage, this analysis resulted in a very significant multiple correlation, .98, indicating that these two variables accounted almost perfectly for the probe tone ratings. Significant contributions were made by both the distribution of tones and the C major key profile. This means that above and beyond the influence of the frequency of tone occurrence, there was a systematic effect of the quantified tonal hierarchy of C major. A similar result was obtained when the analogous analysis was performed on the data for the F ♯ major passage. The multiple correlation was .97, and both the distribution of tones in the passage and the quantified tonal hierarchy of F ♯ major contributed significantly to the correlation. Therefore, for both the single-voice conditions, the ratings reflected both the distribution of tones in the perceptually immediate context, and the hierarchy of tonal stability abstracted from the context.

A different pattern of results was found for the combined C and F ♯ major passage, however. In this case, the probe tone ratings were entered into a multiple regression with the frequency of occurrence of the tones in the combined C and F ♯ major passage, and the C major and F ♯ major key profiles. This resulted in a slightly lower multiple correlation of .93, which, however, was still highly significant. The main difference was that now only the distribution of tones in the context contributed significantly to the multiple correlation. Neither the C major key profile nor the F ♯ major key profile was systematically related to the probe tone ratings once the frequencies of occurrence of the tones in the context were taken into account. This suggests that, when making probe tone ratings following the combined C and F ♯ major passages, listeners relied almost exclusively on the distribution of tones on the perceptually immediate context. Although the ratings showed differentiation among the tones, it was apparently much more strongly determined by the distribution of tones than by a sense of the tonalities abstracted from the sounded events.

This last analysis calls the bitonal interpretation into question. No evidence was found to support the notion that the two tonalities were perceptually functional as organizational entities abstracted from the perceptually immediate context. The distribution of tones in the context more strongly determined the ratings than the tonal hierarchies of the two keys. The next experiments took a somewhat different approach to examining the bitonal interpretation. If listeners do hear the passage in terms of two independent tonalities, then it should be possible for them to attend selectively to one or another of the components in the combined C and F ♯ major passage. This prediction is based on the idea that if listeners interpret the tones in terms of their functions in the two keys, then they should be able to use this information to separate the two voices. Both these experiments employed listeners who were unfamiliar with the passage. It was played dichotically over earphones, with the C major voice played in one ear and the F ♯ major voice in the other ear.

In the first of the selective-attention experiments, the dichotically presented passage was followed by a probe tone presented to a single ear. Listeners were instructed to base their probe tone rating on the voice that had been sounded in the same ear as the probe tone. That is, if the probe tone was presented in the right ear, then they were to judge how well it fit with the voice that had been sounded in the right ear. Because the cue indicating the relevant voice was presented after the passage, it is called a "postcue." Multiple-regression analyses were then performed to determine whether the key of the cued voice had a larger weight than the key of the other voice. The top of Figure 9.15 shows the regression weights for C and F♯ major key profiles for the case in which the cued voice was C major (filled circles) and the case in which the cued voice was F♯ major (open circles). If listeners used the postcue effectively, then the open circles should be upward and to the left of the filled circles. This pattern was not found, suggesting that the two voices could not be separated on the basis of key. Alternatively, it may have been that excessive memory demands were placed on the listeners because the cue indicating the relevant voice was not presented until after the passage.

To eliminate the memory load associated with the postcue task, the second selective-attention experiment informed listeners in advance of the trials which ear would hear the voice on which they were to base their probe tone judgments. Thus, the cue is called a "precue." From trial to trial, the C and F♯ major voices were alternately presented to the different ears in a random fashion. The results of the multiple-regression analyses are shown in the bottom of Figure 9.15. Again, there was absolutely no evidence that listeners were able to attend selectively to one of the two component voices; the weights for the key of the cued voice were no greater than the weights for the key of the other voice. Other informal experiments, in which the voices were presented in different timbres and through spatially separated loudspeakers, produced similar results. Thus, these selective-attention experiments showed that listeners were unable to separate the voices on the basis of key, supporting the notion that the tonalities were not fully functional as separate and independent entities.

Before considering variables that may promote the apparent fusion of the two voices in this passage, the results of the next experiment in the series will be described briefly. Unlike the listeners who participated in the first three experiments, the listeners in this experiment had considerable experience with this particular passage. They were all members of the Cornell University orchestra, which had recently performed the piece in concert. The group included the two clarinetists and the pianist who had played the particular passage. Otherwise, the listeners had music backgrounds similar to those in other experiments. The central questions were whether the component keys would have stronger or weaker effects and whether they would be more or less separable than found previously. The experienced listeners participated in miniature replications of all three experimental designs: no cue, postcue, and precue.

The experienced listeners' results were virtually identical to those for the listeners in the first three experiments. The passage combining the C and F♯ major voices produced probe tone ratings that could be statistically decomposed into C and F♯ major key hierarchies. However, the ratings correlated more strongly with the distribution of tones (their fre-

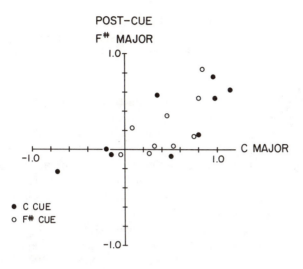

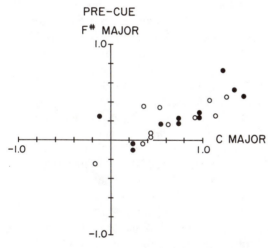

Fig. 9.15. Weights in multiple-regression analysis for C major key profile (horizontal axis) and F♯ major key profile (vertical axis) in postcue experiment (top) and precue experiment (bottom) from Krumhansl and Schmuckler (1986). The filled circles are for cued C major passage and open circles are for cued F♯ major passage. There is no evidence that listeners can use the cues to attend selectively to one component key; if they had, the open circles would have been upward and to the left of the filled circles. Copyright 1986 by the Regents of the University of California. Reprinted by permission of the publisher.

quencies of occurrence) in the passage than with the tonal hierarchies. The listeners were also unable to attend selectively to one component voice on the basis of either the postcue or the precue when the passage was presented dichotically. Thus, extensive experience with the passage apparently did not enable listeners to perceive two abstract, independent tonalities. Instead, the results indicated that the two component voices were solidly fused together in perception and the perceived relative structural significance of tones was determined largely by the degree to which they were emphasized through repetition in the music.

The fusion of the two voices in this passage can be understood in light of research on perceptual organization in audition, which was summarized briefly in Chapter 6. The two voices are presented close together in pitch and have virtually identical rhythms. Various empirical studies have shown that these conditions lead to perceptual fusion. Tones tend to belong to the same perceptual stream when they are close in pitch (Bregman & Campbell, 1971; Bregman & Pinker, 1978; Dowling, 1973; G. A. Miller & G. Heise, 1950; Van Noorden, 1975), and pitch proximity can override information about the location of the sound (Deutsch, 1975). Temporal synchrony is also a variable known to promote fusion (Dannenbring & Bregman, 1978; Bregman & Pinker, 1978; Rasch, 1978), and this is true even for dichotically presented tones (Warren & Bashford, 1976; Steiger & Bregman, 1982a,b). This literature, then, is entirely consistent with the present finding that listeners were unable to attend selectively to the two component voices of this passage.

In addition, it may be that listeners have difficulty perceiving two fully functional and independent tonalities when their hierarchies of stability conflict with one another. Consider the two keys of C and F♯ major suggested by this passage. The tendencies of unstable tones in these keys would often work in opposition. The tone F♯, for example, would be highly unstable in the key of C major (with a strong tendency to resolve to G), but would be the most stable tone in F♯ major. Similarly, the tone C would be highly unstable in F♯ major (with a strong tendency to resolve to C♯), but would be the most stable tone in C major. Listeners may be unable to feel the tendencies of unstable tones in more than one key simultaneously. The movement from instability to stability is one of the fundamental perceptual effects of tonality, and this passage—with its use of keys with conflicting tendencies—may prevent the two keys from becoming fully established. Instead, the materials from the two keys appear to fuse together into a single, complex organization.

Is the complex perceptual organization of this passage consistent with theoretical analyses in terms of the octatonic collection? We approached this question in two ways. First, we conducted an additional experiment in which the octatonic scale was used as context in a probe tone experiment. The octatonic scale was played in either ascending or descending form, and beginning and ending on either C or F♯. The ascending octatonic scale beginning on C is shown at the top of Figure 9.16. There was little effect of whether the scale was played in ascending or descending form, so these data were averaged. However, the tone with which it began and ended had a strong effect, so the data for the C and F♯ octatonic scales were not averaged. The probe tone ratings for the two octatonic scale contexts are shown at the bottom of Figure 9.16. Various analyses of these data suggested that the octatonic scale, in isolation, functioned somewhat like a dominant seventh chord requiring resolution to the tonic; the probe tone ratings following the octatonic scale beginning on C resembled those for F major, and the probe tone ratings following the octatonic scale beginning on F♯ resembled those for B major. This may be interesting in light of Van den Toorn's partition (1983) of the octatonic collection as dominant sevenths.

However, the primary reason for obtaining the probe tone ratings with the octatonic scales was to determine how well they predicted the probe tone ratings for the *Petroushka* passage. The data for all conditions in the

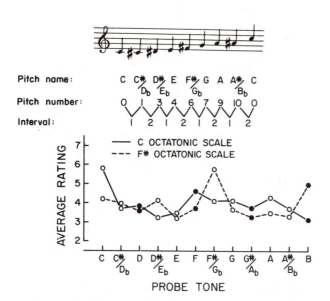

Fig. 9.16.   Tones and intervals in C octatonic scale used as context in the probe tone experiment (top); probe tone ratings for C and F♯ octatonic scale context (bottom) from Krumhansl and Schmuckler (1986). The ratings made following the octatonic scales were not strong predictors of the ratings made following the passage from Stravinsky's Petroushka. Copyright 1986 by the Regents of the University of California. Reprinted by permission of the publisher.

four previous experiments were considered. Each set of probe tone ratings for the combined C and F♯ major passage was entered into a regression analysis using the C and F♯ octatonic scale data as predictors. In no case did the octatonic scale data provide a satisfactory account of the ratings; each multiple correlation was nonsignificant. It should be remembered that the octatonic collection was presented in the probe tone experiment in a musically neutral scalar form. It may be that these contexts were insufficient to evoke the kinds of organizations implicit in more complex music written with reference to the octatonic collection and, thus, the probe tone data for the octatonic scale contexts are not good predictors of those made following the musical passage itself.

Van den Toorn (1983) identified a number of different partitionings of the octatonic collection in Stravinsky's music. The partitioning is determining by how a particular composition emphasizes various tones of the collection, giving rise to a hierarchy of priorities. For the passage considered here, he (p. 53) proposed the following diagram of priorities:

Level 2: 0,6 = C, F♯

Level 3: (0 4 7) on 0,6 = (C E G) (F♯ A♯ C♯)

Level 4: (0 4 7) (6 10 1) = (C E G) (F♯ A♯ C♯)

Level 5: 0 1 (3) 4 6 7 (9) 10 (0) = C C♯ (D♯) E F♯ G (A) A♯ (C)

The tones of greatest priority, C and F♯, are at the highest and most significant level. The next two levels show the major chord partitions on C and F♯. The complete octatonic collection appears at the lowest level; the parentheses indicate that the tones D♯ and A are not operative at this level. It should be noted that the G♯/A♭ tones that appear in the passage are not in the octatonic collection.

Van den Toorn's diagram (1983) for the passage essentially constitutes a set of predictions for the relative structural significance of tones in this passage. In order to compare it to the probe tone data, the diagram was roughly quantified as follows:

Tone:	C	C♯	D	D♯	E	F	F♯	G	G♯	A	A♯	B
(C E G) partition	2	0	0	0	1	0	0	1	0	0	0	0
(F♯ A♯ C♯) partition	0	1	0	0	0	0	2	0	0	0	1	0

The value of 2 was assigned to tones appearing at the highest level, 1 to tones appearing at lower levels, and 0 to tones that do not appear in the diagram. These values were then entered into a multiple regression with the probe tone data for the combined C and F♯ major passage for all four experiments. Despite the rough quantification of the diagram, it accounted quite well for the data. In the six cases (the no-cue, postcue, and precue designs for inexperienced and experienced listeners), all but one of the multiple correlations was significant; the value in the remaining case fell just short of the required level. More importantly, in each case the value of the multiple regression was higher than the corresponding value using the C and F♯ major key profiles (Krumhansl & Kessler, 1982) as predictors. The multiple correlations for the C and F♯ major chord partitions averaged .76 ($p < .05$); those for the C and F♯ major key profiles averaged .67, which was not significant. Thus, the theoretical model produced a better fit than the tonal hierarchies of C and F♯ major.

To summarize, Van den Toorn's theoretical model (1983) provided the most satisfactory account of the perceptual effects of the passage. The probe tone ratings conformed quite well to his diagram of priorities. They also correlated strongly with the relative frequencies with which the tones were sounded in the passage. This convergence suggests that both Van den Toorn's analysis and the listeners' responses were based on the relative emphasis given the tones by their repetition in the music. A hierarchy of priorities was perceptually established by the distribution of tones in the passage, a hierarchy that coincides with the theoretical analysis. Little evidence supported the idea that two tonalities were perceptually functional as abstract and independent organizational entities. The C and F♯ major key profiles were weaker predictors of the probe tone data than either the theoretical model or the distributions of tones in the music, and listeners were unable to attend selectively to one of the component voices. This was true for listeners independent of their prior experience with the musical passage. Grouping principles operate to fuse the two voices together; in addition, it may be difficult to perceive the contradictory tendencies of tones in these two very distantly related keys. These variables appear to prevent the two tonalities from becoming established perceptually, and the tonal hierarchy of this passage mirrors the explicit emphasis given the tones in the music. Experiments presented in the next chapter explore further the question of how tonal hierarchies are formed in styles outside traditional tonal-harmonic music with which listeners may be unfamiliar.

10. Tonal hierarchies in atonal and non-Western tonal music

Music takes extremely diverse forms historically and cross-culturally. The preceding chapters have essentially all been concerned with pitch structures in Western tonal-harmonic music. The rationale for this initial focus was to develop experimental methodologies, and establish basic results, in the context of a musical style that has received extensive theoretical analysis. The methods have produced results generally consistent with theoretical predictions giving them external validation. The experiments reported in this chapter extend the probe tone technique (Krumhansl & Shepard, 1979; Krumhansl & Kessler, 1982; Chapter 2) to music that structures pitch in ways quite different from tonal-harmonic music. The chapter begins with studies in which the materials are written in the style of 12-tone serialism. This music is called atonal because no pitch takes the role of a tonic; in addition, traditional harmonies are not employed. The studies summarized in the remainder of the chapter apply the experimental technique cross-culturally to music that is tonal in the sense of establishing hierarchies of stability. However, the intervals of the scales are different from those of major and minor scales, and the harmonic element of traditional Western music is absent. Comparing the results of the experiments provides information about how these structural differences affect the way the music is organized in perception.

A second motivation was to assess the role of prior experience. In all cases, it was possible to find listeners with varying degrees of familiarity with the style. As has been shown in previous chapters, listeners internalize stylistic norms through experience, and these affect the way music is perceived and remembered. Musicians (e.g., Hindemith, 1952/1961, p. 40; L. B. Meyer, 1956, p. 63) and psychologists (e.g., Dowling, 1978) alike have assumed that listeners will inappropriately impose this knowledge on styles with which they are less familiar. In support of this, those of us most familiar with tonal-harmonic music are aware of the disquieting effect of other styles resulting from the mismatch between our expectations and the music. Our ability to remember and reproduce music in unfamiliar styles is severely limited. However, we may apprehend certain aspects of the music even on first hearing and, from these, begin to understand its underlying organization. This learning process will be facilitated if the listener is able to suspend style-inappropriate expectations and let the perceptual experience guide the search for patterns in the novel style.

The experimental results will be examined with an eye toward identifying strategies listeners bring to music in styles outside their experience.

Tonal hierarchies in 12-tone serial music

This section reviews two probe tone studies that explored the perceptual effects of 12-tone serial music. They were part of a longer series of experiments described in the article by Krumhansl, Sandell, and Sergeant (1987). The stimulus materials were based on two compositions by Schoenberg: the Wind Quintet (op. 26) and the String Quartet No. 4 (op. 37). These pieces are written in the style of 12-tone serialism. This style, the introduction of which is often attributed to Schoenberg, has had a profound effect on Western twentieth-century composition and theory. Its essential characteristic is that each composition is based on a specified order of the 12 tones of the chromatic scale, called the basic set, series, or tone row; each composition uses a different series. The series determines the order in which the tones appear, so that the entire set of 12 chromatic scale tones is presented before any one is repeated.

According to Schoenberg (1948/1975, p. 264), employing a series is advantageous because no pitch is repeated more frequently than any other and, because of this, no tone can be interpreted as a tonic.

The construction of a basic set of twelve tones derives from the intention to postpone the repetition of every tone as long as possible. . . . The emphasis given to a tone by premature repetition is capable of heightening it to the rank of a tonic. But the regular application of a set of twelve tones emphasizes all the others in the same manner, thus depriving one single tone of the priviledge [*sic*] of supremacy. It seemed in the first stages immensely important to avoid a similarity with tonality.

Octave doublings are avoided for the same reason. Other advantages cited by Schoenberg are that the series serves to unify a piece because the same series is used throughout, and that it regulates the appearance of dissonances because all tones are referred to the order of the series.

Despite the apparent limitations imposed by the use of the series, Schoenberg (1941/1975) stresses the compositional freedom of the style. A number of variables generate variety within 12-tone compositions. The series as a whole can be transposed to any pitch, and any tone can appear in any octave. Immediate repetitions of pitches are also allowed. In addition to the basic set (the series in prime form), it can be played in any of three mirror forms: the retrograde (which reverses the temporal order of the tones in the series), the inversion (which reverses the pitch direction of each interval in the series), and the retrograde inversion (which reverses the temporal order of the inversion). (Chapter 6 reviewed a number of studies examining the perceptual effects of these transformations.) The series may be used horizontally (as a melody) or vertically (forming harmonies); it can be divided between the main part and an accompaniment or between several contrapuntal parts. Also, it can be subdivided into smaller groups, such as four groups of three tones, which can be treated independently (e.g., reordered). Finally, all kinds of rhythmic variations are possible.

The Wind Quintet is one of the first compositions in which Schoenberg used the serial technique in a strict way. The series is shown in Figure 10.1. Locally, it has the quality of a whole-tone scale. Notice that the last tone plus the first 5 tones constitute one whole-tone scale, and the remaining tones, 6 through 11, constitute the other whole-tone scale. Also, the last 6 tones are related by a perfect fifth to the first 6 tones; each tone in the second half is transposed up a fifth from its corresponding tone in the first half, except the last tone, which is transposed down a fifth. This makes answers at the fifth (imitation of a sequence at an interval of a fifth) possible, a property exploited by Schoenberg in the piece. The series from the String Quartet No. 4 is also shown in Figure 10.1. It has rather different properties. If the first 6 tones are inverted and transposed down a fifth, the resulting pitches are identical to the last 6 tones (D C♯ A B♭ F E♭, when inverted, becomes D E♭ G F♯ B C♯, which, when transposed down a fifth, becomes G A♭ C B E F♯). Schoenberg (1941/1975, p. 225) recommended using series with this kind of property because they permit accompaniment with a transposed inversion without repeating any tone too soon. Also, at a local level, the series suggests different key regions. For example, the first group of 3 tones might be said to suggest A major or perhaps D major or minor; the second group of 3 tones might suggest B♭ major or E♭ major. These designations are approximate, of course, because the keys are not established through conventional means.

The contexts used in the first probe tone experiment were the first 3, 6, or 9 tones, or all 12 tones of the two series. Each of these contexts was followed by all possible probe tones from the chromatic scale. Listeners were instructed to rate how well the probe tone fit with the preceding context in the sense of the atonal idiom. The tones were all of equal duration, and each tone had components sounded in five octaves (see Figure 2.2), so that the octave in which the tones are notated in Figure 10.1 is arbitrary. The listeners were all musically trained, but varied in terms of their experience with atonal music. More than half had at least an undergraduate degree in music, and a number of the listeners had graduate-level training. The four context lengths were presented in order of increasing length in the first replication. Then, the entire set of context–probe tone combinations was repeated in a second complete replication.

The rationale for this design was threefold. First, context length was varied to investigate whether the probe tone ratings contained invariant patterns independent of how much of the series was presented on the trial. Second, the two replications were included to determine whether experience with the series in the first replication changed the pattern of

Wind Quintet

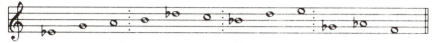

String Quartet no 4

Fig. 10.1.   The series from Schoenberg's Wind Quintet (top) and String Quartet No. 4 (bottom). Contexts in the first probe tone experiment (Krumhansl, Sandell, & Sergeant, 1987) consisted of the first three, six, or nine tones, or the complete series. Tone components were sounded over a five-octave range, so the octave indicated is arbitrary. Copyright 1987 by the Regents of the University of California. Reprinted by permission of the publisher.

responding in the second replication. Third, these musically neutral statements of the series were used to obtain basic data to compare with the second probe tone experiment (described later), which used actual excerpts from the two pieces.

Principles of 12-tone serial composition suggest that a number of variables may influence the probe tone ratings. First, if listeners have internalized the principle that no tone is to be repeated before the series is complete, then ratings for probe tones contained in the incomplete contexts should be lower than tones not yet sounded. Second, listeners may learn the order of the tones in the series in the first replication of the experiment, and give higher ratings to tones immediately following the incomplete contexts in the second replication. The final variable has to do with tonal effects, and there would seem to be two possibilities here. It may be that listeners perceive all tones as equal, consistent with Schoenberg's description, and the ratings will be essentially the same for all tones. Alternatively, it may be that listeners understand the method as seeking to avoid traditional key structures, and will give low ratings to tones that are consistent with local key implications.

A preliminary analysis of the data showed large differences between listeners in the pattern of responding. Two basic patterns, which were in most respects diametrically opposite one another, could be identified. Therefore, the listeners were divided into two groups, called group 1 and group 2, according to these patterns. Intersubject agreement was reasonably high within groups, although considerably higher for group 1 listeners (in fact, all intersubject correlations were individually significant) than for group 2 listeners. The music background questionnaire showed listeners in the first group tended to have more academic training in music (it included all listeners with graduate-level training) and more experience with atonal music. Neither of these background characteristics, nor any others assessed by the questionnaire, sharply defined group membership, however. The discussion here will emphasize the results for group 1 listeners because of their greater interest from the point of view of the theory of 12-tone serialism.

Figure 10.2 shows the group 1 probe tone ratings for the four context lengths for the series from the Wind Quintet and String Quartet No. 4. The probe tones are ordered on the horizontal axis according to their position in the series. Tones actually sounded in the context are to the left of the dashed lines in each case. The position of the probe tone in the series had one of the strongest effects on the ratings. Tones sounded in the incomplete statements of the series were rated lower (with an average of 3.00) than tones not yet sounded (with an average of 4.61). This finding is consistent with the principle requiring the series be complete before any tone is repeated. Among tones contained in the contexts, lowest ratings tended to be given to those sounded most recently. To evaluate this effect statistically, a recency value of 1 was assigned to the last tone, a value of 2 to the second to last tone, and so on. The ratings correlated significantly with the recency of the probe tone in the contexts ($r = .64$ and .79 for the Wind Quintet and String Quartet, respectively, $p < .01$ for both). (The positive sign of these correlations means that the lower ratings were given to more recently sounded tones.) These serial-position effects meant that no invariant patterns were contained in the ratings across the four context lengths.

The second effect of interest was whether higher ratings were given to tones that immediately follow the incomplete contexts in the series than tones that appear later. This effect was assessed by correlating the ratings for tones not contained in the incomplete contexts with how many positions later they appear in the series. For neither of the pieces was the correlation significant for group 1 listeners; nor were the ratings for immediately following tones consistently higher in the second replication than in the first. This analysis looked at the fourth tone of the series when the context contained three tones, the seventh tone of the series when the context contained six tones, and the tenth tone of the series when the context contained nine tones. The ratings for these tones increased by an average of only .55 from the first to the second replication.

Thus, despite the extensive opportunities to become familiar with the order of the tones in the series in the first replication of the experiment, this variable did not consistently influence the ratings in the second replication of the experiment. It should be remembered that the explicit instructions were not to judge how many positions beyond the incomplete contexts the probe tone appears in the series. However, the serial-position effects described earlier suggested that listeners did take order into

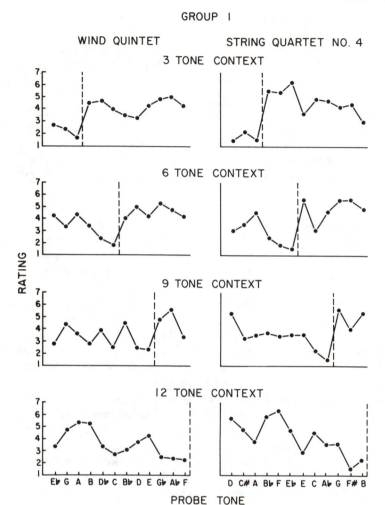

GROUP I

WIND QUINTET STRING QUARTET NO. 4

3 TONE CONTEXT

6 TONE CONTEXT

9 TONE CONTEXT

12 TONE CONTEXT

RATING

PROBE TONE

Fig. 10.2. Probe tone ratings for group 1 listeners from the first probe tone experiment of Krumhansl, Sandell, and Sergeant (1987). These listeners had, on average, more academic training and experience with atonal music. Tones are ordered along the horizontal axis as in the series, and tones sounded in the contexts (consisting of 3, 6, 9, or 12 tones) are to the left of the dashed lines. Copyright 1987 by the Regents of the University of California. Reprinted by permission of the publisher.

account in a very general way in forming their judgments; at least, they reliably differentiated between tones contained in the incomplete contexts and tones not yet sounded. It seems possible, then, that listeners did not precisely remember the order of tones in the series even though they had considerable exposure to it in the first replication of the experiment.

The final analysis examined the probe tone ratings for influences of local key implications of the contexts. More details of this analysis, which is somewhat complicated, can be found in Krumhansl, Sandell, and Sergeant (1987). The first step was to characterize key implications systematically in a way that could be compared to the probe tone ratings. For this purpose, we used the key-finding algorithm described in Chapter 4. In what we called the "unweighted model," the tones sounded in the contexts of this experiment were assigned the value 1; tones not sounded in the contexts were assigned the value 0. These values were then correlated with the 24 major and minor key profiles (Krumhansl & Kessler, 1982, Table 2.1). The correlations gave 24 values, called the key strength vector, for the context in question.

The unweighted model could not be applied to the complete 12-tone contexts (because all tones would have a value of 1, making it impossible to compute a correlation). For this reason, an alternative model, called the "weighted" model, was also used. If a tone was not sounded in the context, then it was assigned the value 0. The first tone in the context was assigned the value 1, the second 2, the third 3, and so on. The weighted model assumes that tones sounded recently are perceptually more salient than tones sounded earlier. For context lengths three, six, and nine (where comparisons between the two models could be made), the models agreed well. Moreover, the key strength values corresponded quite well with musical intuitions and, as would be expected given the nature of the two series, the tonal strengths were greater in general for the String Quartet than for the Wind Quintet.

The second step in the analysis measured the degree to which group 1 listeners' ratings resembled those for any major or minor key. Each of the eight rating profiles (for the four context lengths and the two pieces) was correlated with the tonal hierarchies for all 24 major and minor keys. In general, the probe tone ratings resembled the tonal hierarchy of some key. This was especially true for the String Quartet, for which all four context lengths had some key or keys that correlated significantly with the probe tone ratings. Thus, the ratings in this experiment showed patterns similar to those found in previous experiments with strong key-defining contexts. However, what is the relationship between the keys resembling the listeners' probe tone ratings in this experiment and the local key implications of the contexts?

This question was assessed in the final step of the analysis. The key strength vectors for the contexts (their tonal implications quantified by the unweighted and weighted models) were correlated with the key strength vectors for the listeners' probe tone ratings (the correlations between their data and the tonal hierarchies). The correlations computed in this step would be high to the extent that the probe tone ratings fit with the tonal implications of the contexts. Rather than finding high correlations, the analysis found strong negative correlations, which means that the probe tone ratings resembled the hierarchy of a key that is very distant from the key suggested by the context. Each one of the correlations was individually significant (at $p < .05$) whether the unweighted or weighted model was used.

To summarize this analysis for effects of key implications, a very interesting pattern was found for group 1 listeners: lower ratings were given to tones that fit with local key suggestions and higher ratings were given to tones that work against these suggestions. This had the consequence that the probe tone ratings from this experiment resembled those for keys very distant from the keys implied by the contexts. Listeners were reversing the ordering of the ratings from those appropriate to tonal contexts. It is not clear whether this strategy was conscious or not, although a few of the listeners in this group commented on having used a response rule of this kind. In any case, the results suggest that diatonic tonal hierarchies were psychologically functional, although used in a way opposite to the way they function with tonal music. It would appear, then, that knowledge of tonal structures described in previous chapters was still operative, and listeners inverted the normal tone hierarchies to reflect the denial of key structures associated with 12-tone serial music.

The probe tone ratings for the remaining listeners, who constitute group 2, are shown in Figure 10.3. Their results were, in almost all respects, opposite to those for group 1 listeners. Tones sounded in the incomplete statements of the series were rated higher (with an average of 4.93) than tones not yet sounded (with an average of 4.15). Among tones contained in the contexts, highest ratings tended to be given to those sounded most recently. This effect was substantiated by correlating the ratings with the recency of the probe tone in the excerpt. The correlations were $r = -.75$ and $-.58$ for the Wind Quintet and String Quartet, respectively ($p < .01$ for both); the negative sign means that higher ratings were given to the more recent tones. Thus, these listeners tended to base their response on the extent to which the tones are emphasized in the context.

As for group 1 listeners, there were no serial-position effects for tones not contained in the incomplete contexts; nor were the ratings for tones immediately following the incomplete contexts higher in the second replication than the first (in fact, the ratings for the next tones decreased by an average of .44). Thus, no evidence indicated that these listeners learned, during the first replication of the experiment, to anticipate the tones that follow in the series after the incomplete contexts. Finally, their ratings did not strongly resemble those for unambiguous key-defining contexts, which can be understood because the traditional mechanisms for establishing keys are not present. However, some influence of keys was evident in the ratings, and these were generally consistent with local key implications. The key strength vectors for the contexts (their tonal implications quantified by the unweighted and weighted models) correlated positively with the key strength vectors for the listeners' probe tone

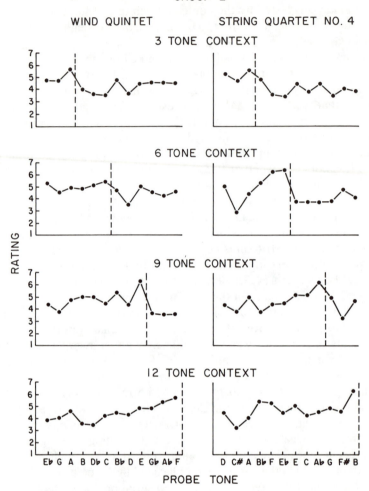

Fig. 10.3. Probe tone ratings for group 2 listeners from the first probe tone experiment of Krumhansl, Sandell, and Sergeant (1987). These listeners had, on average, less academic training and experience with atonal music. Tones are ordered along the horizontal axis as in the series, and tones sounded in the contexts (consisting of 3, 6, 9, or 12 tones) are to the left of the dashed lines. Copyright 1987 by the Regents of the University of California. Reprinted by permission of the publisher.

ratings (the correlations between their data and the tonal hierarchies). For the unweighted model, four of the six correlations were significant; for the weighted model, all eight correlations were significant. In other words, these listeners tended to give higher ratings to probe tones that were consistent with local key implications. This effect, and those of serial position described earlier, sharply distinguished between the two groups of listeners. Before considering the implications of these findings, the results of the second probe tone study will be summarized.

The contexts of the second probe tone experiment were actual excerpts from the two pieces (shown in Figures 10.4 and 10.5). Each excerpt was followed by all possible probe tones selected from a pitch range centered on that of the excerpt. The excerpts stated the complete series (in prime form) from the Wind Quintet and the String Quartet No. 4. They were taken from a single instrumental part, except in one case in which a tone was borrowed from another part to complete the series. Notice the extreme variations in terms of rhythm, number of immediate repetitions, contour, interval size and distribution, pitch range, and tempo. The central question was how these variables would influence the probe tone ratings. Will these surface characteristics produce different tonal hierarchies from those found for the musically neutral statements of the series used in the first experiment? In order to make direct comparisons with the earlier results, listeners were classified into group 1 and group 2 as before.

The results for group 1 listeners were highly consistent with the earlier

Fig. 10.4. Excerpts from Schoenberg's Wind Quintet used in the second probe tone experiment of Krumhansl, Sandell, and Sergeant (1987). Each excerpt presents the tone row in prime form; in the fourth excerpt the row is transposed. Copyright 1987 by the Regents of the University of California. Reprinted by permission of the publisher.

Fig. 10.5. Excerpts from Schoenberg's String Quartet No. 4 used in the second probe tone experiment of Krumhansl, Sandell, and Sergeant (1987). Each excerpt presents the tone row transposed but in prime form. Copyright 1987 by the Regents of the University of California. Reprinted by permission of the publisher.

results. The correlations between the probe tone ratings for the excerpts and the neutral statements of the series averaged .69 ($p < .05$) and were individually significant for all eight excerpts. (These correlations were computed after shifting the data in this experiment to compensate for the different starting tones of the excerpts.) Also, similar patterns were found for the four excerpts from the same piece. The average correlation between the rating profiles for the different excerpts from the same piece was .60 ($p < .05$). As would be expected, the correlations between rating profiles for excerpts from different pieces were lower, in fact, consistently negative. These results suggest that the perceived hierarchy of tones was largely unaffected by surface characteristics of the excerpts.

A number of additional analyses examined the rating data for residual effects of specific properties of the excerpts. These properties are listed in Table 10.1. The first property was the recency of the probe tone in the excerpt (the last tone was scored 1, the second to last tone was scored 2, etc.). The next three properties concerned the pitch height of the probe tone in the excerpt. The first measured its absolute pitch height, the sec-

Table 10.1. Correlations between properties of the 12-tone serial excerpts and the probe tone ratings

Property	Group 1	Group 2
Recency of probe tone in excerpt	.54*	−.18
Absolute pitch height of probe tone in excerpt	.07	.23*
Pitch height of probe tone relative to average height of tones in excerpt	−.07	.14
Absolute value of pitch difference between probe tone and average of tones in excerpt	.12	.02
Absolute duration of probe tone in excerpt	−.05	.30*
Duration of probe tone relative to excerpt duration	−.12	.20*
Number of attacks of probe tone in excerpt	−.23*	.12
Metrical stress of first attack of probe tone in excerpt	−.22*	.07

*Significant at $p < .05$.

ond measured its pitch height relative to the average pitch height of tones in the excerpt, and the third measured the absolute value of the difference between its pitch height and the average pitch height of the tones in the excerpt (how much it deviates in either direction from the average). The next two properties were the absolute duration of the tone and its duration relative to the total duration of the excerpt. The second to last property was the number of attacks of the probe tone in the excerpts, that is, the number of immediate repetitions. The final property was an attempt to characterize metrical stress. We applied the metrical preference rules of Lerdahl and Jackendoff (1983) to assign a metrical grid to each excerpt. The corresponding metrical stress values were assigned to each tone; when there were immediate repetitions, the value taken was for the first attack of the tone.

Table 10.1 shows the correlations between each of these properties and the listeners' probe tone ratings. As in the first probe tone study, group 1 listeners consistently rated more recently sounded tones lower. Only two other properties in the table had a consistent relationship to the ratings. These listeners tended to give lower ratings to tones with more attacks (immediate repetitions) in the excerpts, and lower ratings to tones that appear at points of metrical stress. Both these effects were opposite those that would be expected for tonal music, in which repetitions and metrical stress would be expected to produce higher probe tone ratings. As before, lower ratings were given to tones that fit with local key implications than tones that do not fit with key implications. The correlation between the key strength vectors for the excerpts (using the weighted model) and the key strength vectors for the listeners' ratings, averaged − .67 and were individually significant for each of the eight excerpts (with $p < .01$). Thus, a number of properties showed reversals from the normal results for tonal music: tone repetitions, metrical stress, and key implications.

The probe tone ratings in this experiment for group 2 listeners were marked by a great deal of variability. The ratings did not correlate significantly with those from the first experiment, and the ratings for excerpts from the same piece were not more similar to one another than they were to ratings for excerpts from different pieces. Thus, variations in the excerpts masked the relationship between the excerpts from the same piece, and between the excerpts and the musically neutral statements of the series used in the first experiment. As in the first experiment, this group tended to rate more recently sounded tones higher, although the correlation ($-.18$) was not quite significant. To the extent that properties of the excerpts could be identified as affecting the ratings, it seemed that listeners were basing their responses on very obvious surface characteristics. Only three of the properties had a significant relationship with the ratings, and each of these was positive: absolute tone height, absolute tone duration, and tone duration relative to the total duration of the excerpt. Effects of local key implications were inconsistent; only one of the eight excerpts produced probe tone ratings that correlated significantly with any key. In a number of measures, then, the second group of listeners evidenced difficulty in producing consistent probe tone ratings for these musically complex excerpts.

These two probe tone experiments were preliminary explorations into the perceptual effects of 12-tone serial music. They considered the specific question of what variables affect the perception of tone hierarchies in music of this style. The conclusions that can be drawn are limited to the tone rows from these two compositions and the excerpts drawn from them. Despite these limitations, a number of findings are of potential interest. The most striking finding was the large individual differences in the pattern of responding in the probe tone task. One group of listeners could be identified who produced results that were highly consistent with one another, and also consistent with various principles of 12-tone composition. This group had, on average, more academic training in music and more experience with atonal music. The remaining listeners produced less consistent results that were, in most respects, opposite to those for the first group of listeners.

The first group showed evidence of having internalized the principle that no tone is to be repeated until all 12 tones have been sounded. However, no evidence indicated that they took into account the specific order of the unsounded tones in the series. Also, the results for the musically complex excerpts were similar to those for the neutral statements of the series, and invariant patterns appeared across the excerpts from the same piece. These listeners were apparently able to appreciate the common origin of the excerpts in the basic underlying series, and were largely unaffected by surface characteristics. These findings support the unifying potential of using a single series throughout a composition. To the extent that surface characteristics were influential, the effects were opposite to those that would be expected for tonal music: lower ratings for tones with more attacks and greater metrical stress in the excerpts. These listeners also showed reversals from normal key implications, in that they gave higher ratings to tones that were inconsistent with local key suggestions than to tones that were consistent with them. A number of these results can be understood in terms of the theory of 12-tone serialism, and as reversals from perceptual effects associated with tonal music.

The second group of listeners produced results that were generally more variable. To the extent that reliable patterns could be identified, they suggested that certain basic perceptual strategies were being applied to the contexts used in these probe tone experiments. These listeners gave higher ratings to tones sounded in the contexts than to tones not sounded in the contexts; particularly high ratings were given to tones sounded most recently. They also tended to give higher ratings to tones that were higher in pitch and sounded for longer durations in the excerpts. Thus, their ratings were influenced by the degree to which the tones are emphasized in the perceptually immediate contexts. These effects had the consequence that the results for excerpts from the same piece did not contain invariant patterns. It is doubtful, therefore, that they perceived that the excerpts were based on the same underlying series. Weak effects of local key implications were also evident: they gave higher ratings to tones that were consistent with key implications than those that were inconsistent with these. There was some suggestion, then, that these listeners were processing the materials in terms of perceptual principles more appropriate to tonal music than to 12-tone serial music.

Tonal hierarchies in North Indian music

The next study applied the probe tone method to classical North Indian music. We (Castellano, Bharucha, & Krumhansl, 1984) chose this style because a well-developed music theory describes many of the structural features of the music in a way that facilitates comparisons with Western tonal-harmonic theory. Jairazbhoy (1971) provides a very extensive and useful treatment, giving specific information about such properties as scale structure and relationships between scales. His account also makes predictions about tonal hierarchies. Indian music has certain characteristics in common with Western tonal music, or properties that are in some way analogous. Common to the two systems is the organization of the music around a single tone, the tonic, which in Indian music is called Sa. The Sa serves as the starting point of the scale, and is the most stable of the musical tones. The fifth scale tone, Pa, is an interval of a fifth above the Sa, and is considered second most stable in the system. North Indian music employs a large number of different scales, called thāts. In all scales, however, the Sa and Pa are fixed and are never altered; they represent an invariant of the musical style. Indian music uses a drone, which sounds the Sa (usually accompanied by the Pa) continuously during the melody. This drone may serve an important function of perceptually anchoring the melody to the two fixed structural tones of the scale.

The names of the scale tones, Sa, Re, Ga, Ma, Pa, Dha, and Ni, correspond to the Do, Re, Mi, Fa, Sol, La, and Ti of the Western major diatonic scale, as illustrated in Figure 10.6. The two systems have approximately equal tunings, although Indian music employs considerably more variations in intonation (ornamentations) around these focal tones. In the scale system, the Sa and Pa are the only fixed tones, so that each of the other five scale tones may be altered by a semitone, each in one direction only. The Re, Ga, Dha, and Ni may each be lowered by a half-step, and the Ma may be raised by a half-step. Any combination of these tones can be used, generating a set of 32 possible modal scales of which 10 are currently in common use, according to Jairazbhoy (1971).

Indian music theory also provides descriptions of the degree of relatedness between these scales, which is sometimes expressed geometrically. Figure 10.7 shows Jairazbhoy's spatial configuration (1971) depicting the relations between the 10 basic scales used in North Indian music. Nine of these scales fall on what is called the circle of thāts (thāt no. 7 is not in current use, and thāt Bhairav occupies a position inside the circle). Table 10.2 contains the names of the notes in the thāts on the circle of

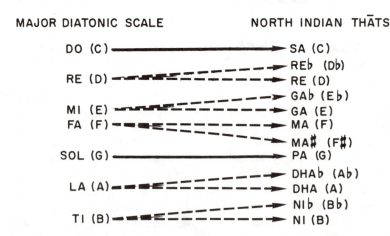

Fig. 10.6. Graphic illustration of correspondence between major diatonic scale tones and tones in North Indian thāts. The Re, Ga, Ma, Dha, and Ni can each appear in two different forms, producing a total of 32 different thāts.

CIRCLE OF THĀTS

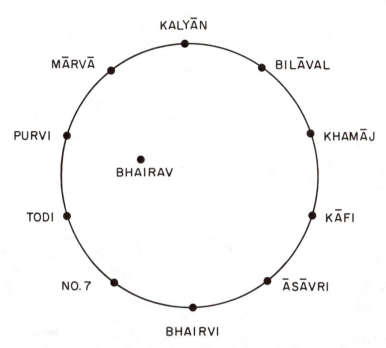

Fig. 10.7. Thāts on the circle of thāts shown according to the theoretical model of Jairazbhoy (1971). Copyright 1984 by the American Psychological Association. Adapted by permission of the publisher.

thāts and thāt Bhairav; Sa is set by convention to be the note C. Around this circle, neighboring scales overlap in all but one scale pitch. In this respect, the circle of thāts is analogous to the circle of fifths with the important difference that the Indian thāts are all based on the same tonic, whereas the keys on the circle of fifths are all based on different tonics.

It is interesting to find this parallel between the system of Western keys and the system of Indian thāts. In contrast to Western tonal-harmonic music, modulations within a piece are very rare in Indian music. Thus, the relations between thāts do not depend on their explicit manifestation in modulations; nor does Indian music use chords in any way analogous to the harmonic system of Western music. Thus, the degree of relatedness between thāts is not determined by either modulations or harmonic functions of chords, but depends solely on scale structure. In contrast, the three variables of scale structure, harmonic functions of chords, and

Table 10.2. Tones in North Indian scales

Scale	Tones						
Circle of thāts							
Bilāval	C	D	E	F	G	A	B
Khamāj	C	D	E	F	G	A	B♭
Kāfī	C	D	E♭	F	G	A	B♭
Āsāvri	C	D	E♭	F	G	A♭	B♭
Bhairvi	C	D♭	E♭	F	G	A♭	B♭
A7	C	D♭	E♭	F♯	G	A♭	B♭
Todi	C	D♭	E♭	F♯	G	A♭	B
Purvi	C	D♭	E	F♯	G	A♭	B
Mārvā	C	D♭	E	F♯	G	A	B
Kalyān	C	D	E	F♯	G	A	B
Bhairav	C	D♭	E	F	G	A♭	B

modulations all converge on the description of interkey distance in Western music; therefore their relative contributions cannot be assessed independently.

North Indian music is largely improvisational, and is exceedingly complex rhythmically and melodically. The melodic component is embodied in the concept of a rāg, which has no counterpart in Western music. There are several hundred rāgs, each with characteristic melodic features. Rāgs are specified by these features, which include a typical catch phrase and ascending and descending lines. In addition, the underlying thāt, or scale, of the rāg may be modified by the addition or deletion of one or more tones. For each rāg, two tones, the vādi and samvādi, are designated. These tones usually form an interval of a fifth (or fourth) with one another; they are usually not the Sa or the Pa, although they may be. These tones are considered structurally significant, with the vādi more important than the samvādi. These tones, particularly the vādi, are sounded frequently and in prominent positions, and are the tones with which variations begin and end. The vādi and samvādi are also said to produce a distinctive affective quality or mood. Rāgs are variously classified according to these affective qualities, the time of day that they are to be performed, the similarity of the melodic characteristics, their underlying scales, and a number of other attributes.

A performance consists of the melodic materials of the rāg set to a particular metrical pattern. At the beginning of the performance, the basic melodic features are presented in a metrically free and improvisatory fashion. When the metrical structure is introduced, the melodic line often follows a set composition, which generally consists of two parts, the sthāyi and the antra. The sthāyi, which will be relevant for what follows, is often played in the lower and middle pitch registers, and focuses on the vādi. The antra is played in the middle and upper pitch registers, and focuses on the samvādi. After the melodic and metrical structures are established, the performers proceed to improvise on the basic materials.

To summarize, Indian music theory suggests that well-defined tonal hierarchies underlie its melodic component. As in Western music, the tonic (Sa) would be expected to dominate in this hierarchy. The tonic would be followed by the fifth degree of the scale (Pa), which has a fixed relationship to the tonic and is usually sounded with the tonic in the drone. Two other tones unique to each rāg, the vādi and samvādi, would also be expected to occupy relatively high positions in the hierarchy, followed by the other thāt tones, and finally the tones not contained in the thāt. Moreover, to the extent that thāt membership is reflected in the listeners' ratings, we should be able to recover the geometric representation of relations between thāts from the rating profiles.

Ten common North Indian rāgs were selected for our investigation. These rāgs are classified by Danielou (1968) as having a number of different underlying thāts. Figure 10.8 shows the rāgs according to the position of their underlying thāts in Jairazbhoy's representation (1971). Table 10.3 indicates for each rāg its parent thāt, the tones in the thāt, the vādi, the samvādi, and the tuning of the rāg (the tones that are added or deleted from the parent thāt). It should be noted that the names of the rāgs and the names of their underlying thāts differ; in some cases, the name of a rāg corresponds to the name of some other thāt. This may reflect inconsistencies in the classification scheme, historical changes, or other variables; in all cases, we followed Danielou's designation.

For each rāg, we used as stimulus materials the sthāyi and theme from Danielou (1968). The theme (roop) is a section that is shorter than the sthāyi; it incorporates the characteristic features of the rāg and can be used to identify it. As an example, Figure 10.9 shows the sthāyi and theme from one of the rāgs. Each block of trials began with the sthāyi, played twice through, to orient the listener to the rāg. Each experimental trial began with the theme. This theme was followed by each of the 12 possible probe tones. The listeners' task was to rate how well each probe tone fit with the preceding context. We used synthesized tones, generated to simulate Indian instruments, with equal-tempered tuning. This was necessary to ensure uniformity of amplitude, duration, tuning, and timbre. The melody was accompanied by a drone consisting of the Sa and Pa; however, the drone did not accompany the probe tone. More details of the method can be found in the published report (Castellano, Bharucha, & Krumhansl, 1984).

Two groups of listeners participated in the experiment. One group, mostly Indian students studying at Cornell University, had training in Indian music. The second group was approximately matched in terms of musical experience, but their experience was limited to Western music

RĀGS ON THE CIRCLE OF THĀTS

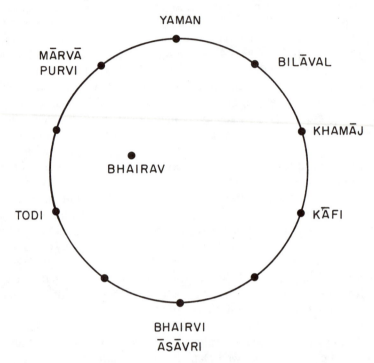

Fig. 10.8. Thāts underlying rāgs used in the probe tone experiment of Castellano, Bharucha, and Krumhansl (1984). The rāgs are shown on circle of thāts from Jairazbhoy (1971). Copyright 1984 by the American Psychological Association. Adapted by permission of the publisher.

and instruments. It would have been desirable to have had a group of listeners familiar only with Indian music (our Indian listeners all had considerable exposure to Western music in addition to their training in Indian music.) Although the selection of listeners was not ideal, it would have been difficult to find listeners unfamiliar with tonal-harmonic music given its wide distribution. However, it is possible to assess the relative strength of Indian and Western influences; the results can be compared to predictions from Indian music theory concerning the tonal hierarchies appropriate to Indian music, and the tonal hierarchies obtained in earlier experiments using Western key contexts.

For each of the 10 rāg contexts, we obtained a profile of probe tone

Table 10.3. Rāgs used in experiment

Rāg	Parent Thāt	Vādi	Samvādi	Tuning
Bhairav	Bhairav	A♭	D♭	Same as thāt
Yaman	Kalyān	E	B	Same as thāt
Bilāval	Bilāval	A	E	B missing
Khamāj	Khamāj	E	B	B added
Kāfi	Kāfi	G	C	Same as thāt
Āsāvri	Bhairvi	A♭	D♭	Same as thāt
Bhairvi	Bhairvi	C	F	D and F♯ added
Todi	Todi	A♭	E♭	Same as thāt
Purvi	Mārvā	E	B	F added
Mārvā	Mārvā	E	A	G missing

ratings, shown in Figure 10.10. The values are those found by averaging across all listeners because the two groups produced remarkably similar results; the average intergroup correlations for the 10 rāgs was .87. This strikingly high value indicates that the two groups of listeners produced very similar responses, a finding that will be considered later. Figure 10.11 summarizes the statistical tests done comparing the various classes of tones, and shows on the left–right dimension the rating for each class of tones averaged over all listeners. In general, tones in the underlying thāt of the rāg were given higher ratings than those not in the thāt. Among the thāt tones, the Sa (tonic) was given the highest rating, followed by the Pa (the fifth scale degree); these two tones are sounded continuously in the drone and are never altered in any of the scales. The vādi followed these and was on average rated higher than the other thāt tones exclusive of the Sa and Pa. The vādi is emphasized in the sthāyi, which was played at the start of each block of trials. The samvādi, however, was not rated higher than the thāt tones remaining after the Sa, Pa, and vādi had been taken out. This can be understood because the samvādi is of secondary importance to the vādi and is not necessarily featured in the musical excerpts used in the experiment. In general, however, the results conformed quite well with theoretical predictions.

However, to what can the surprising degree of agreement between the two groups of listeners be attributed? Two possibilities will be considered. First, it may be that the listeners, who were all familiar with Western music, were assimilating the musical contexts to Western key structure. To determine how similar the rāg rating profiles were to those for major and minor keys, we used the data from the earlier experiment (Krumhansl & Kessler, 1982; Table 2.1). In this analysis, done separately for the two groups of listeners, the Sa of the rāg was set equal to the tonic of the key.

STHĀYI

THEME

Fig. 10.9. The sthāyi and theme from the rāg Yaman (Danielou, 1968) used as one of the 10 rāgs in the probe tone experiment of Castellano, Bharucha, and Krumhansl (1984). Adapted by permission of the publisher.

The correlations are presented in Table 10.4. The average correlation with the major-key profile was .59 for Indian listeners and .61 for Western listeners, a difference that was small and not statistically significant. Moreover, the correlations depended strongly on the particular rāg. For some rāgs, the correlations were quite high, particularly for the rāg (Bilāval) the scale of which is identical to the major diatonic scale. For other rāgs, the correlations approached zero, indicating no consistent relationship. Similar results were found using the minor-key rating profile. The average correlation with the minor-key profile was .45 for the Indian listeners and .50 for the Western listeners. Again, this difference was not statistically significant, and the correlations varied over a wide range depending on the particular rāg. To summarize, these analyses found little to support the idea that listeners were imposing the tonal hierarchies of Western music on these excerpts.

The second possibility is that the ratings of both groups were based on the relative salience of the tones in the theme contexts. One characteristic of the contexts that can be readily quantified and compared to the ratings is the total duration of each of the 12 tones of the chromatic scale. When

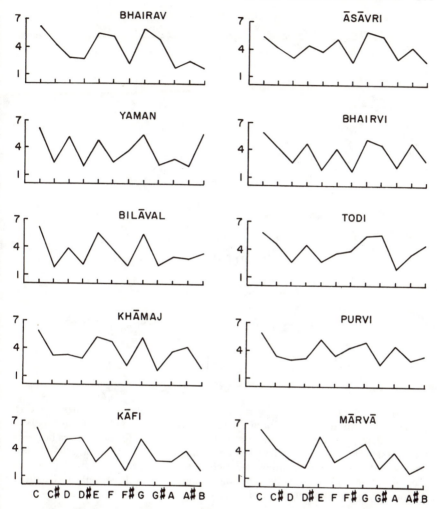

Fig. 10.10. Probe tone ratings for 10 North Indian rāgs from the experiment of Castellano, Bharucha, and Krumhansl (1984). The values shown are averaged across the Indian and Western listeners, because their responses were similar. Copyright 1984 by the American Psychological Association. Adapted by permission of the publisher.

these durations were correlated with the ratings, we found consistently high values (the correlations are given in Table 10.4). They averaged .83 for the Indian listeners and .81 for the Western listeners; these values did not differ statistically. These uniformly high correlations indicate that one variable that was strongly governing the responses of both groups of lis-

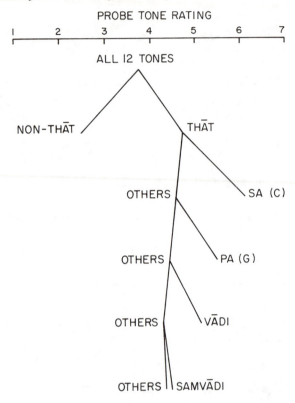

Fig. 10.11. Average probe tone ratings for different classes of tones in North Indian rāgs from the experiment of Castellano, Bharucha, and Krumhansl (1984). The tree diagram summarizes the series of statistical tests for differences between the classes of tones. Thāt tones received higher ratings than non-thāt tones; among thāt tones, highest ratings were given to the Sa, followed by the Pa, and then the Vādi. Copyright 1984 by the American Psychological Association. Adapted by permission of the publisher.

teners was the relative durations with which the various tones are sounded, and this can account in large part for the convergence between the two groups of listeners.

This result indicates that one strategy the inexperienced Western listeners applied to this style was that of registering the relative salience or emphasis given the various tones in the musical contexts. In this case, this strategy produced style-appropriate tonal hierarchies. Thus, it could be used to achieve a sense of tonal organization that, when refined and solidified though experience, would serve as the basis for appreciating and remembering more complex and subtle structural features. For the Indian listeners, the high correlations between the probe tone ratings and

Table 10.4. Correlations between probe tone ratings for rāg contexts and major and minor key tonal hierarchies and tone durations

	Correlation with					
	Major Key		Minor Key		Durations	
Rāg	Western	Indian	Western	Indian	Western	Indian
Bhairav	.65	.65	.45	.43	.77	.76
Yaman	.69	.67	.29	.23	.87	.81
Bilāval	.90	.94	.39	.43	.84	.87
Khamāj	.71	.85	.39	.27	.72	.80
Kāfi	.51	.67	.82	.83	.88	.84
Āsāvri	.46	.36	.59	.73	.84	.94
Bhairvi	.24	.30	.75	.78	.76	.74
Todi	.22	.13	.70	.59	.73	.89
Purvi	.89	.67	.33	.15	.85	.81
Mārvā	.83	.64	.29	.07	.78	.82
Average	.61	.59	.50	.45	.81	.83

the tone durations reflect the convergence between the surface emphasis given the various tones and the underlying tonal organization of the rāgs. Because these musical materials embody the basic melodic characteristics of the rāg, we would expect them to contain features useful for orienting the listener to the appropriate underlying organization.

Beyond the effect of tone duration, only the Indian listeners showed consistent effects of thāt membership. This conclusion is based on multiple-regression analyses that were performed to assess whether or not there was a significant influence of thāt membership in addition to the influence of tone duration. The analyses were done separately for Indian and Western listeners. They found that thāt membership had a regular effect, above and beyond the effect of tone duration, only for the Indian listeners. That is, once the effect of tone duration was taken into account, only the Indian listeners revealed sensitivity to the distinction between tones that function in the underlying thāt of the rāg and those that do not. Apparently, Western listeners internalized information about the relative durations of the tones in the perceptually immediate context, but beyond this they were unable to abstract the Indian musical scale structure.

This difference in sensitivity to thāt structure between the two groups of listeners was brought out clearly in the final analysis. Recall that in the case of Western music, we (Krumhansl & Kessler, 1982; Chapter 2) were able to recover a regular and interpretable map of musical keys from the probe tone ratings. The same approach was taken in this case to assess whether the probe tone ratings for the rāg contexts contained sufficient information to recover the spatial configuration of thāts shown in Figure 10.8. The first step in the analysis was to calculate the correlations between all possible pairs of rating profiles for the 10 rāgs. Some of these correlations were high, but others were low. To give a sense of this variation, Figure 10.12 shows at the top the profiles for two rāgs, Yaman and Bilāval, the underlying thāts of which have all but one tone in common (differing only in the F versus F♯). These two profiles were similar, with a correlation of .78. In contrast, the rāgs Yaman and Bhairvi had dissimilar rating profiles as can be seen at the bottom of Figure 10.12; the correlation between their profiles was − .08. Note that the underlying thāts of these two rāgs differ in all tones except the fixed Sa and Pa, which are common to all thāts. This maximal mismatch between the thāts was reflected in the opposite patterns in the rating profiles for all tones other

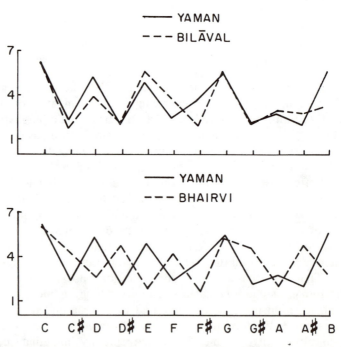

Fig. 10.12. Probe tone ratings for Yaman and Bilāval (top) and for Yaman and Bhairvi (bottom) from Castellano, Bharucha, and Krumhansl (1984). Yaman and Bilāval share all tones except for F♯, and the rating profiles are similar. Yaman and Bhairvi differ in all possible tones, sharing only the Sa and the Pa, which are never changed in any of the North Indian scales; the rating profiles are dissimilar. Copyright 1984 by the American Psychological Association. Adapted by permission of the publisher.

than the Sa and the Pa; the two rāgs are also located on opposite sides of the circle of thāts.

In the second step of the analysis, these correlations (computed separately for the two groups of listeners) were analyzed using multidimensional scaling. A satisfactory fit to the data was obtained in two dimensions. The left panel of Figure 10.13 shows the solution for Indian listeners, in which the predicted configuration was recovered quite exactly. The rāg Bhairav was located near the center of the configuration and the other rāgs were arranged in a circular pattern in the predicted order. The pairs of rāgs, Purvi and Mārvā, and Āsāvri and Bhairvi, which are based on the same underlying thāts, were represented by points in virtually identical positions. This was also true of two other rāgs, Bilāval and Khamāj, which can be understood by considering the tunings of these two rāgs (Table 10.3). Although Danielou (1968) classified them under different parent thāts, their tunings differ only in the seventh degree of the scale; Khamāj contains the seventh degree in both the natural and the lowered (flatted) forms, whereas Bilāval contains neither. Thus, when the tuning, as opposed to the thāt, is taken into account, there is no clear prediction as to the relative ordering of the two rāgs in the spatial configuration.

The right panel of Figure 10.13 shows the results of the multidimensional scaling analysis for the Western listeners' rating profiles. The pat-

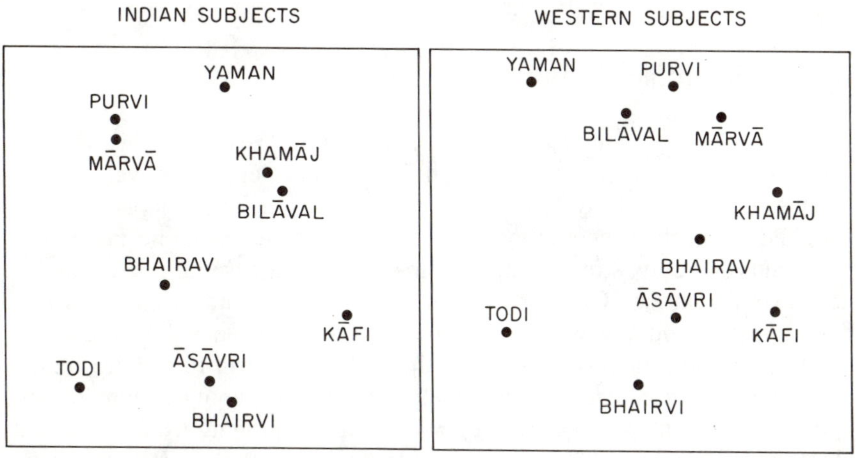

Fig. 10.13. Multidimensional scaling solution for correlations of probe tone ratings for North Indian rāgs for Indian listeners (left) and Western listeners (right) from Castellano, Bharucha, and Krumhansl (1984). The configuration at the left for Indian listeners recovers quite exactly Jairazbhoy's theoretical model (1971) of thāt relations; the configuration at the right for Western listeners shows more deviations from the theoretical predictions. Copyright 1984 by the American Psychological Association. Adapted by permission of the publisher.

tern roughly corresponded to the predictions, with Bhairav located in a somewhat central position and the other thāts arranged in a circular configuration. However, more careful comparisons show a number of discrepancies between the obtained and predicted order of the rāgs. These discrepancies reflect that thāt membership was not consistently related to the ratings of these listeners. To the extent that the predicted pattern was recovered, it would seem to depend on the influence of tone duration, which correlated moderately with thāt membership. From these analyses, it appears that more experience is required than that provided by the experimental contexts for the abstraction of relations between Indian scales.

Despite this difference in sensitivity to the thāt structure, it should be emphasized that the responses of the two groups of listeners were remarkably similar. This finding can be attributed to the use of relatively rich musical contexts and the sensitivity of all listeners to structural features made explicit in the contexts. Larger differences would be expected if the experimental situation placed greater memory or task demands on the listeners. However, by using musically rich contexts and a relatively simple task, we have shown that listeners apply considerable resources to the problem of abstracting conceptual features, particularly the tonal hierarchy, from complex musical materials. The relative durations of the tones was identified as a property that promotes the internalization of style-appropriate tonal hierarchies. This study was an initial attempt to extend the method cross-culturally to a musical system with features quite different from Western tonal music.

Tonal hierarchies in Balinese music

Systems sharing even fewer commonalities with Western music are of a great deal of interest for studying how listeners perceive novel musical styles. One such study, done by Kessler, Hansen, and Shepard (1984), applied the probe tone method to the music of Bali. In Indonesian music, one finds two coexisting tuning systems in gamelan ensembles. A gamelan consists primarily of hanging gongs, gong-chimes, and drums to which string instruments, wind instruments, and vocal parts may be added. The fixed-pitch instruments divide into those that conform to sléndro tuning and those that conform to pélog tuning. The sléndro tuning system is composed of five pitches per octave, with intervals ranging from somewhat less than 200 cents (100 cents is equal to one semitone in Western music) to somewhat less than 300 cents. The interval sizes vary more widely in the pélog tuning, which is composed of seven pitches per octave. These intervals may range from less than 100 cents to more than 300 cents. It should be emphasized that these tunings vary from ensemble to ensemble, giving each a distinctive quality. Different modes are defined on these tuning systems. A mode in sléndro consists of all five of the pitches, but these are hierarchically differentiated with one tone, the gong tone, most important. A mode in pélog consists of a subset of five of the seven pitches, which, again, are hierarchically differentiated. (See Hood, 1944/1969; Hatch, 1986; Dowling and Harwood, 1986, for more discussion of pitch systems in Indonesian music and references to the related literature.)

The study of Kessler, Hansen, and Shepard (1984) included both Western and Balinese listeners, some of whom appeared to be totally unfamiliar with Western music. Their study also included both Western and Balinese musical materials in the probe tone experiment. The contexts consisted of 16-note melodies. Two of these were intended to suggest major and minor keys and were played on a piano. Three others were written in three different modes of pélog tuning, and two others were written in two different modes of sléndro tuning; these were played on Balinese instruments. All the pélog and sléndro contexts began on the gong tone. The major and minor diatonic contexts were followed by all probe tones of the chromatic scale, the pélog contexts by all seven tones of the pélog tuning system, and the sléndro contexts by all five tones of the sléndro tuning systems. Melodies and probe tones were in the same one-octave range, and were tape-recorded for the experiment. All three types of contexts (Western diatonic, Balinese pélog, and Balinese sléndro) were heard by all subjects.

The probe tone ratings showed relatively marked differences in the way listeners responded to the task. This necessitated analyzing the data in a way that was sensitive to different response strategies (see Kessler, Hansen, & Shepard, 1984, for more details). For the Western major diatonic context, three groups of listeners produced similar responses: Western listeners, Balinese listeners familiar with Western music, and a subgroup of Balinese listeners not previously familiar with Western music. Their ratings correlated strongly with the frequency of occurrence of the tones in the melodic context, scale membership, and the tonal hierarchy of Western keys (Krumhansl & Kessler, 1982). These three variables all strongly intercorrelated. This finding suggests that scale membership and the tonal hierarchy were reflected in the relative salience of the tones in the melodies, and that a subgroup of the Balinese listeners unfamiliar with Western music used this information to abstract the style-appropriate tonal hierarchy. Other listeners, however, adopted a strategy of focusing primarily on pitch height.

For the context based on the pélog scale, a similar pattern was found. The ratings for Western listeners and the same two groups of Balinese listeners produced responses that correlated highly with the frequency of occurrence of tones in the melodic context, scale membership, and the tonal hierarchy appropriate to the pélog context. Again, these three variables all strongly intercorrelated, and the Western listeners unfamiliar with Balinese music were able to use frequency of occurrence to produce responses that were consistent with theoretical predictions. Two subgroups of Balinese listeners were also found whose responses were determined primarily by pitch height.

The results for the context based on the sléndro scale further supported the idea that naive Western listeners were basing their responses largely on the frequency of occurrence of tones in the melodic context. The correlation of their probe tone ratings with this variable was stronger than with the theoretical predictions. In this case, the theoretical predictions were mirrored less well in the frequency of occurrence of the tones in the melody, and the latter had a stronger influence on the Western listeners' probe tone ratings. The Balinese listeners, on the other hand, had higher correlations with the theoretical predictions, although again some focused primarily on pitch height. To summarize, this study, like the study of North Indian music, showed that listeners unfamiliar with a specific musical style tended to base their probe tone judgments on the relative emphasis given the tones in the contexts, and in many cases this strategy proved effective for appreciating the style-appropriate tonal hierarchies.

Tonal hierarchies: some generalizations

The studies reviewed in this chapter just begin to sample the great diversity found in music historically and cross-culturally. However, the results suggest some preliminary generalizations concerning the psychological response to music outside the tonal-harmonic tradition. Taken together, the experiments exhibit a wide variety of patterns in the probe tone ratings that, in many cases, conformed to theoretical predictions for the particular musical style. From the methodological point of view, this suggests that the technique can be applied easily to music that structures pitch materials in very different ways. From a psychological point of view, the results suggest that listeners' perceptions adapt quite readily to these differences. Rather than demonstrating a psychological system that imposes a fixed set of expectations based on the style with which the listeners are most familiar, the results showed that listeners can set aside these expectations and hear the pitch events in style-appropriate terms quite independently of their prior musical experience. For example, both Western and Indian listeners produced probe tone ratings that were consistent with the hierarchical differentiation of tones in North Indian music. Western listeners produced probe tone ratings for pélog contexts of Balinese music that were similar to those for Balinese listeners, and some of the Balinese listeners produced probe tone ratings for Western diatonic music that were similar to those for Western listeners. In no case was there evidence of residual influences of the style more familiar to the listeners on ratings of how well the probe tones fit with the musical contexts.

What principles enable listeners to abstract tonal functions in novel musical styles? Evidence bearing on this question comes from the cases just cited in which style-appropriate responses were made, and also from cases in which the patterns of responses do not conform to theoretical predictions. In the first kind of case, the theoretical predictions for tonal hierarchies were mirrored quite directly in the relative emphasis given the tones in the musical contexts. Tones judged as dominating in the hierarchies were sounded more frequently and for longer durations. These variables largely governed the responses of naive listeners when the contexts were melodies based on diatonic scales, themes from North Indian rāgs, and melodies based on Indonesian pélog tuning. In the latter, that the melodies also began on the most important gong tone may also have been influential. Listeners were apparently predisposed to attend to these surface characteristics, which, in many cases, yielded a sense of tonal hierarchies appropriate to the style.

Deviations from theoretical predictions are also informative. Western listeners hearing the melodies based on sléndro tuning did not produce patterns resembling the Balinese listeners or theoretical predictions. They seemed to rely primarily on the number of repetitions of each tone in the context, which, in this case, did not mirror the style-appropriate tonal hierarchy. Tone duration appeared as a variable in the study of 12-tone serial music. Listeners who were on average less familiar with this style tended to give higher ratings to tones sounded longer in the musical excerpts, which meant that the ratings of excerpts from the same piece were not similar even though they contained the same pattern of successive intervals. Another variable governing their responses was the pitch height of the tone, which also influenced the responses of some of the Balinese listeners with both Western and Balinese contexts. Finally, the serial position of tones in the contexts was influential in the study of 12-tone serial music. The listeners who were less familiar with the style tended to give higher ratings to more recently sounded tones, whereas the opposite pattern held for listeners who were more familiar with the style.

In fact, the most striking differences between listeners were found in the two experiments using 12-tone serial materials. Two almost diametrically opposite patterns appeared, suggesting that these materials lend themselves to very different strategies in the probe tone task. One pattern of responding, evident for the listeners with more extensive academic training and experience with atonal music, produced patterns that were, in a number of respects, simple reversals of patterns appropriate to tonal-harmonic music. They tended to give lower ratings to tones sounded in the context (particularly those sounded most recently), to tones that fit with local key implications, to tones that are repeated more often, and to tones that appear in metrically stressed positions. The data for the other listeners reflected the application of principles more appropriate to tonal music than to 12-tone serial music. In particular, they tended to give higher ratings to tones sounded in the context (particularly those sounded most recently), to tones that fit with local key implications, and to (as just mentioned) tones with longer durations. This is the only case studied so far in which listeners were apparently inappropriately processing the materials in terms of knowledge of a more familiar style.

The large intersubject differences found in the study with 12-tone serial materials suggest that the organization of pitch materials in this music may coincide less well with the kinds of perceptual strategies that listeners use with unfamiliar styles. In particular, a basic mismatch may exist between this style's treatment of all 12 chromatic scale pitches equally, and the psychological tendency to relate all pitches to a few stable and unchanging reference pitches. The studies reviewed in previous chapters demonstrated that the tonal hierarchies of Western music have a variety of psychological implications, systematically affecting perceived tonal relations and memory for tones in melodic sequences. The cross-cultural studies reviewed in this chapter showed that when the music organizes the materials around a few reference pitches, this organization is readily apprehended by listeners with little previous experience with the style. Surface characteristics of the music were identified that appear to guide the discovery of style-appropriate tonal hierarchies. These findings suggest that the hierarchical differentiation of musical elements is a basic principle governing pitch perception and memory. The next, and final chapter considers somewhat more broadly the question of how psychological principles are reflected in musical pitch organizations.

11. Music cognition: theoretical and empirical generalizations

This final chapter begins with an analysis of formal properties that are exhibited by a number of different musical pitch systems. My focus is primarily on some properties of diatonic harmony that may be important psychologically for encoding and remembering pitch information. Having established certain notational devices in the context of this familiar system, the same methods of analysis are then applied to other pitch systems to evaluate the extent to which they share similar abstract properties. If commonalities are found, then they may suggest perceptual and cognitive forces shaping the formation of pitch systems. The second part of the chapter gives an overview of what are considered by this author to be the major findings of the empirical work presented in the preceding chapters. Three categories of results will be considered in particular: the hierarchical differentiation of musical elements, the dependency of perceived relations on context, and the mappings between objective and subjective aspects of music. These results indicate that certain basic perceptual and cognitive abilities underlie our musical capacity, abilities that are shared to some extent with other domains of complex human activity.

Properties of the diatonic-harmonic system

The basic properties of the diatonic-harmonic system, shown in Table 11.1, are assumed to be well known. The diatonic scale consists of a seven-tone subset of the chromatic set. The chromatic set is labeled in the first column as 0 through 12 (which designates the tone an octave above the tone 0). The subsequent columns show, respectively: the ratios in equal-tempered tuning of the pitches with the 0 tones, their values in cents, simple-integer ratios approximating the equal-tempered ratios, the names of the intervals (using the same abbreviations as in Table 3.1), and the seven tones constituting the major diatonic scale.

A number of these properties may reflect constraints imposed by the psychological system for perceiving and remembering pitch. Dowling (1978) suggested that the diatonic scale contains only seven discrete pitch classes because this matches our limited ability to remember and label items reliably along continuous dimensions such as pitch frequency. The pattern of intervals, however, is repeated at octave intervals throughout the musical range. This expands the set of tones available without, pre-

Table 11.1. Properties of the diatonic scale

Pitch	Ratio With 0	Cents Above 0	Simple-Integer Ratio			Interval Name	Diatonic Scale
0	1.0000	0	1 : 1	=	1.0000	Unison	0
1	1.0595	100	16 : 15	=	1.0667	m2	
2	1.1225	200	9 : 8	=	1.1250	M2	2
3	1.1892	300	6 : 5	=	1.2000	m3	
4	1.2599	400	5 : 4	=	1.2500	M3	4
5	1.3348	500	4 : 3	=	1.3333	P4	5
6	1.4142	600	45 : 32	=	1.4063	Tritone	
7	1.4983	700	3 : 2	=	1.5000	P5	7
8	1.5874	800	8 : 5	=	1.6000	m6	
9	1.6818	900	5 : 3	=	1.6667	M6	9
10	1.7818	1000	16 : 9	=	1.7778	m7	
11	1.8877	1100	15 : 8	=	1.8750	M7	11
12(0)	2.0000	1200	2 : 1	=	2.0000	Octave	

Cycle of scales (on the cycle of fifths):

	1	8	3	10	5	0	7	2	9	4	11	6	(1)
0-Scale					x	x	x	x	x	x	x		
7-Scale					x	x	x	x	x	x	x	x	
2-Scale	x						x	x	x	x	x	x	x
9-Scale	x	x						x	x	x	x	x	x
4-Scale	x	x	x						x	x	x	x	x
11-Scale	x	x	x	x						x	x	x	x
6-Scale	x	x	x	x	x						x	x	x
1-Scale	x	x	x	x	x	x						x	x
8-Scale	x	x	x	x	x	x	x						x
3-Scale		x	x	x	x	x	x	x					
10-Scale		x	x	x	x	x	x	x	x				
5-Scale			x	x	x	x	x	x	x	x			
0-Scale					x	x	x	x	x	x	x		

sumably, greatly increasing processing difficulty because of the natural identification of tones at octave intervals. This octave identification probably derives from the acoustic appearance of the octave as the first overtone in the harmonic series.

The next property to note is that the pattern of scale degrees is asymmetric in the sense that it maps onto itself only at the interval of an octave. The scale consists of intervals in the following relative sizes: large, large, small, large, large, large, small. If one considers the set of intervals between all possible pairs of diatonic tones, then there are two minor seconds (or major sevenths), five major seconds (or minor sevenths), four minor thirds (or major sixths), three major thirds (or minor sixths), six perfect fourths (or perfect fifths), and one tritone. This can be written in vector notation as $<2,5,4,3,6,1>$, where the first value gives the number of minor seconds (major sevenths), the second the number of major seconds (minor sevenths), and so on. Browne (1981) argued that the asymmetric pattern and the presence of rare intervals (there are only two minor seconds and one tritone) aid the listener in "position finding"—that is, in discovering the appropriate diatonic framework. His argument has been partially substantiated experimentally by Brown and Butler (1981; Butler, 1982; Butler & Brown, 1984; Brown, 1988).

The interval vector, $<2,5,4,3,6,1>$, has two other notable properties. The first is that the most consonant interval, the perfect fourth (or fifth), is the most frequent interval, whereas the least consonant intervals, the minor second (major seventh) and the tritone, are the least frequent. Except at these extremes, the simplicity of the integer ratios (one possible measure of consonance) does not correspond to the number of intervals of each type. The second property is that each entry in the vector is unique; that is, there are no duplicated entries. This means that the number of intervals of any type is different from the number of intervals of any other type. In addition, there is at least one interval of each type; no value in the vector is equal to zero.

The last property concerning scale structure is that it determines in a natural way the relations between scales. The cycle of scales (circle of fifths) is shown at the bottom of Table 11.1. For any scale, raising the fourth scale pitch by a semitone gives the next scale on the cycle. For example, take the 0-scale in which the fourth scale degree is tone 5; raising it by a semitone to 6 gives the tones of the 7-scale. Repeating this process continues to produce scales around the cycle until the initial scale is reached again. A system of scales related in this way might be desirable for expanding the set of tonal resources available beyond the diatonic set of a single scale. It allows shifts to neighboring scales to be effected easily in the music and assimilated readily by listeners because neighboring scales differ only by a one semitone change of a single tone. Numerous empirical results already presented demonstrate that key distance is an important variable in music perception and memory.

The scale cycle possesses a number of curious mathematical properties. It has a generator of 7 (corresponding to a perfect fifth) or, equivalently, a generator of 5 (corresponding to a perfect fourth). This is to say that the cycle is produced by successively adding 7 (modulo 12, which means subtract 12 when needed so that all numbers will be between 0 and 11); starting at 0, this gives the following: 0; $(0 + 7 =) 7$; $(7 + 7 - 12 =) 2$; $(2 + 7 =) 9$; $(9 + 7 - 12 =) 4$; and so on. The diatonic scale tones are adjacent on this cycle; the next scale is obtained by dropping the leftmost pitch and adding one on the right. Any generator that is mutually prime with 12 would generate such a cycle, but it is interesting to note that the only possibility other than the trivial generator of 1 is 7 (or equivalently, 5)—the generator of the circle of fifths. Given that there is this unique, nontrivial generator, one can then go on to ask what scale sizes are such that the adjacent scale is reached by changing a single tone by a semitone. The answer is, just scale sizes 7 (the diatonic scale) and 5 (the pentatonic scale, discussed later). (In contrast, suppose the scale consisted of six adjacent scale tones on the cycle, in particular, the tones 0 2 4 5 7 and 9; the next scale would be produced by deleting the tone 5 and adding the tone 11—not a change of a single tone by a semitone.) The final question is, how many scale tones are needed to give a unique interval vector, that is, an interval vector with all different entries? Here, again, the answer is seven, which gives the interval vector <2,5,4,3,6,1>. For smaller scale sizes, there are some zero entries (e.g., the interval vector for a six-tone scale is <1,4,3,2,5,0>); for larger scale sizes, there are always duplicated values in the vector (e.g., the interval vector for an eight-tone scale is <4,6,5,4,7,2>). More details can be found in Krumhansl (1987).

The scalar properties are complemented by a number of harmonic properties. The present discussion will be limited to triads built on the diatonic scale tones. Table 11.2 shows the chord tones, chord types, and chord functions of the diatonic triads of the 0-scale and their functions in the neighboring scales on the cycle. Roman numerals indicate the scale degree of the root of the triads, and whether the chords are major, minor, or diminished. Triads are formed by selecting every other scale pitch. For example, the triad built on the tonic consists of the first, third, and fifth scale degrees (the tones 0 4 7); the triad built on the second scale degree consists of the second, fourth, and sixth scale degrees (the tones 2 5 9), and so on. This produces relatively consonant intervals of fifths and thirds in the triads, and also a consistent mapping between chord type (major, minor, and diminished) and the scale degree of the root of the triad. Notice also that the chord tones are dispersed fairly evenly throughout the octave range, making smooth voice leading between chords possible. The tones of the major chords can be expressed in terms of the ratios 4 : 5 : 6, those of the minor chords in terms of 10 : 12 : 15, and those of the diminished chord in terms of 160 : 192 : 225 (or 25 : 30 : 36 if the simpler ratio of 36 : 25 is taken for the tritone). The greater simplicity of the ratio for major chords suggests that these, as more consonant chords, might naturally serve as important structural harmonies within the system. This is also consistent with the interlocking pattern of harmonic functions of diatonic triads shown in Table 11.2. Given that the I chord would be expected to be most structurally significant by virtue of having the tonic as root, then one would expect secondary structural significance to be assigned to the IV and V chords, which are the I chords in neighboring keys on the scale cycle. This property, consistent with harmonic practice, would serve to tie strongly together neighboring keys on the cycle. This

Table 11.2. Properties of diatonic triads

Chord Tones	Chord Type	Function in 0-Scale	Function in 5-Scale	Function in 7-Scale
0 4 7	Major	I	V	IV
2 5 9	Minor	ii	vi	—
4 7 11	Minor	iii	—	vi
5 9 0	Major	IV	I	—
7 11 2	Major	V	—	I
9 0 4	Minor	vi	iii	ii
11 2 5	Diminished	vii°	—	—

analysis, and a variety of empirical findings presented earlier, demonstrate strong interdependencies between tonal and harmonic structures.

Properties of pentatonic, octatonic, and North Indian scales

Having noted, in the last section, some formal properties of the diatonic-harmonic system, similar analyses of other pitch systems are presented in this section. Comparisons of this sort are psychologically interesting inasmuch as commonalities among systems may suggest perceptual and cognitive constraints on the formation of pitch structures. L. B. Meyer (1957, p. 413) makes a similar argument, "What remains constant from style to style are not scales, modes, harmonies, or manners of performance, but the psychology of human mental processes—the ways in which the mind operating within the context of culturally established norms, selects and organizes the stimuli that are presented to it." Dowling and Harwood's discussion of properties found universally among musical styles (1986) complements the present treatment, which focuses primarily on more formal aspects.

The first scale to be considered is the pentatonic scale, which is shown in Table 11.3. It consists of five adjacent pitches on the cycle of fifths, which, as can be seen at the bottom of the table, produces a natural cycle of pentatonic scales. The generator of the cycle, 7, is the same as that for the diatonic scales. Beginning with the 0-scale, the next scale on the cycle is reached by lowering the tone 0 by a semitone to 11; continuing the process generates a complete cycle of scales. The interval vector is $<0,3,2,1,4,0>$. Neither of the least consonant intervals, the minor second (major seventh) or the tritone, is present. The most consonant interval, the perfect fourth (fifth), is the most frequent. Ignoring the zero entries, the interval vector contains unique entries (no entries are repeated). The pattern of scale steps is asymmetric, with relative interval sizes: small, small, large, small, large. The pattern of intervals maps onto itself only

Table 11.3. Properties of the pentatonic scale

Pitch	Ratio With 0	Cents Above 0	Simple-Integer Ratio			Interval Name	Pentatonic Scale
0	1.0000	0	1 : 1	=	1.0000	Unison	0
1	1.0595	100	16 : 15	=	1.0667	m2	
2	1.1225	200	9 : 8	=	1.1250	M2	2
3	1.1892	300	6 : 5	=	1.2000	m3	
4	1.2599	400	5 : 4	=	1.2500	M3	4
5	1.3348	500	4 : 3	=	1.3333	P4	
6	1.4142	600	45 : 32	=	1.4063	Tritone	
7	1.4983	700	3 : 2	=	1.5000	P5	7
8	1.5874	800	8 : 5	=	1.6000	m6	
9	1.6818	900	5 : 3	=	1.6667	M6	9
10	1.7818	1000	16 : 9	=	1.7778	m7	
11	1.8877	1100	15 : 8	=	1.8750	M7	
12(0)	2.0000	1200	2 : 1	=	2.0000	Octave	

Cycle of scales (on the cycle of fifths):

	1	8	3	10	5	0	7	2	9	4	11	6	(1)
0-Scale						X	X	X	X	X			
7-Scale							X	X	X	X	X		
2-Scale								X	X	X	X	X	
9-Scale	X								X	X	X	X	X
4-Scale	X	X								X	X	X	X
11-Scale	X	X	X								X	X	X
6-Scale	X	X	X	X								X	X
1-Scale	X	X	X	X	X								X
8-Scale		X	X	X	X	X							
3-Scale			X	X	X	X	X						
10-Scale				X	X	X	X	X					
5-Scale					X	X	X	X	X				
0-Scale						X	X	X	X	X			

at octave intervals. The small number of scale tones would seem to limit the harmonic possibilities of the pentatonic system, therefore, harmonic properties will not be considered. To summarize, the pentatonic scale shares a number of properties with the diatonic scale: a small number of scale tones forming an asymmetric pattern repeating only at the octave, a rough correspondence between consonance and the number of intervals of each kind, a natural cycle of scales with the same generator as the diatonic scale, and an interval vector with nonduplicated values (ignoring the two missing intervals).

In contrast, the octatonic scale, shown in Table 11.4, has virtually no commonalities with the diatonic scale even though it is built from the same chromatic set. The scale consists of an alternating pattern of semitone steps and whole-tone steps. The pattern repeats four times per octave, mapping onto itself with transpositions of three, six, and nine semitones. The interval vector, <4,4,8,4,4,4> shows a great deal of redundancy and no correspondence with consonance. No cycle of scales emerges; in fact, there are just two distinct octatonic scales (shown at the bottom of Table 11.4), which is why Messiaen (1944) called it a mode of limited transposition. The only possible complete cycle of the chromatic set (with generator 7) does not contain the octatonic scale as adjacent pitches. Instead, the scale can be described as the sum of two subcycles: (0 3 6 9) and (1 4 7 10). The presence of major and minor thirds permits the construction of traditional chord types, including major, minor, diminished, and dominant seventh chords. No simple rule, however, determines chord construction in a way analogous to that for diatonic triads (in which triads are formed by selecting every other scale degree). Also, chord type is not consistently mapped to the position of the chord's root in the scale. For the octatonic scale, then, harmonic properties are quite independent of the properties of the scale. Together, these observations suggest that the tonal and harmonic characteristics of the octatonic system need to be determined compositionally rather than following from

Table 11.4. Properties of the octatonic scale

Pitch	Ratio With 0	Cents Above 0	Simple-Integer Ratio		Interval Name	Octatonic Scale
0	1.000	0	1 : 1	= 1.0000	Unison	0
1	1.0595	100	16 : 15	= 1.0667	m2	1
2	1.1225	200	9 : 8	= 1.1250	M2	
3	1.1892	300	6 : 5	= 1.2000	m3	3
4	1.2599	400	5 : 4	= 1.2500	M3	4
5	1.3348	500	4 : 3	= 1.3333	P4	
6	1.4142	600	45 : 32	= 1.4063	Tritone	6
7	1.4983	700	3 : 2	= 1.5000	P5	7
8	1.5874	800	8 : 5	= 1.6000	m6	
9	1.6818	900	5 : 3	= 1.6667	M6	9
10	1.7818	1000	16 : 9	= 1.7778	m7	10
11	1.8877	1100	15 : 8	= 1.8750	M7	
12(0)	2.0000	1200	2 : 1	= 2.0000	Octave	

Two octatonic scales:

0-scale	0	1	3	4	6	7	9	10
1-scale	1	2	4	5	7	8	10	11

inherent structural properties, consistent with theoretical and empirical analyses summarized elsewhere (Van den Toorn, 1983; Krumhansl & Schmuckler, 1986; Chapter 9).

Next, we turn to the scales (thāts) of North Indian music, focusing on the scales on the circle of thāts. According to Jairazbhoy (1971), these include most of the scales in common use (more information about the structural properties of the scales as described by Jairazbhoy can be found in Castellano, Bharucha, and Krumhansl, 1984; Chapter 10). The top of Table 11.5 shows the tones of these scales, all of which contain the tones 0 (Sa) and 7 (Pa). The bottom of Table 11.5 illustrates the cyclic nature of the scale relations, where the scale tones are indicated on the cycle of fifths. As can be seen, neighboring scales differ by a semitone change of a single pitch. The first six scales consist of seven tones adjacent on the cycle. As such, they correspond to diatonic scales, except in all cases, it should be emphasized, the tonic (Sa) is the tone 0. The interval vector for these, <2,5,4,3,6,1>, is the same as that of the diatonic scale, with all entries unique and a rough correspondence between consonance and the relative frequencies of the different intervals, especially at the extremes of the continuum of consonance.

The four remaining scales contain the invariant 0 (Sa) and 7 (Pa) tones and five tones adjacent to one another on the cycle but separated from the 0 and 7 tones. Thus, the five tones constitute a pentatonic scale (compare Table 11.3). The interval vectors for these four scales are the following: <3,4,4,3,5,2> for A7, <4,3,3,4,5,2> for Todi, <4,3,3,4,5,2> for Purvi, and <3,4,4,3,5,2> for Mārvā. These interval vectors show a somewhat less consistent relationship between interval frequency and consonance. However, each scale has an uneven distribution of interval frequencies, with the tritone in each case the least frequent and the perfect fourth (or fifth) the most frequent. There are also duplicated entries in the vectors, although if the 0 and 7 tones (the invariant tones) are omitted, then the resulting vector, <0,3,2,1,4,0>, has unique entries (ignoring the missing intervals). In all cases, the scales form asymmetric patterns repeating only once per octave. The generator of the cycle (7) is the same as that for diatonic and pentatonic scales. Chords are not employed in Indian music in a way that is analogous to diatonic-harmonic music, so harmonic properties will not be considered.

A number of properties emerge from these analyses that are common to diatonic, pentatonic, and North Indian scales. All of these systems employ an asymmetric pattern of scalar intervals that repeats once per octave. In addition, the scales contain an uneven distribution of interval types with certain relatively rare intervals. An influence of consonance is apparent in each case; the least consonant intervals tend to be least frequent, and the most consonant the most frequent. Finally, the relations between scales can, for all these systems, be represented on a cycle of scales with a common generator, 7. This generator is the only nontrivial

Table 11.5. Properties of North Indian scales on the circle of thāts

Kalyān	Bilāval	Khamāj	Kāfi	Āsāvri	Bhairvi	A7	Todi	Purvi	Mārvā
0	0	0	0	0	0	0	0	0	0
					1	1	1	1	1
2	2	2	2	2					
			3	3	3	3	3		
4	4	4						4	4
	5	5	5	5	5				
6						6	6	6	6
7	7	7	7	7	7	7	7	7	7
				8	8	8	8	8	
9	9	9	9						9
		10	10	10	10	10			
11	11						11	11	11

Cycle of scales (on the cycle of fifths):

	1	8	3	10	5	0	7	2	9	4	11	6	(1)
Kalyān						x	x	x	x	x	x	x	
Bilāval					x	x	x	x	x	x	x		
Khamāj				x	x	x	x	x	x	x			
Kāfi			x	x	x	x	x	x	x				
Āsāvri		x	x	x	x	x	x	x					
Bhairvi	x	x	x	x	x	x	x						
A7	x	x	x	x		x	x					x	x
Todi	x	x	x			x	x				x	x	x
Purvi	x	x				x	x			x	x	x	x
Mārvā	x					x	x		x	x	x	x	x
Kalyān						x	x	x	x	x	x	x	

279

generator of the complete chromatic set. On this cycle, the next scale is reached by altering a single tone by a semitone. Only in the case of the diatonic-harmonic system, however, do we see this cycle of scales reflected also in the harmonic functions of chords and, interestingly, this is the only case in which modulations between scales are employed to expand the tonal resources beyond the basic scale set. This suggests that the overlapping functions of chords in related scales may be necessary compositionally and psychologically to successfully effect changes between related scales.

Novel pitch systems proposed recently by Pierce (described in Mathews, Pierce, & Roberts, 1987) and Balzano (1980, 1986) suggest that these kinds of formal properties are not unique to the systems considered here. Briefly, Pierce proposed a 9-tone scale drawn from a full set of 13 tones distributed equally (in log frequency) over an octave and a fifth. A number of intervals in this set can be approximated by small ratios of frequencies, and the system exhibits virtually all the abstract structural characteristics described here of the diatonic system. Primarily, the Pierce system differs from diatonic harmony inasmuch as the interval vector contains redundant entries, chord types are not unambiguously mapped to chord roots, and (as a consequence of the basic construction of the scale) the asymmetric pattern of scalar intervals repeats at an octave and a fifth (rather than at an octave). Balzano proposed a system with 20 equally spaced (in log frequency) microtones per octave; the scale consists of a 9-tone subset. It, too, shares a number of abstract properties with the diatonic system, with the most important difference being the lack of intervals with small frequency ratios. In addition, the generator of the scale cycle is not unique, and the interval vector contains missing entries. Krumhansl (1987) provides a detailed analysis of these two systems, which, with the primary exceptions noted, exhibit a remarkable number of properties in common with the diatonic-harmonic system. Experiments exploring the psychological effects of novel systems such as these provide a special opportunity for testing the connection suggested here: between abstract properties of pitch systems and constraints on our ability to encode and remember pitch information.

Properties emerging from the empirical studies

Until this point, the focus of this chapter has been on properties of musical pitch systems the perceptual effects of which have not, for the most part, been subjected to experimental analysis. A number of abstract characteristics, however, are shared by pitch systems that have provided rich resources for music composition. These may reflect the operation of basic psychological principles in music perception and cognition. In the remainder of the chapter, the major findings of the empirical studies that were presented in previous chapters are summarized. The general orientation taken here is that of cognitive psychology. The basic problem, as initially formulated, was to describe the knowledge listeners have about musical structure and characterize how this knowledge affects the way listeners perceive and remember music. The view was that the experience of music goes beyond registering the acoustic parameters of tone frequency, amplitude, duration, and timbre. Presumably, these are recoded, organized, and stored in memory in a form different from sensory codes. Music was assumed to evoke enduring mental structures to which the sounded events are compared and through which they are interpreted. To the extent that the auditory events conform to knowledge of melodic, harmonic, tonal, rhythmic, and metrical patterns, a well-organized percept and a stable memory representation would result.

The investigations focused on pitch structure, and tonality in particular. This focus on tonality was chosen for a number of reasons. First, it plays a central role in theoretical treatments of Western tonal-harmonic music. Second, most music cross-culturally and historically can be described as tonal in the general sense that pitch materials are centered around one or a few structurally significant tones. Finally, studies of other perceptual and cognitive domains had demonstrated that mental concepts are often organized around a few normative, prototypical, or central elements. This work suggested the operation of a general principle that might apply to music also, and made predictions about specific patterns of results that are taken to reflect the existence of cognitive reference points.

The basic experiments examined the knowledge listeners have of pitch structures in Western tonal-harmonic music at three levels: single tones, chords, and keys. For both tones and chords, the first step was to measure quantitatively how stable or structurally significant each element is heard as being in major and minor key contexts. Descriptions of tonal-harmonic music suggested that a key context imposes a hierarchy of psychological stability on these sets of elements, and provides a qualitative account of the ordering. These predictions were confirmed in the experimentally measured tonal and harmonic hierarchies. Moreover, these hierarchies were sufficiently regular to serve as a basis for a musically interpretable spatial representation of relationships between musical keys. Both tonal and harmonic hierarchies yielded the same measure of interkey distance, suggesting strong interdependencies between these two hierarchies.

A number of scaling experiments were then conducted to quantify the perceived degree of relatedness between tones and between chords. The primary question was whether the tonal and harmonic hierarchies would be reflected in judgments of pairs of successive elements sounded in key-defining contexts. These experiments found that both tones and chords were judged as more closely related when they occupy relatively high positions in the hierarchies of the key. Thus, context enhances the perceived relations among the more stable elements in a key. In addition, strong temporal asymmetries were found, with unstable elements judged as more closely related to stable elements than the reverse. Analogous results arose from memory studies paralleling the scaling studies. The effects of tonal and harmonic hierarchies were consistent enough to be summarized in terms of a small number of principles describing the influence of key context on the perception of tones and chords. The results account, in part, for the sense of coherence produced by well-structured melodic and harmonic sequences and the ability to remember them accurately. These studies demonstrated that listeners have precise knowledge of tonal-harmonic pitch structures. The essential organizational principle governing this knowledge is the hierarchical differentiation of tones and chords; these hierarchies are strongly tied to relations between abstract tonal centers or keys. In this hierarchical differentiation, we see one of the hallmarks of a cognitive system: the categorization and classification of sensory information in terms of a stable, internal system of structural relations.

Gestalt psychology also provided a useful framework for understanding and describing some of the experimental results. The Gestalt principles of grouping have been central to various psychological theories of musical structure. Such variables as pitch and temporal proximity, timbral similarity, and the formation of simple contour patterns are presumed to affect the way in which the elements are perceived in relation to one another and how they join to form larger perceptual units. However, rereading the Gestalt literature uncovered a somewhat deeper affinity with the present program of research. One particular phrase by Wertheimer (W. D. Ellis, 1938, p. 4) seemed particularly apt: "What takes place in each single part already depends upon what the whole is. *The flesh and blood of a tone depends from the start upon its role in the melody*" [italics added]. He is pointing out that the experience of a melody is not simply a consequence of its tones and intervals, but depends also on the function of each tone in the perceptual whole—the melody.

Many of the studies reported here can be described as trying to understand how the "flesh and blood" of the musical elements, the tones and chords, are determined by their functions in larger musical contexts. The results strongly confirmed the notion that the meaning of each element, and how it enters into relations with each of the others, depends on the context. For example, the degree to which each tone is heard as fitting with a tonal context is determined by the tone's function in the tonality. Tonal functions also strongly affect the degree of perceived relatedness between tones; intertone relations could not be described solely in terms of their intervallic distance or other context-invariant properties. Similar conclusions emerged from the studies of chords. Chords, like tones, varied in terms of how well they are heard as fitting with tonal contexts in a way that depended on their harmonic functions in the context. Also, the degree to which chords were heard as related to one another showed regular contextual dependencies. These findings argue strongly that the perceptual organization of music cannot be described in terms of physical properties of the sounded events. Instead, the nature of each single event depends on its role in the whole context, in particular, its tonal organization.

The Gestalt notion of dynamic qualities of elements proved useful for understanding other results. According to Gestalt theory, certain elements are stable, others unstable with dynamic forces that draw them to more stable elements. In music, unstable elements, tones and chords, create a need to move toward or resolve to more stable elements in the system. The degree to which the individual elements were judged as fitting with tonal contexts was taken to be a measure of relative stability. This identification was supported by finding that less stable elements tended to be poorly remembered and frequently confused with more stable elements. In this sense, then, they were assimilated to the more stable elements. In addition, sequences ending on stable elements were preferred to sequences ending on less stable elements. This kind of dynamic quality of pointing forward in time to the stable points of rest engenders in the listener a feeling of tension and resolution that is fundamental to tonal music.

The perception of longer sequences also showed evidence of dynamic qualities. As a sequence of events unfolds in time, the listener is continually engaged in a process of organizing, interpreting, and evaluating each event in terms of the others. One experiment investigated the problem of how the sense of key develops and changes over time. This process could be described as one in which each sounded event was interpreted in light of its possible tonal functions. These interpretations were integrated over time, strengthening some and weakening others, giving rise to an initial sense of the tonality. As subsequent events were sounded that came to suggest another key, the perceived tonal center also shifted. When the new key was closely related to the first, the shift was accomplished easily and without disruption; however, when the new key was more distant, the change occurred later, more abruptly, and in some cases temporarily disrupting the sense of any tonal organization. To use the Gestalt metaphor, it is as though the initial tonal center creates a field of forces that points toward other, closely related centers, but resists movement to more distant centers.

Each sounded event is affected by events both preceding and following it. In other words, the quality of any event is affected both proactively and retroactively by those surrounding it in the temporal context. An experiment that supported this claim introduced in an otherwise tonal sequence an unstable element. This sequence was then compared to one sounded at a later time in which a single event was changed. As would be expected, the unstable element was itself poorly remembered. Moreover, it disrupted the memory for elements that were prior to it and those that followed: when unchanged, they were sometimes judged as changed; conversely, when changed, listeners sometimes failed to detect the change. Thus, a musical event exerts its influence over a temporal interval that exceeds its physical duration, altering the interpretation of events over an extended temporal range. The meaning of any event can be described, then, as dynamically changing as it is interpreted and reinterpreted as the sequence unfolds in time.

These experiments suggest that what is special about the human musical capacity is the ability to relate the sounded events dynamically to one another, and to comprehend the multiplicity of structural functions of the events at many different levels simultaneously. This process evolves continuously as the events unfold in time. Each event is understood as it joins with other events to form larger structural units. At no point is a final, single, or "correct" analysis achieved; no decision or single interpretation is required. Instead, what is essential to the process is the ability to appreciate and to evaluate the various possible functions of the events by understanding them in terms of their melodic, harmonic, and tonal roles. The process must be extremely sensitive to the organization expressed directly in the sounded events, must be continuously active, and must be able to assess the relations of varying strengths at different levels of analysis.

From cognitive psychology came a bias to conceive of knowledge of pitch structures as stable, inflexible, and necessary for the comprehension and memory of musical sequences. The view was that information already present in the mind must be added to the incoming perceptual information for it to become meaningful. The psychological literature on music has generally favored the position that years of experience are required for musical structures to be learned. This position is supported by numerous reports of changes in the ability to perform various musical tasks as a function of the listener's age and musical training. Also, tests of musical aptitude and ability are used to assess what are presumed to be stable individual differences in musical talent. Implicit in these approaches is the assumption that musical knowledge is highly constrained, stable, and permanent. It is presumed to be the consequence of years of exposure to a system of music, which itself may be shaped at a very basic level by acoustic properties and the way they are encoded by the sensory system. Once acquired, this knowledge is thought to impose its organization on all subsequent musical experiences.

However, can it really be concluded that all musical experiences are necessarily and completely assimilated to a system of musical knowledge that is abstracted through extensive experience? If so, how is it that we can recognize different styles, alternate between them, and understand each in its own terms? How is it that the unique characteristics of each piece come to be appreciated, so that even after repeated hearings we discover new patterns—patterns that depend on the way the particular musical composition is constructed? That we have these abilities suggests that we may have coexisting knowledge of multiple style systems, and that we can interpret the sounded musical events in the appropriate stylistic framework. Moreover, it seems that we can, and do, build up a representation of the particular piece in which the elements are coded not only in terms of general knowledge about the relevant style system, but also in terms of the composition's particular characteristics. It may be that sensitivity to distributions of elements in the perceptually immediate stimulus is important for orienting to the appropriate style and appreciating each composition's unique features. L. B. Meyer (1957, 1967, pp. 42–53) and J. E. Cohen (1962) provide useful discussions of these and related issues.

The cross-cultural study in the research program that was summarized here was particularly persuasive in directing my attention to listeners' sensitivity to information in the perceptually immediate musical stimulus. That study found that all listeners, independent of their prior experience with the particular musical style, were able to appreciate the style-appropriate tonal hierarchies. Listeners showed no evidence of assimilating the musical contexts to an inappropriate style system with which they were highly familiar. These findings were attributed to the relatively complex musical contexts having made explicit the tonal hierarchies, by sounding elements dominating in the hierarchies more frequently and for longer durations. Both experienced and inexperienced listeners were sensitive to this information and reflected it in their judgments. This same basic result has now been found for a number of styles with very different underlying pitch structures.

That surface characteristics of the music, such as tone frequency and duration, produced a sense of style-appropriate tonal hierarchies in listeners unfamiliar with the style suggested that perceived tonal and harmonic relations in traditional Western music might also conform to stylistic regularities. The literature contained a number of statistical treatments of music, often couched in information-theoretical terms. These studies counted the number of occurrences of single tones, successive pairs of tones, and chords in a large corpus of tonal-harmonic compositions. Each of the statistical summaries was compared with the corresponding empirical results. For example, the distribution of frequency of occurrence of the 12 chromatic scale tones was compared to the tonal hierarchy of the appropriate key. A strong relationship was found: tones sounded most frequently were those that occupy high positions in the tonal hierarchy. In a similar way, the frequencies of occurrence of successive tones were compared to listeners' judgments of successive tones in tonal contexts. Again, the comparison showed good agreement. The frequencies of diatonic triads also corresponded to the degree to which the chords were judged as fitting with key-defining contexts, and a qualitative account of the likelihood of successive pairs of chords resembled listeners' judgments about pairs of chords in key contexts.

Statistical measures of this kind, although somewhat crude, summarize stylistic regularities in Western tonal-harmonic music in a way that matches well the experimental results. The correspondences were really quite striking, with statistical distributions in all cases mirrored in the empirical data. Listeners appear to be very sensitive to the frequency with which the various elements and their successive combinations are employed in music. It seems probable, then, that abstract tonal and harmonic relations are learned through internalizing distributional properties characteristic of the style. This sensitivity to distributions of elements was central to L. B. Meyer's account (1956) of how cultural norms determine the listener's experience of the music. He claims the feeling of tension and resolution, activity and rest, instability and stability, and the pointing of certain events to others, are a consequence of the probability relations in the style system that listeners have learned through experience.

The psychological literature on learning, both human and animal, demonstrates remarkable sensitivity to the frequency with which events occur. Given this, it may not be surprising that the distributions of tones and chords in tonal-harmonic music are reflected so directly in listeners' perceptual judgments of these elements presented singly and in combination. What does seem striking is that this information about frequency of occurrence is represented so accurately in hierarchies of tones and chords that they can be used to generate a very regular and interpretable spatial representation of musical keys. That is, the distributions over the sets of tones and chords determine structure at the abstract level of musical keys. This measure of interkey distance was also reflected in a variety of other experimental measures of perceived relations and memory accuracy. Thus, music seems to have made very special use of a biological system for encoding frequency of occurrence, using correlated patterns to generate structure at a level abstracted from the sounded events.

At many points in the research, the experiments have strongly confirmed music-theoretical predictions. The convergence between these two approaches to understanding music suggest that they are complementary, despite their distinctly different methodologies. What are the prospects for a fruitful synthesis? From the point of view of music cognition, music theory is an invaluable source of information concerning musically significant characteristics that might be subjected to experimental investigation. In some cases, theoretical treatments make detailed predictions that can be tested with appropriate experimental designs. Occasionally, these are couched in psychological terms, speculating on the effects on the listener of certain compositional techniques. Descriptions such as these are extremely useful to psychological investigators for selecting appropriate materials and experimental tasks, and for understanding and interpreting the results. That empirical methods have largely confirmed these observations suggests that the theory offers important psychological insights.

In the other direction, psychological investigations may suggest a psychological basis for certain of the compositional regularities theorists have uncovered through extensive analysis of music. Framing the problem in perceptual terms may bring into focus the information available to the listener, as distinguished from information derived largely from analyses of written scores. To the extent that the theory is intended to characterize perceptual effects, it is important to consider how a piece is organized by the listener as it unfolds in time. The psychological evidence so far suggests that the percept undergoes continuous reorganization as successive events are sounded. Although the memory capacity for isolated events is limited, listeners have impressive abilities to organize the sounded events into larger units when they conform to certain basic structural principles. Moreover, they appear to be able to appreciate the musical functions of the events on several different levels simultaneously. Results such as these may lead to specification of musical properties in more psychologically relevant terms.

Second, psychological studies may suggest new methods for representing musical structure. Experiments provide a systematic body of observations in a form quite different from the descriptive systems that have been used in music theory. The experimental data are usually expressed in quantitative terms permitting the application of various analytical techniques. These techniques can be useful for summarizing and discovering underlying patterns that may be difficult to characterize using the kinds of discrete symbolic representations predominantly employed in music theory. Alternative modes of representations, such as hierarchical trees and spatial representations that can be recovered from quantitative data, may provide the means of expressing structural features that could not be expressed in other forms. Developing a sufficiently rich and precise representational system is a central problem for any domain. Approaching this problem with the techniques of both music theory and music psychology may stimulate new developments in the domain of music.

Finally, applying experimental methods may yield new insights into the forms of musical expression that are currently less well understood from a theoretical point of view. Cross-cultural studies, for example, have often focused on local measurable physical attributes, such as tuning systems. Perceptual measures may provide an avenue for discovering and describing larger units of musical organization. Underlying psychological principles may be uncovered that extend across diverse musical styles. Although the styles may have extremely different surface characteristics, analogous patterns may be found when regularities are formulated in more abstract, psychological terms. Music cognition may also guide the development of new compositional techniques. Perceptual studies can describe the kinds of features to which listeners are sensitive when first hearing a piece in an unfamiliar style. They can also elucidate the process through which more subtle properties come to be appreciated with more extensive experience, yielding stable and coherent conceptual representations.

References

Allen, D. (1967) Octave discriminability of musical and nonmusical subjects. *Psychonomic Science, 7*, 421–22.

Ashby, F. G., & Perrin, N. A. (1988) Toward a unified theory of similarity and recognition. *Psychological Review, 95*, 124–50.

Attneave, F., & Olson, R. K. (1971) Pitch as medium: A new approach to psychophysical scaling. *American Journal of Psychology, 84*, 147–66.

Bachem, A. (1950) Tone height and tone chroma as two different pitch qualities. *Acta Psychologica, 7*, 80–88.

Backus, J. (1969/1977) *The acoustical foundations of music* (2nd ed.). New York: Norton.

Balch, W. R. (1981) The role of symmetry in the good continuation of two-part melodies. *Perception & Psychophysics, 29*, 47–55.

Balzano, G. J. (1980) The group-theoretic description of 12-fold and microtonal pitch systems. *Computer Music Journal, 4*, 66–84.

Balzano, G. J. (1986) What are musical pitch and timbre? *Music Perception, 3*, 297–314.

Bartlett, J. C., & Dowling, W. J. (1980) The recognition of transposed melodies: A key-distance effect in developmental perspective. *Journal of Experimental Psychology: Human Perception and Performance, 6*, 501–15.

Bartlett, J. C., & Dowling, W. J. (1988) Scale structure and similarity of melodies. *Music Perception, 5*, 285–314.

Benjamin, W. E. (1984) A theory of musical meter. *Music Perception, 1*, 355–413.

Berger, A. (1968) Problems of pitch organization in Stravinsky. In B. Boretz and E. T. Cone (Eds.), *Perspectives on Schoenberg and Stravinsky*. Princeton, NJ: Princeton University Press.

Bharucha, J. J. (1984a) Anchoring effects in music: The resolution of dissonance. *Cognitive Psychology, 16*, 485–518.

Bharucha, J. J. (1984b) Event hierarchies, tonal hierarchies, and assimilation: A reply to Deutsch and Dowling. *Journal of Experimental Psychology: General, 113*, 421–25.

Bharucha, J. J. (1987) Music cognition and perceptual facilitation: A connectionist framework. *Music Perception, 5*, 1–30.

Bharucha, J. J., & Krumhansl, C. L. (1983) The representation of harmonic structure in music: Hierarchies of stability as a function of context. *Cognition, 13*, 63–102.

Bharucha, J. J., & Stoeckig, K. (1986) Reaction time and musical expectancy: Priming of chords. *Journal of Experimental Psychology: Human Perception and Performance, 12*, 403–410.

Bharucha, J. J., & Stoeckig, K. (1987) Priming of chords: Spreading activation or overlapping frequency spectra? *Perception & Psychophysics, 41*, 519–24.

Bingham, W. V. (1910) Studies in melody. *Psychological Monographs, 12* (3, Whole No. 50).

Boomsliter, P., & Creel, W. (1961) The long pattern hypothesis in harmony and hearing. *Journal of Music Theory*, **5**, 2–31.

Bregman, A. S. (1978) The formation of auditory streams. In J. Requin (Ed.), *Attention and performance* (Vol. 7). Hillsdale, NJ: Erlbaum.

Bregman, A. S. (1981) Asking the "what for" question in auditory perception. In M. Kubovy & J. Pomerantz (Eds.), *Perceptual organization*. Hillsdale, NJ: Erlbaum.

Bregman, A. S., & Campbell, J. (1971) Primary auditory stream segregation and perception of order in rapid sequences of tones. *Journal of Experimental Psychology*, **89**, 244–49.

Bregman, A. S., & Pinker, S. (1978) Auditory streaming and the building of timbre. *Canadian Journal of Psychology*, **32**, 19–31.

Brooks F. P., Jr., Hopkins, A. L., Jr., Neumann, P. G., & Wright, W. V. (1957) An experiment in musical composition. *I R E Transactions on Electronic Computers*, **EC-7**, 175–82.

Brown, H. (1988) The interplay of set content and temporal context in a functional theory of tonality perception. *Music Perception*, **5**, 219–50.

Brown, H., & Butler, D. (1981) Diatonic trichords as minimal tonal cue-cells. *In Theory Only*, **5(6,7)**, 39–55.

Browne, R. (1981) Tonal implications of the diatonic set. *In Theory Only*, **5(6,7)**, 3–21.

Budge, H. (1943) *A study of chord frequencies*. New York: Bureau of Publications, Teachers College, Columbia University.

Burns, E. M., & Ward, W. D. (1982) Intervals, scales, and tuning. In D. Deutsch (Ed.), *The psychology of music*. New York: Academic.

Butler, D. (1982) The identification of tonal centers in music. Paper presented at the NATO Conference on the Acquisition of Symbolic Skills, Keele, England.

Butler, D., & Brown, H. (1984) Tonal structure versus function: Studies of the recognition of harmonic motion. *Music Perception*, **2**, 6–24.

Carroll, J. D. (1972) Individual differences in multidimensional scaling. In R. N. Shepard, A. K. Romney, & S. Nerlove (Eds.), *Multidimensional scaling: Theory and application in the behavioral sciences* (Vol. 1). New York: Academic.

Carroll, J. D. (1976) Spatial, non-spatial, and hybrid models for scaling. *Psychometrika*, **41**, 439–63.

Castellano, M. A., Bharucha, J. J., & Krumhansl, C. L. (1984) Tonal hierarchies in the music of North India. *Journal of Experimental Psychology: General*, **113**, 394–412.

Cazden, N. (1945) Musical consonance and dissonance: A cultural criterion. *The Journal of Aesthetics & Art Criticism*, **4**, 3–11.

Chafe, C., Mont-Reynaud, B., and Rush, L. (1982) Toward an intelligent editor of digital audio: Recognition of musical constructs. *Computer Music Journal*, **6**, 30–41.

Clarke, E. F., & Krumhansl, C. L. (1990) Perceiving musical time. *Music Perception*, **7**, 213–52.

Cliff, N. (1966) Orthogonal rotation to congruence. *Psychometrika*, **31**, 33–42.

Cohen, A. J. (1977) Tonality and perception: Musical scales prompted by excerpts from *Das Wohl temperierte Clavier* of J. S. Bach. Paper presented at the Second Workshop on Physical and Neuropsychological Foundations of Music, Ossiach, Austria.

Cohen, J. E. (1962) Information theory and music. *Behavioral Science*, **7**, 137–63.

Cooper, G. W., & Meyer, L. B. (1960) *The rhythmic structure of music*. Chicago: University of Chicago Press.

Cuddy, L. L., Cohen, A. J., & Miller, J. (1979) Melody recognition: The experimental application of rules. *Canadian Journal of Psychology, 33*, 148–57.

Cuddy, L. L., & Lyons, H. I. (1981) Musical pattern recognition: A comparison of listening to and studying tonal structures and tonal ambiguities. *Psychomusicology, 1*, 15–33.

Cunningham, J. P. (1978) Free trees and bidirectional trees as representations of psychological distance. *Journal of Mathematical Psychology, 17*, 165–88.

Danielou, A. (1968) *The rāga-s of Northern Indian music*. London: Barrie & Rockliff.

Dannenbring, G. L., & Bregman, A. S. (1978) Streaming vs. fusion of sinusoidal components of complex tones. *Perception & Psychophysics, 24*, 369–76.

Deliège, I. (1987) Grouping conditions in listening to music: An approach to Lerdahl & Jackendoff's grouping preference rules. *Music Perception, 4*, 325–60.

Deliège, I. (1989) Recognition of musical forms through listening. *Contemporary Music Review, 14*, 214–30.

Demany, L., & Armand, F. (1984) The perceptual reality of tone chroma in early infancy. *Journal of the Acoustical Society of America, 76*, 57–66.

Deutsch, D. (1972a) Effect of repetition of standard and comparison tones on recognition memory for pitch. *Journal of Experimental Psychology, 93*, 156–62.

Deutsch, D. (1972b) Octave generalization and tune recognition. *Perception & Psychophysics, 11*, 411–12.

Deutsch, D. (1975) Musical illusions. *Scientific American, 233*, 92–104.

Deutsch, D. (1978) Delayed pitch comparisons and the principle of proximity. *Perception & Psychophysics, 23*, 227–30.

Deutsch, D. (1982a) Grouping mechanisms in music. In D. Deutsch (Ed.), *The psychology of music*. New York: Academic.

Deutsch, D. (1982b) The processing of pitch combinations. In D. Deutsch (Ed.), *The psychology of music*. New York: Academic.

Deutsch, D. (1986a) A musical paradox. *Music Perception, 3*, 275–80.

Deutsch, D. (1986b) Auditory pattern recognition. In K. R. Boff, L. Kaufman, & J. P. Thomas (Eds.), *Handbook of perception and human performance*. Vol. 2, *Cognitive processes and performance*. New York: Wiley.

Deutsch, D. (1987) The tritone paradox: Effects of spectral variables. *Perception & Psychophysics, 41*, 563–75.

Deutsch, D., & Feroe, J. (1981) The internal representation of pitch sequences in tonal music. *Psychological Review, 88*, 503–22.

Deutsch, D., Kuyper, W. L., & Fisher, Y. (1987) The tritone paradox: Its presence and form of distribution in a general population. *Music Perception, 5*, 79–92.

Deutsch, D., Moore, F. R., & Dolson, M. (1986) The perceived height of octave-related complexes. *Journal of the Acoustical Society of America, 80*, 1346–53.

Dewar, K. M., Cuddy, L. L., & Mewhort, D. J. K. (1977) Recognition memory for single tones with and without context. *Journal of Experimental Psychology: Human Learning and Memory, 3*, 60–67.

Dowling, W. J. (1972) Recognition of melodic transformations: Inversion, retrograde, and retrograde inversion. *Perception & Psychophysics, 12*, 417–21.

Dowling, W. J. (1973) The perception of interleaved melodies. *Cognitive Psychology, 5*, 322–37.

Dowling, W. J. (1978) Scale and contour: Two components of a theory of memory for melodies. *Psychological Review,* **85,** 341–54.

Dowling, W. J. (1988) Tonal structure and children's early learning of music. In J. Sloboda (Ed.), *Generative processes in music.* Oxford: Clarendon.

Dowling, W. J., & Bartlett, J. C. (1981) The importance of interval information in long-term memory for melodies. *Psychomusicology,* **1,** 30–49.

Dowling, W. J., & Harwood, D. L. (1986) *Music cognition.* Orlando, FL: Academic.

Draeger, H. H. (1967) A quantitative analysis of music as exemplified by Beethoven's sketches for his Opus 131. *Festschrift für Walter Wiora.* Basel: Barenreiter Kassel.

Ellis, C. J. (1965) Pre-instrumental scales. *Ethnomusicology,* **9,** 126–44.

Ellis, W. D. (Ed. & trans.) (1938) *A source book of Gestalt psychology.* London: Routledge & Kegan Paul.

Ennis, D. M., & Mullen, K. (1986) A multivariate model for discrimination methods. *Journal of Mathematical Psychology,* **30,** 206–19.

Estes, W. K. (1950) Toward a statistical theory of learning. *Psychological Review,* **57,** 94–107.

Estes, W. K. (1972) Research and theory in the learning of probabilities. *Journal of the American Statistical Association,* **67,** 81–102.

Estes, W. K. (1976) The cognitive side of probability learning. *Psychological Review,* **83,** 37–64.

Farnsworth, P. R. (1925) Atonic endings in melodies. *American Journal of Psychology,* **36,** 394–400.

Farnsworth, P. R. (1926a) The effect of repetition on ending preferences in melodies. *American Journal of Psychology,* **37,** 116–22.

Farnsworth, P. R. (1926b) Ending preferences in two musical situations. *American Journal of Psychology,* **37,** 237–40.

Fernald, A. (1985) Four-month-old infants prefer to listen to Motherese. *Infant Behavior and Development,* **8,** 181–95.

Fokker, A. D. (1949) *Just intonation.* The Hague: Martinus Nijhoff.

Forte, A. (1970) The structure of atonal music: Practical aspects of a computer-oriented research project. In B. S. Brook (Ed.), *Musicology and the computer: Musicology 1966–2000: A Practical program.* New York: The City University of New York Press.

Forte, A. (1973) *The structure of atonal music.* New Haven, CT: Yale University Press.

Francès, R. (1958) *La perception de la musique.* [The perception of music (W. J. Dowling, trans.). Hillsdale, NJ: Earlbaum] Paris: J. Vrin.

Fucks, W. (1962) Mathematical analysis of the formal structure of music. *I R E Transactions on Information Theory,* **8,** S225–28.

Garner, W. R. (1970) Good patterns have few alternatives. *American Scientist,* **58,** 34–42.

Garner, W. R. (1981) The analysis of unanalyzed perceptions. In M. Kubovy and J. R. Pomerantz (Eds.), *Perceptual organization.* Hillsdale, NJ: Erlbaum.

Garner, W. R., Hake, H. W., & Eriksen, C. W. (1956) Operationism and the concept of perception. *Psychological Review,* **63,** 149–59.

Goldmeier, E. (1982) *The memory trace: Its formation and its fate.* Hillsdale, NJ: Erlbaum.

Gower, J. C. (1977) The analysis of asymmetry and orthogonality. In J. R. Barra et al. (Eds.), *Recent developments in statistics.* Amsterdam: North-Holland.

Hahn, J., & Jones, M. R. (1981) Invariants in auditory frequency relations. *Scandinavian Journal of Psychology,* **22**, 129–44.

Hall, D. (1973) The objective measurement of goodness-of-fit for tunings and temperaments. *Journal of Music Theory,* **17**, 274–90.

Hall, D. (1974) Quantitative evaluation of musical scale tunings. *American Journal of Physics,* **48**, 543–52.

Harshman, R. (1978) Models for analysis of asymmetrical relationships among N objects or stimuli. Paper presented at the First Joint Meeting of the Psychometric Society and the Society for Mathematical Psychology, McMaster University, Hamilton, Ontario, Canada.

Hasher, L., & Zacks, R. T. (1979) Automatic and effortful processes in memory. *Journal of Experimental Psychology: General,* **108**, 356–88.

Hasher, L., & Zacks, R. T. (1984) Automatic processing of fundamental information: The case of frequency of occurrence. *American Psychologist,* **39**, 1372–88.

Hatch, M. (1986) Southeast Asia, and related articles. In D. Randel (Ed.), *The new Harvard dictionary of music.* Cambridge, MA: Harvard University Press.

Helmholtz, H. L. F. (1954) *On the sensations of tone as a physiological basis for the theory of music* (A. J. Ellis, Ed. & trans.). New York: Dover. (Revised edition originally published, 1885.)

Hiller, L., & Fuller, R. (1967) Structure and information in Webern's Symphonie Op. 21. *Journal of Music Theory,* **11**, 60–115.

Hiller, L. A., Jr., & Isaacson, L. M. (1959) *Experimental music.* New York: McGraw-Hill.

Hindemith, P. (1961) *A composer's world.* Garden City, NJ: Anchor. (Originally published, 1952.)

Hintzman, D. L. (1976) Repetition and memory. In G. Bower (Ed.), *The psychology of learning and motivation* (Vol. 10). New York: Academic.

Hintzman, D. L. (1988) Judgments of frequency and recognition memory in a multiple-trace memory model. *Psychological Review,* **95**, 528–51.

Hirsh-Pasek, K., Kemler Nelson, D. G., Jusczyk, P. W., Cassidy, K. W., Druss, B., & Kennedy, L. (1987) Clauses are perceptual units for young infants. *Cognition,* **26**, 269–86.

Holtzman, S. R. (1977) A program for key determination. *Interface,* **6**, 29–56.

Hood, M. (1969) Bali, Java, and related articles. In W. Apel (Ed.), *The Harvard dictionary of music.* Cambridge, MA: Harvard University Press. (Originally published, 1944.)

Houtsma, A. J. M., & Goldstein, J. L. (1972) Perception of musical intervals: Evidence for the central origin of the pitch of complex tones. *Journal of the Acoustical Society of America,* **51**, 520–29.

Hughes, M. (1977) A quantitative analysis. In M. Yeston, (Ed.), *Readings in Schenker analysis and other approaches.* New Haven, CT: Yale University Press.

Hutchinson, W., & Knopoff, L. (1978) The acoustic component of Western consonance. *Interface,* **7**, 1–29.

Hutchinson, W., & Knopoff, L. (1979) The significance of the acoustic component of consonance in Western music. *Journal of Musicological Research,* **3**, 5–22.

Jairazbhoy, N. A. (1971) *The rāgs of North Indian music: Their structure and evolution.* London: Faber & Faber (and Wesleyan University Press).

Jenkins, G. M., & Watts, D. G. (1968) *Spectral analysis and its applications.* San Francisco: Holden-Day.

Johnson, S. C. (1967) Hierarchical clustering schemes. *Psychometrika, 32*, 241–54.

Jordan, D. S. (1987) Influence of the diatonic tonal hierarchy at microtonal intervals. *Perception & Psychophysics, 41*, 482–88.

Julesz, B., & Hirsh, I. J. (1972) Visual and auditory perception—An essay of comparison. In E. E. David, Jr., & P. B. Denes (Eds.), *Human communication: A unified view.* New York: McGraw-Hill.

Kameoka, A., & Kuriyagawa, M. (1969) Consonance theory Part II: Consonance of complex tones and its calculation method. *Journal of the Acoustical Society of America, 45*, 1460–69.

Kessler, E. J., Hansen, C., & Shepard, R. N. (1984) Tonal schemata in the perception of music in Bali and the West. *Music Perception, 2*, 131–65.

Knopoff, L., & Hutchinson, W. (1978) An index of melodic activity. *Interface, 7*, 205–29.

Knopoff, L., & Hutchinson, W. (1981) Information theory for musical continua. *Journal of Music Theory, 25*, 17–44.

Knopoff, L., & Hutchinson, W. (1983) Entropy as a measure of style: The influence of sample length. *Journal of Music Theory, 27*, 75–97.

Koffka, K. (1935) *Principles of Gestalt psychology.* New York: Harcourt, Brace, & World.

Köhler, W. (1947) *Gestalt psychology.* New York: Liveright.

Krantz, D. H., Luce, R. D., Suppes, P., & Tversky, A. (1971) *Foundations of measurement* (Vol. 1). New York: Academic.

Krumhansl, C. L. (1978) Concerning the applicability of geometric models to similarity data: The interrelationship between similarity and spatial density. *Psychological Review, 85*, 445–63.

Krumhansl, C. L. (1979) The psychological representation of musical pitch in a tonal context. *Cognitive Psychology, 11*, 346–74.

Krumhansl, C. L. (1982) A quantitative description of musical key structure. Paper presented at the meeting of the Society for Mathematical Psychology, Princeton, NJ.

Krumhansl, C. L. (1983) Set-theoretic and spatial models of similarity: Some considerations in application. Paper presented at the meeting of the Society for Mathematical Psychology, Boulder, CO.

Krumhansl, C. L. (1987) General properties of musical pitch systems: Some psychological considerations. In J. Sundberg (Ed.), *Harmony and tonality.* Stockholm: Royal Swedish Academy of Music (Publication No. 54).

Krumhansl, C. L., Bharucha, J. J., & Castellano, M. A. (1982) Key distance effects on perceived harmonic structure in music. *Perception & Psychophysics, 32*, 96–108.

Krumhansl, C. L., Bharucha, J. J., & Kessler, E. J. (1982) Perceived harmonic structure of chords in three related musical keys. *Journal of Experimental Psychology: Human Perception and Performance, 8*, 24–36.

Krumhansl, C. L., & Castellano, M. A. (1983) Dynamic processes in music perception. *Memory & Cognition, 11*, 325–34.

Krumhansl, C. L., & Jusczyk, P. W. (1990) Infant's perception of phrase structure in music. *Psychological Science, 1*, 1–4.

Krumhansl, C. L., & Keil, F. C. (1982) Acquisition of the hierarchy of tonal functions in music. *Memory and Cognition, 10*, 243–51.

Krumhansl, C. L., & Kessler, E. J. (1982) Tracing the dynamic changes in perceived tonal organization in a spatial representation of musical keys. *Psychological Review,* **89**, 334–68.

Krumhansl, C. L., Sandell, G. J., & Sergeant, D. C. (1987) The perception of tone hierarchies and mirror forms in twelve-tone serial music. *Music Perception,* **5**, 31–78.

Krumhansl, C. L., & Schmuckler, M. A. (1986) The *Petroushka* chord. *Music Perception,* **4**, 153–84.

Krumhansl, C. L., & Shepard, R. N. (1979) Quantification of the hierarchy of tonal functions within a diatonic context. *Journal of Experimental Psychology: Human Perception and Performance,* **5**, 579–94.

Kruskal, J. B. (1964) Nonmetric multidimensional scaling: A numerical method. *Psychometrika,* **29**, 28–42.

Kruskal, J. B., & Wish, M. (1978) *Multidimensional scaling.* Beverly Hills, CA: Sage Publications.

Kubovy, M. (1981) Concurrent-pitch segregation and the theory of indispensable attributes. In M. Kubovy and J. R. Pomerantz (Eds.), *Perceptual organization.* Hillsdale, NJ: Erlbaum.

Lakner, Y. (1960) A new method of representing tonal relations. *Journal of Music Theory,* **4**, 194–209.

Lerdahl, F. (1988) Tonal pitch space. *Music Perception,* **5**, 315–50.

Lerdahl, F., & Jackendoff, R. (1983) *A generative theory of tonal music.* Cambridge, MA: M. I. T. Press.

Levelt, W. J. M., Van de Geer, J. P., & Plomp, R. (1966) Triadic comparisons of musical intervals. *The British Journal of Mathematical and Statistical Psychology,* **19**, 163–79.

Lipps, Th. (1885) Das Wesen der musikalischen Harmonie und Disharmonie. *Psychologische Studien,* 92–161.

Lockhead, G. R., & Byrd, R. (1981) Practically perfect pitch. *Journal of the Acoustical Society of America,* **70**, 387–89.

Longuet-Higgins, H. C. (1962a) Letter to a musical friend. *Music Review,* **23**, 244–48.

Longuet-Higgins, H. C. (1962b) Second letter to a musical friend. *Music Review,* **23**, 271–80.

Longuet-Higgins, H. C., & Lee, C. S. (1984) The rhythmic interpretation of monophonic music. *Music Perception,* **1**, 424–41.

Longuet-Higgins, H. C., & Steedman, M. J. (1971) On interpreting Bach. *Machine Intelligence,* **6**, 221–41.

Luce, R. D., & Krumhansl, C. L. (1988) Measurement, scaling, and psychophysics. In R. C. Atkinson, R. J. Herrnstein, G. Lindzey, & R. D. Luce (Eds.), *Stevens' handbook of experimental psychology* (2nd ed.). Vol. 1, *Perception and motivation.* New York: Wiley.

Malmberg, C. F. (1918) The perception of consonance and dissonance. *Psychological Monographs,* **25** (2, Whole No. 108), 93–133.

Mathews, M. V., Pierce, J. R., & Roberts, L. A. (1987) Harmony and new scales. In J. Sundberg (Ed.), *Harmony and tonality.* Stockholm: Royal Swedish Academy of Music (Publication No. 54).

McAdams, S. (1984) The auditory image: A metaphor for musical and psychological research on auditory organization. In W. R. Crozier & A. J. Chapman (Eds.), *Cognitive processes in the perception of art.* Amsterdam: North-Holland.

Meehan, J. R. (1980) An artificial intelligence approach to tonal music. *Computer Music Journal*, **4**, 60–65.

Messiaen, O. (1944) *Technique de mon langage musical.* Paris: Alphonse Leduc.

Meyer, L. B. (1956) *Emotion and meaning in music.* Chicago: University of Chicago Press.

Meyer, L. B. (1957) Meaning in music and information theory. *Journal of Aesthetics & Art Criticism,* **15**, 412–24.

Meyer, L. B. (1967) *Music, the arts, and ideas.* Chicago: University of Chicago Press.

Meyer, L. B. (1973) *Explaining music: Essays and explorations.* Berkeley: University of California Press.

Meyer, M. (1900) Elements of psychological theory of melody. *Psychological Review,* **7**, 241–73.

Meyer, M. (1903) Experimental studies in the psychology of music. *American Journal of Psychology,* **14**, 456–78.

Miller, G. A., Heise, G. (1950) The trill threshold. *Journal of the Acoustical Society of America,* **22**, 637–38.

Miller, L. K. (1985) Sensitivity to tonal structure in a developmentally disabled musical savant. Paper presented at the meeting of the Psychonomics Society, Boston.

Miller, L. K. (1987) Determinants of melody span in a developmentally disabled musical savant. *Psychology of Music,* **15**, 76–89.

Moran, H., & Pratt, C. C. (1926) Variability of judgments of musical intervals. *Journal of Experimental Psychology,* **9**, 492–500.

Mullen, K., & Ennis, D. M. (1987) Mathematical formulation of multivariate Euclidean models for discrimination methods. *Psychometrika,* **52**, 235–49.

Nettl, B. (1964) *Theory and method in ethnomusicology.* London: Free Press of Glencoe.

Nosofsky, R. M. (1986) Attention, similarity, and the identification–categorization relationship. *Journal of Experimental Psychology: General,* **115**, 39–57.

Palmer, C., & Krumhansl, C. L. (1987a) Independent temporal and pitch structures in perception of musical phrases. *Journal of Experimental Psychology: Human Perception and Performance,* **13**, 116–26.

Palmer, C., & Krumhansl, C. L. (1987b) Pitch and temporal contributions to musical phrase perception: Effects of harmony, performance timing, and familiarity. *Perception & Psychophysics,* **41**, 505–18.

Parncutt, R. (1987) Sensory bases of harmony in Western music. Unpublished doctoral dissertation, University of New England, Australia.

Parncutt, R. (1988) Revision of Terhardt's psychoacoustical model of the root(s) of a musical chord. *Music Perception,* **6**, 65–94.

Pedersen, P. (1975) The perception of octave equivalence in twelve-tone rows. *Psychology of Music,* **3**, 3–8.

Pikler, A. G. (1966) Logarithmic frequency systems. *Journal of the Acoustical Society of America,* **39**, 1102–10.

Pinkerton, R. C. (1956) Information theory and melody. *Scientific American,* **194**, 77–86.

Piston, W. (1978) *Harmony* (4th ed.). New York: Norton. (Originally published, 1941.)

Plomp, R., & Levelt, W. J. M. (1965) Tonal consonance and critical bandwidth. *Journal of the Acoustical Society of America,* **38**, 548–60.

Pollard-Gott, L. (1983) Emergence of thematic concepts in repeated listening to music. *Cognitive Psychology,* **15**, 66–94.

Pomerantz, J. R. (1981) Perceptual organization in information processing. In M. Kubovy & J. R. Pomerantz (Eds.), *Perceptual organization.* Hillsdale, NJ: Erlbaum.

Pruzansky, S., Tversky, A., & Carroll, J. D. (1982) Spatial versus tree representations of proximity data. *Psychometrika, 47,* 3–24.

Rahn, J. (1980) *Basic atonal theory.* New York: Longman.

Rameau, J. P. (1971) *Treatise on harmony* (P. Gossett, trans.). New York: Dover. (Originally published, 1722.)

Rasch, R. A. (1978) The perception of simultaneous notes, such as in polyphonic music, *Acustica,* **40**, 21–33.

Reger, M. (1903) *On the theory of modulation.* (Kalmus Publication No. 3841). Melville, NY: Belwin Mills.

Revesz, G. (1954) *Introduction to the psychology of music.* Norman, OK: University of Oklahoma Press.

Rips, L. J., Shoben, E. J., & Smith, E. E. (1973) Semantic distance and the verification of semantic relations. *Journal of Verbal Learning and Verbal Behavior,* **12**, 1–20.

Roberts, F. S. (1979) *Measurement theory with applications to decision making, utility, and the social sciences.* Reading, MA: Addison-Wesley.

Roberts, L. A., & Mathews, M. V. (1984) Intonation sensitivity for traditional and nontraditional chords. *Journal of the Acoustical Society of America,* **75**, 952–59.

Roberts, L. A., & Shaw, M. L. (1984) Perceived structure of triads. *Music Perception, 2,* 95–124.

Roederer, J. G. (1973) *Introduction to the physics and psychophysics of music* (2nd ed.). New York: Springer-Verlag.

Rosch, E. (1975) Cognitive reference points. *Cognitive Psychology,* **7**, 532–47.

Rosch, E. (1978) Principles of categorization. In E. Rosch & B. B. Lloyd (Eds.), *Cognition and categorization.* Hillsdale, NJ: Erlbaum.

Rosch, E., & Mervis, C. B. (1975) Family resemblances: Studies in the internal structure of categories. *Cognitive Psychology,* **7**, 573–605.

Rosner, B. S., & Meyer, L. B. (1982) Melodic processes and the perception of music. In D. Deutsch (Ed.), *The psychology of music.* New York: Academic.

Rosner, B. S., & Meyer, L. B. (1986) The perceptual roles of melodic process, contour, and form. *Music Perception, 4,* 1–39.

Ruckmick, C. A. (1929) A new classification of tonal qualities. *Psychological Review, 36,* 172–80.

Sattath, S., & Tversky, A. (1977) Additive similarity trees. *Psychometrika,* **42**, 319–45.

Schenker, H. (1954) *Harmony* (O. Jones, Ed., and E. M. Borgese, trans.). Cambridge, MA: M. I. T. Press. (Originally published, 1906.)

Schmuckler, M. A. (1988) Expectation in music: Additivity of melodic and harmonic processes. Unpublished doctoral dissertation, Department of Psychology, Cornell University.

Schoenberg, A. (1978) *Theory of harmony* (R. E. Carter, trans.) Berkeley: University of California Press. (Originally published, 1922.)

Schoenberg, A. (1975) Composition with twelve tones (1). In L. Stein (Ed.), *Style and idea.* London: Faber & Faber. (Originally published, 1941.)

Schoenberg, A. (1975) Composition with twelve tones (2). In L. Stein (Ed.), *Style and idea*. London: Faber & Faber. (Originally published, 1948.)

Schoenberg, A. (1969) *Structural functions of harmony*. (Rev. ed.). New York: Norton. (Originally published, 1954.)

Shackford, C. (1961) Some aspects of perception, Part I: Sizes of harmonic intervals in performance. *Journal of Music Theory, 5*, 162–202.

Shackford, C. (1962a) Some aspects of perception, Part II: Interval sizes and tonal dynamics in performance. *Journal of Music Theory, 6*, 66–90.

Shackford, C. (1962b) Some aspects of perception, Part III: Addenda. *Journal of Music Theory, 6*, 295–303.

Shepard, R. N. (1962) The analysis of proximities: Multidimensional scaling with an unknown distance function. I & II. *Psychometrika, 27*, 125–40, 219–46.

Shepard, R. N. (1964) Circularity in judgments of relative pitch. *Journal of the Acoustical Society of America, 36*, 2346–53.

Shepard, R. N. (1982) Geometrical approximations to the structure of musical pitch. *Psychological Review, 89*, 305–33.

Simon, H. A., & Sumner, R. K. (1968) Pattern in music. In B. Kleinmuntz (Ed.), *Formal representation of human judgment*. New York: Wiley.

Sloboda, J. A. (1981) The uses of space in music notation. *Visible Language, 25*, 86–110.

Sloboda, J. A. (1985) *The musical mind: The cognitive psychology of music*. Oxford: Oxford University Press.

Smoliar, S. W. (1980) A computer aid for Schenkerian analysis. *Computer Music Journal, 4*, 41–59.

Speer, J. R., & Adams, W. E. (1985) The effects of musical training upon the development of the perception of musical pitch. Paper presented at the meetings of the Society for Research in Child Development.

Speer, J.R., & Meeks, P.U. (1985) School children's perception of pitch in music. *Psychomusicology, 5*, 49–56.

Steiger, H., & Bregman, A. S. (1982a) Competition among auditory streaming, dichotic fusion and diotic fusion. *Perception & Psychophysics, 32*, 153–62.

Steiger, H., & Bregman, A. S. (1982b) Negating the effects of binaural cues: Competition between auditory streaming and contralateral induction. *Journal of Experimental Psychology: Human Perception & Performance, 8*, 602–13.

Stravinsky, I., & Craft, R. (1962) *Expositions and developments*. New York: Doubleday.

Stuckenschmidt, H. H. (1969) *Twentieth century music*. New York: McGraw-Hill.

Tenney, J., & Polansky, L. (1980) Temporal Gestalt perception in music. *Journal of Music Theory, 24*, 205–41.

Terhardt, E. (1974) Pitch, consonance and harmony. *Journal of the Acoustical Society of America, 55*, 1061–69.

Terhardt, E. (1984) The concept of musical consonance: A link between music and psychoacoustics. *Music Perception, 1*, 276–95.

Terhardt, E., Stoll, G., & Seewan, M. (1982a) Pitch of complex signals according to virtual-pitch theory: Tests, examples, and predictions. *Journal of the Acoustical Society of America, 71*, 671–78.

Terhardt, E., Stoll, G., & Seewan, M. (1982b) Algorithm for extraction of pitch and pitch salience from complex tonal signals. *Journal of the Acoustical Society of America, 71*, 679–88.

Thompson, W. F. (1986) Judgements of key change in Bach chorale excerpts: An investigation of the sensitivity to keys, chords, and voicing. Unpublished doctoral dissertation, Department of Psychology, Queen's University, Kingston, Ontario, Canada.

Thorndike, E. L. (1921) *Teacher's word book of 10,000 words*. New York: Bureau of Publications, Teachers College, Columbia University.

Thurlow, W. R., & Erchul, W. P. (1977) Judged similarity in pitch of octave multiples. *Perception & Psychophysics, 22*, 177–82.

Trehub, S. E. (1987) Infants' perception of musical patterns. *Perception & Psychophysics, 41*, 635–41.

Tversky, A. (1977) Features of similarity. *Psychological Review, 84*, 327–52.

Tversky, A., & Hutchinson, J. W. (1986) Nearest neighbor analysis of psychological spaces. *Psychological Review, 93*, 3–22.

Ueda, K., & Ohgushi, K. (1987) Perceptual components of pitch: Spatial representations using a multidimensional scaling technique. *Journal of the Acoustical Society of America, 82*, 1193–1200.

Van den Toorn, P. C. (1975) Some characteristics of Stravinsky's diatonic music. *Perspectives of New Music, 14*, 104–38.

Van den Toorn, P. C. (1977) Some characteristics of Stravinsky's diatonic music (II). *Perspectives of New Music, 15*, 58–95.

Van den Toorn, P. C. (1983) *The music of Igor Stravinsky*. New Haven, CT: Yale University Press.

Van Noorden, L. P. A. S. (1975) *Temporal coherence in the perception of tone sequences*. Eindhoven, The Netherlands: Institute for Perception Research.

Ward, W. D., & Burns, E. M. (1982) Absolute pitch. In D. Deutsch (Ed.), *The psychology of music*. New York: Academic.

Warren, R. M., & Bashford, J. A. (1976) Auditory contralateral induction: An early stage of binaural processing. *Perception & Psychophysics, 20*, 380–86.

Watt, H. J. (1923–1924) Functions of the size of intervals in the songs of Schubert and of the Chippewa and Teton Sioux Indians. *British Journal of Psychology, 14*, 370–86.

Welker, R. L. (1982) Abstraction of themes from melodic variations. *Journal of Experimental Psychology: Human Perception and Performance, 8*, 435–47.

Wertheimer, M. (1938) Gestalt theory. In W. D. Ellis (Ed. and trans.), *A source book of Gestalt psychology*. London: Routledge & Kegan Paul.

Werts, D. (1983) A theory of scale references. Unpublished doctoral dissertation, Department of Music, Princeton University.

White, B. (1960) Recognition of distorted melodies. *American Journal of Psychology, 73*, 100–107.

Whitlow, J. W., Jr., & Estes, W. K. (1979) Judgments of relative frequency in relation to shifts of event frequencies: Evidence for a limited-capacity model. *Journal of Experimental Psychology: Human Learning and Memory, 5*, 395–408.

Whitlow, J. W., Jr., & Skaar, E. (1979) The role of numerosity in judgments of overall frequency. *Journal of Experimental Psychology: Human Learning and Memory, 5*, 409–21.

Winograd, T. (1968) Linguistics and the computer analysis of tonal harmony. *Journal of Music Theory, 12*, 2–49.

Winold, A., & Bein, J. (1985) Banalyze, An artificial intelligence system for harmonic analysis. Unpublished manuscript.

Youngblood, J. E. (1958) Style as information. *Journal of Music Theory, 2*, 24–35.

Zipf, G. K. (1965) *Human behavior and the principle of least effort*. New York: Hafner Publishing Company. (Originally published, 1949.)

Author index

Subject index

304